2-29-96

Dear Harriett—(and Jack)
What can I say
to such a dear
friend!!
L'chiam!!!
Love
Harriet

# Harriet Roth's Deliciously Healthy Jewish Cooking

350 New Low-Fat,
Low-Cholesterol, Low-Sodium Recipes
for Holidays and Every Day

# HARRIET ROTH'S
# DELICIOUSLY
# HEALTHY JEWISH
# COOKING

A DUTTON BOOK

DUTTON
Published by the Penguin Group
Penguin Books USA Inc., 375 Hudson Street, New York, New York 10014, U.S.A.
Penguin Books Ltd, 27 Wrights Lane, London W8 5TZ, England
Penguin Books Australia Ltd, Ringwood, Victoria, Australia
Penguin Books Canada Ltd, 10 Alcorn Avenue, Toronto, Ontario, Canada M4V 3B2
Penguin Books (N.Z.) Ltd, 182–190 Wairau Road, Auckland 10, New Zealand

Penguin Books Ltd, Registered Offices: Harmondsworth, Middlesex, England

First published by Dutton, an imprint of Dutton Signet, a division of Penguin Books USA Inc.
Distributed in Canada by McClelland & Stewart Inc.

First Printing, April, 1996
10  9  8  7  6  5  4  3  2  1

REGISTERED TRADEMARK—MARCA REGISTRADA

LIBRARY OF CONGRESS CATALOGING-IN-PUBLICATION DATA
Roth, Harriet.
    Harriet Roth's deliciously healthy Jewish cooking : 350 new low-fat, low-cholesterol, low-sodium recipes
for holidays and every day / Harriet Roth.
        p.   cm.
    Includes index.
    ISBN 0-525-93931-8 (acid-free paper)
    I. Cookery, Jewish. 2. Low-fat diet—Recipes. 3. Low-cholesterol diet—Recipes. I. Title. II. Title: Deli-
ciously healthy Jewish cooking.
    TX724.R587    1996
641.5′67—dc20                                                                                                95-11429
                                                                                                                    CIP

Printed in the United States of America
Set in Goudy Old Style
Designed by Eve L. Kirch

This book is dedicated to my mother,
Sarah Lebovitz Sobel,
May 12, 1885–November 4, 1943,
whose memory continues to give my life special meaning.

# Contents

*Acknowledgments*   xi

*Introduction*   xv

## HOLIDAYS   1

*Shabbat*  3  •  *Rosh Hashanah*  11  •  *Yom Kippur*  26
*Sukkot*  40  •  *Thanksgiving*  44  •  *Chanukah*  56  •  *Purim*  61
*Passover*  67  •  *Shavuot*  100  •  *Fourth of July*  106

## APPETIZERS   113

## SOUPS   135

## SALADS   175

## NOODLES AND GRAINS   203

## VEGETABLES   231

## FISH   279

## POULTRY   299

BEEF, LAMB, AND VEAL    333

OODLES OF STRUDELS    347

BAKING    369

FRUIT DESSERTS    397

THE BAKER'S "DEADLY" DOZEN    413

Metric Equivalents    434

Glossary of Yiddish Terms    435

Bibliography    441

Index    443

# Acknowledgments

When word got around that I was writing a book about Jewish cooking that was low in fat and cholesterol, most people responded by saying, "Healthy Jewish cooking—that's an oxymoron."

In spite of this, I started receiving recipes from far and wide that I would revise and add to my burgeoning supply of family favorites. Recipes were accompanied by notes saying, "I know that this is too high in fat and/or cholesterol. After you cut the fat by eliminating the chicken fat, butter, and egg yolks, do you think there is some way to keep the flavor?"

I tested and revised these recipes until they passed the taste test but were still healthful. Most of the recipes come from my years of cooking, but my nostalgic memories of the tastes and smells of my mother's cooking have provided the basis of many of the recipes you will enjoy.

Over the years, I have developed a deep concern for my family's health. Both my insatiable interest in food and cooking, and my professional background as a nutritionist have led me to discover new ways to prepare and enjoy deliciously healthy kosher-style Jewish cooking.

My thanks to the many wonderful, supportive friends, friends of friends, and family members who have encouraged me from the very start. They have searched, re-searched, suggested, and digested recipes. Much of the flavor of this book comes from the kitchens of Jewish cooks, who meet the daily challenge of getting another meal on the table for yet another day or holiday and doing it (mostly) with pleasure and love.

I have been so fortunate in having incredible assistance on all my books, this time is no different. The only change is in the cast of some of the characters. My publisher, Elaine Koster, has remained the same, much to my joy. Since two heads are better than one, I now have two new bright, perceptive editors, Julia Moskin and Carole DeSanti. Each brings her own special qualities to this book. Scott Terranella and Rena Kornbluh also made major contributions. In addition, my thanks to Dolores Simon, the consummate professional copy editor who helped to fine-tune my book so that it works. Kate Cambridge, my publicist, knew all the right doors to open. My secretary, Sharon Berryhill, is still in place. I could never have completed the manuscript without her consistent, dependable help. And still quietly working behind the scenes is Arnold Dolin, my friend and advocate for many years.

To all of the following unsung heroes, a special "dunka schoen" in appreciation of your ongoing support: Helen Aaron, Irene Baron, Ani Chakmakian, R.D., Leonard Davis, M.D., Connie Reif Davis, Linda Elstad, Dorothy Essick, Harriet Friedman, Dorothy Hartstein, R.D., Rabbi Meyer Heller, Renee Holland, Bill Kizner, Gayle Kohl, Rabbi Arthur J. Kolatch, Helen Kolatch, Ruth Sobel Litt, Shirley Mantell, Griselda Mendoza, Nanette Nathanson, Harriet Root, Barbara Rosove, Rabbi John Rosove, Jake Roth, Eva Silver, Marilyn Sobel, Marcy Steinberg, Marilyn Steinberg, and Edith Sobel Wahl.

My children, Sally, Larry, and Eileen, were honest critics, and my granddaughter Molly's smiling face brought joy that made each day special.

And of course my gratitude to my husband, Harold, who, for these many years, has been there to share both my laughter and tears. His unconditional love, patience, and encouragement throughout my professional and personal lives continue to spark an endless source of creative energy.

H.R.

*God could not be everywhere,*
*and therefore he made mothers.*

—Jewish Proverb

# Introduction

## WHAT IS JEWISH COOKING?

What is Jewish cooking? Ask people whose parents or ancestors came from Russia, France, Poland, Austria, Germany, Czechoslovakia, Hungary, Spain, England, Persia, and Israel and you will hear completely different answers. Ashkenazi and Sephardic Jews have different culinary traditions and different ways of preparing the same dishes. To write a cookbook that covered the entire world of Jewish cooking would be as unwieldy an undertaking as writing a useful travel guide to the whole globe.

For me, Jewish cooking is linked inextricably with memories of my mother's kitchen. I can still smell the challah and kuchen baking in her oven in preparation for the Sabbath. I remember her taking a little round of dough and stretching it paper thin on the large dining room table; filling it with a mixture of chopped apples, cinnamon, sugar, and nuts, and then using the white tablecloth underneath to roll this wondrous mixture into long rolls of strudel. I can still hear the pronouncements and admonitions she passed on as she cooked.

I remember her yearly twenty-four-hour vigil, during which she got up on the hour through the night to stir huge cauldrons of Italian plums, which were available only for about two weeks in September, to make plum butter (Lekvar, page 411). It was then sealed in jars and used for baking and for filling blintzes throughout the year. My sisters and I still take turns carrying out this ritual.

I remember my mother's homemade noodles drying on the kitchen table and her delight when she bought a little machine, resembling a miniature sewing machine, that spat out mountains of noodles with a turn of the wheel. I felt lucky when, sometimes, I was even allowed to help.

The kitchen was a magical kingdom, presided over by my mother and aunt, and cooking was a family affair. I remember the approach of Shabbat, ushered in by a cooking marathon at our home that started on Thursday night and continued until just a few hours before sundown on Friday. The sound of my Aunt Ella chopping liver and eggs in a large, well-worn wooden bowl securely cradled between her knees reverberates in my mind whenever I see a plate of chopped liver. I recall instantly the overwhelming seduction of the smells that would greet me when I returned from school: challah in the oven, chicken soup simmering on the stove, a platter overflowing with crispy *fritlach* or some other treat lightly dusted with powdered sugar and waiting to melt in your mouth. Some days, I didn't even have to open the door to savor the smell of the gefilte fish.

As evening approached, the big, round oak table in the kitchen was covered with a bright white linen tablecloth and crowned with the polished brass candlesticks. The table was set with the "good dishes" and matching silverware. The whole Sobel family—my parents, brothers Herb, George, and Irv, sisters Ruth and Edie, Aunt Ella, and even my dog Jack—seemed to be preparing for the Sabbath. It looked so festive, solemn, and peaceful that I could hardly wait to bathe and put on a freshly starched and ironed dress and my patent leather shoes. Then, personally prepared for Shabbat, I returned to the kitchen—my safe haven, then and now.

Happily, cooking and eating are cornerstones of tradition in many Jewish families besides my own. Sadly, the way our parents and grandparents ate was not terribly healthful and probably contributed to the health problems that are the source of some sorrowful memories as well. My father developed heart disease at an early age—in his early fifties—and my mother died young of cancer. I'm convinced that had there been more information regarding *preventive* nutrition, they both might have lived longer and healthier lives.

# JEWISH COOKING YOU CAN LIVE WITH

Medical science tells us that the single most important change we can make in our diet is to reduce the total fat that we consume. This means eating less of foods that are naturally high in fat and adding less fat when we cook. Now, suggesting this to a traditional Jewish cook is like telling a painter not to use any blue: it makes the whole exercise seem slightly pointless. Most cooks would tell you that it is impossible to prepare the traditional foods any other way. At one time, I would have said the same thing. In fact, when my husband developed a coronary problem, I regretfully eliminated from our diets all the traditional foods as prepared by my mother and his (stuffed *derma*, chopped liver, *griebenes*, and *schmaltz* in abundance: did we really eat like that?).

Now, seventeen years later, I have tested and collected endless variations and adaptations of traditional Jewish dishes. I am happy to report that all the old favorites can be made low in fat and cholesterol, and still taste delicious.

The incidence of heart disease, diabetes, high blood pressure, and colon cancer in the Jewish population—Orthodox, nonobservant, and in between—is inordinately high. There is no conclusive evidence to determine whether the critical factor is genetic or cultural, but since we can't manipulate our genes, we owe it to ourselves to eat healthily. Diabetes especially has strong patterns of inheritance in the Jewish population. Since we now know that regulating fat consumption is as critical as regulating sugar consumption when trying to stabilize blood sugar levels, controlling diabetes and other debilitating diseases with diet is a stronger possibility than ever before. Recognize that a low-fat, low-cholesterol, high-fiber diet will not only lengthen your life but also improve its quality. Make this style of eating the habit of a lifetime. It's not the occasional indulgence at a bar mitzvah or wedding that affects your health: it's what you eat day in and day out that matters. Here are a few simple but important guidelines to help you on your way.

## Focus on Total Fat, Not Calories

By limiting *all* animal protein to no more than four to five ounces daily (a portion about the size and thickness of a deck of cards), and eating more vegetables, fruits, cereal, and grain products, we can easily limit our fat intake to *20 percent or less* of our total calories. (Nutritionists and medical researchers widely agree that this is the optimum percentage for health. Only pressure from the meat and dairy industries has kept the new USDA guidelines at 30 percent.) Try to make *at least* three days a week days when none of your food comes from animal sources. Eat soups, salads, vegetables, breads, cereals, grains, and pasta dishes. The reduction of fat will be a boon to your health. A side benefit, of course, will be a reduction in your weight, because all calories are not created equal.

**There are 9 calories in every gram of fat—
twice as many as in every
gram of protein or carbohydrate!**

Fat calories are converted to body fat more easily than calories from protein or carbohydrates. Still, a low-fat diet is not a magic bullet against obesity. Low-fat cooking is not a license to overeat! However, fighting the fat is essential to any weight-loss or healthy eating plan.

## SATURATED FAT: THE DANGEROUS CULPRIT

Saturated fat contributes to heart disease by raising the level of cholesterol in the blood. In fact, eating foods high in saturated fat raises blood cholesterol *more* than eating foods high in cholesterol does!

All saturated fats are solid at room temperature. They are found primarily in foods of animal origin, such as dairy products (whole milk, butter, cream, sour cream, ice cream, yogurt, and cheeses), and in any meat or poultry fat. Saturated fats are also found in tropical oils, such as coconut oil, palm oil, palm kernel oil, cocoa butter, and any vegetable oil that has been hydrogenated, such as stick margarine or solid vegetable shortening. When any oil is hydrogenated, it becomes more solid and saturated, and thus is more likely to raise your cholesterol level. Tropical oils and hydrogenated fats are used frequently in processed foods, because they are cheap and have longer shelf lives than other fats.

## DAILY INTAKE OF FAT AND CALORIES

To determine the number of calories you should consume to reach your optimum weight, multiply your desired weight by 15 calories. Formula:

**Desired weight × 15 calories =
daily calories needed for optimum weight.**

How many grams of fat should you eat each day?

**Formula: Daily calories × .20 (20 percent)**
**divided by 9 (calories in 1 gram of fat) =**
**total grams of fat you should consume daily.**

This formula is based on fat consumption of 20 percent of calories per day. Like the FDA, the American Heart Association recommends a maximum consumption of 30 percent of daily calories from fat, but most experts believe that 30 percent is too high. Whichever guideline you follow, remember less fat is better.

| | Daily Fat Gram Consumption | | | |
|---|---|---|---|---|
| Total Calorie Level | Target: 10% from fat | 15% from fat | 20% from fat | 30% from fat |
| 1200 | 13 | 20 | 26 | 40 |
| 1500 | 17 | 25 | 33 | 50 |
| 1800 | 20 | 30 | 40 | 60 |
| 2000 | 22 | 33 | 44 | 66 |
| 2200 | 24 | 37 | 49 | 73 |
| 2500 | 28 | 42 | 56 | 83 |
| 3000 | 33 | 50 | 67 | 100 |

# A Few Words about Cholesterol

Cholesterol is a fatty, waxlike substance that can be found only in foods of animal origin. A food can be high in fat, like avocado, chocolate, or nuts, but contain no cholesterol. Or it can be low in fat, like turkey breast or some fish, yet still contain cholesterol. Other foods, especially some that are high in saturated fat, may not contain cholesterol per se, but can still raise the cholesterol level in your blood.

**To *prevent* heart disease, limit your cholesterol**
**intake to less than 100 mg per day.**

Once you limit your consumption of meat, fish, or poultry to a small portion and accompany it with soups, salads, pasta, potatoes, dried peas, beans, or lentils, legumes, grains, or vegetables in larger portions, you are on the right track.

# HOW'S YOUR CHOLESTEROL?

People twenty years old and over should have their cholesterol checked at least every five years. The doctor should also check your HDL (high-density lipoprotein), sometimes called "good" cholesterol, which helps to remove "bad" cholesterol (see below) from your blood. Higher levels of HDL help promote healthier arteries, and recent studies suggest that high HDLs may even have the ability to remove plaque previously deposited on artery walls, thereby reversing atherosclerosis. LDL (low-density lipoprotein), also known as the "bad" cholesterol, deposits plaque on your artery walls. A total blood cholesterol level of 200 or less is desirable, but if yours is higher, reducing the amount of saturated fat and cholesterol in your diet can help lower it. Remember that the saturated fat you eat actually raises your blood cholesterol *more* than the cholesterol you eat does. Don't worry about getting too *little* cholesterol—your body makes all that it needs!

**Ideal cholesterol test results:**
1. Total cholesterol count of *under 200*
2. LDL count of *under 130*
3. HDL count of *45 or over*

# AVOID TOO MUCH SODIUM AND SALT

Scientists may disagree about the specific dangers of salt, but every major health authority from the U.S. Surgeon General to the National Academy of Sciences has encouraged us to cut down on salt and sodium compounds. We should all be concerned about our consumption of salt, whether occurring naturally in foods and water; in medications, added commercially as a preservative (sodium benzoate, sodium nitrate, or sodium nitrite, commonly found in smoked meat or fish), MSG (monosodium glutamate), or HVP (hydrolized vegetable protein), which contains MSG; or the salt we add ourselves in cooking and at the table (frequently without tasting first).

I am not suggesting that all foods should be prepared entirely without salt. However, adding a little salt at the end of cooking makes its taste more effective. Try filling your salt shakers with herbs or saltless seasonings for the same flavor-enhancing effect without the added sodium. No one should use a potassium-based salt substitute without doctor's approval. And anyone using kosher meats should be extra careful to limit their meat consumption as well as added salt because of the amount of salt used in koshering. Definitely stop eating poultry skin, because of its high fat, cholesterol, and sodium contents.

All of us, whether hypertensive or salt sensitive, should limit our sodium intake to no more than about 1,800 mg or less per day. (One teaspoon of salt contains about 2,000 mg of sodium.) It's not only high blood pressure that we should be concerned about; the risk of osteoporosis and colon cancer are both increased by excess sodium consumption. Cooking fresh food is one of the best ways of reducing sodium intake, since most of the sodium we consume comes from processed foods. Salt and sugar are the most commonly added preservatives in prepared or commercial foods.

---

### PROCESSED FOODS HIGH IN SODIUM

*Meats:* Corned beef, salami, smoked turkey, hot dogs
*Fish:* Canned fish, frozen or smoked fish
*Condiments:* Salad dressings, ketchup, mustard, pickles, olives
*Milk Products:* Most cheeses
*Commercially Prepared Products:* Canned, frozen, and dried soups, gravies, and vegetables
*Breakfast Foods:* Most dry and instant cereals
*Snack Foods:* Pretzels and chips

---

# LIMIT YOUR SUGAR

Sugar contributes to tooth decay and obesity and provides empty calories without essential vitamins and minerals. Its influence becomes even more pernicious because of the bad company it keeps. Sucrose tends to appear along with loads of fat and cholesterol in desserts like cookies, cakes, pies, and ice cream. Be aware that sugar is frequently added as the first ingredient in no- or low-fat foods, particularly cakes and cookies. Refined simple sugars also tend to increase triglyceride levels in the blood—a contributing factor for heart disease. In light of all this negative information, I've decreased the amount of simple sugars in all the recipes—though not eliminated them completely.

# LOAD UP ON COMPLEX CARBOHYDRATES AND FIBER

Foods that are high in fiber—fruits, vegetables, dried legumes (peas, beans, and lentils), whole grains, breads, cereals—are lower in caloric density than sugary, high-fat foods, and tend to slow down the rapid intake of calories that contribute to weight gain. A high-fiber style of eating is a natural protection against colon cancer, diverticulitis, diabetes, and heart disease. Both soluble fiber and insoluble fiber are important for health. So while you're decreasing the fat, increase the fiber!

Obviously, *sensible portions are essential in maintaining weight and health*. Overeating any food is not a good idea.

# MAINTAINING A HEALTHY WEIGHT

The shift in the updated suggested weight tables for adults takes the emphasis off appearance in favor of a focus on health and avoidance of the health problems associated with carrying excess weight. Adults thirty-five or over will find a slightly higher acceptable weight range. The new chart also puts men's and women's weights together, with the assumption that most healthy women will fall at the lower end of the range and most healthy men will fall at the higher end. This is because a man will tend to have more muscle and bone (which are heavy) than a woman of the same height.

Dr. C. Wayne Callaway, a member of the committee that developed the new federal guidelines, says, "Our definition of healthy weight says that you also have to know your other health numbers, such as blood cholesterol and blood pressure, and then consider them along with weight and body shape."

The following chart lists suggested weight levels. But remember: each person's optimum weight is affected by his or her age, activity level, and other individual differences.

| Height | USFDA SUGGESTED WEIGHT (without clothes or shoes) 19–34 years | 35 years and over |
|--------|-------------|-------------------|
| 5'0" | 97–128 | 108–138 |
| 5'1" | 101–132 | 111–143 |
| 5'2" | 104–137 | 115–148 |
| 5'3" | 107–141 | 119–152 |
| 5'4" | 111–146 | 122–157 |
| 5'5" | 114–150 | 126–162 |
| 5'6" | 118–155 | 130–167 |
| 5'7" | 121–160 | 134–172 |
| 5'8" | 125–164 | 138–178 |
| 5'9" | 129–169 | 142–183 |
| 5'10" | 132–174 | 146–188 |
| 5'11" | 136–179 | 151–194 |
| 6'0" | 140–184 | 155–199 |
| 6'1" | 144–189 | 159–205 |
| 6'2" | 148–195 | 164–210 |
| 6'3" | 152–200 | 168–216 |
| 6'4" | 156–205 | 173–222 |

# What Is Kosher?

Misconceptions aside, the word kosher does not just mean clean. A correct literal definition of the word kosher is "proper; ritually fit for use."

Certain foods are forbidden entirely under the laws of *kashruth*. Other foods (mainly meats) can be kosher as long as they are correctly prepared before cooking. There are no restrictions on plant foods. All regulations pertain to animal foods: flesh of any kind and dairy products. The strict prohibitions are based on categories of creatures as described in the Old Testament Book of Leviticus. Flying creatures with feathers are acceptable; flying creatures without feathers (insects) are not. Birds of prey are also forbidden. If it swims, it must have fins and removable scales; shellfish or crustaceans are forbidden. Land animals must have split hooves and chew their cud; therefore cattle, sheep, deer, and goats are acceptable, but swine, horses, camels, rabbits, reptiles, and all carnivorous beasts are not.

To be rendered kosher, animals must be slaughtered and the meat prepared in accordance with certain rituals *(shekhitah)* under rabbinic supervision. The underlying principle is that we may not cause pain to any living thing. Kosher butchers, in the main, sell only the forequarter of the animal. Centuries ago, Ashkenazi authorities ruled that most butchers were not competent to perform the required excision of the sciatic nerve, so to be safe, the meat from the hindquarter was outlawed altogether. However, in Israel and in Sephardic communities around the world, there are specialists (called *menakrim*) who are trusted to remove the sciatic nerve and render the hindquarter kosher. Hence, leg of lamb from these Sephardic kosher butchers can be considered kosher.

Jewish tradition dictates that animal blood must not be consumed. Therefore, the process of koshering requires the following:

1. Soaking meat in water for half an hour.
2. Salting meat on all sides with kosher salt.
3. Draining meat on an inclined, perforated surface for one hour.
4. Rinsing off all salt.

Certain meats cannot be prepared in this way. It is permissible, therefore, to salt certain meats and broil them immediately. Liver, for instance, is koshered by broiling with the flame below. In most kosher butcher shops today, you will see a sign indicating that the meat and poultry have been koshered as an accommodation for the customers.

# THE KOSHER KITCHEN

Dairy products (*milchig*) and meat products (*fleischig*) must be kept separate and must not have even secondhand contact. That is why a kosher kitchen must have not only separate sets of dishes, silverware, and pots and pans, but also separate bars of soap with which to wash them, and two sets of dish towels. The high-tech or professional kosher kitchen has two dishwashers.

Kosher law prohibits the consumption of meat and milk foods at the same meal. Generally, observant Jews wait six hours after eating a meat meal before eating a dairy food. However, there is no wait required after eating a dairy meal.

The third category of foods is *pareve*, neutral foods that can be eaten with either milk foods or meat foods. Vegetables, fruits, grains, cereals, breads, coffee, nuts, certain *pareve* margarines and milk substitutes, fish, and eggs are all *pareve*. (Eggs that contain a speck of blood, however, are unacceptable.) Eating a healthful low-fat, low-cholesterol diet means drawing the bulk of your nutrition from these foods (all except egg yolks!).

# STOCKING THE HEALTHY KOSHER KITCHEN

Over the last twenty years, the number of kosher products on supermarket shelves in the U.S. has skyrocketed to twenty thousand, with estimated annual sales of $30 billion. Some 30 percent of these products are purchased by Jews for religious reasons. Another 30 percent are purchased by Muslims, whose own religious dietary law is very similar to kashruth. The remainder are purchased by people who associate the term kosher with purity and wholesomeness, believing that foods twice inspected—that is, by a USDA government inspector and a trained Jewish food inspector (called a *mashgeich*)—are of a higher quality than nonkosher, and they will pay the occasionally higher prices.

Orthodox rabbis generally oversee the koshering of processed foods, but in some instances Conservative rabbis and community organizations have assumed the responsibility. Each certifying agency has its own symbol for food that is kosher. If a "P" or a "D" appears next to a symbol, it stands for "Pareve" or "Dairy." Foods that are kosher for Passover must be labeled as such.

None of the kosher inspections and their attendant label codes have anything to do with a food's nutritional value.

Although there are more than one hundred and thirty symbols used by commercial food processors to mark products as kosher, only five symbols are widely accepted on a national level:

 A star with a K in the center—certified by the Orthodox Jewish Council of Baltimore, Md.

Ⓤ An O with a U in the center, underneath marked "ou"—certified by Union of Orthodox Jewish Congregations, New York, N.Y.

Ⓚ A circle with a K in the center, underneath marked "ok"—certified by Organized Kashrus Laboratories, Brooklyn, N.Y.

The Hebrew symbol KOF-K—certified by Kosher Supervision Service, Teaneck, N.J., and New York, N.Y.

△K̲ A triangle with a K in the center marked "adequate for Conservative but not for Orthodox Jewry"—certified by Rabbi Joseph Ralbag

If you notice a symbol on foods that you are buying other than the ones listed, and keeping kosher is important to you, check its credibility with the manufacturer or your rabbi or the following publications:

### Orthodox Jews:

*Kashruth: A Handbook for Home and School,* published by the Union of Orthodox Jewish Congregations Rabbinical Council of Americas.

### Conservative Jews:

*The Jewish Dietary Laws,* by Samuel Dresner and David Pollock, published by the Rabbinical Assembly or United Synagogues Commission on Jewish Education.

## ABOUT THIS BOOK

This book is not, strictly speaking, a kosher cookbook in that some very Orthodox Jews may find preparations and some ingredients not to their liking. I have made every effort, however, to make sure the recipes could be used by an experienced kosher-observant cook in a kosher kitchen. Every recipe is marked either "Meat," "Dairy," or "Pareve." If a recipe can be prepared in more than one way, I have marked it accordingly. There is no reason why religious law and modern, *healthy* eating cannot go hand in hand.

### The Recipes

Measuring cups and spoons were unknown to our mothers' (or grandmothers') traditional Jewish cooking, as they were to the home cooks of all nationalities in the days before Fannie Farmer. I do remember my mother using the same teacup and spoons, which consequently became the standard measures in her recipes. Other measures were a handful of this, a pinch of that, an eggshell filled with water, or a certain bowl filled up to here. The most technical instruction in most Jewish kitchens was *meschittarein* ("just throw it in"). Sometimes, when sharing a treasured recipe, the cook might "inadvertently" omit a critical ingredient—but that's another story.

### Guide to Nutrition Information

The nutrition information given for each recipe in this book is made available by analysis by Computrition, Inc., in Chatsworth, California. It is based upon the most current data available from the USDA and individual food processors.

The analysis is for a single serving based upon the largest number of servings listed for the specific recipe. It also is for a suggested portion, such as a tablespoon of salad dressing, a cup of soup, or one cookie. The nutrition information does not include optional ingredients, garnishes, or ingredients with no specific amount stated. When alternative ingredients appear in the recipe, the analysis is based upon the first choice listed. If a range is listed for amounts, such as ¼ to ½ cup flour, values are based upon the first, lower amount stated.

The listed nutrition information for each recipe includes:

**Calories**          **Total Fat**          **Saturated Fat**          **Calories from Fat**
**Percentage of**          **Cholesterol**          **Sodium**          **Fiber**
**Calories from Fat**

## Check Your Labels

The new FDA food labels mean it's easier than ever to make good, healthful food choices. Nutrition claims are now clearly defined by federal regulations in order to help you determine how your food selections fit into a healthy lifestyle.

| Label | Definition (Based on the Referred Serving Size) |
| --- | --- |
| Calorie-free | Less than 5 calories |
| Low-calorie | 40 calories or less |
| Reduced-calorie | At least 25% fewer calories when compared with the reference food |
| Sugar-free | Less than ½ gram of sugar |
| Light or Lite | ⅓ fewer calories or 50% less fat when compared to the reference food. If more than half the calories are from fat, fat content must be reduced by 50% or more |
| Fat-free | Less than ½ gram of fat |
| Low-fat | 3 grams or less of fat |
| Reduced-fat | At least 25% less fat when compared with the reference food |
| Cholesterol-free | Less than 2 mg cholesterol and 2 grams or less saturated fat |
| Low-cholesterol | 20 mg or less cholesterol and 2 grams or less saturated fat |
| High-fiber | 5 grams or more fiber |

The nutrition claims are based upon standardized serving size as listed on the label.

# STOCKING THE LOW-FAT, LOW-CHOLESTEROL KITCHEN

Following a low-fat, low-cholesterol, healthful lifestyle doesn't mean that you have to forgo all of your favorite foods forever, but it does mean that you have to exercise good judgment on a daily basis. It starts with what you buy at the market and keep on your shelves at home. Nothing is more frustrating than not having all the ingredients you need when you start to cook. It would be impossible, of course, to list everything needed in all the recipes. However, I have listed some basic pantry supplies I like to keep on hand. All brand names supplied are for kosher products, but local brands can be substituted by those who do not keep kosher.

## In the Refrigerator

Nonfat or skim milk
Nonfat plain or fruited yogurt (no gelatin added)
Low-fat tofu
Part-skim or nonfat ricotta cheese or hoop cheese
Nonfat cottage cheese
Nonfat sour cream
Fat-free nondairy creamer
Fat-free cream cheese
Fat-free Italian or vinaigrette salad dressing
Fat-free mayonnaise
A tub of light margarine or Smartbeat no-fat margarine
Extra-virgin olive oil
Onion-flavored olive oil (page 255)
Canola oil
Extra-large eggs
Brown sugar
Gold's grated horseradish
Dried prunes and apricots (perferably organic)
Dark raisins
Fresh seasonal fruits (especially lemons)
Fresh seasonal vegetables (especially carrots, celery, cucumbers)
Rapid-rise dry yeast
Dried bread crumbs
Hungarian paprika

## In the Pantry

Vegetable oil cooking spray (plain, butter flavored, and olive oil)
Dried split peas, lentils, and beans
Cholent mix
Brown rice (if kept more than three months, store in refrigerator to keep from becoming rancid), white rice, barley, wild rice, bulgur, kasha
Pasta, farfel, and noodles (made without egg yolks)
Unbleached all-purpose flour
Baking powder
Baking soda
Granulated sugar and confectioners' sugar
Cornmeal, oatmeal, oat bran
Cocoa
Whole-grain hot and cold cereals
Potatoes, onions, shallots, and garlic
Nonfat powdered milk
Powdered buttermilk
Matzo meal, cake meal, potato starch

## Canned Goods

Nonfat evaporated milk
Gefilte fish
Salmon
White tuna in water
Fruit in natural juice
Quartered artichoke hearts
Salt-free whole-kernel corn
Salt-free beets
Sodium-reduced kidney and garbanzo beans
Vegetarian baked beans
Low-sodium V-8 juice
Sodium-reduced tomato juice
Kosher *pareve* gravy
Sodium-reduced marinara sauce (no meat)
Salt-free tomato paste
Sodium-reduced tomato sauce
Sodium-reduced diced tomatoes in juice
Sodium-reduced chicken broth
Low-calorie beet borscht or schav

Instant noodle soup (chicken flavor)
Low-sodium onion soup mix
Quick jelly dessert

## *Seasonings*

Balsamic, red, rice, apple cider, and distilled white vinegars
Sodium-reduced soy sauce
Salt-free herb and vegetable seasonings
Worcestershire sauce
Kosher salt
Garlic and onion powder (no salt)
Dried thyme, dill, bay leaves, and other favorite herbs
Ground white pepper
Black peppercorns for grinding
Crushed red pepper flakes
Ground cinnamon
Ground ginger
Whole nutmeg (to be used in grinder or grater)
Poppy seeds
Sesame seeds
Pure vanilla extract and/or vanilla beans
Imported dried mushrooms

## *Snacks*

Salt-free pretzels
Bagel chips
Salt-free, fat-free popcorn
Fat-free potato chips
Matzos (no egg)
Matzo crackers
Melba toast
Fat-free cinnamon crackers
Caramel corn fat-free corn cakes

## In the Freezer

You can put together healthful meals without making a trip to the store if you make good use of your freezer. With a little thought, your freezer can produce wonders for last-minute meals or unexpected guests.

Egg substitute
Onion Helper (page 254)
Phyllo leaves (will keep up to 3 months)
Frozen vegetables like broccoli, cauliflower, tiny peas, spinach, and mixed vegetables
    (avoid those in butter or other sauces)
Natural fruit juice bars
Unsweetened frozen fruits (like blueberries, mangoes, peaches, pineapple)
Unsweetened frozen fruit juice concentrate
Skinned chicken breast fillets or turkey breast slices (4 to 5 ounces raw)
Skinned chicken or turkey legs
Ground turkey breast
Gefilte Fish Roll (page 289)
Lox
2½-pound broiler or Cornish hen, skinned, defatted, and quartered
Head green cabbage (for stuffed cabbage)
Tabachnik no-salt frozen soups
Grated Parmesan cheese or non-dairy alternative
Fresh gingerroot
Nonfat frozen yogurt
Fruit sorbet
Walnuts, almonds, or hazelnuts
Fat- and sodium-reduced margarine
Bagels, bagel chips, and bialys
Water challah
Corn rye bread
Whole wheat bread
Pumpernickel
Any homemade soups
Stick margarine

## A Last Word

Despite the standardization of recipes today, and despite all of our measuring calories and fat grams and sodium intake, cooking remains an alchemical process, a reminder of the interplay between seen and unseen forces in our lives. I have had this feeling about food since I was a child; so while I will provide the instructions and the measurements and the nutritional information, you must provide the magic and the love that will transform your food and all who share it.

# HERBS: ADD A LITTLE SPICE TO YOUR LIFE

Jewish cooking has always relied heavily on fat and salt for flavor. Fat, in fact, is a flavor carrier, so low-fat cooks need to think a little more carefully about flavor when cooking. Salt in *moderation* is a flavor enhancer, but too much salt is a palate deadener. Using less salt will allow you to discover many new tastes that were previously masked by oversalting or would have been too subtle. Try to spark the flavors of your dishes using herbs, saltless seasonings, and flavor enhancers such as lemon juice and good wine. (No cooking wine; it's high in sodium.)

Fresh herbs, more than any other ingredient, give a lift to foods. They are at their most fragrant and flavorful when freshly cut. Consider planting a little herb garden: herbs do just as well in pots on the windowsill as they do in a big garden.

Good-quality dried herbs are obviously a help. They should be stored in a cool, dry, dark place or in your freezer and generally replaced every 6 to 8 months. A sprinkling of fresh herbs just before serving will enhance any dish.

Here are a few herbs that you may find enhance the taste of your cooking:

*Basil:* Intensely herbaceous and aromatic. Combines well with tomatoes, salads, vinaigrette dressing, and most vegetables.

*Bay leaves:* Imported bay leaves are superior. They need long simmering, as in soups and stews. *They are not meant to be eaten; remember to remove before serving.* May also be used in marinades for fish or meat.

*Chervil:* Delicate flavor with the look and taste of parsley. Add freshly chopped to eggs, spinach, peas, carrots, mushrooms; use the whole leaf in salads.

*Chives:* Long, slender blades. Add freshly snipped chives to vegetables (particularly potatoes), soups, salads, and vinaigrette dressing.

*Dill:* Fine, feathery leaves. Fresh is best. Use in yogurts, soups, sauces, and dressings, on fish, in borscht and chowders, and sprinkle on vegetables, such as carrots, cucumbers, beets, and green beans.

*Italian or flat-leaf parsley:* Much more flavorful than curly parsley, and one of the most nutritious herbs. Add freshly chopped to any savory preparation during or after cooking, to salads before serving, and to add special flavor to soups.

*Lovage:* Strong-tasting, easy to grow, with long, celerylike leaves. Flavor reminiscent of both celery and parsley. Wonderful accent to potatoes, corn, or green salads.

*Marjoram:* Fresh is best—sweet, mild, and summery taste, a bit like oregano. Use fresh or dried on tomatoes, mushrooms, and potatoes.

*Mint:* Large, pointed green, sometimes fuzzy, leaves. Potent flavor. Essential for the tart, spicy salads of the Middle East and Asia. Can be used on fresh fruit, broiled tomatoes, in tomato sauce, with garlic and oil over fish.

*Oregano:* A bittersweet, spicy green taste. Use fresh or dried in most marinades, tomato sauces, beans and rice, and yogurt dishes.

*Rosemary:* Needlelike leaves have a piney taste. Fresh or dried, whole or chopped. Add to marinades, simmered sauces and soups, chicken and veal. Wonderful on roasted potatoes or green beans.

*Sage:* Velvety green leaves. Use fresh, not powdered. Flavor can be overpowering, so use judiciously. Use in pasta, tomato or meat sauces, under skin of chicken or turkey before roasting.

*Sorrel:* Fresh, faintly lemon taste. A small amount can lift puréed vegetable soup or salad greens. Sorrel is the main ingredient in Schav Borscht (page 147).

*Tarragon:* Long, slender, dark green leaves with a spicy licorice taste. Fresh is preferred. Add to tomato soup, mushrooms, beets, corn. Steep fresh to flavor vinegar.

*Thyme:* Small, pointed leaves, pleasant taste that seems to fit everywhere. Essential herb in cooking. Used in soups, stocks, sauces, marinades, or mixed green salads.

# HOLIDAYS

*Although many Jewish cooks have updated their daily meals, many still return to the tradition of "cooking Jewish" on holidays and special family occasions.*

# SHABBAT

## Make it a special time.

*Remember the sabbath day, to keep it holy.*
—Exodus 20:8

Shabbat, the Sabbath, a day set aside for prayer, reflection, and the reinforcement of family ties, has been a source of strength for Jews throughout the centuries.

When I was growing up, Shabbat was the one night that we all had dinner together. From the time I was old enough to sit at that big oak table with the rest of the family, I could hardly wait for sundown, which heralded that lovingly prepared, delicious (and labor-intensive) meal. Everything was special, everybody was in attendance, no excuses accepted. My mother's expression—a mixture of exhaustion and pleasure—as she surveyed her progeny is indelibly etched in my treasury of sweet memories. At the end of every busy week, my parents required that we take at least these few hours to jest, joke, grouse, gourmandize, and just be together. I wonder occasionally if I have idealized these Shabbat dinners in memory, but no matter: idealized or not, my past has provided the nourishment for my future. As my children were growing up, I tried—even with the demands and distractions of modern living—to continue the traditions of Shabbat. If their childhood memories are as nourishing as mine, it will have been worth the effort.

❦

## A SHABBAT MENU

*Mother Mollie's No-Cholesterol Challah (page 5)*

*Wine*

*Vegetarian Chopped Liver (page 7) or Gefilte Fish Roll (page 289)*

*My Mother's Chicken Soup (page 138) with No-Yolk Noodles*

*Hungarian Vegetable Salad (page 193)*

*Edie Wahl's Brisket (page 337)*

*Potato Kugel (page 256) with Applesauce*

*Nita Williams' Stuffed Zucchini (page 277)*

*Spiced Baked Pears (page 404)*

*Marbled Mandelbrot (page 386)*

# SABBATH EVE

### Prayer for Candle Lighting

At sundown on Friday, technically eighteen minutes before sunset, the Sabbath candles are lit and the following blessing is said:

*Baruch atah Adonai Elohenu melech ha'olam, asher kideshanu bemitzvotav vetzivanu lahadlik ner shel Shabbat.*

Blessed art Thou, O Lord our God, king of the universe, who has sanctified us by Thy commandments and instructed us to kindle the Sabbath candles.

### Prayer on Drinking Wine

*Baruch atah Adonai Elohenu melech ha'olam, boray prei hagafen.*

Blessed art Thou, O Lord our God, king of the universe, who creates the fruit of the vine.

### Prayer over the Sabbath Challah Beginning the Meal

This blessing over bread, known as the *hamotzi*, is recited at the beginning of any meal where bread is served. It covers all food items eaten at the meal.

*Baruch atah Adonai Elohenu melech ha'olam, hamotzi lechem min ha'aretz.*

Blessed art Thou, O Lord our God, king of the universe, who brings forth bread from the earth.

# ❦ Mother Mollie's No-Cholesterol Challah ❦
## (PAREVE)
*Yield: Three 9 × 5-inch loaves (about 45 slices)   (1 slice = 1 serving)*

Challah is the traditional Jewish braided egg bread which is served at weekly Shabbat meals. In accordance with an ancient custom, my mother always removed a small piece of dough before the loaf was shaped. This little piece, the *challah* (Hebrew for "priest's share"), was set aside to rise and bake on its own until it was charred beyond use.

I love making challah. I love the way it feels, smells, and tastes, and of all the challahs I have ever tasted (bought or homemade), this one is the most delicious. Served fresh, its texture and taste are a special treat. The next day, it makes toast that simply melts in your mouth.

The recipe comes originally from my mother-in-law, Mollie Hollander Roth, who made challahs as easily as I used to make brownies. Shortly after my husband and I were married, my in-laws came to visit us for the Thanksgiving holiday. We were living in Cleveland, Ohio, at the time. It started snowing Thanksgiving eve and continued for four days. Under its blanket of snow, the city came to a grinding halt. Fortunately, we had a good supply of yeast, flour, and eggs on hand, and my mother-in-law provided all of our delighted apartment neighbors with daily loaves of freshly baked challah.

With the necessary changes from Crisco to a bit of canola oil, and egg yolks to egg whites, I've lowered the fat and cholesterol while managing to preserve the integrity of Mollie's marvelous challah.

If you are not a bread maker, water (eggless) challah may be purchased at some Jewish bakeries on Fridays. Most times I make challah in loaf pans because the slices are more even, but you can bake the braided dough on baking sheets if you prefer.

    3 envelopes rapid-rise yeast
    ¼ cup sugar or honey
    1 tablespoon kosher salt
    2¾ cups warm water (about 105° to 115°)
    ¼ cup canola oil
    6 extra-large egg whites plus 1 extra-large egg, slightly beaten
7 to 7½ cups unbleached all-purpose flour or bread flour
    1 egg white, slightly beaten, for glazing
    3 tablespoons poppy seeds, sesame seeds, or charnitchka (black caraway
      seeds) (optional)

1. Coat three 9 × 5 × 3-inch loaf pans with cooking spray or canola oil.

2. Place the yeast, sugar, salt, and water in the large bowl of an electric mixer and stir to dissolve. Let stand 5 to 10 minutes or until the yeast is creamy and bubbles.

3. Add the oil and egg white mixture and beat, using the dough hook, until well mixed.

4. Stir in 3½ cups of flour and beat on medium speed with the dough hook for 1 minute.

5. Add 4 more cups of flour, ½ cup at a time, beating on medium speed until a soft dough is formed. Knead with the dough hook for 5 to 6 minutes until the dough is smooth and elastic. Scrape down the sides of the bowl.

6. Sprinkle the top of the dough with about 1 tablespoon of flour, cover the bowl with a clean kitchen towel and let rise in the bowl for about 15 to 20 minutes or until indentation of fingers will remain in the dough.

7. Lightly flour hands and push the dough down in the bowl. Work the dough in the bowl about 1 minute.

8. Turn the dough out on a lightly floured surface and divide into 3 portions. Knead each lightly into a round ball. Flatten 1 round of dough and cut into 3 pieces. Lightly dust the strips of dough with flour and roll into 3 ropes about 10 inches in length. Join 3 strips at the top and braid, placing the braided bread in a prepared pan.

9. Repeat with the remaining dough and cover the 3 pans with damp towels. The pans should be placed in the warm, draft-free place in the kitchen. Let rise 30 minutes. The dough will double or reach close to the top of the pan. Meanwhile preheat the oven to 375°.

10. Brush lightly with slightly beaten egg white and avoid letting the glaze drip onto the pan or the bread will stick. Sprinkle with poppy seeds, sesame seeds, or charnitchka, if desired.

11. Place the pans on the middle rack and bake at 375° for 15 minutes. Reduce the heat to 350°. Bake for about 30 to 35 minutes, or until golden brown.

12. Loosen the loaf with a metal spatula and remove from the pan. If sufficiently baked, the loaf will make a hollow sound when thumped on the bottom. Cool the challahs on a rack.

*To Serve:* Cool before slicing (if you can wait that long). If you are fortunate enough to have some left, this freezes beautifully if carefully wrapped in foil then placed in a freezer bag.

---

PER SERVING

| | | | |
|---|---|---|---|
| 1.9 gm total fat | .20 gm saturated fat | .8 gm fiber | 114 calories |
| 4 mg cholesterol | 15.4% fat | 143 mg sodium | 17 calories from fat |

# ❦ Vegetarian Chopped Liver ❦

## (PAREVE)

*Yield: 4 cups*

*Serves: 12 as a first course    (2 tablespoons = 1 serving as an appetizer)*

Whenever people heard that I was writing a low-fat, low-cholesterol Jewish cookbook, they asked facetiously if I had a recipe for low-fat, low-cholesterol chopped liver. My answer was, of course, no. But when my publisher, Elaine Koster, requested a vegetarian spread that would *taste* like chopped liver I was happy to oblige. For a delicious nonvegetarian version, substitute 1 cup finely chopped roast brisket for the walnuts.

  1 medium eggplant (about 1¼ pounds), peeled and sliced into ¼-inch rounds
  ⅓ cup green lentils
  1 large Vidalia onion or 3 yellow onions, chopped fine (2 cups)
  1 tablespoon olive oil
1½ cups (about ½ pound) coarsely chopped mushrooms (portobello, shiitake, and/or button mushrooms)
  2 tablespoons balsamic vinegar
  2 large cloves garlic, smashed or minced
  2 teaspoons salt-free vegetable seasoning
  ½ teaspoon ground white pepper
  1 cup egg substitute mixed with 2 extra-large egg whites
  6 extra-large hard-cooked egg whites (discard yolks)
  ½ cup coarsely chopped, toasted walnuts
  ¼ cup nonfat mayonnaise
    Salt and freshly ground black pepper, to taste
    Chopped fresh thyme leaves, for garnish

1. Preheat the broiler. Place the eggplant slices on a baking sheet, coat with olive oil cooking spray, and broil until lightly browned. Turn the slices over and repeat. Quarter the slices when cool enough to handle.

2. Cook the lentils in 1 cup water for 20 minutes or until soft. Drain.

3. Combine 1 cup of chopped onion and the olive oil in a nonstick skillet, cover, and wilt for 2 to 3 minutes. Uncover and sauté until soft, about 3 minutes.

4. Add the mushrooms, balsamic vinegar, garlic, seasoning, and white pepper; sauté 5 minutes. Add the lentils, stir, and cool.

5. Pour 1 cup of the egg substitute mixture into a 6-inch nonstick skillet. Cover and cook over low heat for about 10 minutes or until firm, but not browned. Let stand 10 minutes, remove the cover, cut into eighths, and cool.

6. Put the eggplant, sautéed onion mixture, remaining cup of chopped raw onion, hard-cooked egg whites, nuts, and cooked, cooled egg substitute in a food processor. Using the steel blade, process with pulsing action until blended and finely chopped or puréed. Or use a food grinder.

7. Remove the mixture to a bowl. Add the mayonnaise, stir, and adjust seasoning with salt and pepper; cover and refrigerate several hours, or overnight, before serving.

*To Serve:* Mound on a lettuce-lined platter or individual plates. Sprinkle with chopped thyme leaves and surround with thin slices of mild onion and tomato. Accompany with squares of matzo, challah, and/or pumpernickel.

| PER SERVING AS AN APPETIZER | | | |
|---|---|---|---|
| .7 gm total fat | .12 gm saturated fat | .5 gm fiber | 25 calories |
| 0 mg cholesterol | 25.2% fat | 67 mg sodium | 7 calories from fat |

# ❦ Cholent ❦
## (MEAT)
### Serves: 10 to 12

I first tasted cholent (the name comes from the Yiddish *shul-ente,* meaning the conclusion of the synagogue services) when I visited the home of my cousins in Rehovot, Israel, many years ago. When mealtime arrived, Esther extended a drop-leaf table that managed to seat cousins by the dozens as they arrived. The tastes and smells were nearly as wonderful as the joy my husband, daughter, and I experienced upon meeting our newfound relations.

This distinctively Jewish dish has origins as early as the fourth century A.D. Because lighting fires and cooking on Saturday—a day of rest—were prohibited, this one-dish meal for Shabbat lunch was prepared on Friday, sealed with a paste of flour and water, and taken to a neighborhood bakery for slow cooking overnight. Whether you call it *chamin* (a warmed food), *adafini,* cassoulet, or cholent, this dish has flexibility, and its specific character can be determined by the individual cook. Choose lima beans, chickpeas (a favorite in Israel), fava, navy, or cannellini beans, barley, or potatoes; eliminate the meat if you prefer and use other vegetables, such as onions, carrots, celery, tomatoes, or Swiss chard, for a vegetarian dish. Whether you add meatballs, matzo balls, eggs in their shells, kugel, flanken, kishka or helzel, turkey, chicken, brisket, or lamb shanks, it's your call. The only rule: don't stir—just shake the dish from time to time and enjoy.

One story that is told about cholent concerns a priest and a rabbi who were very good friends. The priest complained that he had insomnia, and the rabbi suggested that he try eating cholent as a cure. Several days later, they met and the unhappy priest said, "I understand how you fall asleep from this dish, but what I don't understand is how do you get up?!"

In the Ashkenazi recipe below, I've created a tasty, low-fat cholent with marrow bones and skinned chicken added to the vegetables and other ingredients. If overnight cooking doesn't suit your lifestyle, this may be cooked for three to four hours on top of the stove. It makes a special Sunday night supper as well as a Sabbath luncheon meal.

  1 tablespoon olive oil
  4 large onions, peeled and chopped fine
¼ cup barley, washed
  1 pound dried large lima beans, rinsed and drained (see Note)
    Salt and freshly ground pepper to taste
  5 (2-inch) slices marrow bones
  3 large carrots, peeled and cut into 1-inch chunks
  2 large tomatoes, peeled, seeded, and diced
  3 ribs celery with leaves, chopped
  1 (2½-pound) broiler, skinned, defatted, and cut into 10 pieces,
    or 3 to 4 turkey legs, skinned
  1 tablespoon sweet or hot Hungarian paprika
  6 cloves garlic, unpeeled
10 pitted prunes
    Vegetarian Kishkes (page 132): Make 1 large roll (kishka), wrap in plastic, and pierce several times with a fork (optional)
  4 new or Yukon Gold potatoes, peeled and quartered
  2 tablespoons sugar
    Boiling water or sodium-reduced, fat-free chicken broth, to cover
    Chopped Italian parsley, for garnish

1. Place a cholent heavy roaster pot or a Dutch oven with a tight-fitting lid over low heat. Coat the bottom and sides with olive oil spray. Add the oil and heat. Add the onion and sauté until soft, about 10 minutes. Mix in the barley.

2. Layer ingredients in the cholent pot in the following order: drained lima beans sprinkled lightly with salt and pepper, marrow bones, carrots, tomatoes, celery, chicken pieces sprinkled with pepper and paprika, garlic cloves, prunes, kishka, and potatoes.

3. Melt the sugar in a small dry skillet until it turns deep brown. Remove from the heat, carefully add 2 tablespoons of water, and pour the syrup over the potatoes.

4. Add boiling water and/or chicken broth to cover.

5. Bring to a boil, cover, and simmer for 30 minutes. Meanwhile, heat the oven to low (225°).

6. Shake the pan, and place in the oven to bake overnight. If you need more liquid, add no more than ½ cup at a time.

7. Before serving, remove the cover and transfer the kishka to a cutting board. Raise the oven temperature to 500° and bake the cholent until a crust forms. Crush the crust down into the beans and juices, then allow a crust to form a second time. Arrange the kishka slices on top of the cholent before serving, and sprinkle with parsley.

NOTE: One package of Unger's mixed dried beans for cholent may be used.

---

PER SERVING

| 4.8 gm total fat | 1.17 gm saturated fat | 5.9 gm fiber | 236 calories |
| 32 mg cholesterol | 18% fat | 78 mg sodium | 44 calories from fat |

# ROSH HASHANAH

## It's Late This Year . . .

*And in the seventh month, on the first day of the month, ye shall have a holy convocation. . . . It shall be the day of blowing the horn unto you.*
—NUMBERS 29:1

Why is it that Rosh Hashanah never seems to be on time? It is always either early or late. Rosh Hashanah marks the beginning of the Jewish year. Since the Hebrew calendar is lunar, the date of Rosh Hashanah is that of the new moon closest to the holiday of Sukkot. In other words, there is a perfectly good reason why the new year falls sometimes as early as the beginning of September and sometimes as late as early October.

Rosh Hashanah is also the opening of the Days of Awe, a ten-day period of prayer and introspection, culminating in Yom Kippur, a time to reflect, take stock of our lives, give thanks for the good times in the year just ended, and express hope for peace and happiness for the whole world in the year to come.

Jewish cooks have created holiday menus that incorporate family traditions as well as the traditions of their ancestral homelands. Symbolic foods vary from one nation to another. Both of the following menus, one Ashkenazi, one Syrian Sephardic, are traditional; their common elements reflect the bond that joins the Jews as one people, while their differences reflect the extraordinary variety of Jewish experience around the world.

*"L'shanah tovah tikatevu."* (May you be inscribed [in the Book of Life] for a good year.)
—TRADITIONAL ROSH HASHANAH GREETING

❧❧

## ASHKENAZI ROSH HASHANAH DINNER
**The Symbolic Foods include:**
A round challah with raisins—*the symbol of the kingship of God*
*(it resembles a crown), and of the cycle of the year*
Apples dipped in honey—*for a sweet new year*
Carrots, raisins, honey, apples, prunes—*sweet dishes that are reminders of hope*

❧❧

### DINNER
*Mother Mollie's No-Cholesterol Challah (page 5) with Honey*
*Gefilte Fish Loaf (page 71) with Chrain (page 73)*
*My Mother's Chicken Soup (page 138) with No-Yolk Noodles*
*Roasted Chicken Italian Style (page 13)*
*Farfel Ring (page 15) with Peas and Snow Peas*
*Spinach Kugel (page 16)*
*Carrot and Prune Tzimmes (page 272)*
*Marinated Cucumbers (page 178) with Fresh Dill*
*Rhubarb Sauce (page 412)*
*Mollie Roth's Honey Chiffon Cake (page 17)*
*Almost Aunt Dora's Strudel (page 362)*

❧❧

# ❧❧ Round Challah with Raisins ❧❧
### (PAREVE)
*Yield: 2 round challahs*

On Rosh Hashanah Jewish bakery shelves are filled with spiral, dome-shaped loaves symbolic of the continuity of life. They are filled with raisins to symbolize the hope of a sweet year. Using the same recipe as for my loaf challahs, I prepare this round challah as the centerpiece of the holiday dinner.

1 recipe Mother Mollie's No-Cholesterol Challah (page 5)
½ cup dark raisins, rinsed and dried
1 large egg white, beaten until foamy

1. Follow steps 1 through 7 in the challah recipe and divide the dough in half. Roll one half into a ball, cover with a kitchen towel, and set aside. Place the other half on a floured work surface and knead it lightly. Roll out with a rolling pin into a 9 × 12-inch rectangle.

2. Sprinkle with raisins and roll the dough up tightly, jelly roll fashion, starting at a 12-inch side. Roll the dough back and forth with the hands into a rope about 32 to 34 inches long.

3. Form the rope into a spiral shape, starting at the center, on a baking sheet coated with vegetable oil cooking spray or cornmeal. (The baking sheet should be large enough to hold 2 loaves.) Tuck the end of the rope under the bread. Cover with a slightly dampened kitchen towel and place in a draft-free spot. Repeat with the remaining dough.

4. Let the loaves rise about 30 to 45 minutes, or until doubled in bulk. Meanwhile, heat the oven to 375°.

5. Brush each loaf lightly with beaten egg white. Place the baking sheet on the middle rack of the oven and bake for 15 minutes. Reduce the heat to 350° and bake about 30 minutes longer, or until the bread sounds hollow when tapped on the bottom.

6. Transfer to a rack and cool.

## ❦ Roasted Chicken Italian Style (Italkin) ❦
### (MEAT)
*Serves: 8 (1 chicken breast half = 1 serving)*

It's always convenient to have a "company dish," whether for holidays or other entertaining, that can be prepared ahead of time. In this recipe I've chosen chicken breasts and drumsticks over thighs, because of the lower fat content. You may also use boneless chicken breasts; however, meat cooked on the bone is more flavorful.

 8 chicken breast halves (around 4 pounds), or 16 drumsticks (or half and half), skinned and defatted, washed in cold running water, and dried with paper towels
 2 shallots, minced
 6 large cloves garlic, smashed, peeled, and minced
 2 large onions, peeled, halved, and sliced thin
 2 tablespoons olive oil
½ cup fresh lemon juice
 4 bay leaves
12 fresh plum tomatoes, quartered, or 1 (28-ounce) can whole plum tomatoes, drained
 4 fennel bulbs (greens removed, sliced thin)
¼ cup chopped Italian flat-leaf parsley
 1 cup sodium-reduced chicken broth, defatted
 2 teaspoons Hungarian paprika
   Salt and freshly ground pepper to taste

1. Place the chicken parts in a large bowl or plastic bag. Combine the remaining ingredients and pour over the chicken. Cover or seal and marinate in the refrigerator overnight.

2. Preheat the oven to 375°.

3. Arrange the chicken and vegetables in a single layer in a roasting pan or an attractive 3-quart casserole. Place in the upper third of the oven and bake uncovered for about 1 hour, or until the chicken and vegetables are tender and lightly browned.

*To Serve:* Garnish with watercress and accompany with farfel ring filled with steamed young carrots and snow peas, and fresh rhubarb or applesauce.

───────────── PER SERVING ─────────────

| | | | |
|---|---|---|---|
| 4.5 gm total fat | 1.03 gm saturated fat | 1.6 gm fiber | 216 calories |
| 73 mg cholesterol | 18.7% fat | 208 mg sodium | 41 calories from fat |

---

### ❦ HARRIET'S HINTS ❦

*Defatting poultry or meat: Use stainless steel kitchen shears for trimming fat or skin from poultry. It's easier, quicker, and safer than using a knife.*

---

# ❦ Farfel Ring ❦
## (MEAT)
### *Serves: 12*

When I was a newlywed living in Cleveland, Ohio, my friend Harriet Krause gave me this recipe. We have enjoyed it all these years, and so have all the friends we've shared it with. It can be made the day before, and it also freezes beautifully for future use.

- 4 cups sodium-reduced chicken broth, defatted (see Note)
- 2 (7-ounce) packages brown farfel (toasted egg barley) (or use regular farfel browned briefly under the broiler)
- 2 tablespoons olive oil
- 1 large onion, peeled and minced
- ½ pound fresh mushrooms, cleaned and sliced
- ½ cup chopped Italian flat-leaf parsley
- ½ teaspoon ground white pepper
- Salt to taste

1. Bring the chicken broth to a boil in a saucepan; add the farfel and simmer over medium heat until almost dry.

2. Heat the olive oil in a nonstick sauté pan over medium heat. Add the onion and sauté for 5 minutes, or until wilted. Add the mushrooms and sauté 2 to 3 minutes.

3. Add the farfel to the mushroom-onion mixture. Blend. Add the parsley and pepper. Taste and add salt if needed. Heat the oven to 350°.

4. Coat a 2½-quart ring mold with olive oil cooking spray. Add the farfel mixture and cover the mold with foil.

5. Place the mold in a large baking pan. Fill the pan with 1 inch of hot water, transfer to the oven, and bake for 1 hour.

6. Remove the farfel from the water bath and let stand for 15 minutes. Remove foil, loosen the edges of the farfel with a spatula, and unmold.

*To Serve:* Unmold the ring on a round platter and fill the center with any desired vegetables, such as peas and carrots in the center, surrounded with broccoli and cauliflower florets.

NOTE: One package of low-sodium soup mix with or without noodles, combined with 4½ cups boiling water, may be substituted for the chicken broth.

| PER SERVING | | | |
|---|---|---|---|
| 3.4 gm total fat | .67 gm saturated fat | 1.3 gm fiber | 114 calories |
| 22 mg cholesterol | 27.4% fat | 58 mg sodium | 31 calories from fat |

## ❦ Spinach Kugel ❦
### (PAREVE)
*Serves: 10 to 12*

I frequently use versatile Passover products, like potato starch, matzo meal, matzo farfel, and matzos throughout the year. This recipe uses matzo farfel.

    2 cups chopped leek (white part only) or onion
    1 tablespoon olive oil or canola oil
    2 (10-ounce) packages frozen chopped spinach, thawed and squeezed dry
    ¾ cup egg substitute
    2 tablespoons chopped fresh dill
    2 tablespoons chopped fresh chives or scallion
    2 cups matzo farfel
    2 cups defatted sodium-reduced chicken broth
    4 extra-large egg whites
    ½ teaspoon freshly ground pepper
    ¼ teaspoon freshly grated nutmeg
      Salt to taste
      Hungarian paprika

1. Preheat the oven to 350°.

2. Sauté the leek in the oil in a nonstick skillet. Cover for 3 minutes, remove the cover, and sauté until soft. Remove from the heat and add the spinach.

3. Place the egg substitute, dill, chives and the spinach mixture in the food processor and process briefly.

4. Mix the matzo farfel with the chicken broth; add the spinach mixture to the farfel and let stand 5 to 10 minutes.

5. Beat the egg whites until they are shiny and form soft peaks. Fold the whites into the spinach mixture along with the pepper and nutmeg. Taste and adjust seasonings.

6. Coat a 13 × 9 × 2-inch glass baking dish with olive oil cooking spray.

7. Pour the mixture into the dish, sprinkle with paprika, and bake for about 45 minutes or until firm.

*To Serve:* Cut into 10 to 12 portions and serve *hot* as an accompaniment to roast veal, turkey, or chicken.

---

PER SERVING

| | | | |
|---|---|---|---|
| 2.62 gm total fat | .33 gm saturated fat | 3.5 gm fiber | 200 calories |
| 0 mg cholesterol | 7% fat | 160 mg sodium | 23 calories from fat |

# ❧ Mollie Roth's Honey Chiffon Cake ❧ (Low-fat, No-cholesterol Lekach)

## (PAREVE)

### Serves: 14 to 16

No Rosh Hashanah dinner at my mother-in-law's house ended without this delicious light honey cake as one of the many desserts. Until she was eighty-seven years old, Mother prepared the whole holiday dinner: challah, gefilte fish, chicken soup, kreplach, roast chicken and/or veal, homemade applesauce, strudel, and honey cake. She was an amazing, energetic, caring woman. Everybody left those evenings with their favorite care package.

1¼ cups honey
1¼ cups hot, strong coffee
3½ cups unbleached all-purpose flour
¾ cup sugar
2½ teaspoons baking powder
1 teaspoon baking soda
2 teaspoons ground cinnamon
½ teaspoon ground allspice
¼ teaspoon ground ginger
¼ teaspoon freshly grated nutmeg
¼ cup canola oil
½ cup egg substitute
4 extra-large egg whites, at room temperature
¼ teaspoon cream of tartar
½ cup sliced almonds, for garnish (optional)
Confectioners' sugar

1. Dissolve the honey in the hot coffee; cool. Meanwhile, heat the oven to 350°.

2. Sift together the flour, ½ cup sugar, the baking powder, baking soda, cinnamon, allspice, ginger, and nutmeg into a large mixing bowl.

3. Add the oil, egg substitute, and cooled coffee mixture; stir until smooth.

4. Beat the egg whites and cream of tartar until foamy; add the remaining sugar, 1 tablespoon at a time, beating until stiff and glossy.

5. Pour one third of the batter over the beaten egg whites and fold gently until blended. Repeat 2 times with the remaining batter.

6. Pour and scrape into an ungreased 10-inch tube pan. Sprinkle with almonds.

7. Bake in the middle of a preheated oven for about 1 hour 15 minutes, or until the top springs back when lightly touched.

8. Invert the pan on a bottle or funnel and let cool completely.

9. Loosen the sides of the cake with a thin knife and remove from the pan. Dust with confectioners' sugar before serving.

VARIATION: Lightly coat bottoms of 2 loaf pans with vegetable oil spray and line with wax paper. Scrape the batter into the pans. Bake in a preheated 350° oven for about 50 minutes or until the cake starts to pull away from the sides of the pans.

This cake freezes well.

| PER SERVING | | | |
|---|---|---|---|
| 3.9 gm total fat | .35 gm saturated fat | .8 gm fiber | 271 calories |
| 0 mg cholesterol | 12.8% fat | 131 mg sodium | 36 calories from fat |

❧

## A SYRIAN SEPHARDIC ROSH HASHANAH DINNER

*Sephardic Jews from the Arab countries of the Middle East have unique customs and traditions. The Arabic Sephardim are more Orthodox than other Sephardim, and their rituals and language have a decidedly Arabic flavor. As in many Jewish homes, food and holiday celebration are a way of sharing hospitality. My Sephardic cooking specialist, Renée Holland, is a first-generation American Jew. She is carrying on the traditions of her parents, who came from Syria. For Rosh Hashanah she prepares a sumptuous holiday feast for her family and many guests, starting with a ceremonial platter of symbolic foods.*

❧

### The Symbolic Foods Include:

A calf's tongue—*May we surge forward in all our endeavors*
Dates, apple slices, and honey—*May there be happiness and peace for all men*
Pomegranate—*May our good deeds be as numerous as the seeds within
this fruit are plentiful*
A round raisin challah with honey—*To make the coming year sweet*

❧

### HORS D'OEUVRES

*Cracked Wheat Dip (page 20) with Vegetable Crudités*
*Phyllo Triangles Filled with Spinach or Mashed Potatoes and Onion*
*Hummus (page 123) with Pita Bread*

❧

### BUFFET TABLE

*Roast Turkey*
*Mechshe (Stuffed Zucchini) (page 21)*
*Rizib Chicken (page 22)*
*Renée Holland's Kibbe (page 23)*

*Sautéed Button Mushrooms with Onions and Celery*

*Steamed String Beans and Asparagus*

*Black-Eyed Peas with Garlic*

*Syrian Gelatin Mold with Apricots and Almonds (page 24)*

DESSERTS

*Fresh Fruit*

*Syrian Sponge Cake*

*Date Cake*

## Cracked Wheat Dip

(PAREVE)

*Yield: 1½ cups (1 tablespoon = 1 serving)*

**1 cup cracked wheat**
**1 large onion, peeled and chopped**
**1 tablespoon canola oil**
**¼ cup finely chopped Italian flat-leaf parsley**
**1 fresh or canned tomato, peeled and seeded**
**1 (6-ounce) can salt-free tomato paste**
**¼ cup toasted pine nuts (optional)**
**2 tablespoons liquid tamarind (see Note)**
**1 teaspoon ground cumin**
**Few grains ground red pepper (cayenne)**
**Salt to taste**

1. Wash the cracked wheat in cold water; allow to drain, leaving a little water (about 2 tablespoons).
2. Sauté the chopped onion in canola oil until light golden.
3. Combine all the ingredients in a food processor and process just to blend.

*To Serve:* This may be refrigerated, but it should be brought to room temperature at serving time. Serve with crudités (assorted crisp raw vegetables).

NOTE: If you are not able to find liquid tamarind in your local market, try a Middle Eastern market; or substitute 2 tablespoons ketchup mixed with 1 tablespoon lemon juice.

—————— PER SERVING ——————

| | | | |
|---|---|---|---|
| .7 gm total fat | .06 gm saturated fat | 1.3 gm fiber | 36 calories |
| 0 mg cholesterol | 16.3% fat | 30 mg sodium | 6 calories from fat |

## ❦ Mechshe (Stuffed Zucchini) ❦
### (PAREVE)
*Serves: 12*

12 small zucchini (3 pounds), halved lengthwise
¼ cup uncooked short-grain rice
 1 pound ground turkey
½ teaspoon kosher salt
½ teaspoon ground allspice
½ teaspoon ground cinnamon
2½ cups water, or as needed
18 dried apricots
¼ cup fresh lemon juice
 2 tablespoons sugar

1. Hollow the zucchini with a grapefruit spoon.
2. Combine the rice, turkey, spices, and ½ cup water.
3. Fill the zucchini loosely with the rice mixture. Place side by side in an ovenproof 12-inch sauté pan. Top with apricots.
4. Place a plate over the zucchini to weight them down.
5. Mix the lemon juice and sugar with 2 cups water and pour into the pan. Then pour in enough additional water to come to the level of the plate.

6. Bring to a boil, cover, and cook over low heat for 15 minutes. Meanwhile, heat the oven to 350°.

7. Transfer to the oven and bake, covered, for about 1½ hours.

*To Serve:* Remove carefully with a slotted spatula and arrange on a heated serving platter.

---

PER SERVING

| | | | |
|---|---|---|---|
| 3.3 gm total fat | .88 gm saturated fat | 1.2 gm fiber | 114 calories |
| 30 mg cholesterol | 25.1% fat | 136 mg sodium | 30 calories from fat |

# ❧ Rizib Chicken ❧
# (Syrian Chicken and Rice)
### (MEAT)
*Serves: 12*

If you cook the chicken the day before, it will be easier to remove the meat from the bone and the fat from the stock.

1 (2½- to 3-pound) fryer, quartered
2 cups uncooked rice
1 teaspoon kosher salt
1 cup pine nuts, toasted

1. Cook the chicken in enough water to cover until tender (about 45 minutes).

2. Drain and defat the chicken broth. Skin the chicken, remove the bones, and dice the meat.

3. Place the rice in a flameproof casserole pan and cover with 4 cups of defatted broth from the cooked chicken. Add the salt and bring to a boil.

4. Add the diced chicken to the rice and cook, stirring frequently, until there is about ¼ inch of liquid on top of the rice. Meanwhile, preheat the oven to 300°.

5. Cover the casserole and place in the oven for 45 minutes.

6. Just before serving, press the rice mixture into a 6-cup mold and pack tightly.

*To Serve:* Turn the mold out onto a heated serving platter and sprinkle with pine nuts.

---
————————————— P E R   S E R V I N G —————————————

| | | | |
|---|---|---|---|
| 14.1 gm total fat | 2.50 gm saturated fat | 1.2 gm fiber | 290 calories |
| 30 mg cholesterol | 42.3% fat | 241 mg sodium | 127 calories from fat |

---

# ❦ Renée Holland's Kibbe ❦ (Crescent-shaped Meatballs)
### (MEAT)
*Yield: 32 pieces (1 piece = 1 serving)*

This dish may be served as an appetizer or as part of a buffet.

*Outside Shell:*
- 1 pound very lean ground veal or turkey
- 1 (12-ounce) package uncooked cream of rice cereal
- ½ teaspoon kosher salt, or to taste
- 1 tablespoon canola oil
- Few drops fresh lemon juice

*Filling:*
- ⅓ pound extra lean ground beef
- 1 teaspoon ground cinnamon
- 1 teaspoon ground allspice
- ½ cup finely chopped celery with leaves

*Sauce:*
- 8 ribs celery, cut into 1-inch chunks
- 3 large cloves garlic, smashed, peeled, and minced
- ½ cup minced fresh mint leaves or ¼ cup crushed dried
- 1 quart water
- 1 cup fresh lemon juice or 10 to 12 ounces (about 1¼ cups) bottled lemon juice
- 2 tablespoons sugar
- Salt to taste

1. Make the outside shell: Combine the veal with the cream of rice and salt; mix well.

2. Place 1 tablespoon canola oil and a few drops of fresh lemon juice in a shallow plate. Dip your fingers in this mixture to prevent the shells from sticking while you form the shell mixture into 32 balls about 1 inch round.

3. Make the filling: Combine the beef, cinnamon, allspice, and celery; mix well.

4. Make a hollow in each ball with your finger and fill with ½ teaspoon of filling. Close the opening by pinching it firmly and form the ball into a crescent shape.

5. Make the sauce: Boil all the sauce ingredients uncovered for ½ hour. Taste and adjust seasonings. The sauce should be quite tart.

6. Add formed kibbe to the boiling lemon sauce; return to a boil and simmer for ½ hour.

NOTE: If desired, raw kibbe may be frozen without the lemon sauce and used at a future date.

--- PER SERVING ---

| | | | |
|---|---|---|---|
| 1.3 gm total fat | .45 gm saturated fat | .2 gm fiber | 74 calories |
| 15 mg cholesterol | 16.2% fat | 82 mg sodium | 12 calories from fat |

# ❧ Syrian Gelatin Mold ❧ with Apricots and Almonds
## (PAREVE)
### Serves: 12

To lower the fat content of this fruit mold, cut the amount of almonds in half.

3 (3-ounce) boxes kosher apricot or lemon gelatin
8 ounces dried apricots
8 ounces (1⅔ cups) blanched almonds
   Watercress, for garnish

1. Mix the gelatin according to package directions and chill briefly until syrupy.
2. Boil the apricots in water to cover for 5 minutes. Drain, cool, and purée.

3. Mix the chilled, syrupy gelatin with the purée.
4. Scatter the blanched almonds on the bottom of an oiled 6-cup mold.
5. Spoon the gelatin mixture on top.
6. Refrigerate until firm.

*To Serve:* Unmold and serve as a side dish with meat or chicken, garnished with watercress and fresh pineapple chunks.

| PER SERVING | | | |
|---|---|---|---|
| 11.0 gm total fat | 1.04 gm saturated fat | 3.6 gm fiber | 242 calories |
| 0 mg cholesterol | 11.0% fat | 204 mg sodium | 99 calories from fat |

# YOM KIPPUR (DAY OF ATONEMENT)

## A Time for Reflection

*Howbeit on the tenth day of this seventh month is the day of atonement: It shall be a holy convocation unto you; and ye shall afflict your souls. . . . And ye shall do no manner of work in that same day, for it is the day of atonement. . . .*

—LEVITICUS 23:27–28

With the stirring strains of the Kol Nidre prayer, we begin the great fast of Yom Kippur. But abstinence from food is of no value without true reflection and the atonement that comes with it. To prepare ourselves for fasting on Yom Kippur, we keep our foods before the fast as bland as possible.

### EREV YOM KIPPUR DINNER

*Eggs and Onions (page 28)*

*Mother Mollie's No-Cholesterol Challah (page 5)*

*My Mother's Chicken Soup (page 138) with No-Yolk Noodles*

*Relish Tray of Red, White, and Black Radishes*

*Roast Chicken with Brussels Sprouts (page 29)*

*Sarah's Rice Kugel (page 218)*

*Prune-Apricot Compote (page 400)*

After the blast of the shofar officially closes the long day of prayer and introspection, people head for home, a little weary, but spiritually uplifted. All are looking forward to breaking the fast. Most families serve a dairy "brunch" type of meal, while others prefer a traditional holiday dinner.

While I was growing up, the girls were expected to leave synagogue early and see that the table was set appropriately. *Kuchen*, challah, and coffee were served first to break the fast, and then usually a complete *fleischig* (meat) meal, from soup to dessert, followed.

In recent years, although the custom of having coffee and *kuchen* remains, we have changed and lightened the succeeding meal with a *milchig* (dairy) menu. The following is a buffet that expands to feed unlimited numbers, and the food can be prepared the day before so that you can stay for the beautiful concluding Neilah service, and then return to your home and family to enjoy breaking the fast.

❦

## BUFFET FOR FAMILY AND FRIENDS

*Beet–Gefilte Fish Mold (page 34) with Cucumber Sauce*

*Herring Antipasto (page 119)*

*Mother Mollie's No-Cholesterol Challah (page 5)*

*Sliced Tomatoes, Cucumbers, Onions, and Nonfat Cream Cheese with Bagels*

*Poached Salmon (page 295) with Green Sauce (page 296)*

*Fresh Fruit Salad*

*Israeli Vegetable Salad (page 184)*

*Atlanta Honey Cake (page 35)*

*Reformed Rugelach (page 37)*

*Mama's Danish (page 418)*

*Mock Strudel (page 38)*

❦

# ❦ Eggs and Onions ❦
## (PAREVE)
### *Serves: 8 as a first course*

My sister-in-law Helen Kolatch in San Francisco and I were talking food and recipes one day, and she mentioned that her husband, Arthur, really missed eating eggs
and onions mixed with "you-know-what" (*schmaltz*, or rendered chicken fat). Being
the devoted wife that she is, she brainstormed and came up with the idea of using egg
substitute in place of egg yolks. I thought that perhaps a bit of onion-flavored olive
oil might replace the fat. Arthur loves it. What do you think?

10 **extra-large eggs**
 1 **(8-ounce) carton egg substitute**
 1 **large onion, chopped fine and drained of juice (1½ cups)**
 1 **tablespoon Onion-flavored Olive Oil (page 255) (and some of the cooked
    browned onions if you like)**
 ½ **teaspoon ground white pepper, or to taste**
   **Salt to taste**

1. Place 8 eggs in a 1½-quart saucepan, add warm tap water to cover them by 1
inch, and bring to a boil. Reduce the heat to a simmer and cook for 20 to 25 minutes.
Cool immediately under cold running water; crack the shells to speed cooling. Peel
the eggs, halve, and remove the yolks. (Discard the yolks, or save for your dog.)

2. Cook the egg substitute mixed with 2 egg whites covered in a 6-inch nonstick
skillet over low heat for 10 minutes, or until firm. Allow it to stand, covered, without
heat for 10 minutes and cool for 10 additional minutes before cutting into chunks. Or
microwave on High in a shallow soup bowl for 3 minutes; cool and cut into chunks.

3. Grate or chop the egg whites and cooked, cooled egg substitute in a food processor, using pulsing action (not too fine).

4. In a bowl, combine the chopped egg mixture, chopped onion, flavored olive oil,
and pepper. Mix well.

5. Taste and adjust seasonings. Chill before serving.

*To Serve as a First Course:* Place one scoop on a leaf of radicchio or butter lettuce.
Garnish with sliced tomato, a thin slice of red onion, and a spear of dill pickle. Accompany with challah, pumpernickel, or corn rye bread.

VARIATIONS: This may also be mounded in a pretty bowl sprinkled with snipped chives, surrounded with matzo wafers, and served with thoroughly chilled sodium-reduced V-8 juice or tomato juice. Or it may be used as a sandwich filling or in pita bread.

Six grated red radishes *or* 2 small finely chopped potatoes that have been cooked in their jackets may be added to the mixture, if desired.

| ――――― P E R   S E R V I N G ――――― | | | |
|---|---|---|---|
| 3.7 gm total fat | .60 gm saturated fat | .8 gm fiber | 93 calories |
| 0 mg cholesterol | 36.1% fat | 243 mg sodium | 33 calories from fat |

# ❦ Roast Chicken with Brussels Sprouts ❦
## (MEAT)
### *Serves: 4*

1 medium onion, peeled, halved, and sliced
2 ribs celery with leaves, sliced
4 carrots, peeled and sliced
2 cloves garlic, smashed, peeled, and minced
1 (2½-pound) broiler, skinned, quartered, all visible fat removed
3 tablespoons fresh lemon juice
1½ teaspoons saltless vegetable seasoning
1 tablespoon Hungarian paprika
  Freshly ground pepper
16 brussels sprouts
1 cup defatted sodium-reduced chicken broth (optional)

1. Heat the oven to 350°. Scatter the sliced onion, celery, carrots, and garlic in the bottom of a small roasting pan.

2. Season the chicken with lemon juice, vegetable seasoning, paprika, and pepper on both sides.

3. Arrange the seasoned chicken on the vegetables. Cover and bake for 30 minutes.

4. Remove the cover and broil the chicken until lightly browned on both sides. Transfer the chicken to a plate.

5. Add the brussels sprouts to the vegetables in the roasting pan, season with ad-

ditional paprika and pepper, and place the chicken pieces with juice on top. At this point, if mixture seems dry you may add 1 cup of chicken broth. Cover and bake for 30 additional minutes.

*To Serve:* Spoon the chicken onto a heated platter, surround with the cooked brussels sprouts and vegetables, and top with gravy.

---

PER SERVING

| | | | |
|---|---|---|---|
| 8.4 gm total fat | 2.20 gm saturated fat | 4.1 gm fiber | 310 calories |
| 91 mg cholesterol | 23.9% fat | 140 mg sodium | 75 calories from fat |

# ❦ Never-fail Kuchen ❦
## (DAIRY)

*Yield: Three 9-inch loaves (about 30 slices [1 slice = 1 serving])*
*or two 10-inch round coffee cakes*

We all know the feeling of sheer pleasure that comes from eating a favorite comfort food. Coffee cake made from a yeast dough has always been my family's favorite. I have a recipe of my mother's that I used for years; however, I hesitated about including this recipe, since it does take more time than a cake made from batter. But I thought perhaps some of you might enjoy the taste and smell of a yeast dough as much as I do.

It just would not seem like the high holidays if I didn't prepare some *kuchen* for the family to enjoy, especially when breaking the fast after Yom Kippur services. My mother's old recipe is out of the question because of all its fat and cholesterol. Before you start, compare the difference, and see how easy it is to enjoy a delicious coffee cake by making a few substitutions and modifying the recipe just a bit.

## Yesterday's Kuchen

    8 cups unbleached all-purpose flour
    2 teaspoons kosher salt
    1 cup sugar
    3 packages active dry yeast
    1 cup whole milk

     8 ounces (2 sticks) unsalted butter
    12 extra-large egg yolks
    ⅔ cup sour cream

*Filling:*
     4 ounces (1 stick) unsalted butter, melted
     1 cup sugar
     2 teaspoons ground cinnamon
    1½ cups ground toasted walnuts
     1 cup golden raisins

*Streusel Topping:*
    5⅓ tablespoons (⅓ cup) cold unsalted butter
    ½ cup sugar
     2 teaspoons ground cinnamon
     1 cup coarsely chopped walnuts
    1¼ cups unbleached all-purpose flour

## Today's Kuchen

     4 cups unbleached all-purpose flour plus 4 cups sifted cake flour or whole
       wheat pastry flour
     2 teaspoons kosher salt
    ½ cup sugar
     3 packages rapid-rise yeast
    1¼ cups 1 percent milk or low-fat evaporated milk
     4 ounces (1 stick) light margarine
     3 whole eggs, slightly beaten with 4 extra-large egg whites
    ½ cup light sour cream

*Filling:*
     4 extra-large egg whites, slightly beaten
    ⅔ cup granulated sugar or ½ cup brown sugar
     2 teaspoons ground cinnamon
    ⅔ cup ground toasted walnuts or hazelnuts
    1½ cups dark raisins, plumped in hot water

*Streusel Topping:*

> 2 to 3 tablespoons cold unsalted light margarine
> ¼ cup sugar
> 1 teaspoon ground cinnamon
> ½ cup coarsely chopped nuts
> ¾ cup unbleached all-purpose flour

### To Prepare Dough:

1. Remove 1 cup unbleached flour and set aside. Combine the remaining flour, salt, sugar, and yeast in the large bowl of an electric mixer. Mix together until blended.

2. Heat the milk and butter or margarine to 130°.

3. Stir the hot liquid into the flour, add the slightly beaten eggs and sour cream, and beat with the dough hook to combine.

4. Add enough of the reserved flour to form a medium soft dough.

5. Knead with the dough hook for 5 minutes or until the dough is satiny and no longer sticky. If necessary, add more flour, a tablespoon at a time.

6. Cover with a kitchen towel and let rest in a draft-free place 20 to 25 minutes, or until it leaves an impression when two fingers are poked into the center.

7. Punch down the dough* and knead briefly.

### To Make Streusel Topping:

Combine all the ingredients and work together with a pastry blender, food processor, two knives, or your fingers until the mixture resembles coarse crumbs.

### To Shape and Fill Dough:

1. Divide the dough into thirds and knead each section briefly. Work with one section of dough at a time, keeping the remainder lightly covered.

2. Roll the section of dough out into a large square about 12 × 14 inches and ¼ inch thick. Brush with the melted butter (if you are following Yesterday's Kuchen recipe) or with the slightly beaten egg whites (Today's Kuchen), sprinkle with sugar, cinnamon, nuts, and raisins. Roll up *tightly*, jelly roll style. Cut the roll evenly into 6 slices.

3. Grease three 9-inch loaf pans with margarine or butter-flavored cooking spray. Sprinkle several spoonfuls of streusel on the bottom of one pan. Fit the slices cut side

---

*At this point the dough can be covered and placed in the refrigerator for up to 2 days. It *must be punched down* each time it rises, which is *often during the first 3 to 4 hours*. Once thoroughly chilled, it needs to be punched down only twice a day. I usually prepare the dough one day and bake it the next day.

up into the pan, squeezing them in if necessary. Press the slices down slightly into the pan so that in rising they will grow together. Sprinkle with 2 more tablespoons of streusel topping.

4. Repeat with the two other pieces of dough and the remaining pans. Cover the pans with a damp towel and let the dough rise until it is almost doubled in bulk. Meanwhile, heat the oven to 350°.

5. Bake in the preheated oven for about 45 minutes, or until the streusel tops are lightly browned. *Do not overbake*. Remove from the pans and cool on a rack.

NOTE: This kuchen freezes beautifully. It should be wrapped airtight, first in plastic, then in foil or another plastic bag.

## Cheese Kuchen

   Today's Kuchen dough (page 31)
   Cheese filling (page 102)
 1 tablespoon sugar mixed with ¼ teaspoon cinnamon or 3 tablespoons Streusel topping (page 32)

1. Preheat the oven to 350°.
2. Grease a 9- or 10-inch layer cake or tart pan.
3. Roll or pat the dough to fit into the pan. Let the dough rise until puffy, about 15 minutes.
4. Spread with the cheese filling. Sprinkle with the cinnamon-sugar mixture or streusel.
5. Bake in the preheated oven about 40 minutes or until lightly browned.

### YESTERDAY'S KUCHEN PER SERVING

| | | | |
|---|---|---|---|
| 19.7 gm total fat | 8.84 gm saturated fat | 2.2 gm fiber | 412 calories |
| 121 mg cholesterol | 42.3% fat | 122 mg sodium | 177 calories from fat |

### TODAY'S KUCHEN PER SERVING

| | | | |
|---|---|---|---|
| 6.1 gm total fat | 1.07 gm saturated fat | 1.5 gm fiber | 257 calories |
| 24 mg cholesterol | 21.4% fat | 144 mg sodium | 55 calories from fat |

# ❧ Beet–Gefilte Fish Mold ❧
## (PAREVE)
### *Serves: 8 to 10*

This mold is great for a buffet or brunch. It can be prepared ahead of time, freeing you for other last-minute preparations.

*Fish Mold:*
1 (16-ounce) can salt-free beets, julienne cut
1 (1-pound 8-ounce) jar gefilte fish balls
1 (3-ounce) package lemon-flavored gelatin
3 tablespoons fresh lemon juice
1 (6-ounce) jar beet horseradish (no sulfites added)

*Cucumber Dressing:*
 1 cup nonfat sour cream
½ cup peeled, grated, seeded cucumber
 2 teaspoons grated onion
   Freshly ground pepper to taste
 1 teaspoon sugar
 2 tablespoons chopped fresh dill
   For garnish: 4 hard-cooked eggs, whites only, halved; 8 fish balls or small whole beets; European cucumber slices; celery curls; mixed greens or bunches of fresh dill

1. Drain and chop the beets, reserving their liquid. Drain the fish balls and pour the liquid into a large measuring cup. Add the beet juice and enough water to make 2¾ cups of liquid.

2. In a medium saucepan, heat 1 cup of the liquid to boiling. Add the lemon gelatin and stir until dissolved. Add the remaining liquid and the lemon juice. Chill until syrupy.

3. Stir in the horseradish and chopped beets. Pour into an 8-cup ring or fish mold coated with vegetable oil cooking spray.

4. Reserve 8 of the fish balls for garnish, if desired. Arrange the remainder evenly throughout the mixture. Cover and chill 4 to 6 hours or overnight before serving.

5. Make the cucumber dressing: Combine all the dressing ingredients and mix thoroughly. Cover and chill 1 to 2 hours before serving.

*To Serve:* Unmold on a serving platter. Surround with bunches of fresh dill, European cucumber slices, celery curls, and halved egg whites with either small beets or fish balls in the center. Sprinkle with fresh chopped dill. Pour the cucumber dressing into a bowl and place in the center of the mold.

---

**—— PER SERVING ——**

| | | | |
|---|---|---|---|
| 1.3 gm total fat | .3 gm saturated fat | .6 gm fiber | 131 calories |
| 20 mg cholesterol | 8.8% fat | 442 mg sodium | .2 calories from fat |

---

**—— ❧ HARRIET'S HINTS ❧ ——**

*To make gefilte fish from jars taste more like homemade: Drain liquid from two 24-ounce jars gefilte fish into a saucepan and add 1 cup water. Add 3 carrots, 2 potatoes, and 1 rib celery with leaves, all sliced ½-inch thick, and 3 slices of onion. Bring to a boil, reduce the heat, and simmer, uncovered, for 20 minutes. Add fish balls and 2 tablespoons chopped flat-leaf parsley or dill, and simmer for 15 minutes. Remove from heat and let cool. Strain out solids and chill separately. Serve chilled fish topped with carrot and potato slices, a spoonful of jellied broth, and grated horseradish.*

# ❧ Atlanta Honey Cake (Lekach) ❧
## (PAREVE)
### Serves: 20

The Jewish New Year wouldn't be complete without a Rosh Hashanah honey cake to start the new year and finish the meal. Everybody has a favorite recipe, and the lineage of this one is really quite impressive. Both Sunny Steinberg and cousin Millie Deich say this cake is a variation of grandmother Sarah Jacobson Raskin's recipe. It comes out perfectly no matter what size pan you use. I have cut the fat and sugar and deleted the egg yolks without any sacrifice of taste.

  4 extra-large egg whites
  ½ cup egg substitute
  ¾ cup sugar
  1 cup honey
  ⅓ cup canola oil
  ½ cup very strong coffee
  3 tablespoons blackberry or grape jelly
  3 tablespoons strawberry preserves
  3 tablespoons orange marmalade
3¼ cups unbleached all-purpose flour
  2 teaspoons baking powder
  1 teaspoon baking soda
  1 teaspoon ground allspice
    Grated zest of 1 orange
  ½ cup sliced almonds or chopped pecans

1. Coat a 15 × 10 × 2-inch pan with vegetable oil cooking spray. Line the bottom with wax paper and coat the paper as well. Preheat the oven to 350°.

2. Beat the egg whites in the large bowl of an electric mixer until light and soft peaks form. Add the egg substitute while beating.

3. Gradually add the sugar, honey, oil, coffee, and preserves, while beating.

4. Sift the dry ingredients together and add the orange zest.

5. Add the flour mixture to the egg mixture and beat until blended.

6. Pour and scrape the batter into the prepared pan. Sprinkle with sliced almonds or chopped pecans and bake on the middle rack of the oven for about 35 minutes or until a toothpick inserted near the center comes out clean. Do not overbake. Cool in the pan.

*To Serve:* Cut into squares or diamond shapes.

VARIATION: This cake may be made in a 13 × 9 × 2-inch pan and baked for about 1 hour. I'm told it can be frozen for up to 1 year. It never stays around our house that long!

| PER SERVING | | | |
|---|---|---|---|
| 6.3 gm total fat | .55 gm saturated fat | 1 gm fiber | 237 calories |
| 0 mg cholesterol | 23.3% fat | 118 mg sodium | 57 calories from fat |

# ❦ Reformed Rugelach ❦
## (PAREVE)
*Yield: 60 pastries (1 pastry = 1 serving)*

In the past few years, there has been a rugelach renaissance, not just in Jewish kitchens, bakeries, and delicatessens, but in all manner of markets, mail-order catalogs, and coffee houses. These easy-to-prepare pastries originated in Eastern Europe. My favorite recipe has a cream cheese dough as a base. They freeze well before or after baking. You can also freeze the dough for future use. In fact, the only difficulty with traditional rugelach is their high fat and cholesterol content. When made with fat-reduced cream cheese (no-fat cream cheese just does not make it) and light margarine (⅓ fat-reduced), the fat content will be considerably lower than my original recipe. Then I used ½ pound of butter and ½ pound of cream cheese—quite a difference!

**Cream Cheese Dough:**
- 2½ cups unbleached all-purpose flour
- 8 ounces (2 sticks) butter-flavored light margarine, well chilled and cut into 8 cubes
- 1 (8-ounce) package light cream cheese, well chilled and cut into 8 cubes
- 2 teaspoons fresh orange juice (optional)

**Nut Filling:**
- ⅓ cup sugar
- 1 tablespoon ground cinnamon
- 1 cup toasted walnuts or pecans, chopped fine
- ⅔ cup dark raisins

### To Prepare Dough:

1. Place the flour in a food processor. Add the chilled margarine pieces and process with the pulsing action until the mixture resembles coarse meal. Add the chilled cream cheese and process very briefly until the dough starts to hold together.

2. Shape the dough in plastic wrap—do not touch with the hands. Divide into 5 equal portions and flatten each portion into a disk. Wrap each disk in plastic and place in a plastic bag. Chill 4 hours or overnight before using. The dough may also be frozen 4 to 6 weeks for future use.

### To Prepare Rugelach:

1. Mix the sugar and cinnamon thoroughly. Sprinkle 1 to 1½ tablespoons of cinnamon sugar on a clean work surface. Roll out a dough disk into a 9-inch circle about ⅛ inch thick, directly on the cinnamon sugar.

2. Divide the nuts and raisins into 5 portions. Sprinkle the rolled-out dough with one portion; press in with floured hands or a rolling pin.

3. Cut into 12 wedges (a pizza cutter works well); roll each wedge tightly from the wide to the pointed end. Keep the raisins inside the dough—they will burn if exposed.

4. Place the rugelach point down on a nonstick baking sheet coated with butter-flavored cooking spray. Curve to crescent shape if desired. Refrigerate 30 minutes before baking or freeze to bake at a later date.

5. Bake in a preheated 350° oven for 20 to 25 minutes or until lightly browned. Repeat with the remaining dough and filling.

NOTE: You may also make rugelach by rolling each portion of dough into a 12 × 7-inch rectangle between 2 sheets of wax paper. Spread the dough with the cinnamon, nut, and raisin filling, roll tightly jelly-roll style, and cut into ten 1½-inch pieces. Place on a baking sheet, refrigerate 30 minutes, then bake in a 350° oven for 15 to 20 minutes.

## Variation #1: My Favorite Mock or Simple Strudel

1. Prepare one recipe rugelach dough through Step 2. Roll each disk into a rectangle about 12 × 7 inches between two sheets of wax paper that has been lightly dusted with confectioners' sugar. Lift and reverse the paper several times while rolling to prevent sticking.

2. Spread the dough with about ¾ cup sugar-free apricot, peach, strawberry, or

boysenberry preserves, leaving a 1-inch border at each edge. Sprinkle the preserves with ¼ cup of rugelach nut filling mixture (no raisins).

3. Fold the dough over 2 times along the 12-inch side of dough to meet the 1-inch border, then fold the 1-inch border over the dough. Flatten with your hand or the rolling pin.

4. Place seam side down on a baking sheet coated with vegetable oil cooking spray. Chill for 30 minutes. Brush with lightly beaten egg white. Puncture with a fork diagonally at 1-inch intervals.

5. Bake in a preheated 350° oven for about 35 minutes or until golden brown.

6. Cool on a rack. Cut into 1-inch diagonal slices with a serrated knife and sprinkle with confectioners' sugar. These freeze beautifully if you can manage to secrete them from your family.

## Variation #2: Mini Fruit Tarts

1. Form twelve 1-inch balls from one disk of rugelach dough and mold them into the bottom and sides of a 1½-inch nonstick mini muffin tin. Prick several times with a fork, chill for 20 to 30 minutes, and bake in a preheated 350° oven for 12 to 15 minutes or until they just start to brown.

2. Cool the tart shells, remove from the tin, and fill with fresh blueberries, raspberries, blackberries, or 1 large strawberry. Glaze with melted currant or crabapple jelly.

| PER SERVING | | | |
|---|---|---|---|
| 2.9 gm total fat | .65 gm saturated fat | .3 gm fiber | 54 calories |
| 2 mg cholesterol | 48% fat | 51 mg sodium | 26 calories from fat |

# SUKKOT

## The Jewish Thanksgiving

*Thou shalt keep the feast of tabernacles seven days, after that thou hast gathered in thy wine press. And thou shalt rejoice in thy feast. . . .*
— DEUTERONOMY 16:13–14

Sukkot, a Hebrew word meaning booths, huts, or tents, celebrates the fall harvest and commemorates the Hebrews' years of wandering in the desert after the exodus from Egypt. It lasts for a week, beginning on the fifteenth day of Tishri. The sukkah, a temporary hut, has a roof loosely covered with willow branches or corn stalks so as not to block out the sky. The inside of the sukkah is decorated with apples, clusters of grapes, pumpkins, squash, ears of corn, and any other fruits or vegetables appropriate to the season. Traditionally, family meals are eaten in the sukkah. Stuffed cabbage (also called *holishkes, pratkes,* or *galuptze*), *kreplach*, and strudel—all making use of the bounty of the season and all transportable out of doors—are traditional foods that are served on this holiday.

## SUKKOT MENU

*Sweet and Sour Stuffed Cabbage (page 41)*

*Mashed Potatoes with Onions and Garlic (page 242)*

*Sliced Zucchini and Corn*

*Helen Kolatch's Fruit Kugel (page 43)*

*Gisele Pollak's No-Fat Apple Strudel (page 364)*

# ❧ Sweet and Sour Stuffed Cabbage ❧

## (MEAT)

*Serves: 6 (12 cabbage rolls; 2 rolls = 1 serving as entrée)*

A wonderful make-ahead dish for family or guests, this recipe may be prepared a day before serving and reheated or frozen for future use. Or double the recipe, using one right away and freezing the other.

1 medium onion, peeled and halved
1 carrot, peeled and grated
1 teaspoon grated fresh gingerroot (optional)
2 large cloves garlic, smashed, peeled, and minced
   Freshly ground pepper to taste
1 teaspoon salt-free vegetable seasoning
1 teaspoon Hungarian paprika
2 extra-large egg whites
1 tablespoon low-sodium ketchup mixed with ¼ cup water
½ cup chopped Italian flat-leaf parsley
⅓ cup dried bread crumbs, nonfat cracker crumbs, or matzo meal
½ cup uncooked white or parboiled brown rice
1 pound ground turkey breast (see Note)
1 head green cabbage, cored

*Sauce Ingredients:*

1 (12-ounce) bottle chili sauce
1 (12-ounce) bottle low-sodium ketchup
6 cups water
   Juice of 2 lemons
¼ cup packed brown sugar

1. Mince half the onion. Combine with the grated carrot, ginger, garlic, seasonings, egg whites, and ketchup mixture until well blended.

2. Add the parsley, bread crumbs, rice, and meat, using a fork to mix.

3. Dip the cored cabbage in a large pot of boiling water to ease removal of leaves. Drain and separate 12 large leaves and trim off the ribs. Shred the remaining cabbage and reserve.

4. Place about ½ cup of the filling mixture in each cabbage leaf. Fold over one side, roll up, and tuck in the remaining side.

5. Chop the remaining onion half. Sprinkle the shredded cabbage and chopped onion on the bottom of a 3-quart oval or rectangular casserole or roaster. Place the cabbage rolls on top of the cabbage, seam side down.

6. Combine the sauce ingredients and pour over the cabbage rolls. Cover with foil or the top of the roaster.

7. Place in a preheated 325° oven and cook for 2 to 2½ hours. (Place the casserole on a foil-lined baking sheet to collect drips.)

*To Serve:* Garnish with chopped fresh parsley and accompany with peas, mashed potatoes, and chilled applesauce.

Note: If desired, ⅓ pound each of ground turkey breast, ground veal, and lean ground beef may be substituted for 1 pound of ground turkey breast.

## Other Sauces

*Sauce #1:*
   1 (16-ounce) can whole cranberry sauce
   1 (16-ounce) can salt-free tomato sauce
   2 cups water
   ½ cup dark raisins

*Sauce #2:*
   2 (12-ounce) bottles chili sauce
   2 cups water
      Juice of 1 lemon
   1 (8-ounce) jar currant or grape jelly

| PER SERVING | | | |
|---|---|---|---|
| 1.4 gm total fat | .42 gm saturated fat | 3.4 gm fiber | 301 calories |
| 89 mg cholesterol | 4.2% fat | 575 mg sodium | 13 calories from fat |

# ❧ Helen Kolatch's Fruit Kugel ❧

## (PAREVE)

*Serves: 12*

  4 extra-large egg whites
  1 cup egg substitute
  1 (16-ounce) can crushed pineapple in natural juice
 ⅓ cup sugar
2½ tablespoons canola oil
 ½ cup matzo meal
  3 apples, peeled and chopped
10 ounces pitted prunes, quartered
 ½ cup chopped dried apricots

1. Heat the oven to 350°. Coat a 13 × 9 × 2-inch baking dish with vegetable oil cooking spray.

2. Beat the egg whites with the egg substitute, add the pineapple with juice, and blend. Add the remaining ingredients and stir until well blended. Pour into the prepared baking dish.

3. Bake for 30 minutes or until nicely browned. Allow to set for 10 to 15 minutes before cutting into 12 serving portions.

| PER SERVING | | | |
|---|---|---|---|
| 4 gm total fat | .4 gm saturated fat | 3.4 gm fiber | 201 calories |
| 0 mg cholesterol | 16.4% fat | 57 mg sodium | 36 calories from fat |

# THANKSGIVING

## A Special Day for American Jews

If it were not for my mother and father's spirit of adventure and their courage, I would not have the good fortune to celebrate this holiday. Both of my parents immigrated to America alone, my mother at thirteen from Hungary and my father at fifteen from Czechoslovakia. Both would almost certainly have been victims of the Holocaust, like the families they left behind. This presents yet another reason for me and my family to give thanks each year.

As Jews, we feel special gratitude for living in a country where we can peacefully enjoy the fruits of freedom. Since Jewish tradition dictates that the gathering of families at holidays should include friends without families of their own, for many years we had upward of forty guests for dinner. I could always count on my son Larry to sneak into the kitchen to taste my mother's bread stuffing while the turkey was still roasting. Today his wife Eileen and daughter Molly help fill our family circle.

The menu has also been adjusted a bit to accommodate our healthier style of eating, without sacrificing the pleasures of a hearty Thanksgiving dinner. We've cut down on the protein and increased the number of vegetable choices. My mother's stuffing recipe remains. Compare the difference:

🌿

## YESTERDAY'S MENU

*Crudités (Fresh Vegetables) with Sour Cream Dip*

*Guacamole and Corn Chips*

*Chopped Liver Pâté*

*Potato Knishes*

*Mini Meatballs*

*Roast Turkey with Giblet Gravy*

*My Mother's Bread Stuffing (page 304)*

*Spinach Casserole*

*Minted Carrots*

*Mashed Potatoes*

*Persimmon Pudding*

*Cranberry-Pineapple Freeze*

*Sponge Cake Roll with Raspberry Sauce*

*Pecan Pie*

*Pumpkin Pie with Whipped Cream*

*Mile-High Lemon Meringue Pie (page 425)*

🌿

## TODAY'S MENU

*Tofu Dill Dip (page 46) with Crudités (Fresh Vegetables)*

*Fresh Tomato Salsa and Baked Corn Chips*

*Hummus (page 123) and Pita Bread*

*Ricotta and Artichoke Flowers (page 354)*

*Spinach Cups (page 122)*

*Roast Breast of Turkey (page 48) and Turkey Legs*

*My Mother's Bread Stuffing (page 304)*

*Mashed Potatoes with Onions and Garlic (page 242) with Turkey Gravy (page 49)*

*Fruited Sweet Potato Tart (page 51)*

*Acorn Squash Rings with Peas and Pimiento*

*Layered Vegetable Kugel (page 52)*

*Brussels Sprouts with Toasted Almonds*

*Cranapple Sauce (page 54)*

*Cranberry or Lemon Sorbet with*

*Dorothy Essick's Poppy Seed Crisps (page 388)*

*A Very Good Chocolate Cake (page 391)*

*Low-fat Pumpkin Pie with Glazed Pecans*

*A Basket Filled with Varied Grapes*

🌱

The menu has been changed to lower its fat content. By not roasting a whole turkey, using just the breast and legs, I've eliminated the high-fat turkey thighs. The hors d'oeuvres are fewer and simpler. Vegetarian side dishes are in abundance. Desserts are now lower in fat. I wouldn't think of cheating my daughter Sally out of her pumpkin pie: I still use the Never-Fail Pie Crust (page 423), but the filling uses only egg whites and nonfat evaporated milk.

# 🌱 Tofu Dill Dip 🌱
## (PAREVE)
*Yield: 1½ cups (1 tablespoon = 1 serving)*

"Years of study have confirmed that when soy protein replaces animal protein in the diet, cholesterol levels tend to drop." So says the *Environmental Nutrition Newsletter*. Soy products also contain many cancer-fighting compounds. Tofu, the oft-neglected pareve protein, has little flavor of its own. It picks up flavor from sauces and seasonings. Try stir-frying tofu with vegetables and serve over rice or noodles; prepare an Eggless Egg Salad (page 195); or make a tasty corn soup (page 170). Whatever your choice, bear in mind that the health-enhancing qualities of tofu ask for its inclusion in our daily diets.

1 (10½-ounce) cake low-fat firm tofu
1 cucumber, peeled, seeded, and cut into eighths
2 large cloves garlic, smashed and peeled
2 slices onion
¼ teaspoon ground white pepper
2 tablespoons chopped fresh dill
½ red bell pepper, seeded and diced fine
  Hungarian paprika, for garnish

1. Combine the tofu, cucumber, garlic, onion, ground white pepper, and dill in a food processor or blender. Process until smooth.

2. Pour into a bowl and mix in the diced bell pepper. Sprinkle with paprika, cover, and chill in the refrigerator at least 1 hour before serving.

*To Serve:* Place the bowl in the center of a large salad basket or platter. Surround with mounds of fresh vegetables such as carrots; celery or zucchini spears; red, yellow, or green bell pepper slices; cherry tomatoes; sliced, peeled black radish; red radishes; scallions; sliced rutabaga, turnip, or fennel; sugar snap peas or snow peas; slim asparagus; broccoli florets or cauliflowerets; or any vegetable that you enjoy. Baked corn chips, bagel chips, no-fat potato chips, or matzo crackers can also be offered.

---
PER SERVING
---

| | | | |
|---|---|---|---|
| .6 gm total fat | .09 gm saturated fat | .2 gm fiber | 12 calories |
| 0 mg cholesterol | 41.6% fat | 2 mg sodium | 6 calories from fat |

---
HARRIET'S HINTS
---

*Unused portions of tofu should be stored in the refrigerator in cold water to cover. The water should be changed every few days.*

# ❦ Roast Breast of Turkey ❦

## (MEAT)

*Serves: 12*

Roasted turkey breast is not only lower in fat and easier to handle than a whole bird, it is also quicker to cook. The white meat comes out moister since it doesn't have to wait for the dark meat to finish cooking. I season the turkey under the skin so that flavors are not lost when the skin is discarded.

     1 (5-pound) fresh bone-in turkey breast, washed and patted dry
       Juice of 1 lemon
     3 large cloves garlic, smashed, peeled, and minced
     2 teaspoons onion powder
     2 tablespoons minced fresh thyme or 2 teaspoons dried thyme, crumbled
       Ground white pepper
    10 fresh sage leaves, optional (do not use dried sage)
     2 teaspoons Hungarian paprika
     1 onion, peeled and chopped coarse
     1 carrot, chopped coarse
     1 rib celery, chopped coarse

**The Day Before:**

1. Loosen the breast skin with your fingers and rub the turkey with lemon juice under the skin.

2. Sprinkle the turkey under the skin with minced garlic, onion powder, thyme, and pepper. Place sage leaves under the skin on each side of the breast. Rub the skin with lemon halves and sprinkle with paprika.

3. Cover lightly with plastic wrap and allow to stand in the refrigerator overnight.

**To Cook Turkey:**

1. Preheat the oven to 325°.

2. Sprinkle the onion, carrot, and celery on the bottom of a shallow, slotted broiler pan. Arrange the turkey breast on top, bone side down. Roast about 2 hours, or until the thickest portion registers 155° to 160° on an instant-read thermometer. (Be careful not to hit the bone.)

3. Remove from the oven. Tent with foil and allow to rest 20 minutes before removing the skin and carving.

*To Serve:* Arrange the turkey slices on a heated platter; surround with lemon cups filled with cranberry-orange relish.

---

PER SERVING

| | | | |
|---|---|---|---|
| 3.1 gm total fat | .98 gm saturated fat | .6 gm fiber | 160 calories |
| 65 mg cholesterol | 18.4% fat | 66 mg sodium | 28 calories from fat |

# ❧ Turkey Gravy ❧
## (MEAT)

*Yield: 3 to 4 cups (2 tablespoons = 1 serving)*

This delicious gravy may be prepared and frozen for future use. It is a must with mashed potatoes and/or turkey.

Neck and giblets (except liver) from 12- to 14-pound turkey, washed under cold water
4 cups cold water
2 cups sodium-reduced fat-free chicken broth
½ cup dry white wine
1 small onion, peeled and quartered
1 carrot, quartered
1 rib celery with leaves, quartered
1 bay leaf
1 large clove garlic, smashed
1 teaspoon dried thyme, crushed
6 peppercorns
¼ cup unbleached all-purpose flour
Salt and freshly ground pepper to taste
Onion or garlic powder to taste
Worcestershire sauce to taste (optional)

1. In a large saucepan, combine the giblets, water, chicken broth, wine, onion, carrot, celery, bay leaf, garlic, thyme, and peppercorns. Bring to a boil over high heat. Skim off the foam as it accumulates. Reduce the heat, cover partially, and simmer until the giblets are tender, about 1½ hours.

2. Strain and measure the stock. You should have about 3½ cups; if not, boil until reduced. Discard the neck and giblets or save for the dog!

3. When the turkey is roasted, remove from the oven and transfer to a platter. Cover with foil and allow to stand at least 20 minutes to set the juices before carving.

4. Add 1 cup of turkey stock to the drippings and vegetables in the roasting pan. Scrape the browned particles up from the bottom of the pan with a wooden spoon. Strain, pressing juices from the vegetables.

5. Pour the mixture into a measuring cup and remove the fat when it rises to the top, or use a gravy separator.

6. Add the defatted drippings to the reserved stock. Stir 1 cup of the stock into the flour in a small bowl. Mix until free of lumps.

7. Add the flour mixture to the stock. Stir over medium-high heat until the mixture coats the spoon or whisk.

8. Taste and adjust seasonings with salt, pepper, onion or garlic powder, and Worcestershire sauce, if desired.

NOTES: Canned defatted sodium-reduced chicken broth may be substituted for turkey stock. Stock may be made, cooled, and refrigerated 2 days in advance or frozen for future use.

---

**PER SERVING**

| | | | |
|---|---|---|---|
| 0 gm total fat | 0 gm saturated fat | 0 gm fiber | 11 calories |
| 0 mg cholesterol | 2.0% fat | 2 mg sodium | 0 calories from fat |

---

❦ HARRIET'S HINTS ❦

*Stuffing from the bird's cavity tastes even better because of the turkey's juices that are absorbed; however, you do lose some of the moisture from the bird. I also sometimes place some of the stuffing under the skin and roast it that way, in addition to making an extra casserole of stuffing.*

# ❧ Fruited Sweet Potato Tart ❧

## (PAREVE)

*Serves: 14 (⅔ cup = 1 serving)*

This wonderfully tasty recipe makes a beautiful presentation for company. It could even satisfy your sweet tooth as a dessert.

4 pounds Golden Delicious or Spartan apples, cored, peeled, and sliced ¼ inch thick

½ cup frozen unsweetened apple juice concentrate, thawed

3½ pounds sweet potatoes, scrubbed and baked in their skins until tender

2 tablespoons packed dark brown sugar

Grated zest of 2 oranges and 1 lemon

¼ cup sherry

1 teaspoon ground cinnamon

1 teaspoon freshly grated nutmeg

3 firm bananas, sliced (sprinkled with 3 tablespoons orange juice)

2 ripe pears, peeled, halved, cored, and cut into ¼-inch slices

1 bunch dark grapes in season or 12 pitted prunes, poached in sherry and halved

½ cup melted cranberry or currant jelly, for glaze

1. Preheat the oven to 375°.

2. Layer the apples in rows in a 3-quart rectangular or oval casserole sprayed with vegetable oil cooking spray. Brush with apple juice, cover, and bake for about 20 minutes (or in a microwave oven on High for about 5 minutes).

3. Peel the baked sweet potatoes and purée in a blender or food processor. When puréed, add the brown sugar, orange and lemon zest, sherry, cinnamon, and nutmeg. Blend well.

4. Place half the sweet potato mixture over the cooked apples and smooth the surface.

5. Arrange half the banana slices, sliced pears, and grapes in diagonal rows over the sweet potato mixture.

6. Cover with the remaining sweet potato mixture and arrange the remaining fruit in rows on top.

7. Glaze the fruit with melted jelly, using all of the glaze.

8. Bake at 375° for about 30 minutes.

NOTE: This may be prepared the day before through Step 7, covered tightly with plastic, and refrigerated. The next day, bring the casserole to room temperature and bake for 40 minutes.

| PER SERVING | | | |
|---|---|---|---|
| 1.1 gm total fat | .26 gm saturated fat | 7.7 gm fiber | 256 calories |
| 0 mg cholesterol | 3.5% fat | 18 mg sodium | 10 calories from fat |

## ❧ Layered Vegetable Kugel ❧
### (PAREVE)
*Serves: 8 to 10*

This vegetable dish is nice for any company or holiday dinner, since it can be prepared the day before and is a different and attractive way to present vegetables. Vary the combination to suit your family.

    1 pound carrots, peeled and cut into 2-inch chunks
    1 large head cauliflower, separated into florets
    2 (10-ounce) packages frozen chopped spinach or broccoli, thawed and drained
    ¾ cup egg substitute
    6 teaspoons olive oil
      Salt and freshly ground pepper to taste
    1 teaspoon dried thyme
    1 clove minced garlic
    ½ teaspoon freshly grated nutmeg
    ¾ cup matzo meal or bread crumbs (plus extra as needed)
      Fresh Tomato Sauce (page 53) (optional)
      Fresh thyme leaves or flat-leaf parsley leaves, for garnish
      Steamed broccoli and cauliflower florets (optional)

1. Steam or microwave the carrots and cauliflower in separate pots until just tender.

2. Purée the carrots in a food processor or blender and return to their pot. Rinse the processor or blender container and purée the cauliflower; return to its pot. Purée

the spinach; place in a small saucepan. To each vegetable add ¼ cup of egg substitute and 2 teaspoons of olive oil. Season with salt and pepper.

3. At this point add the thyme to the carrots; the garlic and nutmeg to the spinach. Add ¼ cup matzo meal or bread crumbs to each and purée.

4. Coat individual glass soufflé cups or an 8-inch springform pan with olive oil cooking spray; sprinkle with matzo meal or bread crumbs.

5. Make layers in this order: first cauliflower, then spinach, then top with carrots. (The dish may be prepared a day in advance up to this point.)

6. Bake in a preheated 400° oven 40 minutes for a large mold or 15 minutes for custard cups or until a knife inserted in the center comes out clean.

*To Serve:* Let stand 5 minutes before removing pan ring. Place on platter and if desired, serve topped with fresh tomato sauce and sprinkled with fresh thyme leaves or parsley; surround with steamed broccoli and cauliflower florets.

─────────── V E G E T A B L E   K U G E L   P E R   S E R V I N G ───────────

| | | | |
|---|---|---|---|
| 3.1 gm total fat | .46 gm saturated fat | 4.5 gm fiber | 93 calories |
| 0 mg cholesterol | 27.7% fat | 117 mg sodium | 28 calories from fat |

# Fresh Tomato Sauce
( P A R E V E )

*Serves: 8 to 10*

2 shallots, minced
¼ cup water
¾ cup dry white wine or vermouth
6 canned Italian plum tomatoes, drained and seeded
1 tablespoon olive oil or canola oil
¼ cup chopped fresh mint (½ cup leaves) (optional)
1 teaspoon sugar
   Few grains of salt
   Freshly ground pepper to taste

1. In a saucepan, simmer the shallots in the water and wine 2 minutes, so that the alcohol evaporates.

2. Purée 3 of the tomatoes and chop the other 3. Add to the saucepan and simmer 2 to 3 minutes.

3. Add a bit of oil at a time, while whisking the sauce.

4. Add the mint, sugar, salt, and pepper. Reduce the heat and simmer gently for 3 to 4 minutes.

5. Spoon over the vegetable kugel or serve on the side.

—————— TOMATO SAUCE PER SERVING ——————

| | | | |
|---|---|---|---|
| 1.4 gm total fat | .19 gm saturated fat | 0 mg fiber | 25 calories |
| 0 mg cholesterol | 47.5% fat | 78 mg sodium | 12.5 calories from fat |

## ❧ Cranapple Sauce ❧
### (PAREVE)
*Serves: 12 (½ cup = 1 serving)*

In apple season, my mother used to can her wonderful applesauce. She used a Foley food mill, an indispensable tool for applesauce (and potato *shlishkas*, page 243). I use her food mill to this day. With a food mill, you can cook the apples in their skins and get all the flavor plus a nice bit of color, and you save time by not having to peel. My mother-in-law taught me the delights of combining berries and apples or rhubarb in a sauce that is a bit chunkier but also delicious.

          4 pounds apples (McIntosh, Spartan, or Jonathan), washed
            and quartered
       1¼ cups reduced-calorie cranapple juice
          1 pound fresh cranberries
    2 to 3 tablespoons sugar, or to taste

1. Place the apples, juice, cranberries, and sugar in a saucepan. Simmer, covered, for about 15 to 20 minutes or until the apples are soft. Cool.

2. Put through a food mill; discard the skins and seeds. Taste and adjust sweetening.

3. Chill before serving or freeze in plastic containers for future use.

NOTE: For a chunkier sauce, peel and core the apples, place all the ingredients in a microwave-safe bowl, cover, and microwave on High for 10 minutes or until soft. Mix with a fork to obtain the desired consistency.

| PER SERVING | | | |
|---|---|---|---|
| .5 gm total fat | .07 gm saturated fat | 4.0 gm fiber | 98 calories |
| 0 mg cholesterol | 3% fat | 3 mg sodium | 4 calories from fat |

# Chanukah

## All the Latkes You Can Eat

*And on the 25th day of Kislev . . . The sanctuary of God was dedicated anew with song and music . . . moreover, Judah the Maccabean and his brethren, with the whole congregation of Israel, ordained that the day of the dedication of the altar should be celebrated from year to year for eight days in gladness and thanksgiving.*

—Apocrypha–I Maccabees 4:52–59

Chanukah, the festival of lights, is a joyous holiday that celebrates an ancient victory for freedom and peace. This celebration is as timely today as it was thousands of years ago. It is still marked by lighting the candles on the menorah, feasting, singing, and the lighthearted exchange of gifts, particularly for the children. Unfortunately for nutrition-watchers and fat-counters, it is also a holiday celebrated by the eating of foods cooked in oil!

For many years, Chanukah was our extended family's special holiday. With guests numbering in the forties, we planned, decorated, and cooked for days with eagerness and anticipation. Today, the food processor and freezer are standard in many of our homes, but once upon a time, Chanukah was very labor-intensive. I would have the potatoes (20 to 30 pounds!) already peeled, my husband grated them all by hand, and my mother-in-law, who was the premier potato latke–maker of all time, worked her magic with several skillets, producing piles of crispy golden-brown latkes. The unbeatable aroma of these potato pancakes frying led everybody into the kitchen to "say hello" first. Of course, a sample or two from Nana was always in order to see if the latkes were as good as last year's. In fact, I don't know how any latkes made it to the buffet table—and who cared? If we ran out of latkes, there was no shortage of fun and *gemütlichkeit* or good spirits.

We stopped doing this production number when our children were teenagers. Ten years later we decided to give it a try once more. The setting and cast of characters were different. We were in a smaller home. Some of the children had children of their own. So we adjusted: The guests came laden, not with gifts, but with food to fill the waiting boxes that would be taken off to centers where needy people could be helped to enjoy the season. Though the smell of frying potatoes wasn't as strong in the air, freezing the latkes ahead of time gave us more time out of the kitchen.

One year, we sat down after dinner to a showing of the Roth Chanukah film retrospective: my husband's spliced and edited video collage of years of home movies. There was Sally at six months continually falling off Poppie's lap; Abby in her little velvet dress; the way we looked (we were so young); our dated hairstyles; our then-fashionable dress (Linda's "Stella Dallas" jewelry, my high-heeled shoes)—and our tears because some of those on the screen were no longer with us. But the important thing was that we were still a family, changing with the times and celebrating another Chanukah season.

❧

## CHANUKAH FEAST

*Marilyn Lewis's Roast Brisket with Prunes and Garlic (page 58)*

*Lemon Chicken for a Crowd (page 314)*

*Mollie's Potato Pancakes (page 59) with Applesauce*

*Broccoli Noodle Kugel (page 219)*

*Marinated Vegetables (page 239)*

*Ellen Batzdorf's Red Cabbage (page 240)*

*Salad of Mixed Greens and Fresh Herbs*

*Almost Aunt Dora's Strudel (page 362)*

*Pogachels (Pogácsa) (page 417)*

*Mrs. Katz's Devil's Food Cake (page 428)*

*Lemon Squares (page 430)*

*Fresh Fruit*

❧

# ❧ Marilyn Lewis's Roast Brisket ❧ with Prunes and Garlic
## (MEAT)
*Serves: 20*

Marilyn Lewis is the innovative and creative force behind Kate Mantilini's Restaurant in Los Angeles. Her talent as a cook is demonstrated in this extraordinary recipe for a rather ordinary cut of beef. By using a lean cut of meat, trimming the fat before roasting, defatting the gravy, and serving smaller portions of meat with more generous portions of grains, vegetables, and fruits, you can hold your fat and cholesterol content at a more prudent level.

  8 medium carrots, peeled and cut into chunks
  3 medium onions, peeled and cut into chunks
 20 cloves garlic, smashed and peeled
  2 (3½-pound) first-cut lean briskets or 1 (8-pound) flat cut brisket
    with deckal removed and fat trimmed
    Freshly ground pepper to taste
  1 14½-ounce bottle sodium-reduced ketchup or chili sauce
  1 cup water
 ½ cup dried pitted prunes
 ½ cup plus 1 tablespoon red wine vinegar or balsamic vinegar
  3 cups port wine
  8 dried pitted prunes, for garnish

1. Preheat the oven to 450°.
2. Throw the carrots, onions, and garlic into a roaster. Coat vegetables lightly with olive oil cooking spray and roast, uncovered, for 20 minutes. Stir occasionally.
3. Wash the brisket under cold running water, place on top of the roasted vegetables, and season with freshly ground pepper.
4. Cover the brisket with the ketchup or chili sauce. Add the water.
5. Reduce the oven heat to 325° and place the covered roaster in the oven. Roast for 2 hours.
6. Throw in the ½ cup prunes, cover, and roast 30 additional minutes. Test the meat with a fork. It should be very tender.
7. Remove the brisket to a carving board and let stand until room temperature.

8. Strain and defat the drippings left in the roaster. Purée the strained vegetables, garlic, and prunes. Add to the drippings.

9. In a small saucepan, bring the vinegar and port to a boil. Reduce to a simmer and heat about 10 minutes.

10. Add the drippings mixture to the reduced wine mixture and add a few extra prunes to use as garnish. Bring to a boil, reduce the heat, and simmer while stirring for about 10 minutes. Adjust seasonings to your taste.

*To Serve:* Trim meat of any visible fat and cut into ¼-inch diagonal slices, turning to make a herringbone pattern. Arrange on a warmed serving plate, pour the superb sauce, and garnish with prunes. Accompany with Mollie's Potato Pancakes (below), applesauce flavored with skillet-browned fresh-grated horseradish, and Baked Apples Muscatel (page 401), all arranged attractively on a large platter.

VARIATION: For an even lower fat version, boil the onions, carrots, and garlic in water to cover (like a soup) until tender. Roast the brisket with plenty of sliced onions, chili sauce or ketchup, and prunes. Discard the grease and sliced onions. Purée the vegetables and prunes and proceed as in Steps 8 to 10. This way the brisket cooks off some of its fat, the onions flavor the brisket, and you then throw out everything that cooked in the brisket fat.

| PER SERVING | | | |
|---|---|---|---|
| 15.2 gm total fat | 5.97 gm saturated fat | .6 gm fiber | 284 calories |
| 87 mg cholesterol | 48.9% fat | 80 mg sodium | 137 calories from fat |

# ❦ Mollie's Potato Pancakes (Latkes) ❦ (Everybody's Favorite)
## (PAREVE)
*Yield: 24 pancakes (2 pancakes = 1 serving)*

Potato latkes are a favorite food served at Chanukah. They have a high fat content when fried the old-fashioned way. In fact, the old-fashioned way is symbolic of the one jug of oil which miraculously burned for eight days. (In Israel, fried jelly donuts are traditional Chanukah fare for the same reason.) Without breaking terribly with tradition, these latkes are not fried; instead they are sautéed in a minimal amount of canola oil in a nonstick skillet, drained on paper towels, and placed on a rack in a heated oven to keep warm and further drain off any excess fat before serving. They are still crisp and delicious.

    4 extra-large egg whites
    1 small onion, peeled and cubed
    4 large Russet potatoes (about 2½ pounds or 6 cups), peeled,
        cut into 1-inch cubes, and covered with cold water
    ⅓ cup fine dried bread crumbs, matzo meal, or white flour
    ¼ teaspoon ground white pepper
      Salt to taste
      Canola oil

1. Put the egg whites, onion, and 2 cups of drained potato cubes in a food processor with blade in place. Process 3 to 4 seconds, or until finely chopped.

2. Add the remaining, well-drained potatoes and process, using pulsing action, until finely minced. Do not purée or overblend.

3. Pour into a mixing bowl; add the bread crumbs, pepper, and salt. Stir to blend.

4. Pour 2 to 3 tablespoons canola oil into a 10- to 12-inch heavy nonstick skillet coated with nonstick vegetable spray. Place over medium-high heat. When hot, drop heaping tablespoons of the potato mixture into the oil, using the back of a spoon to flatten the latkes. Fry until brown and crisp, about 4 minutes. Turn only once, to avoid greasy latkes, and do not crowd the skillet.

5. When golden brown on both sides and crisp, drain on a large brown paper bag or paper towels. Place on a cake rack set on a shallow baking sheet and put in a 250° oven to keep warm, and to further drain fat, while you cook the remaining latkes.

*To Serve:* Serve with nonfat sour cream, nonfat yogurt, sugar-free applesauce, or any of your favorite chutneys or sauces.

*To Freeze Latkes:* After draining, arrange the latkes on a cookie sheet and place in the freezer until frozen solid. Stack in a plastic bag and seal. To reheat, place the frozen latkes on a nonstick foil-lined baking sheet and bake at 450° in the upper third of the oven for 5 to 7 minutes or until crispy and hot.

| PER SERVING | | | |
|---|---|---|---|
| 4.8 gm total fat | .38 gm saturated fat | 1.8 gm fiber | 142 calories |
| 0 mg cholesterol | 29.8% fat | 67 mg sodium | 43 calories from fat |

# PURIM

*The Jews of the villages . . . make the fourteenth day of the month Adar a day of gladness and feasting and a good day, and of sending portions one to another.*

—ESTHER 9:19

Purim is the spring holiday that commemorates Esther, the favorite Jewish queen of Persia, and her rescue of the Jews from the evil Haman, an adviser in the court of Ahasuerus of Sushan. Haman sought to annihilate the Jews because they would not bow down to him.

Therefore, Purim is a holiday that shows good triumphant over evil. It is celebrated with great enthusiasm, especially by children. At the *magillah* reading, children cheer Esther and her courageous deeds and spin their "groggers" to drown out the cruel Haman's name.

Tradition dictates that on this holiday we give special gifts to the poor, and gifts of food to relatives, friends, and neighbors. These plates of Purim baked goods are known as *shalack manot* (sending of portions). The recipient, whether a child or an adult, reciprocates in kind with a plate of at least two sweets, one of which is usually *hamantaschen*, the classic Purim pastry. I remember impatiently looking forward to coming home from school so that I could deliver these gifts.

Purim comes with special festivities for adults as well as children. The miraculous salvation of the Jewish community by Esther and her uncle Mordecai is celebrated as a day to mark a person's right to be different, even if he or she is in the minority.

Since Purim is the last holiday before Passover, it provides a good opportunity to use up our flour and leavening agents in baking before making Pesach.

❦

## PURIM MENU

*Sarah's Lima Bean and Barley Soup with Mushrooms (page 155)*

*My Family's Favorite Veal Roast (page 342)*

*Kasha Varnishkes (page 218)*

*Radish, Celery, and Cucumber Salad*

*Chick-Peas (Nahit) (page 274)*

*Banana Pineapple Sherbet (page 408)*

*Hamantaschen (below)*

*Dr. Harvey Mendess's Mother's Date Bars (page 64)*

*Poppy Seed Komitzbrodt (page 65)*

❦

## ❦ Hamantaschen (Haman's Hat) ❦
### (PAREVE)

*Yield: about 30 pastries (1 hamantasch = 1 serving)*

Hamantaschen are three-cornered pastries inspired by Haman's three-cornered hat. They can be made of cookie dough or yeast dough. The traditional filling is poppy seed (*mohn*) or plum butter (Lekvar, page 411).

2½ cups sifted unbleached all-purpose flour
¼ teaspoon kosher salt
2 tablespoons sugar
5⅓ tablespoons (⅓ cup) chilled butter-flavored margarine, cubed
¼ cup egg substitute
2 teaspoons pure vanilla extract
3 tablespoons ice water or cold fresh orange juice
3 tablespoons distilled white vinegar
3 tablespoons canola oil
Filling (see below)

### To Prepare Dough:

1. Combine 1½ cups of the flour, the salt, sugar, and margarine in a food processor bowl. Using the steel blade, process with pulsing action until the flour resembles coarse cornmeal.

2. Mix the egg substitute, vanilla, water, vinegar, and oil with a fork. Add the remaining 1 cup of flour and mix lightly to blend.

3. Combine the two mixtures and stir with a fork just until blended.

4. Cover with plastic wrap and store in the refrigerator overnight.

### To Prepare Hamantaschen:

1. When ready to use, pinch off a piece of dough the size of a walnut. Roll on a lightly floured surface into a 2½-inch round.

2. Place 1 teaspoonful of filling in the center; fold over three sides of the dough, forming a triangle over the filling. Pinch the edges to close, leaving a little of the filling showing.

3. Place on an ungreased nonstick baking sheet.

4. Repeat with the remaining dough.

5. Bake in a preheated 400° oven for 20 minutes, or until lightly browned.

SUGGESTED FILLINGS:

## Lekvar

See page 411.

## Poppy Seed (Mohn) Filling

  2 cups poppy seeds
  1 cup nonfat or skim milk
  ½ cup honey
  ¼ cup sugar
  ½ cup dark raisins (½ cup grated apples and ¼ cup finely chopped nuts may be
      substituted for raisins)
  2 teaspoons grated lemon zest

1. Wash the poppy seeds in a fine strainer several times; drain.
2. Combine the poppy seeds with the milk, honey, and sugar in a saucepan.

3. Cook over moderate heat until thick (about 10 minutes), stirring occasionally to prevent scorching.

4. Add the raisins and lemon zest; *let cool* before using.

## Prune Apricot Filling

 5 ounces sun-dried apricots
10 ounces pitted prunes
½ cup frozen unsweetened apple juice concentrate
 1 cup water
   Grated zest of 1 lemon

Combine all the ingredients in a microwave-safe bowl or saucepan and cover. Microwave on High for 12 to 15 minutes. Stir well to blend. Cool before using.

NOTE: All fillings can be prepared in advance, covered, and stored in the refrigerator. Prepared prune or poppy seed filling may be substituted for your own.

FOR YEAST DOUGH: See page 419. Form balls the size of a small apple and roll out ¼ inch thick and 4 to 6 inches in diameter. Fill, form triangles, let rise until doubled in bulk, and bake in a preheated 350° oven for 30 to 40 minutes or until lightly browned.

—————————— PER SERVING ——————————

| | | | |
|---|---|---|---|
| 4.6 gm total fat | .62 gm saturated fat | 1.1 gm fiber | 102 calories |
| 0 mg cholesterol | 40.4% fat | 95 mg sodium | 42 calories from fat |

# ❦ Dr. Harvey Mendess's Mother's Date Bars ❦ (Winnipeg Style)
## (PAREVE)
### Yield: 32 bars (1 bar = 1 serving)

This recipe was sent to me from Winnipeg, Manitoba, Canada. Dr. Harvey Mendess got this straight from his mother. It read: "Add some flour, a little butter, not a lot, maybe an egg or two, and don't forget to stir. Also some flavoring. What do you mean how much? Enough!! Enough so it tastes good. Leave me alone already. I told you how, so go and do it."

10 to 12 ounces pitted dates, cut into small pieces
      1 cup cold water
        Juice of ½ lemon
      ¾ cup packed brown sugar
      ½ cup unbleached all-purpose flour
      ½ teaspoon baking soda
    1½ cups rolled oats or oatmeal
      ⅓ cup canola oil

1. Combine the dates, water, lemon juice, and ¼ cup of the brown sugar in a saucepan and cook over medium heat until mushy. Set aside to cool.

2. Combine the flour, baking soda, and rolled oats in a small bowl. Mix and set aside. Preheat the oven to 350°.

3. Beat the canola oil with the remaining ½ cup brown sugar in a medium bowl. Add the dry ingredients and stir. Blend well.

4. Coat an 8-inch square pan lightly with butter-flavored cooking spray. Sprinkle lightly with half the dry mixture; pat down. Spread the date mixture over it. Crumble the rest of the dry mixture on top.

5. Bake for 35 to 40 minutes, or until the top has browned and crisped.

6. Remove from the oven, cool, and slice into 2 × 1-inch bars. Remove from the pan with a spatula and arrange on a platter.

--- PER SERVING ---

| 2.6 gm total fat | .22 gm saturated fat | 1.2 gm fiber | 79 calories |
| 0 mg cholesterol | 27.9% fat | 21 mg sodium | 23 calories from fat |

# ❧ Poppy Seed Komitzbrodt ❧
## (PAREVE)
### Yield: 48 slices (1 slice = 1 serving)

I've added whole wheat flour, used one whole egg or egg substitute, and eliminated the oil completely. The result is a flavorful, crispy confection that has no cholesterol and practically no fat.

1 cup whole wheat pastry flour
1¼ cups unbleached all-purpose flour
1 cup sugar
⅓ cup poppy seeds
1 teaspoon baking powder
½ teaspoon baking soda
¼ cup egg substitute or 1 extra-large egg
3 extra-large egg whites
3 tablespoons fresh orange juice
1 teaspoon pure orange extract or 2 teaspoons grated orange zest

1. Preheat the oven to 325°. Spray a baking sheet with butter-flavored cooking spray.

2. Combine the flours, sugar, poppy seeds, baking powder, and baking soda. Mix with a slotted spoon.

3. Whisk together the eggs, orange juice, and orange extract; add to the dry ingredients and mix well.

4. Divide the dough into 2 portions. With floured hands on a lightly floured work surface, roll into 2 logs about 12 inches long and 1½ inches thick.

5. Place on the prepared pan 3 inches apart and bake 25 minutes, or until firm to the touch.

6. Remove from the pan and cool slightly on a rack. Using a serrated knife, cut into ½-inch diagonal slices and return to the baking sheet cut side down. Bake at 300° for about 15 minutes on each side, or until lightly browned. Cool thoroughly before storing or freezing.

VARIATION: Three tablespoons of fresh lemon juice and 2 teaspoons of grated lemon zest may be substituted for the orange.

—————— PER SERVING ——————

| .4 gm total fat | .05 gm saturated fat | .1 gm fiber | 36 calories |
| 0 mg cholesterol | 10.6% fat | 16 mg sodium | 4 calories from fat |

# PASSOVER

## The Jewish Kitchen at Pesach: "Why Are These Recipes Different from All Other Recipes?"

*Remember this day, in which ye came out of Egypt, out of the house of bondage; for by strength of hand the Lord brought you out from this place: there shall no leavened bread be eaten.*

—EXODUS 13:3

Many traditions and customs are passed down informally from generation to generation. Eating offers a wonderful window into our culture where there is no written record, but the special dietary restrictions of Pesach pose an extra challenge to the health-conscious cook. In researching this chapter, I discovered that virtually every Jewish person I know has different ideas about what foods can and cannot be eaten during Passover. For example, my Sephardic friends eat rice, corn, and legumes during Passover—but in my Ashkenazic household the rice goes out right along with the bread. Therefore, the recipes in this chapter rely for bulk on matzos, matzo meal, fruits, and vegetables. Any packaged food that is specifically marked "kosher for Passover" can be eaten by all, but if you keep a strictly kosher home, I recommend that you consult your rabbinic authority about any specific foods whose use you question.

Passover rituals center on stories. To celebrate the seder is, of course, to obey the commandment to retell the story of the release from slavery in Egypt. For many families, the traditional stories are stories about food: Are the matzo balls heavier or lighter than last year's? What brand of matzo is best? Can we get away with using gefilte fish from a jar? Is the horseradish too strong?

The telephone is busy with calls to and from friends and relatives. "Do you have a good recipe for matzo kugel?" "Can I make the matzo balls without eggs and oil?" "How can we avoid the dozens and dozens of eggs this year?" And, at the eleventh hour, there's always someone who calls to ask, "Do you have any Haggadahs that you can bring?" You'll have to provide your own Haggadahs, but the following pages contain recipes that will answer most of your nutritional/culinary questions for Passover.

### The Seder Plate

*Maror* (bitter herbs) symbolize the bitterness of the lives of the Israelites when they were enslaved in Egypt.

*Haroset* (fruit and nut paste) represents the mortar the Israelites were forced to use in building.

*Zero'a* (a roasted lamb shankbone or neck of fowl) is a reminder of the Paschal lamb used as a sacrifice in the days of the Temple.

*Karpas* (a fresh spring vegetable like parsley, radish, celery, or new potato) reminds us that spring is a season of renewal and hope. During the seder, it is dipped in salt water as a reminder of tears shed during slavery.

*Beitza* (a hard-boiled or roasted egg) is also a symbol of the yearly renewal of life, and a reminder of the offerings brought to the Temple on festival days.

❧

### THE SEDER MEAL

*Wine and Matzo*

*Haroset (page 70)*

*Gefilte Fish Loaf (page 71) with Homemade Beet Horseradish (page 73)*

*My Mother's Chicken Soup (page 138) with Marvelous Matzo Balls (page 76)*

*Nanette Nathanson's Stuffed Chicken Breasts with Apricot Glaze (page 85)*

*Steamed Asparagus*

*Dorothy Hartstein's Passover Onion Puff (page 79)*

*Jean Berenson's Apple-Carrot Passover Pudding (page 81)*

*Almost Dorothy Hartstein's Passover Chocolate Torte (page 88)*

*Fresh Strawberries*

*Spicy Meringues (page 91)*

*Apricot Squares (page 95)*

❧

ᴡ

## PASSOVER RECIPES

Sally's Ashkenazic Haroset (page 70)

Sephardic Haroset (Date Nut Spread) (page 70)

Gefilte Fish Loaf (page 71)

Homemade Beet Horseradish (page 73)

Falsher Fish (page 74)

Potato Knaidlach (page 75)

Marvelous Matzo Balls (Knaidlach) (page 76)

Bootsie Segal's Feather-Light Matzo Balls (page 77)

Farfel and Asparagus Risotto (page 78)

Dorothy Hartstein's Passover Onion Puff (page 79)

Marge Taylor's Matzo Kugel (page 80)

Jean Berenson's Apple-Carrot Passover Pudding (page 81)

Lillian Tabor's Matzo Kugel (page 82)

Pear-Pineapple Matzo Kugel (page 83)

Basic Matzo Stuffing (page 84)

Nanette Nathanson's Stuffed Chicken Breasts with Apricot Glaze (page 85)

Passover Tzimmes with Mini Matzo Balls (page 87)

Almost Dorothy Hartstein's Passover Chocolate Torte (page 88)

Passover Brownies (page 90)

Spicy Meringues (page 91)

Pesach Mandelbrot (page 92)

Date and Nut Bars from West Bloomfield (page 93)

Dorothy Essick's Vienna Torte (Not Just for Passover) (page 94)

Apricot Squares (page 95)

Dorothy Essick's Passover Rolls (page 96)

Harold's Matzo Brei (page 97)

Passover Granola (page 99)

ᴡ

## ❦ Sally's Ashkenazi Haroset ❦
### (PAREVE)
*Serves: 10*

 2 large Red Delicious or Granny Smith apples, peeled, cored, and quartered
½ cup finely chopped toasted walnuts and/or almonds
 1 teaspoon honey
 1 teaspoon ground cinnamon
 3 tablespoons kosher sweet red wine (or use fresh orange juice and 1 teaspoon grated orange zest)

1. Chop the apples in a food processor.
2. Put the apples and the remaining ingredients in a bowl and blend.
3. Cover with plastic and refrigerate until needed.

| — PER SERVING — | | | |
|---|---|---|---|
| 3.6 gm total fat | .24 gm saturated fat | 1.3 gm fiber | 60 calories |
| 0 mg cholesterol | 52.8% fat | 1 mg sodium | 33 calories from fat |

## ❦ Sephardic Haroset (Date Nut Spread) ❦
### (PAREVE)
*Yield: about 4 cups*

 1 pound pitted dates and dried figs
 4 apples, peeled, cored, and quartered
   Water to cover
 2 cups coarsely ground toasted pecans, almonds, and/or pistachios
½ cup kosher sweet red wine
   Ground cinnamon to taste
 2 tablespoons matzo meal (optional)

1. Put the dates, figs, and apples in a saucepan and add water to cover. Cook over medium heat, stirring occasionally, until the apples are tender and the water evaporates.

2. Remove from the heat. When cool enough to work with, transfer to a food processor, blender, or grinder and process to a coarse consistency.

3. Place in a bowl and add the nuts, wine, cinnamon, and, if desired, matzo meal.

4. Taste and adjust seasonings. Refrigerate. If too thick at serving time, add more wine.

| PER SERVING | | | |
|---|---|---|---|
| 3.4 gm total fat | .29 gm saturated fat | 1.4 gm fiber | 67 calories |
| 0 mg cholesterol | 43.5% fat | 1 mg sodium | 31 calories from fat |

# ❦ Gefilte Fish Loaf ❦
## (PAREVE)

*Yield: Two 9-inch loaves or 20 slices*
*(1 slice = 1 serving)*

Pesach brings thoughts of gefilte fish, and no Jewish cookbook could be complete without a recipe for it. I have omitted the egg yolks and oil, and I think you'll find this recipe very pleasing. I know my family does.

3½ pounds ground (see Note) fish fillets (whitefish, pike, and mullet)
 3 large onions, chopped fine
 1 rib celery, chopped fine
 3 large carrots, peeled and grated
 1 teaspoon kosher salt or to taste
 ½ teaspoon ground white pepper
 2 tablespoons sugar (optional)
 ¼ cup ice water or low-sodium seltzer
 ½ cup matzo meal
 6 extra-large egg whites
 ½ cup snipped chives or fresh dill as garnish (optional)

1. Place the ground fish, onions, celery, carrots, salt, and pepper (and sugar if desired) in a large bowl; stir to blend. Stir in the ice water and matzo meal.

2. In another large bowl, beat the egg whites with an electric mixer until soft peaks form. Gradually add the fish, 1 cup at a time, while beating.

3. Coat two 9 × 5 × 3-inch nonstick loaf pans with vegetable oil cooking spray and line the bottoms with parchment paper, wax paper, or foil. Spray the lining.

4. Spoon the mixture into the pans; spread smooth on top.

5. Place the loaf pans in a larger pan at least 2 inches deep and set in a preheated 325° oven. Pour 1½ inches of boiling water into the larger pan.

6. Bake uncovered for about 50 to 60 minutes, or until the center of a loaf feels firm when pressed.

7. Remove the pans from the water; cool, cover, then chill in the pans for 6 to 8 hours or overnight.

*To Serve:* Slide a knife between the fish and the pan sides. Drain off any juices. Invert the loaf onto a platter, tap to release, and remove the paper. For a buffet, slice the loaf. Place slices on a fish-shaped platter, garnish generously with fresh dill, sprinkle with chives, and accompany with horseradish.

The fish may also be served in individual slices on chilled butter lettuce leaves with a sprig of dill and Homemade Beet Horseradish (page 73).

NOTE: If the fish is not already ground, cut it into 1-inch cubes and chop into a smooth purée in a food processor using blade with pulsing action.

VARIATION: For gefilte fish balls, make above recipe through step 2. Combine 3 pounds of fish bones, 2 ribs of celery, a sliced onion, 3 peeled and sliced carrots, a handful of Italian flat-leaf parsley, and 3 quarts of cold water in a heavy Dutch oven. Bring to a boil and simmer for 30 minutes. Remove any foam and place a plate face down over the ingredients to keep bones and vegetables from sticking to the fish. Wet your hands with cold water and shape the raw fish mixture into 3-inch ovals. Drop them into the simmering broth and simmer, partially covered, for about 2 hours or until liquid is reduced by half. Baste fish balls as they cook. Allow the fish balls to cool slightly in the broth, then gently remove them to a platter. Top with the sliced carrots, cover with plastic wrap then foil, and chill. Strain the fish broth and return it to the saucepan and reduce by half. Store separately in the refrigerator. Jellied broth may be served with the fish balls for those who enjoy.

---

PER SERVING

| | | | |
|---|---|---|---|
| 4.8 gm total fat | .74 gm saturated fat | 1.0 gm fiber | 140 calories |
| 48 mg cholesterol | 31.3% fat | 179 mg sodium | 43 calories from fat |

# ❧ Homemade Beet Horseradish (Chrain) ❧
## (PAREVE)
*Yield: 4 cups (1 tablespoon = 1 serving)*

Not just for Passover. At the farmers market in Los Angeles there is a stall called Magee's, where they have been making positively delicious fresh horseradish right before your eyes for over twenty-five years. Since this is not convenient for most people, you will have to resort to the product available at your local market or use the recipe below. People's tastes for horseradish *(chrain)* varies from mild to very strong. I love it strong enough to clear my sinuses. It is difficult to find bottled horseradish that does not have either preservatives (usually a sulfiting agent), sugar, or oil added. You have to be a label detective to find one that is free of these additives and tastes good. One excellent brand is Gold's, made in Brooklyn and nationally distributed.

1½ **pounds horseradish root, scrubbed clean, peeled, and diced**
 3 **small raw beets, peeled and diced**
 1 **(16-ounce) can salt-free julienned beets, drained**
 1 **teaspoon kosher salt**
 1 **teaspoon sugar (optional)**
¾ **cup distilled white vinegar**

1. Process the cubed horseradish and raw beets in a food processor, using the steel blade, until the desired consistency is reached. Pour into a mixing bowl.
2. Finely chop the drained beets and stir into the horseradish mixture.
3. Add the salt, sugar, and vinegar; mix thoroughly.
4. Taste and adjust seasonings and store in jars with tightly closed lids. This usually keeps 3 to 4 days before it starts to lose its strength.

VARIATIONS:
*Horseradish Sauce for Poached Fish:* Mix ½ cup of plain grated horseradish with 1½ cups of nonfat sour cream and 1½ tablespoons of lemon juice. Taste and adjust seasonings.
*Horseradish Apple Relish:* Mix ½ cup grated plain horseradish with 1 cup shredded

sweet apple, such as McIntosh, Spartan, or Baldwin. This is delicious served as an accompaniment to smoked trout.

---

PER SERVING

| | | | |
|---|---|---|---|
| 0 gm total fat | 0 gm saturated fat | .3 gm fiber | 13 calories |
| 0 mg cholesterol | 2.6% fat | 43 mg sodium | 0 calories from fat |

---

# ❦ Falsher Fish (Mock Gefilte Fish) ❦
## (MEAT)
### Yield: 16 balls (1 ball = 1 serving)

Years ago, most Jews found it too expensive to feed fish to a whole family for Shabbat dinner. They stretched the servings by adding other ingredients to the fish or substituting relatively inexpensive ground chicken. This was called *falsher*, or "false" fish. The flavor, surprisingly, is very much the same.

*Rich Poaching Stock:*
    8 cups defatted sodium-reduced chicken or vegetable broth or water
    1 cup dry white wine or vermouth
    1 large unpeeled onion, sliced
    6 ribs celery with leaves, sliced
    4 carrots, peeled and cut into 2-inch diagonal slices
    1 parsnip, cut into chunks
    6 peppercorns
    1 bay leaf

*Poultry Meatballs:*
    1 medium onion, peeled and quartered
    2 cloves garlic, smashed and peeled
    3 carrots, peeled and quartered
    2 pounds ground turkey breast or chicken breast (no skin or fat)
    ¼ cup egg substitute
    2 extra-large egg whites
    ⅔ cup matzo meal
    ⅓ cup of the prepared stock, cooled

⅛ teaspoon ground white pepper
¾ teaspoon kosher salt
½ bunch Italian flat-leaf parsley, tied with string


1. Make the stock: Combine all the stock ingredients in a 6-quart Dutch oven. Bring to a boil and simmer 30 minutes.

2. Make the meatballs: Mince the onion, garlic, and carrots in a food processor. Add the ground turkey and egg substitute, and blend well in the processor.

3. Beat the egg whites in an electric mixer until soft peaks form. Gradually add the turkey mixture to the egg whites while beating. Add the matzo meal and about ⅓ cup of the stock you have prepared, cooled. Season with salt and pepper.

4. Shape the mixture into 3-inch ovals with hands wet with cold water. Add to the simmering stock. Add the parsley and bring to a boil; reduce to a simmer and cover partially. Continue cooking slowly for 2 hours.

5. Cool slightly. Remove the "fish balls" to a 3-quart shallow casserole with a slotted spoon. Reduce the stock, then strain over the "fish balls." Top with the carrot slices; discard the remaining solids.

6. Cool, cover tightly with plastic wrap, and refrigerate.


*To Serve:* Place a chilled "fish ball" on a lettuce leaf, top with a carrot slice, sprinkle with paprika, and accompany with Homemade Beet Horseradish (page 73) or plain horseradish.

--- PER SERVING ---

| | | | |
|---|---|---|---|
| .6 gm total fat | .15 gm saturated fat | 2.0 gm fiber | 125 calories |
| 38 mg cholesterol | 4.4% fat | 170 mg sodium | 5 calories from fat |


# ❧ Potato Knaidlach ❧
## (PAREVE)
### *Yield: 18 balls (1 ball = 1 serving)*


When my husband and I were in Prague, we were served a huge variety of *knaidlach* (dumplings). These are delicious as a side dish with defatted chicken, turkey, or brisket gravy, or vegetable gravy. They also go well as a main course accompanied by vegetables.

¼ cup egg substitute or 1 whole egg
2 extra-large egg whites
2 tablespoons grated onion
¼ teaspoon kosher salt
⅛ teaspoon ground white pepper
¼ cup matzo meal
⅓ cup potato starch
4 cups grated raw potatoes, drained

1. Beat the eggs, onion, salt, and pepper together in a mixing bowl.

2. Stir in the matzo meal, potato starch, and grated potatoes. Cover tightly with plastic wrap and refrigerate for 20 to 30 minutes until firm enough to handle.

3. Shape into 1-inch balls and drop into a 4- to 5-quart saucepan filled with boiling salted water.

4. Simmer for about 20 minutes. When done the *knaidlach* will rise to the top. Remove with a slotted spoon, drain, and serve hot with gravy.

*To Serve:* As an entree, serve several *knaidlach* napped with gravy and accompany with red cabbage (page 240) and peas and carrots. Fresh fruit or fruit sorbet would be a refreshing dessert.

--- PER SERVING ---

| | | | |
|---|---|---|---|
| .2 gm total fat | .04 gm saturated fat | .6 gm fiber | 54 calories |
| 0 mg cholesterol | 3.4% fat | 48 mg sodium | 2 calories from fat |

## ❦ Marvelous Matzo Balls (Knaidlach) ❦
### (MEAT)
*Yield: 12 to 14 medium balls (1 ball = 1 serving)*

Planning the Passover meal always brings to mind visions of matzo balls. Be they light and fluffy or hard as rocks, each family has its favorite. This healthful recipe is my family's favorite.

4 extra-large egg whites
¾ teaspoon kosher salt
½ cup egg substitute
1 tablespoon canola oil or extra-virgin olive oil
2 tablespoons defatted sodium-reduced chicken broth

  1 teaspoon onion powder
⅛ teaspoon ground white pepper
¼ cup finely chopped Italian flat-leaf parsley or dill (optional)
  1 cup matzo meal

1. Beat the egg whites until frothy; add the salt and beat until stiff.

2. In a separate bowl, beat the egg substitute, oil, broth, onion powder, and pepper together to blend.

3. Fold the egg substitute mixture into the beaten egg whites, with the parsley, if desired.

4. Add the matzo meal and stir to combine. *Note: The more you stir, the firmer the matzo ball.*

5. Cover the mixture and chill in the refrigerator for 1 to 2 hours.

6. Shape into balls about the size of walnuts (using your hands that have been dipped into cold water) and drop into a kettle of lightly salted boiling water. Cover and simmer 45 minutes. Stir gently from time to time to prevent sticking to the bottom of the pan.

7. Remove from the water with a slotted spoon, drain, and add to soup for more flavor.

*To Freeze:* Place well-drained matzo balls on a nonstick baking sheet, cool, and freeze. When frozen solid, place in an airtight zip-lock bag and store in the freezer.

| PER SERVING | | | |
|---|---|---|---|
| 1.7 gm total fat | .18 gm saturated fat | .9 gm fiber | 68 calories |
| 0 mg cholesterol | 21.7% fat | 185 mg sodium | 15 calories from fat |

# ❧ Bootsie Segal's Feather-Light Matzo Balls ❧
## (PAREVE)
*Serves: 6 to 8 (1 matzo ball = 1 serving)*

1½ tablespoons canola oil
½ cup egg substitute
½ cup matzo meal
  1 teaspoon salt
⅛ teaspoon ground white pepper
  2 tablespoons seltzer

1. Combine the oil and egg substitute in a mixing bowl.

2. Add the matzo meal, salt, and pepper and mix thoroughly.

3. Add the seltzer and stir.

4. Cover the bowl with plastic wrap and refrigerate the batter for 30 minutes or more.

5. Bring 3 quarts of salted water to a boil. Form the dough into balls the size of walnuts and drop into the boiling water.

6. Cover, lower the heat, and simmer for 30 to 40 minutes.

7. Drain and place in soup or cool and flash-freeze for future use.

─────── PER SERVING ───────

| | | | |
|---|---|---|---|
| 3.2 gm total fat | .31 gm saturated fat | .2 gm fiber | 68 calories |
| 0 mg cholesterol | 41.5% fat | 323 mg sodium | 29 calories from fat |

## ❦ Farfel and Asparagus Risotto ❦
### (MEAT)
*Serves: 8*

When Passover approaches, people are always asking me for new side dish recipes. This one is just a bit different, but tasty and simple. It is a wonderful accompaniment to roast chicken, turkey, or brisket.

> 3 cups matzo farfel or crumbled whole wheat matzo
> 1 tablespoon olive oil
> 1 small onion, minced
> 6 thin asparagus spears cut into ½-inch diagonal slices, plus additional spears, steamed, for garnish
> 2½ to 3 cups defatted sodium-reduced chicken or vegetable broth
> Freshly ground pepper
> ½ cup minced Italian flat-leaf parsley

1. Lightly brown the matzo farfel in a nonstick skillet, stirring frequently. (It may also be browned under the broiler *if you watch it carefully.*)

2. Heat the oil in a medium saucepan and sauté the onion till translucent, about 3 to 4 minutes. Add the asparagus; sauté 1 minute.

3. Add the browned farfel; stir. Add the broth ½ cup at a time. Stir and cook for 1 minute after each addition. Cook until the farfel is tender.

4. Season with pepper and sprinkle with parsley. Serve hot and garnish with additional asparagus spears, steamed.

VARIATION: One and one-half cups of sliced fresh mushrooms may be added or substituted for the asparagus in step 2.

—————————— PER SERVING ——————————

| | | | |
|---|---|---|---|
| 2.5 gm total fat | .24 gm saturated fat | 1.3 gm fiber | 251 calories |
| 0 mg cholesterol | 9.0% fat | 11 mg sodium | 23 calories from fat |

# ❧ Dorothy Hartstein's Passover Onion Puff ❧
## (PAREVE)
### Serves: 6

My friend Dorothy happens to be an excellent cook—and also a registered dietitian. Although she lives in Long Beach, California, our cooking roots keep us connected. She has graciously allowed me to modify the fat in the original recipe. (It's still a bit high!)

2 cups finely chopped yellow onions
3 tablespoons plus 2 teaspoons canola oil
½ cup egg substitute
6 extra-large egg whites
⅓ cup matzo meal
¾ teaspoon salt
⅛ teaspoon ground white pepper

1. Sauté the onions in 2 teaspoons of oil until transparent, about 5 minutes; set aside to cool. Meanwhile, preheat the oven to 350°.

2. Beat the egg substitute with 1 egg white until it starts to thicken; stir in the onions, the 3 tablespoons of oil, matzo meal, salt, and pepper. Blend well.

3. Beat the remaining 5 egg whites until stiff. Stir one-fourth of the whites into the matzo meal mixture, then fold in the rest.

4. Pour into a 2-quart soufflé dish coated with vegetable oil cooking spray and bake for 25 minutes, or until light brown on top.

NOTE: This dish should be served immediately in order to have a beautiful presentation.

---

**PER SERVING**

| | | | |
|---|---|---|---|
| 9.2 gm total fat | .76 gm saturated fat | .9 gm fiber | 150 calories |
| 0 mg cholesterol | 54.4% fat | 385 mg sodium | 83 calories from fat |

---

# ❦ Marge Taylor's Matzo Kugel ❦
## (PAREVE)
### Serves: 8

Matzo kugel is almost as representative of Passover as matzo balls. This is one of several recipes from which you may choose.

4 thin matzos, 4 cups matzo farfel, or 12 ounces cooked Passover noodles
¾ cup egg substitute mixed with 4 extra-large egg whites
4 tablespoons sugar
1 teaspoon ground cinnamon
4 tart green apples, peeled, cored, and grated coarse
  Grated zest and juice of 1 orange
½ cup chopped walnuts or almonds
½ cup dark raisins

1. Break up the matzos or farfel into a colander, cover with water, and drain. Preheat oven to 350°.
2. In a large mixing bowl, beat the eggs with 3 tablespoons of the sugar and ½ teaspoon of the cinnamon. Add the matzo, farfel, or noodles and let stand 10 minutes.
3. Add the apples, orange zest and juice, nuts, and raisins.
4. Coat a 13 × 9 × 2-inch glass baking dish with vegetable oil cooking spray. Mix the remaining 1 tablespoon of sugar and ½ teaspoon of cinnamon. Sprinkle the dish with the sugar and cinnamon mixture.

5. Turn the kugel mixture into the prepared dish and bake for 45 minutes. Serve hot.

```
─────────────── P E R   S E R V I N G ───────────────
5.7 gm total fat      .53 gm saturated fat   3.2 gm fiber      226 calories
0 mg cholesterol      21.4% fat              72 mg sodium      51 calories from fat
```

# ❦ Jean Berenson's Apple-Carrot ❦ Passover Pudding
## (PAREVE)
### Serves: 6 to 8

My friend Jean Berenson has been making this pudding for friends and family for Passover for over twenty years. The only change, she reports, is in the additional quantities she has been asked to prepare!

¼ cup egg substitute
¼ cup canola oil
½ cup slivered almonds plus ⅓ cup for topping
1 large tart apple, peeled and shredded
1 cup shredded carrots
½ cup chopped dried figs
½ cup diced dried apricots
½ cup matzo meal
⅓ cup sugar
3 tablespoons fresh lemon juice
2 teaspoons grated lemon zest
1½ teaspoons ground cinnamon
   Freshly grated nutmeg
3 extra-large egg whites

1. Preheat the oven to 375°. Spray an 8-inch square glass baking dish or quiche dish with vegetable oil cooking spray.

2. Combine the egg substitute, oil, ½ cup of almonds, the apple, carrots, figs, apri-

cots, matzo meal, 1 tablespoon of the sugar, the lemon juice and zest, cinnamon, and nutmeg. Blend well.

3. Beat the egg whites until foamy and gradually add the remaining sugar, continuing to beat until the whites are stiff.

4. Fold the beaten whites into the pudding mixture. Turn into the prepared dish and smooth the top. Sprinkle with the ⅓ cup of slivered almonds and bake for 40 minutes.

NOTE: This recipe may be doubled or tripled successfully for a crowd. Just use a larger shallow casserole and increase the baking time by 20 to 30 minutes.

| PER SERVING | | | |
|---|---|---|---|
| 11 gm total fat | 1 gm saturated fat | 4.1 gm fiber | 216 calories |
| 0 mg cholesterol | 43% fat | 38 mg sodium | 107 calories from fat |

# ❦ Lillian Tabor's Matzo Kugel ❦
## (PAREVE)
### Serves: 10 to 12

Here's a matzo kugel recipe that's deliciously reminiscent of the savory bread stuffing that I make at other times of the year.

    1 large onion, peeled and chopped fine
    4 ribs celery with leaves, chopped fine
    1 tablespoon olive oil
    ½ cup chopped Italian flat-leaf parsley
    ¾ cup egg substitute
    8 extra-large egg whites, slightly beaten
      Salt and pepper to taste
   10 sheets matzo, broken up and soaked in warm water
      Hungarian paprika

1. Preheat the oven to 350°. Coat a 13 × 9 × 2-inch glass baking dish with olive oil cooking spray.

2. Sauté the onion and celery in olive oil 5 minutes or until transparent. Add the chopped parsley.

3. In a large bowl, beat together the egg substitute, egg whites, salt, and pepper.

4. Squeeze the water out of the matzos and add to the beaten eggs.

5. Add the vegetable mixture and blend. Pour into the prepared baking dish. Sprinkle with paprika and bake for 1 hour or until firm and browned.

—— PER SERVING ——

| | | | |
|---|---|---|---|
| 2.2 gm total fat | .34 gm saturated fat | 1.3 gm fiber | 139 calories |
| 0 mg cholesterol | 13.6% fat | 106 mg sodium | 20 calories from fat |

## ❧ Pear-Pineapple Matzo Kugel ❧
### (PAREVE)
#### Serves: 12

There is no special reason—religious or otherwise—why matzo kugel cannot be served at times other than Passover. This recipe has particular appeal, and I serve it with roast chicken from time to time throughout the year.

½ cup egg substitute
5 extra-large egg whites
2 tablespoons sugar
8 ounces crushed pineapple in natural juice
2 apples, peeled and shredded
1 firm pear, peeled, cored, and shredded
1 cup dark raisins soaked in ½ cup Passover wine
2 tablespoons canola oil
  Grated zest and juice of 2 lemons
1 teaspoon ground cinnamon
2 teaspoons pure vanilla extract
5 sheets matzo, crumbled, soaked in warm water, and drained, or 12 ounces cooked Passover noodles
½ cup sugar-free apricot preserves (optional)

1. Preheat the oven to 325°. Coat a 13 × 9 × 2-inch glass baking dish with vegetable oil cooking spray.

2. Beat the egg substitute and whites with a fork in a large bowl.

3. Add the sugar, pineapple and its juice, apples, pear, raisin mixture, oil, lemon zest and juice, cinnamon, and vanilla. Stir to blend.

4. Add the drained matzo or noodles and mix thoroughly. Transfer the mixture to the prepared baking dish.

5. Bake for 45 minutes. If desired, dot the kugel with the apricot jam during the last 10 minutes of baking.

VARIATION: You may use 12 stewed apricots on top of the pudding instead of jam for an attractive garnish.

---

**PER SERVING**

| | | | |
|---|---|---|---|
| 3.0 gm total fat | .30 gm saturated fat | 2.1 gm fiber | 165 calories |
| 0 mg cholesterol | 15.7% fat | 45 mg sodium | 27 calories from fat |

---

# ❧ Basic Matzo Stuffing ❧
## (MEAT)

*Yield: Enough for a 12- to 14-pound turkey*
*Serves: 14 to 16*

If your family enjoys stuffing as much as mine does, double the recipe and stuff under the skin, in the cavity, and arrange the rest around the bird.

1 large onion, peeled and minced (about 1 cup)
2 ribs celery, diced fine
2 tablespoons olive oil
2 cloves garlic, smashed, peeled, and minced
7 cups matzo farfel or about 10 finely broken matzo sheets
¼ teaspoon ground white pepper
1 tablespoon Hungarian paprika
½ cup egg substitute or 3 extra-large egg whites
¼ cup chopped Italian flat-leaf parsley
2 cups defatted sodium-reduced chicken broth (use 3 cups broth if you like moist dressing)

1. Sauté the onion and celery in the oil in a covered nonstick sauté pan for 3 to 5 minutes. Remove the cover, add the garlic, and continue to sauté until wilted and tender. (Do not brown.)

2. Add the matzo farfel and stir until lightly toasted.

3. Combine the seasonings, egg substitute, parsley, and chicken broth in a bowl.

4. Add to the matzo mixture, mix, and use to stuff the bird under the skin and/or in the seasoned body cavity. Secure with toothpicks or metal skewers.

VARIATIONS:

*Mushroom Stuffing:* Sauté 2 cups of sliced fresh mushrooms with the onion. You may add 1 teaspoon of crushed dried thyme or 1 tablespoon of chopped fresh thyme to this mixture.

*Nut Stuffing:* One cup coarsely chopped toasted walnuts and/or almonds may be added to the onion with the matzo farfel.

*Fruit Stuffing:* Ten drained, pitted, chopped prunes or apricots; 2 cups peeled, cored, and diced apples; and ½ cup dark raisins may be added with the seasonings and broth.

---

— PER SERVING —

| | | | |
|---|---|---|---|
| 2.8 gm total fat | .27 gm saturated fat | 1.2 gm fiber | 286 calories |
| 0 mg cholesterol | 2.8% fat | 40 mg sodium | 25 calories from fat |

# ❦ Nanette Nathanson's Stuffed ❦ Chicken Breasts with Apricot Glaze
## (MEAT)
### *Serves: 8 (½ chicken breast = 1 serving)*

These delicious chicken breasts can be prepared before the seder and baked while the seder services are in progress. They make a beautiful, festive Passover platter. You eliminate half the fat if you remove the skin before eating. You may also substitute halved Cornish game hens for chicken breasts.

4 (1-pound) whole chicken breasts with skin, all visible fat removed
Juice of 1 lemon
1 teaspoon garlic powder
1½ cups crumbled whole wheat matzo
1½ cups matzo farfel
1½ cups diced onion
1½ cups diced celery
1 tablespoon olive oil
¾ pound white mushrooms, sliced
3 tablespoons toasted pine nuts (optional)
Freshly ground pepper
¼ cup chopped Italian flat-leaf parsley
1 tablespoon Hungarian paprika
½ teaspoon ground ginger
½ teaspoon dried oregano, crushed
½ teaspoon dried thyme, crushed
2 extra-large egg whites, slightly beaten
1¾ cups defatted sodium-reduced chicken broth
1 teaspoon onion powder

*Apricot Glaze (optional)*
1 cup defatted sodium-reduced chicken broth
1 cup dry white Passover wine
1 large shallot, minced
½ cup sugar-free apricot preserves

1. Loosen the skin from the chicken breasts without tearing it. Season under the skin with lemon juice and garlic powder.

2. Toast the matzo and farfel under the broiler until *lightly* browned.

3. Sauté the onion and celery in olive oil until wilted, about 5 minutes. Add the mushrooms and sauté 2 or 3 additional minutes.

4. Add the pine nuts and matzo-farfel mixture and mix well.

5. Combine ⅛ teaspoon of pepper, the parsley, 1 teaspoon of the paprika, the ginger, oregano, thyme, egg whites, and broth. Add to the farfel mixture. Let stand about 2 minutes to absorb moisture. Taste and adjust seasonings.

6. Stuff the mixture under the skin of the chicken breasts. If necessary, secure the skin with a toothpick. Season the breasts with onion powder, pepper to taste, and the remaining teaspoon of paprika.

7. Place in a shallow baking dish and bake 1 hour in the upper third of a pre-heated 350° oven.

### To Prepare Glaze:

1. Simmer the broth, wine, and shallot until reduced by half. Add the apricot preserves and mix until smooth.

2. Force the mixture through a tea strainer to produce a smooth glaze.

3. Using a pastry brush, paint the chicken breasts with glaze 5 minutes before they are finished roasting.

*To Serve:* Cut the breasts in half and arrange on a bed of watercress on a serving platter.

---

PER SERVING

| | | | |
|---|---|---|---|
| 16.1 gm total fat | 3.98 gm saturated fat | 6.3 gm fiber | 531 calories |
| 102 mg cholesterol | 26.7% fat | 132 mg sodium | 145 calories from fat |

---

# ❧ Passover Tzimmes ❧
# with Mini Matzo Balls

### (PAREVE)

*Serves: 12 to 14*

1 (2-pound) can sweet potatoes, drained
1 (1-pound) package peeled baby carrots, cooked until barely tender
1 pound pitted prunes, cooked
1 (16-ounce) can pineapple chunks, drained and juice reserved
½ cup packed brown sugar
½ teaspoon ground cinnamon
½ teaspoon freshly grated nutmeg (optional)
½ recipe Bootsie Segal's Feather-Light Matzo Balls (page 77), made the size of walnuts

1. Preheat the oven to 400°. Spray a 13 × 9 × 2-inch glass baking dish with vegetable oil cooking spray.

2. Arrange the sweet potatoes, carrots, prunes, and pineapple chunks in the prepared dish.

3. Sprinkle with the brown sugar, cinnamon, and nutmeg; arrange the matzo balls on top.

4. Pour the drained juice from the pineapple over the entire mixture.

5. Bake for about 45 minutes or until brown. Baste with juices from time to time.

---

**PER SERVING**

| | | | |
|---|---|---|---|
| 1.2 gm total fat | .16 gm saturated fat | 4.3 gm fiber | 198 calories |
| 0 mg cholesterol | 5.0% fat | 116 mg sodium | 10 calories from fat |

---

# ❦ Almost Dorothy Hartstein's ❦ Passover Chocolate Torte
## (PAREVE)
### Serves: 20

This is a change from the usual Passover sponge cake we've served for years. Although I have lowered the fat and cholesterol content, its delicious flavor is almost the same. A small serving goes a long way and will please all—especially unreformed chocoholics. Serve with fresh strawberries. It is best baked, and refrigerated, at least a day ahead.

⅓ cup blanched almonds

½ cup sugar

⅓ cup walnuts or pecans

⅓ cup potato starch

3 ounces semisweet or unsweetened chocolate

1 cup unsweetened cocoa powder

2 tablespoons instant coffee powder

½ cup boiling water

1 tablespoon pure vanilla extract

⅓ cup egg substitute

3 tablespoons pareve margarine, cut into cubes and at room temperature

3 tablespoons chopped dried apricots steeped in ¼ cup apricot brandy

3 extra-large egg whites

¼ teaspoon cream of tartar

*Chocolate Glaze:*
   1 ounce semisweet chocolate (optional)
   ½ cup unsweetened cocoa powder
   1 cup confectioners' sugar
   ¼ cup boiling water
     Toasted sliced or slivered almonds (optional)


1. Coat an 8-inch springform pan with butter-flavored cooking spray. Line the bottom with wax paper and spray lightly. Preheat the oven to 375°.

2. In a food processor, grind the almonds with 2 tablespoons of the sugar until very fine. Remove to a bowl.

3. Repeat with the walnuts and 2 tablespoons of sugar. Combine the two nut mixtures, add the potato starch, and mix.

4. Melt the chocolate carefully in a microwave. In a small saucepan, combine the chocolate, cocoa powder, coffee, boiling water, and vanilla. Stir in the egg substitute 1 tablespoon at a time, stirring well after each addition.

5. Place the saucepan over low heat; stir gently until the chocolate mixture is slightly thickened.

6. Remove from the heat and beat in the margarine one piece at a time. Add the nut mixture and stir (it will be very thick). Add the apricot mixture.

7. Beat the egg whites in a glass or metal bowl with the cream of tartar until soft peaks form. Slowly beat in the remaining ¼ cup of sugar. Beat until firm and glossy.

8. Fold about ⅓ of the egg whites gently into the chocolate mixture to lighten it. Fold in the remaining egg whites quickly and gently. Pour into the prepared pan and distribute the batter evenly. Bake for 25 to 30 minutes, or until a toothpick inserted at the edge comes out clean. The torte will be firm at the edge but soft in the center when done.

9. Cool on a wire rack about 45 minutes before frosting. The cake will shrink from the sides of the pan when cool. Carefully loosen the edges and remove the springform sides. Invert and remove the wax paper from the cake.


*To Prepare Glaze:*

1. Melt the chocolate and combine with the cocoa powder, confectioners' sugar, and boiling water in a bowl. Stir until smooth.

2. Frost the top and sides of the cake and decorate with toasted sliced or slivered almonds if desired.

NOTE: The cake may be baked several days ahead and refrigerated or frozen. Glaze on the day of serving.

---

**———— PER SERVING ————**

| | | | |
|---|---|---|---|
| 7.2 gm total fat | 2.10 gm saturated fat | 3.0 gm fiber | 151 calories |
| 0 mg cholesterol | 39.8% fat | 41 mg sodium | 65 calories from fat |

---

## ꩜ Passover Brownies ꩜
### (PAREVE)
*Yield: 20 pieces (1 piece = 1 serving)*

This recipe is not only acceptable for Passover but so delicious that you will want to make it year round. It seems almost impossible that this simple recipe should result in a delicious brownie. It is substantially lower in saturated fat and cholesterol than the usual recipe.

⅓ cup canola oil
1 cup sugar
1 extra-large egg or ¼ cup egg substitute
2 extra-large egg whites
1 teaspoon pure vanilla extract
⅓ cup unsweetened cocoa powder
¾ cup matzo cake meal
¼ cup potato starch
½ cup plus 3 tablespoons coarsely chopped walnuts, almonds, or dates

1. Preheat the oven to 350°. Coat an 8-inch square glass baking dish with butter-flavored cooking spray.
2. Beat the oil and sugar together until well blended.
3. Beat the egg and egg whites together and add to the sugar mixture with the vanilla. Blend well.
4. Sift the cocoa, cake meal, and potato starch together, using a single-mesh strainer (not a traditional sifter) and add to the sugar-egg mixture with the chopped nuts or dates. Blend well.
5. Pour the batter into the prepared baking dish, sprinkle with remaining nuts and

bake in the middle rack of the oven for about 25 minutes or until done. If desired, drizzle with 1 ounce melted chocolate.

*To Serve:* Remove from the oven and cut into 20 portions while still warm. They may be frozen for future use.

| ——— P E R   S E R V I N G ——— | | | |
|---|---|---|---|
| 5.0 gm total fat | .51 gm saturated fat | .9 gm fiber | 121 calories |
| 12 mg cholesterol | 35.8% fat | 10 mg sodium | 45 calories from fat |

# ❦ Spicy Meringues ❦
## (PAREVE)
*Yield: 55 to 60 cookies (1 meringue = 1 serving)*

  2 **extra-large egg whites, at room temperature**
1¼ **teaspoons ground cinnamon**
  ⅛ **teaspoon ground allspice**
  ½ **cup superfine sugar**
1½ **cups finely chopped toasted walnuts or chopped dates**

1. Preheat the oven to 250°.
2. Beat the egg whites until soft peaks are formed.
3. Mix the spices with the sugar and add by tablespoons to the egg whites while beating.
4. Beat until stiff but still shiny. Fold in the walnuts.
5. Drop by teaspoonfuls onto a nonstick baking sheet or one that has been lined with parchment, or a regular sheet sprayed with butter-flavored cooking spray.
6. Bake 1¼ hours; turn off the oven, open the door slightly (secure with a wooden spoon), and allow the cookies to cool in the oven overnight.
7. Store in a tightly covered container.

| ——— P E R   S E R V I N G ——— | | | |
|---|---|---|---|
| 1.8 gm total fat | .11 gm saturated fat | .2 gm fiber | 26 calories |
| 0 mg cholesterol | 57.3% fat | 2 mg sodium | 16 calories from fat |

# ❦ Pesach Mandelbrot ❦

## (PAREVE)

*Yield: about 48 slices (1 slice = 1 serving)*

2 tablespoons sugar
2½ teaspoons ground cinnamon
¼ cup egg substitute
4 extra-large egg whites
2 tablespoons canola oil
¼ cup fresh orange juice or lemon juice
1 tablespoon grated orange or lemon zest
1 cup matzo cake meal
¼ cup potato starch
¼ cup matzo meal
¾ cup coarsely chopped toasted almonds

1. Mix the sugar with 1 teaspoon of the cinnamon. In a large bowl, beat the eggs and sugar mixture together thoroughly. Beat in the oil, orange juice, and zest.

2. Mix the cake meal, potato starch, and remaining 1½ teaspoons of cinnamon together. Add the matzo meal and almonds.

3. Mix all the dry ingredients into the egg batter to form a soft dough.

4. Cover the dough with plastic wrap and refrigerate for 1 hour or overnight.

5. Preheat the oven to 350°. Place the dough on a work surface and shape it into a 1-inch-thick cylinder. Cut into rolls approximately 6 inches long. Place on a non-stick baking sheet.

6. Bake the rolls for 30 minutes or until lightly browned.

7. Cool slightly; slice the rolls diagonally into ½-inch slices and place cut side up on the cookie sheet. Return to the oven and brown for 15 minutes.

8. Turn off the heat and let stand in the oven until lightly browned and crisp.

VARIATION: A mixture of 2 tablespoons sugar and ½ teaspoon cinnamon may be sprinkled over the sliced rolls before returning to the oven. You may also just dust lightly with powdered sugar before serving.

—————— PER SERVING ——————

| | | | |
|---|---|---|---|
| 1.8 gm total fat | .12 gm saturated fat | .3 gm fiber | 40 calories |
| 0 mg cholesterol | 1.8% fat | 7 mg sodium | 16 calories from fat |

# ❦ Date and Nut Bars from West Bloomfield ❦
## (PAREVE)
### *Yield: 20 bars (1 bar = 1 serving)*

This recipe for date and nut bars has traveled all the way from West Bloomfield, Michigan, to Los Angeles, California. It's easy to prepare and delicious to eat.

½ cup matzo cake meal plus additional for coating pan
4 extra-large egg whites
¾ cup egg substitute
1 cup sugar
2 cups chopped dates (preferably Medjhool)
2 cups chopped toasted walnuts
1 teaspoon ground cinnamon
2 tablespoons sweet Passover wine
Grated zest of 1 lemon
Grated zest of 1 orange

1. Preheat the oven to 325°. Coat an 11 × 7 × 2-inch glass baking dish with vegetable oil cooking spray and flour lightly with cake meal.

2. Beat the egg whites; when thick, add the egg substitute and sugar gradually while beating until stiff and glossy.

3. Stir in the dates, nuts, ½ cup cake meal, cinnamon, wine, and lemon and orange zests. Turn the batter into the prepared baking dish.

4. Bake for 45 minutes. Cool and cut into 20 bars.

--- PER SERVING ---

| | | | |
|---|---|---|---|
| 7.5 gm total fat | .55 gm saturated fat | 2.5 gm fiber | 190 calories |
| 0 mg cholesterol | 33.2% fat | 28 mg sodium | 67 calories from fat |

# ❧ Dorothy Essick's Vienna Torte ❧
# (Not Just for Passover)
### (PAREVE)

*Yield: Two 9-inch round cakes*
*Serves: 16 to 18*

There are some recipes, like those for good matzo balls and this cake, that are too good to be saved for just one holiday. Dorothy and I played with this recipe to make it "legal," and the result is superb in texture as well as taste. For baking, we used a wonderful old aluminum loaf pan (16 × 5 × 4 inches) that I have used for many years to bake a large challah or kuchen; in this case, it made a delicate and delicious torte. However, you can successfully use two 9-inch round cake pans.

1 cup egg substitute
Grated zest of 1 orange
1 cup sugar
2 cups (½ pound) finely ground toasted pecans or walnuts
1 tablespoon instant coffee granules, crushed
1 tablespoon unsweetened cocoa powder
1 teaspoon ground cinnamon
⅓ cup matzo cake meal
6 extra-large egg whites

*Filling and Topping:*
½ cup sugar-free raspberry jam, heated with 1 tablespoon framboise liqueur
Confectioners' sugar
Fresh raspberries for garnish

1. Preheat the oven to 350°. Line two 9-inch round cake pans with wax paper.
2. Beat the egg substitute with the orange zest until foamy; add ¾ cup sugar gradually, beating until thick.
3. In a separate bowl, mix the pecan meal with the coffee granules, cocoa, cinnamon, and matzo cake meal. Add to the thick egg mixture and mix to blend.
4. Beat the egg whites until soft peaks start to form. Gradually add the remaining ¼ cup sugar, 1 tablespoon at a time, beating well after each addition. Beat until stiff and glossy, but not dry.

5. Gently fold the egg whites into the cake mixture.

6. Pour equal amounts of batter into the prepared pans and bake for about 20 minutes, or until a toothpick inserted in the center comes out clean.

7. Remove from the oven and invert the pans onto a cake rack to cool completely. Loosen the sides of the cakes with a spatula and remove from the pans. Peel off the wax paper.

*To Serve:* Cut each cooled cake horizontally in half with a serrated knife and spread with raspberry jam filling. Return the top of the cake and dust lightly with confectioners' sugar. Place the cake on a round platter and surround with fresh raspberries. I used to add a dollop of whipped cream; however, you can use a spoonful of softened frozen vanilla nonfat yogurt when served with a dairy meal.

---

### PER SERVING

| | | | |
|---|---|---|---|
| 7.8 gm total fat | .77 gm saturated fat | 1.0 gm fiber | 168 calories |
| 0 mg cholesterol | 40% fat | 47 mg sodium | 70 calories from fat |

---

## ❦ Apricot Squares ❦
### (PAREVE)
*Yield: 24 squares (1 square = 1 serving)*

Although this is a Pesach recipe, I bake these tasty pastries throughout the year, using Lekvar (page 411).

1⅔ cups matzo cake meal
⅓ cup sugar
⅓ cup finely ground toasted almonds
⅓ cup canola oil
2 tablespoons fresh lemon juice
1 tablespoon grated lemon zest
1 teaspoon pure vanilla extract
2½ to 3 cups sugar-free apricot preserves or Lekvar (page 411)

1. Coat a 13 × 9 × 2-inch glass baking dish with vegetable oil cooking spray. Preheat the oven to 350°.

2. Combine the cake meal, sugar, and almonds in a bowl. Stir to blend.

3. In a separate bowl, mix the oil, juice, zest, and vanilla. Add to the dry ingredients and stir with a fork.

4. Press down two thirds of the mixture firmly on the bottom of the baking dish.

5. Bake for 15 minutes. Remove from the oven and cool slightly.

6. Spread the preserves over the baked crust and sprinkle with the remaining cake meal mixture.

7. Return to the oven and bake for 25 additional minutes. Cool before cutting into squares. These pastries freeze nicely.

---

PER SERVING

| | | | |
|---|---|---|---|
| 4.7 gm total fat | .33 gm saturated fat | .7 gm fiber | 174 calories |
| 0 mg cholesterol | 23.2% fat | 19 mg sodium | 42 calories from fat |

---

## ❦ Dorothy Essick's Passover Rolls ❦
### (PAREVE)
*Yield: 10 rolls (1 roll = 1 serving)*

The absence of bread during Passover always means no sandwiches for lunch! These rolls make a delicious package for your favorite sandwich fillings. I've eliminated the egg yolks, making them cholesterol-free and, by the way, cutting down on the fat. (There are 5 grams of fat in each egg yolk!)

    1 cup water
    ½ cup canola oil
    ½ teaspoon kosher salt
    1 cup matzo meal
    ½ cup matzo cake meal
    ¼ cup egg substitute plus 7 extra-large egg whites, slightly beaten with a few
        grains of salt
        Poppy seeds, sesame seeds, and/or caraway seeds

1. Bring the water, oil, and salt to a boil; add the matzo meal and cake meal, and stir to blend.

2. Remove from the heat and add approximately 2 tablespoons of egg white mixture at a time while beating with an electric hand beater to blend.

3. Using a tablespoon, spoon the mixture onto a nonstick baking sheet in 10 portions. Brush lightly with slightly beaten egg white. Sprinkle with poppy seeds.

4. Bake in a preheated 400° oven for 35 to 40 minutes. Puncture each roll after baking with the tip of a paring knife or skewer to allow steam to escape.

VARIATIONS:

*Passover Seeded Rolls:* Add 2 tablespoons poppy seeds to the batter.

*Passover Onion Rolls:* Spread 1 tablespoon of chopped red or white onion on top of each roll before baking or add 1 tablespoon of onion powder to the batter.

*Passover Dessert Puffs:* Use 1 cup of matzo cake meal and ½ cup matzo meal, and substitute 1 cup of orange or apple juice for 1 cup water. Drop by the teaspoonful and bake in a preheated 400° oven for 20 to 25 minutes. At serving time, split and fill with fresh berries; place on a bed of strawberry sauce (page 408) and sprinkle with confectioners' sugar.

*Passover Canapés:* Drop batter by the teaspoonful and bake in a preheated 400° oven. Fill baked rolls with Gefilte Fish Balls, tuna salad, salmon salad, Smoked Salmon Tartare (page 116), or Eggs and Onions (page 28).

---

**PER SERVING**

| | | | |
|---|---|---|---|
| 12.2 gm total fat | .94 gm saturated fat | .7 gm fiber | 204 calories |
| 0 mg cholesterol | 52.8% fat | 168 mg sodium | 110 calories from fat |

---

# ❦ Harold's Matzo Brei ❦
## (DAIRY)
### *Serves: 6*

My husband has become the local *matzo brei* maven (expert). Friends from miles around call to find out when he's making his traditional *matzo brei* brunch. My daughter Sally, who is a particularly devoted fan, wonders why he only makes it at Passover. Maybe it's because anticipating this dish makes it even more delicious.

6 squares plain or whole wheat matzo, crumbled
  Nonfat or skim milk to cover, warmed
¾ cup egg substitute
6 extra-large egg whites
  Salt and/or cinnamon to taste
1 tablespoon soft light margarine or canola oil (optional)

1. Place the crumbled matzo in a mixing bowl. Add milk to cover and soak 15 minutes.

2. Beat the egg substitute and whites with a fork to blend. Add seasoning.

3. Squeeze the matzo dry and add to the egg white mixture. Let soak another 15 minutes.

4. Coat a nonstick skillet with butter-flavored cooking spray and place over medium heat. Add margarine to the hot pan if desired. Add the egg and matzo mixture.

5. Scramble as you would eggs or allow to cook pancake-style, browning on both sides.

*To Serve:* Serve immediately with cinnamon, applesauce, orange slices and/or nonfat sour cream.

VARIATION:

*Matzo Brei with Onions:* Place crumbled matzo in a bowl with warm water instead of milk. Proceed as in steps 2 through 4, omitting the cinnamon and adding 1¼ cups of sautéed onions (page 254).

―――――― PER SERVING ――――――

| 1.6 gm total fat | .31 gm saturated fat | .9 gm fiber | 161 calories |
| 1 mg cholesterol | 8.7% fat | 169 mg sodium | 14 calories from fat |

# ❦ Passover Granola ❦
## (PAREVE)

*Yield: 12 cups (½ cup = 1 serving as cereal; 1 tablespoon = 1 serving as a snack)*

Some Pritikin participants and I brainstormed and came up with this cereal when I was at the Pritikin Longevity Center. This granola may be served with milk for breakfast or used as a snack during Passover or throughout the year.

    5 **extra-large egg whites**
  ⅛ **teaspoon cream of tartar**
    3 **tablespoons packed light brown sugar or frozen unsweetened apple juice concentrate**
    2 **teaspoons ground cinnamon**
      **Freshly grated nutmeg to taste**
    8 **squares whole wheat matzo, crumbled**
 1¼ **cups assorted nuts (almonds, pecans, and/or walnuts), chopped coarse**
1½ to 2 **cups assorted dried fruits (dark raisins; cherries, blueberries, cranberries; apricots; and/or dates)**

1. Beat the egg whites with the cream of tartar until slightly thickened. Add the brown sugar gradually with the cinnamon and nutmeg and continue beating until soft peaks form.

2. Add the crumbled matzo and nuts; mix well and spread on 2 nonstick baking sheets.

3. Bake in a preheated 350° oven, stirring every 20 minutes, until crisp and lightly browned on all sides. (Break into chunks as it crisps.)

4. Remove from the oven and cool. Mix in the fruit and store in plastic zip-lock bags or airtight containers. The granola may be frozen for future use.

---
PER SERVING
---

| | | | |
|---|---|---|---|
| 2.8 gm total fat | .26 gm saturated fat | 2.6 gm fiber | 95 calories |
| 0 mg cholesterol | 23.7% fat | 14 mg sodium | 25 calories from fat |

# Shavuot

## "The Land of Milk and Honey"

*And thou shalt observe the feast of weeks, even of the first-fruits of wheat harvest, and the feast of ingathering at the turn of the year.*

—Exodus 34:22

The Talmud considers Shavuot a concluding holiday to Passover and identifies this as the day that Moses received the Ten Commandments on Mount Sinai. Originally celebrated as an agricultural holiday at the time of the barley harvest, Shavuot has become a time to celebrate the Torah. Because the Torah is as pure as milk and honey, it is customary to serve only dairy products at Shavuot. Such tempting dishes as blintzes, noodle kugel, cheese kreplach, cheese knishes, and cheesecake make for delicious dairy meals—and you'll see that they can be low in fat and cholesterol, too.

### SHAVUOT MENU

*Mother Mollie's No-Cholesterol Challah (page 5) or Pumpernickel*

*Schav Borscht (page 147) or Blender Beet Borscht (page 145) with Boiled Potatoes*

*Never-Fail Blintzes (page 101) with Nonfat Sour Cream*

*Renée Holland's Spinach Soufflé (page 103)*

*Salmon Croquettes (page 104)*

*Hungarian Wilted Lettuce and Tomato Salad (page 191)*

*Fresh Strawberries*

*Cheese Kuchen*

# ❦ Never-Fail Blintzes ❦

(DAIRY)

*Yield: 24 blintzes (2 blintzes = 1 serving)*

No Jewish cookbook would be complete without a recipe for blintzes. You might call them crepes, *palacsinken*, or *blini*, and fill them with apricot preserves, blueberries, lekvar, cottage cheese, or mashed potatoes with sautéed onions, but they're still blintzes. The *blatlach* (crepes) may be made ahead of time and kept in the refrigerator for 2 to 3 days or frozen for future use. You can also freeze them filled. They make a wonderful addition to a dairy meal, whether for Shavuot or a Sunday brunch for neighbors. They are more healthful and delicious than the store-bought frozen blintzes, and really quite simple to make. It just takes a little time.

These *blatlach* are cholesterol- and saturated fat–free, and the cheese filling is lowered in fat and cholesterol by using hoop cheese, nonfat cottage cheese, 35 percent fat–reduced or fat-free cream cheese, egg substitute, and nonfat sour cream. They can be browned in a nonstick skillet coated with buttery cooking spray, and you can even indulge yourself with a dollop of nonfat sour cream to top them off.

## Blatlach (Crepes)

1 cup unbleached all-purpose flour, or matzo meal at Passover
1 cup nonfat milk
1 cup club soda or water
⅛ teaspoon kosher salt
½ cup egg substitute mixed with 2 extra-large egg whites
2 tablespoons canola oil

1. Place all the ingredients in a blender or food processor and mix until smooth.
2. Pour into a bowl, cover, and refrigerate for 1 hour or more.
3. Coat a 6-inch nonstick skillet with butter-flavored cooking spray and heat until hot (a few drops of water will dance on the surface). Pour about 3 tablespoons of batter into the center of the skillet. Tilt quickly so that the batter covers the bottom of the pan. Cook until lightly browned on the bottom. Remove to a clean kitchen towel, brown side up, and cool. Before making each crepe, stir the batter and add cooking spray as needed. Continue until all the batter is used, stacking the crepes after they cool. If they are to be frozen, place wax paper between crepes, wrap in foil, and seal in a plastic bag.

## Cheese Filling for Blintzes

8 ounces fresh nonfat hoop cheese, farmer cheese, or ricotta
4 ounces fat-reduced cream cheese or nonfat cream cheese
½ cup nonfat cottage cheese
1 tablespoon nonfat sour cream, plus additional for garnish if desired
2 tablespoons egg substitute
2 tablespoons sugar
2 teaspoons pure vanilla extract
1 teaspoon ground cinnamon
½ cup dark raisins soaked in fresh orange juice (optional)

*Topping:*

3 tablespoons sugar mixed with 1 teaspoon ground cinnamon

Place all the filling ingredients in a food processor or blender and blend just until smooth and of a spreading consistency.

### To Assemble Blintzes:

1. Place a crepe, browned side up, on a flat surface. Place 1 tablespoon of filling in the center. Turn down the top of the crepe, fold in the sides, and fold into a small rectangle. Repeat with the remaining crepes and filling.

2. Place the blintzes, seam side down, in a shallow pan or casserole coated with butter-flavored spray and sprinkle with the sugar-cinnamon topping. Broil until browned. Or brown on both sides in a spray-coated or lightly greased nonstick skillet and sprinkle on topping afterwards.

*To Serve:* Serve hot with nonfat sour cream, fruit preserves, or chopped stewed Prune-Apricot Compote (page 400).

VARIATIONS:

*Pareve Blatlach:* Use all water in the batter so the crepes can be filled with either a meat or dairy filling. Serve topped with Fresh Tomato Sauce (page 53).

*Meat-Filled Crepes:* Chopped leftover meat or chicken may also be used to fill crepes (see page 356 for chicken phyllo filling).

*Dessert Crepes:* Apricot preserves flavored with apricot brandy make a nice dessert filling.

*Lemon Crepes:* For a simple dessert, sprinkle crepes with fresh lemon juice, roll up, and sprinkle with confectioners' sugar. Serve with additional lemon juice and sugar.

---

**PER SERVING**

| | | | |
|---|---|---|---|
| 5.9 gm total fat | 2.17 gm saturated fat | .3 gm fiber | 143 calories |
| 12 mg cholesterol | 37.9% fat | 185 mg sodium | 53 calories from fat |

---

# ❦ Renée Holland's Spinach Soufflé ❦
## (DAIRY)
### *Serves: 8 to 10*

A quick and easy recipe that's ideal for the dairy days of Shavuot.

    2 medium onions, chopped (2 cups)
    1 tablespoon canola oil
    3 (10-ounce) packages frozen chopped spinach, thawed and drained
    1 pound (16 ounces) nonfat cottage cheese or ricotta cheese
      Freshly ground pepper
2½ cups egg substitute
    2 extra-large egg whites

1. Preheat the oven to 350°. Spray a 13 × 9 × 2-inch baking dish with butter-flavored cooking spray.
2. Sauté the onions in the oil until translucent, about 5 minutes.
3. In a large mixing bowl, combine the spinach, cottage cheese, pepper, eggs, and onions. Mix thoroughly and transfer to the prepared baking dish.
4. Bake for about 1 hour, or until puffy and lightly browned.

---

**PER SERVING**

| | | | |
|---|---|---|---|
| 3.7 gm total fat | .56 gm saturated fat | 3.2 gm fiber | 127 calories |
| 3 mg cholesterol | 25.3% fat | 353 mg sodium | 33 calories from fat |

---

# ❧ Salmon Croquettes ❧
## (DAIRY)
*Yield: 8 croquettes (2 croquettes = 1 serving)*

My mother's salmon croquettes, hot or cold, can't be beat for flavor. Don't forget to remove the skin and dark portions of the salmon, and to mash all the bones.

     1 small carrot, peeled and quartered
    ½ onion, peeled and quartered
    ½ green bell pepper, seeded and quartered
     1 (6-ounce) baking potato, baked or boiled, peeled and quartered
     2 extra-large egg whites
     3 tablespoons fresh lemon juice
     1 tablespoon Worcestershire sauce
     1 (15½-ounce) can red salmon, drained, skin removed
    1½ cups dried bread crumbs
    ¼ cup nonfat or skim milk
     2 tablespoons soy-based Parmesan cheese alternative
     4 teaspoons canola oil
     4 lemon wedges dipped in chopped parsley, for garnish

1. Place the carrot, onion, and green pepper in a food processor and mince.
2. Add the cooked potato and the egg whites and process slightly.
3. Add the lemon juice, Worcestershire sauce, salmon, ½ cup of the bread crumbs, and the milk. Process just to blend.
4. Mix the remaining 1 cup of bread crumbs with the Parmesan alternative. Shape the salmon mixture into 8 patties and coat with the bread crumb mixture.
5. Coat a nonstick skillet with butter-flavored cooking spray. Add 2 teaspoons of the oil and heat over medium-high heat. When hot, add the croquettes, brown on one side, turn, drizzle 2 teaspoons oil into the pan, and brown on the other side.
6. Place on a nonstick baking sheet and bake in a preheated 375° oven for about 5 minutes.

*To Serve:* Arrange the croquettes on a platter and garnish with lemon wedges. Accompany with steamed broccoli or cauliflower, carrots, sweet and sour beets, and baked potatoes.

---

**PER SERVING**

| | | | |
|---|---|---|---|
| 7.5 gm total fat | 1.91 gm saturated fat | 2.1 gm fiber | 281 calories |
| 46 mg cholesterol | 24.6% fat | 804 mg sodium | 68 calories from fat |

# FOURTH OF JULY

Ten years ago, my husband and I were invited by friends to attend a Fourth of July fireworks celebration at the Rose Bowl in Pasadena. While waiting for dusk to fall and the fireworks to begin, we overheard the spectators in front of us speaking in another language. They turned out to be a group of Russians here to march in a parade sponsored by the Simon Wiesenthal Holocaust Center in Los Angeles, commemorating the liberation of Auschwitz.

We asked, through their interpreter, if they would like to attend a Fourth of July barbecue at our home the next day. We ended up with fourteen guests, including a celebrated Russian general and his attaché, who were to lead the parade, and a representative from the Russian Tass news agency in San Francisco. We decided to invite some friends who had direct ties to the Holocaust as well.

The following is the meal we served, with one exception. When I described my menu plan to my friend Eva, she was horror-stricken when I came to the corn on the cob. "Harriet," she said, "in Europe we feed this to the cattle." Scratch the corn on the cob.

Whenever the Fourth of July rolls around, I'm reminded of that memorable evening filled with toasts, questions, high emotions, and the appreciation of freedom.

✌

## A FOURTH OF JULY CELEBRATION BARBECUE

*Mini Knishes (page 351)*

*Baba Ghanouj (below) with fresh vegetables and pita bread*

*Barbecued Chicken on the Grill*

*Onion Cabbage Slaw (page 108)*

*Barbecued Vegetables*

*Vegetarian baked beans or Vegetarian Chili (page 263)*

*Edie's Streusel Coffee Cake (page 109)*

*Russian Raisin Nut Slices (page 111)*

*Busy Day Chocolate Cake (page 395)*

*Fresh Peach Dessert Salad (page 112)*

✌

# ✌ Baba Ghanouj ✌

## (PAREVE)

*Yield: 2 cups (1 tablespoon = 1 serving)*

This popular Middle Eastern dish has Arabic roots—the name means "father of greediness." When you eat it as an appetizer with warm pita bread, your palate will soon understand its meaning.

1 large eggplant (about 1¼ pounds)
2 large cloves garlic, smashed and peeled
About 3 tablespoons tahini (sesame paste)
5 to 6 tablespoons fresh lemon juice
Dash of Tabasco or ground red pepper (cayenne)
Hungarian paprika

1. Char the whole eggplant on all sides under the broiler.
2. When the skin is blackened and the eggplant soft, cool under cold running water and peel.

3. Remove the seeds and squeeze out excess moisture.

4. Place the pulp in a food processor or blender with the garlic, tahini, lemon juice, and Tabasco or red pepper. Purée until smooth.

*To Serve:* Spoon onto a shallow saucer-like plate, sprinkle with paprika, and surround with pita triangles.

---

**PER SERVING**

| | | | |
|---|---|---|---|
| .8 gm total fat | .10 gm saturated fat | .3 gm fiber | 12 calories |
| 0 mg cholesterol | 50.3% fat | 2 mg sodium | 7 calories from fat |

---

## ❧ Onion Cabbage Slaw ❧
### (PAREVE)
*Serves: 8*

A high-fiber salad that adds flavor and texture to any meal.

> 1 head green cabbage (about 1½ pounds), shredded
> 1 medium red onion, peeled, sliced thin, and separated into rings, or diced
> 3 carrots, peeled and sliced thin
> ½ cup chopped Italian flat-leaf parsley
> 2 to 3 tablespoons sugar
> Freshly ground pepper to taste
> Salt (optional)
> ¾ cup nonfat mayonnaise (see Note)
> ½ cup rice vinegar or apple cider vinegar
> 2 teaspoons white horseradish (optional)

1. Place the cabbage, onion rings, carrots, and parsley in a large salad bowl; toss.
2. Sprinkle with sugar and pepper; add salt if desired.
3. Combine the mayonnaise, vinegar, and horseradish; blend well.
4. Pour the dressing over the slaw. Toss. Taste and adjust seasonings; cover and chill in the refrigerator until serving time.

NOTE: When this is served with a dairy meal, nonfat yogurt or nonfat sour cream may be substituted for half of the mayonnaise.

| PER SERVING | | | |
|---|---|---|---|
| .3 gm total fat | .04 gm saturated fat | 3.7 gm fiber | 94 calories |
| 0 mg cholesterol | 2.5% fat | 332 mg sodium | 3 calories from fat |

# ᴡ Edie's Streusel Coffee Cake ᴡ
## (DAIRY)
*Yield: 1 cake cut into 32 slices*
*(1 slice = 1 serving)*

The original recipe for this cake came from my sister Edie. This is one of my favorite cakes, whether it's made for my family or to take to a friend's house. I've made the original recipe more healthful by substituting nonfat yogurt or sour cream for regular sour cream, egg whites for whole eggs, light butter-flavored margarine for butter, and reducing the sugar by one third. Adding whole wheat pastry flour improves the texture, nutritional value, and flavor of the cake.

    8 tablespoons (1 stick) light butter-flavored margarine
1⅔ cups sugar
    1 tablespoon pure vanilla extract
    6 extra-large egg whites, slightly beaten
¼ cup egg substitute
1¾ cups whole wheat pastry flour
1¾ cups unbleached all-purpose flour or cake flour
    1 tablespoon baking powder
    2 teaspoons baking soda
    2 cups (16 ounces) nonfat plain yogurt or nonfat sour cream
    1 cup seeded dark raisins, chopped dates, and/or dried apricots, plumped
        in 3 tablespoons apricot brandy or fresh orange juice (see below)

*Streusel Topping:*
⅓ cup finely chopped walnuts or hazelnuts
⅓ cup unbleached all-purpose flour
⅓ cup chopped rolled oats
    2 tablespoons packed brown sugar
    2 teaspoons ground cinnamon
    1 tablespoon light butter-flavored margarine

1. Preheat the oven to 375°. Coat a 10-inch tube pan (angel food cake pan) with butter-flavored cooking spray.

2. Cream the margarine in the bowl of an electric mixer. Add the sugar and beat until smooth. Add the vanilla and blend.

3. Add the egg whites and egg substitute gradually and beat the batter for 3 minutes.

4. In a separate bowl, combine the flours, baking powder, and baking soda and mix thoroughly with a whisk or slotted spoon.

5. Alternately blend one third of the flour mixture, then half of the yogurt, into the batter, starting and ending with the flour. Beat until smooth after each addition.

6. With your fingers, mix together the streusel ingredients until crumbly.

7. Place one third of the batter in the bottom of the prepared tube pan. Sprinkle with one third of the streusel and half of the raisins. Repeat; then top with the remaining third of the batter and streusel.

8. Bake at 375° for 25 minutes. Lower the temperature to 325° and bake for about 40 minutes more, or until the cake starts to pull away from the side of the pan.

9. Cool in the pan on a rack, then loosen with a metal spatula and remove from the pan. The cake may be wrapped in plastic, then foil, and frozen for future use.

| PER SERVING | | | |
|---|---|---|---|
| 4.0 gm total fat | .68 gm saturated fat | .7 gm fiber | 160 calories |
| 0 mg cholesterol | 22.3% fat | 138 mg sodium | 36 calories from fat |

### HARRIET'S HINTS

*To plump dried fruit, place in a single layer on a plate, sprinkle with 2 tablespoons orange juice, and cook in the microwave oven for 40 seconds on High, covered with microwave plastic wrap. Or cover with boiling water and let stand about 5 minutes, or until soft. If your raisins or other fruits are really fresh, just combine them with hot brandy or juice.*

# ❦ Russian Raisin Nut Slices ❦
## (DAIRY)
*Yield: 40 slices (1 slice = 1 serving)*

It's so convenient to have these delicious confections in your freezer, whether to serve unexpected guests or just as a treat for yourself with a cup of tea. Their flavor is a cross between rugelach and mandelbrot.

4 tablespoons (½ stick) light butter-flavored margarine, at room temperature
1 cup minus 2 tablespoons sugar
1 extra-large egg, beaten, or ¼ cup egg substitute
3 tablespoons canola oil
¼ cup light sour cream
1 teaspoon pure vanilla extract
½ teaspoon ground cinnamon
2 cups unbleached all-purpose flour
¾ cup chopped walnuts
1 cup dark raisins, plumped, or dried cherries
Confectioners' sugar, for garnish

1. Preheat the oven to 350°.
2. Cream the margarine and sugar together until fluffy. Add the egg and blend.
3. Add the oil, sour cream, vanilla, and cinnamon and mix thoroughly.
4. Stir in the flour, nuts, and raisins and blend well.
5. Divide the dough into thirds. With floured hands, shape the dough into logs about 1½ inches in diameter. Place on a nonstick baking sheet.
6. Bake in the upper third of the oven for 35 to 40 minutes, or until lightly browned.
7. Remove from the oven; sprinkle generously with confectioners' sugar while still warm.
8. Cool and cut into ¾-inch diagonal slices.

*To Serve:* I like to heat these cookies slightly just before serving.

| ——— PER SERVING ——— | | | |
|---|---|---|---|
| 3.9 gm total fat | .55 gm saturated fat | .5 gm fiber | 88 calories |
| 6 mg cholesterol | 38.4% fat | 16 mg sodium | 35 calories from fat |

# 🌱 Fresh Peach Dessert Salad 🌱

## (PAREVE)

*Serves: 10 to 12*

When fresh, ripe peaches are macerated in fresh citrus juices and scented with mint leaves, they provide just the right simple dessert for any summer meal.

**4 cups peeled, sliced (½ inch) fresh ripe peaches**
**4 kiwis, peeled and sliced into ¼-inch rounds**
   **Juice of 3 to 4 oranges**
   **Juice of 1 lemon**
**6 fresh mint leaves**

1. Place the sliced peaches and kiwi in a large, attractive serving bowl.
2. Add the juices; toss gently, just to blend.
3. Place the mint leaves on top, cover with plastic wrap, and chill several hours in the refrigerator before serving.

---

**PER SERVING**

| | | | |
|---|---|---|---|
| .2 gm total fat | .03 gm saturated fat | 1.9 gm fiber | 51 calories |
| 0 mg cholesterol | 3.8% fat | 0 mg sodium | 2 calories from fat |

# APPETIZERS

*From Nibbles to Noshes*

Smoked Salmon Tartare     116
Red Salmon, Tomato, and Onion Spread     117
Tuna and White Bean Antipasto     118
Herring in Cream     118
Herring Antipasto     119
Mollie Roth's Chicken Fricassee with Dumplings     120
Middle Eastern Chopped Eggplant     121
Spinach Cups     122
Hummus     123
Artichoke Squares     124
Quick and Easy Potato Latkes with Dill Sauce     125
Petcha (Jellied Calf's Foot)     127
Little Meatballs     128
Mrs. Schneider's Chopped Herring (Gehackte Hering)     129
Green Pea Dip with Fresh Vegetables     130
Syrian Meatballs and Cherries     131
Vegetarian Kishkes     132
Chinese Chicken Drumettes     133

Traditionally, appetizers or first courses (known in Yiddish as *vorspeise*) in Jewish cooking have been on the heavy side. Fricassee, gefilte fish, and chopped liver are frequently served as a first course, preceding a main dish of animal protein: hardly what you'd call a light beginning. For those occasions when you want a multi-course service, I'd like to make these suggestions: keep it simple, lighten your choice, and reduce the portion. Do try my Vegetarian Chopped Liver (page 7) or Eggs and Onions (page 28); you'll love the taste.

Often, I think the term "appetizer" seems misplaced. Most of us don't need anything to stimulate our appetites! Remember, it's just supposed to be a nibble or nosh; not a dish so substantial as to satisfy your guests' appetites before they have even started their dinner.

# ❧ Smoked Salmon Tartare ❧

## (DAIRY)

*Serves: 6 (¼ cup = 1 serving)*

In preparing this appetizer I use smoked salmon tails (usually including odd-shaped slices), which are just as flavorful but about half the price of fillets. Be advised that all smoked salmon is relatively high in salt or sodium, depending on the brand or curing method. The FDA requires that a certain amount of salt be added as a preservative. You can, however, purchase smoked salmon *that does not have nitrites or nitrates added* (see Note below). If you are hypertensive it is advisable to limit not only the portions but the frequency with which you eat smoked salmon.

8 ounces smoked salmon tails
3 tablespoons finely chopped red onion or mild white onion
1 tablespoon drained chopped capers (in vinegar, not brine)
2 tablespoons chopped Italian flat-leaf parsley
1 tablespoon fresh lemon juice
2 tablespoons nonfat sour cream
   Radicchio or butter lettuce leaves

1. Chop the smoked salmon fine and place in a bowl.
2. Add the onion, capers, parsley, lemon juice, and sour cream and mix together well with a fork. Taste and adjust seasonings.

*To Serve:* Mound the tartare on a serving plate lined with radicchio or butter lettuce and surround with toast points (see below) or thinly sliced pumpernickel.

## To Prepare Toast Points:

Remove crusts from thinly sliced white bread. Place on a baking sheet and toast in a 375° oven for 10 minutes, or lightly toast in a toaster. Cut into diagonal slices. I frequently use a baguette cut into ¼-inch slices and lightly toasted.

NOTE: Be advised that nitrites and nitrates used as preservatives in some smoked salmon, delicatessen meats, and hot dogs are believed by some to be carcinogenic. It is wise to read your labels for ingredient information.

---

PER SERVING

| | | | |
|---|---|---|---|
| 1.7 gm total fat | .35 gm saturated fat | .2 gm fiber | 50 calories |
| 9 mg cholesterol | 30.2 % fat | 411 mg sodium | 15 calories from fat |

# ❦ Red Salmon, Tomato, and Onion Spread ❦

## (PAREVE)

*Yield: 2½ cups (1 tablespoon = 1 serving)*

1 (8-ounce) can red salmon, drained, skinned, boned, and flaked
5 fresh ripe Italian plum tomatoes, diced
4 whole scallions, sliced thin, or ½ cup finely chopped red onion
2 to 3 tablespoons red wine vinegar, fresh lemon juice, or 1 tablespoon
    balsamic vinegar
    Freshly ground pepper
    Chopped fresh dill, for garnish

1. Place the salmon, tomatoes, and scallions in a mixing bowl.

2. Sprinkle with vinegar and freshly ground pepper. Stir with a fork to blend.

3. Cover and refrigerate for at least 30 minutes before serving. It will keep for 4 to 5 days in the refrigerator.

*To Serve:* Place in a serving bowl, sprinkle with chopped fresh dill, and surround with squares of pumpernickel or melba toast.

| — PER SERVING — | | | |
|---|---|---|---|
| .3 gm total fat | .05 gm saturated fat | .2 gm fiber | 12 calories |
| 4 mg cholesterol | .3% fat | 6 mg sodium | 3 calories from fat |

## ❦ Tuna and White Bean Antipasto ❦
### (PAREVE)
*Serves: 6 (½ cup = 1 serving)*

1 teaspoon extra-virgin olive oil
1 (7½-ounce) can light tuna in water, drained and flaked
1 (16-ounce) can cannellini beans, drained and rinsed
2 tablespoons capers in vinegar (not brine), drained
½ small red onion, chopped fine
⅓ cup nonfat Italian dressing mixed with 1 teaspoon balsamic or red wine
 vinegar
2 tablespoons finely chopped Italian flat-leaf parsley

1. Sprinkle the oil over the drained tuna.
2. Combine the tuna, beans, capers, onion, and Italian dressing mixture.
3. Cover and marinate in the refrigerator for 3 to 4 hours.

*To Serve:* Place in a serving bowl and sprinkle with chopped parsley. Serve with toast rounds made from sourdough baguette or bread sticks.

| PER SERVING | | | |
|---|---|---|---|
| 2.0 gm total fat | .39 gm saturated fat | 2.9 gm fiber | 160 calories |
| 15 mg cholesterol | 11.5% fat | 492 mg sodium | 18 calories from fat |

## ❦ Herring in Cream ❦
### (DAIRY)
*Serves: 10 (1 tablespoon = 1 serving)*

1 (12-ounce) jar herring snacks in wine, drained and cut into ½-inch cubes
1 small green bell pepper, seeded and diced
1 small red bell pepper, seeded and diced
1 bunch scallions, sliced into ½-inch rounds
⅔ cup nonfat sour cream or nonfat plain yogurt
1 small red apple, cored and diced

1 teaspoon fresh lemon juice
1 teaspoon sugar
1 teaspoon celery seed
2 tablespoons minced Italian flat-leaf parsley, for garnish

1. In a mixing bowl, combine the herring with the diced peppers, scallions, sour cream or yogurt, and apple. Add the lemon juice, sugar, and celery seed. Mix well.

2. Transfer to a serving bowl, cover, and refrigerate at least 3 to 4 hours. May be kept in the refrigerator for 1 week.

*To Serve:* Garnish with minced parsley. Accompany with pumpernickel, corn rye squares, or bagel chips.

---
PER SERVING
---

| | | | |
|---|---|---|---|
| 3.5 gm total fat | .77 gm saturated fat | .9 gm fiber | 83 calories |
| 22 mg cholesterol | 37.2% fat | 43 mg sodium | 31 calories from fat |

## ❦ Herring Antipasto ❦
### (PAREVE)
*Serves: 12 (2 tablespoons = 1 serving)*

1 (16-ounce) jar herring in dill sauce, well drained and cut into ¼-inch strips (save onions)
1 small green bell pepper, seeded and diced
1 small red bell pepper, seeded and diced
1 small red onion, chopped fine
1 (6-ounce) jar water-packed artichoke hearts, drained and sliced
1 cup drained salt-reduced kidney beans or garbanzo beans
½ to ⅔ cup sodium-reduced ketchup
Chopped fresh dill, for garnish

1. Place the herring, peppers, onion, artichoke hearts, and beans in a mixing bowl and add the ketchup. Stir to combine.

2. Cover and chill in the refrigerator 4 to 6 hours or overnight before serving. This will keep for up to 2 weeks in the refrigerator—*do not freeze.*

*To Serve:* Place in a serving bowl, sprinkle with chopped dill, and surround with squares of rye bread, pumpernickel bread, or crackers.

| PER SERVING | | | |
|---|---|---|---|
| 4.5 gm total fat | 1.03 gm saturated fat | .6 gm fiber | 86 calories |
| 29 mg cholesterol | 39.2% fat | 235 mg sodium | 40 calories from fat |

# ❦ Mollie Roth's Chicken Fricassee ❦ with Dumplings
## (MEAT)
### *Serves: 10 (3 dumplings = 1 serving)*

When we were first married, my husband told me how he adored his mother's chicken fricassee. He particularly used to search out the *pupiks* (gizzards) as a favorite delicacy. Being a dutiful bride, I thought that if I made the entire fricassee out of gizzards, it would be extra special. I bought a pound of pupiks and prepared the love-inspired dish. It was a disaster as a culinary achievement; however, my husband has never forgotten my loving intentions.

1 tablespoon olive oil
1 large onion, diced
2 large cloves garlic, minced
1 teaspoon salt-free vegetable seasoning
2 (8-ounce) chicken breasts with bones, skinned, all visible fat removed, cut into 1½-inch pieces
1½ pounds chicken drumettes, skinned
3 chicken necks, skinned, cut into 3 or 4 pieces each (optional)
4 chicken gizzards, defatted, cut into 4 pieces each (optional)
Seasoning: 1 teaspoon onion powder, 1 teaspoon garlic powder, ⅛ teaspoon ground white pepper, and 1½ tablespoons Hungarian paprika
3 cups fat-free sodium-reduced chicken broth or water, or as needed

*Dumplings:*
1 extra-large egg
2 half eggshells filled with water

¾ cup plus 1 tablespoon all-purpose flour
Pinch of baking powder
Pinch of salt

1. Put the oil, onion, and garlic in a large nonstick saucepan. Add the vegetable seasoning and sauté over medium heat until the onion is translucent, about 5 minutes.

2. Dry the chicken pieces on paper towels and add to the onion. Sprinkle with seasonings.

3. Brown the chicken pieces with the onion, stirring from time to time to prevent sticking to the pan. If necessary, add broth or water. When browned, add remaining broth, cover and simmer over low heat for 30 minutes or until tender.

4. For dumplings: Beat the egg and water well with a fork; add the flour, baking powder, and salt and beat to the consistency of matzo ball batter. Drop by ½ teaspoonfuls into the simmering fricassee, cover, and cook 20 minutes.

*To Serve:* The portion is quite adequate as an appetizer, and makes a full meal when accompanied by a hearty lentil or split pea soup and a tasty green salad. Don't forget the bread to sop up the remaining sauce. Serve over kasha, farfel, or rice for an entrée if you don't want to take the time to prepare the dumplings.

| PER SERVING | | | |
|---|---|---|---|
| 5.6 gm total fat | 1.35 gm saturated fat | .7 gm fiber | 159 calories |
| 71 mg cholesterol | 32.4% fat | 55 mg sodium | 50 calories from fat |

# ❧ Middle Eastern Chopped Eggplant ❧
## (PAREVE)
*Yield: 5 to 6 cups (2 tablespoons = 1 serving)*

1 (1¼-pound) eggplant
  Juice of 1 lemon
8 cloves garlic, minced fine
1 cucumber, peeled, seeded, and diced
1 medium green bell pepper, seeded and diced
1 large tomato, cored and diced
1½ tablespoons olive oil
  Salt and freshly ground pepper to taste

1. Preheat the oven to 400°. Put the eggplant on a baking sheet and roast about 45 minutes, or until soft. Allow to cool.

2. Peel off the skin, remove the seeds, and dice the eggplant.

3. Place in a bowl and add the remaining ingredients. Mix with a fork, cover, and chill in the refrigerator overnight.

4. Taste and adjust seasonings before serving.

*To Serve:* Accompany with matzo crackers or warm pita bread triangles.

Variation: To serve as a first course, place a slice of a large tomato on a leaf of butter lettuce or radicchio. Top with ½ cup of the eggplant mixture and sprinkle with chopped chives.

---

PER SERVING

| | | | |
|---|---|---|---|
| .5 gm total fat | .06 gm saturated fat | .2 gm fiber | 9 calories |
| 0 mg cholesterol | 41.6% fat | 26 mg sodium | 4 calories from fat |

# ❦ Spinach Cups ❦
## (DAIRY)
*Yield: 24 cups (1 cup = 1 serving)*

A quick, easy, and low-calorie appetizer that you can prepare ahead, freeze, and microwave to heat and serve.

¼ cup egg substitute mixed with 2 extra-large egg whites
½ cup non-fat ricotta cheese
1 (4-ounce) jar chopped pimientos, drained
2 scallions, sliced thin
⅛ teaspoon ground white pepper
¼ teaspoon freshly ground nutmeg
2 (10-ounce) packages frozen chopped spinach, thawed and drained
1 tablespoon grated Parmesan cheese alternative
Cherry tomatoes, for garnish

1. Coat two 1¾-inch muffin tins with olive oil cooking spray. Preheat the oven to 375°.

2. Combine the egg mixture, ricotta cheese, pimientos, scallions, pepper, and nutmeg. Mix thoroughly.

3. Add the spinach and blend.

4. Fill muffin tins with the mixture. Sprinkle with the Parmesan.

5. Bake for about 12 to 15 minutes.

*To Serve:* Remove from the muffin tins and arrange on a doily-lined platter. Garnish with cherry tomatoes.

---

**PER SERVING**

| | | | |
|---|---|---|---|
| .28 gm total fat | .12 gm saturated fat | .8 gm fiber | 17 calories |
| .6 mg cholesterol | 17.6% fat | 50 mg sodium | 3 calories from fat |

---

## ❧ Hummus ❧
### (PAREVE)
*Yield: 3 cups (1 tablespoon = 1 serving)*

This is a very popular and traditional Israeli appetizer. It's easy to make, high in soluble fiber, and similar to Baba Ghanouj (page 107), except that you use garbanzo beans as a base instead of eggplant.

2 (15 ½-ounce) cans sodium-reduced garbanzo beans (chick-peas), drained (save ¼ cup liquid and reserve 2 tablespoons beans for garnish)
⅓ cup fresh lemon juice
1 to 2 tablespoons extra-virgin olive oil
1 teaspoon garlic powder
¼ teaspoon ground white pepper
¼ teaspoon Hungarian paprika
3 tablespoons tahini (sesame paste)
¼ cup chopped Italian flat-leaf parsley, for garnish

1. Purée the drained garbanzo beans in a food processor or blender. Add ¼ cup liquid for smoother consistency.

2. Transfer to a deep bowl. Add the lemon juice and olive oil, 1 tablespoon at a time. Stir well after each addition.

3. Season with garlic powder, pepper, and paprika. Gradually add the tahini and stir well.

4. Let the hummus stand at least 30 to 40 minutes before serving, or cover and store in the refrigerator for future use.

*To Serve:* Place a mound of hummus on a shallow serving dish and use the back of a spoon to spread it evenly over the plate. Garnish with a few whole beans in the center and sprinkle with chopped parsley. Accompany with warmed pita bread cut in triangles and vegetable crudités of red and green bell pepper strips, carrots, radish slices, broccoli florets and cauliflowerets for dipping.

---

### PER SERVING

| | | | |
|---|---|---|---|
| 1.1 gm total fat | .14 gm saturated fat | .5 gm fiber | 28 calories |
| 0 mg cholesterol | 33.4% fat | 2 mg sodium | 10 calories from fat |

## ❧ Artichoke Squares ❧
### (PAREVE)
*Yield: 20 servings (1 piece = 1 serving)*

1 small onion, chopped (about ⅔ cup)
1 large clove garlic, minced
1 tablespoon olive oil
2 (8-ounce) cans quartered hearts of artichoke, drained and chopped
6 nonfat saltine crackers, crumbled, or ½ cup bread crumbs or matzo meal
½ cup egg substitute plus 2 extra-large egg whites
1 teaspoon dried Italian herb blend, crushed, or 1 tablespoon chopped fresh oregano
   Dash of Tabasco
1 tablespoon Worcestershire sauce
1 teaspoon Hungarian paprika

1. Coat an 8-inch square glass baking dish with olive oil cooking spray. Preheat the oven to 350°.

2. Sauté the onion and garlic in olive oil until transparent, 3 to 4 minutes. Add the chopped artichoke and sauté 1 minute.

3. Add the cracker crumbs, egg mixture, herbs, Tabasco, and Worcestershire. Blend well.

4. Pour into the prepared baking dish and sprinkle with paprika.

5. Bake for 35 to 40 minutes. Cut into 20 servings and serve. This may be served either warm or at room temperature.

—————————————— P E R   S E R V I N G ——————————————

| | | | |
|---|---|---|---|
| 1.0 gm total fat | .15 gm saturated fat | .3 gm fiber | 32 calories |
| 0 mg cholesterol | 26.2% fat | 46 mg sodium | 9 calories from fat |

# ❦ Quick and Easy Potato Latkes ❦ with Dill Sauce

(DAIRY; or PAREVE without Dill Sauce)

*Yield: 30 small latkes as an appetizer, 12 large latkes as a vegetable*
*(2 small latkes = 1 serving, 1 large latke = 1 serving)*

Sometimes peeling potatoes seems like a chore. This shortcut makes delicious latkes, and the frozen hash browns may be kept on hand in the freezer for last-minute preparation. Of course, you may also just add chopped or sliced onions and sauté the hash browns, using even less oil. Served as an appetizer with either plain nonfat sour cream or the deliciously herbal Dill Sauce, these will be crowd-pleasers.

3 cups frozen hash-brown potatoes, thawed and well drained
3 extra-large egg whites
½ small onion, peeled and quartered
¼ cup all-purpose flour
¼ teaspoon baking powder
¼ teaspoon kosher salt
⅛ teaspoon ground white pepper
2 tablespoons canola oil

*Dill Sauce (optional)*
   1 (6-ounce) container nonfat cream cheese or ¾ cup nonfat plain yogurt
   ¼ cup nonfat sour cream
   1 tablespoon nonfat mayonnaise
   1 tablespoon chopped fresh dill
   3 tablespoons chopped smoked salmon (optional)
   1 tablespoon chopped fresh chives (optional)
   Fresh dill sprigs, for garnish


   1. Place the potatoes, egg whites, and onion in a food processor. In a small bowl, whisk together the flour, baking powder, salt, and pepper. Add to the potato mixture and process, using the steel blade and a pulsing action, until the potatoes and onion are chopped fine.
   2. Coat a large nonstick skillet with vegetable oil cooking spray. Add the canola oil and heat.
   3. Spoon teaspoons of the potato mixture into the hot pan. Fry until golden brown, *turning once*. Drain on paper towels or large brown paper bags. Keep warm on a baking sheet in a 200° oven. Repeat with the remaining potato mixture.
   4. Combine the sauce ingredients and mix well.
*To Serve:* Spoon the sauce into a bowl or a hollowed-out red pepper cup. Surround with warm latkes and garnish with sprigs of fresh dill; serve immediately.


   NOTES: For large potato latkes, spoon a scant ¼ cup of the potato mixture into the hot oil, flattening with the back of a spoon. Proceed as in step 3 for small latkes.
   These may be placed on a cookie sheet, flash-frozen, and stored in tightly sealed plastic bags for future use. To serve, reheat frozen latkes in a preheated 425° oven for 3 to 5 minutes.


————— PER SERVING AS AN APPETIZER —————

| | | | |
|---|---|---|---|
| 2.2 gm total fat | .20 gm saturated fat | 1.0 gm fiber | 62 calories |
| 0 mg cholesterol | 29.7% fat | 58 mg sodium | 18 calories from fat |


————— PER SERVING FOR DILL SAUCE —————

| | | | |
|---|---|---|---|
| 0 gm total fat | 0 gm saturated fat | 0 gm fiber | 6 calories |
| 1 mg cholesterol | 0% fat | 41 mg sodium | 0 calories from fat |

# ❦ Petcha (Jellied Calf's Foot) ❦
## (MEAT)
*Serves: 6 to 8*

1 whole calf's foot, cracked
1 onion, peeled and sliced
2 large cloves garlic, smashed and peeled
2 stalks celery with leaves, sliced
1 teaspoon black peppercorns
2 bay leaves
3 sprigs thyme
2 tablespoons fresh lemon juice
3 hard-cooked eggs (discard yolks)
Watercress, lemon wedges, sliced tomato, and mild onion slices, for garnish

1. Wash the calf's foot in cold water and lay it flat in a Dutch oven. Cover with cold water, bring to a boil, and simmer for 10 minutes. Skim off the froth with a strainer.

2. Add the onion, garlic, celery, peppercorns, bay leaves, and thyme, and simmer, partially covered, for 2 hours or until the meat comes away from the bone.

3. Remove the meat and bones from the broth; cut the meat into ½-inch cubes and discard the bones. Strain the remaining liquid and return to a clean pan along with the lemon juice and diced meat. Bring to a second boil and remove from the heat.

4. Pour the mixture into a 9 × 5 × 3-inch loaf pan or a 1½-quart ring mold and sprinkle with sliced egg whites. Cover and chill in the refrigerator overnight or until firm.

*To Serve:* Unmold the *petcha* onto a platter and garnish with watercress, lemon wedges, sliced tomato, and mild onion slices. Cut into thin slices when serving.

---

PER SERVING

| | | | |
|---|---|---|---|
| 2.4 gm total fat | .67 gm saturated fat | .6 gm fiber | 87 calories |
| 42 mg cholesterol | 25.5% fat | 61 mg sodium | 21 calories from fat |

# ❧ Little Meatballs ❧
## (MEAT)
### *Yield: 48 meatballs (2 meatballs = 1 serving)*

Convenient and delicious. Keep them in the freezer and you're always ready for a party or a celebration.

> **Thinly sliced corn rye bread, cut into 48 (1½-inch) circles**
> ¼ **cup seltzer**
> 1 **slice water challah or rye bread, crust removed, crumbled**
> 1 **pound ground turkey breast or ½ pound ground turkey breast and ½ pound extra-lean ground veal**
> 3 **tablespoons chopped fresh Italian flat-leaf parsley**
> 3 **tablespoons grated onion**
> 1 **large clove garlic, smashed, peeled, and minced**
> 2 **teaspoons Worcestershire sauce**
> 1 **teaspoon salt-free vegetable seasoning**
> ¼ **teaspoon ground white pepper**
> **Dash of ground red pepper (cayenne)**
> 3 **tablespoons sodium-reduced chili sauce or ketchup**
> **Chopped fresh oregano, thyme, chives, for garnish**

1. Place the bread circles on a baking sheet and coat lightly with olive oil cooking spray. Toast lightly under the broiler on both sides.

2. Pour the seltzer over the bread crumbs and let stand until absorbed.

3. Combine the meat with the parsley, onion, garlic, Worcestershire, seasoning, and white and red pepper. Mix thoroughly with a fork.

4. Roll into 48 balls approximately 1 inch in diameter, using hands dipped in cold water to prevent sticking.

5. Place the balls on the toasted circles. Make a ¼-inch indentation with your little finger in the center of each ball.

6. Broil 3 to 4 minutes. Fill the centers with a dab of chili sauce or ketchup and sprinkle with fresh herbs.

*To Freeze:* Make balls through step 4, place raw on a shallow baking sheet or foil pan, and flash-freeze. When frozen, place the balls in an airtight plastic bag to store. They may be stored in the freezer for 2 months.

VARIATION FOR MEATBALLS: Broil partially thawed meatballs, heat in one of the following sauces, and serve as an appetizer.

*Sauce #1:* Mix 1 (12-ounce) jar of currant jelly with 1 (13¼-ounce) bottle of Heinz light ketchup.

*Sauce #2:* Mix 2 (8-ounce) cans of salt-free tomato sauce, the juice of 2 lemons, and 3 to 4 tablespoons packed brown sugar.

---

### PER SERVING

| | | | |
|---|---|---|---|
| .4 gm total fat | .08 gm saturated fat | 1.7 gm fiber | 87 calories |
| 12 mg cholesterol | 4.1% fat | 186 mg sodium | 4 calories from fat |

---

# ❦ Mrs. Schneider's Chopped Herring ❦ (Gehackte Hering)

## (PAREVE)

### Yield: 5 cups

*(2 tablespoons = 1 serving as an appetizer; ½ cup = 1 serving as a main dish)*

Whenever my family had a potluck supper, Harriet Friedman was always asked to bring her mother's delicious chopped herring. Mrs. Pauline Schneider was born in Poland, but her children and grandchildren enjoy her herring here in the United States!

1 (32-ounce) jar herring snacks in wine, drained (remove pickling spices) (see Note)
1 large mild onion, cut into eighths
1 large tart green apple, peeled, cored, and cut into eighths
3 slices rye bread, toasted, crusts removed, soaked in 4 tablespoons red or white wine vinegar or lemon juice
3 extra-large hard-cooked eggs, yolks discarded
   Freshly ground pepper
2 teaspoons chopped Italian flat-leaf parsley, for garnish

1. Place *well-drained* herring fillets and onion pieces in a food processor; process until chopped fine and put into a bowl.

2. Put the apple and soaked bread in the processor and chop fine. Add the mixture to the chopped herring.

3. Put the egg whites in the processor and chop fine. Remove 2 tablespoons of chopped egg whites and add the remaining whites to herring mixture. Add the pepper. Using a fork or slotted spoon, blend all the ingredients thoroughly. Taste and adjust seasonings.

*To Serve:* Mound in a shallow bowl and make a ring of chopped egg white around the perimeter of the bowl. Sprinkle chopped parsley over the center. Serve with pumpernickel or corn rye bread squares.

NOTE: Be advised that herring is relatively high in fat, even though the fat is in the form of omega-3 fatty acid, which is believed to help clotting and lessen the risk of heart attacks and strokes. Because of the pickling process, herring is also high in sodium. It should be eaten sparingly as an appetizer, and avoided if you have a problem with high blood pressure.

VARIATION: The ingredients may be ground together instead of being chopped in a food processor.

---

——— PER SERVING ———

| | | | |
|---|---|---|---|
| 2.2 gm total fat | .50 gm saturated fat | .3 gm fiber | 48 calories |
| 15 mg cholesterol | 42.1% fat | 36 mg sodium | 20 calories from fat |

---

# ❦ Green Pea Dip with Fresh Vegetables ❦
## (DAIRY)
*Yield: about 2 cups (1 tablespoon = 1 serving)*

1 (17-ounce) can salt-free green peas, drained
3 ounces nonfat whipped cream cheese
⅔ cup nonfat plain yogurt
⅓ cup nonfat mayonnaise
½ cup finely minced onion
1 teaspoon fresh lemon juice
1 teaspoon salt-free vegetable seasoning and 1 clove garlic, minced
    Dash of ground red pepper (cayenne)

**Assorted fresh vegetable suggestions: celery sticks, carrot sticks, green and red pepper strips, radishes, scallions, rutabaga slices, turnip slices, fennel strips, jicama strips, zucchini sticks, cherry tomatoes, cucumber slices**

1. Purée the drained peas in a food processor or blender till smooth.
2. Add the cream cheese, yogurt, mayonnaise, onion, lemon juice, and seasonings and blend briefly.
3. Chill in the refrigerator for several hours before serving.

*To Serve:* Place the dip in a chilled bowl and surround with colorful fresh vegetables on a platter or in a serving basket with nonfat chips or pita bread triangles.

---

PER SERVING

| | | | |
|---|---|---|---|
| .1 gm total fat | .01 gm saturated fat | 1.0 gm fiber | 17 calories |
| 1 mg cholesterol | 3.1% fat | 78 mg sodium | 1 calorie from fat |

---

# ❦ Syrian Meatballs and Cherries ❦
## (MEAT)
*Yield: 48 (Serves 16 to 18 as an appetizer, 10 as an entrée)*

3 medium onions, peeled, halved, and sliced (3 to 4 cups)
2 teaspoons canola oil
1 recipe Little Meatballs (page 128)
½ cup sweet red kosher wine
1 (17-ounce) can pitted tart cherries, drained, or 1 pound fresh pitted Bing cherries mixed with ½ cup frozen apple juice concentrate
2 tablespoons sugar
Juice of ½ lemon
½ teaspoon ground allspice
½ teaspoon ground white pepper
½ cup dried apricots, quartered

1. Sauté the onions in the oil in a nonstick skillet until golden. Remove the onions, add the meatballs, and sauté or broil.

2. Add the remaining ingredients to the meatballs and stir in the onions. Cover and simmer about 1 hour or until the liquid is thick.

*To Serve:* Place in a chafing dish and serve as an appetizer—or as an entrée with steamed rice.

---

PER SERVING

| | | | |
|---|---|---|---|
| .5 gm total fat | .06 gm saturated fat | 1.3 gm fiber | 60 calories |
| 6 mg cholesterol | 7.6% fat | 94 mg sodium | 5 calories from fat |

---

# ❦ Vegetarian Kishkes ❦
## (PAREVE)
### *Serves: 12 to 14*

This is stuffed derma without the skin!

|   |   |
|---|---|
| 1 | medium onion, peeled and minced |
| 3 to 4 | tablespoons olive oil |
| 1 | rib celery with leaves, quartered |
| 1 | carrot, peeled and quartered |
| 1 | clove garlic, smashed and peeled |
| ½ | teaspoon kosher salt |
| ¼ | teaspoon ground white pepper |
| 1½ | teaspoons Hungarian paprika |
| 1 | teaspoon dried basil, crushed |
| 2 | cups matzo meal, unbleached all-purpose flour, or dried bread crumbs |
| ¼ | cup low-sodium tomato juice, V-8 juice, or sodium-reduced Vegetable Broth (page 141) |

1. Sauté the onion in the oil until golden brown.
2. Place the celery, carrot, and garlic in a food processor. Process until finely minced—not puréed.
3. Add the sautéed onion, minced vegetables, salt, pepper, paprika, and basil to the matzo meal. Stir in the tomato juice.

4. Shape into 2 rolls about 1½ inches wide. Place each roll on a sheet of aluminum foil coated with olive oil cooking spray. Shape, wrap, and seal the foil.

5. Place on a baking sheet and bake in a preheated 375° oven for 50 to 60 minutes.

*To Serve:* Remove the foil, slice into ¾-inch pieces, sprinkle with paprika, and serve hot as an appetizer.

---

PER SERVING

| | | | |
|---|---|---|---|
| 3.7 gm total fat | .46 gm saturated fat | 1.0 gm fiber | 114 calories |
| 0 mg cholesterol | 27.9% fat | 92 mg sodium | 33 calories from fat |

# ❦ Chinese Chicken Drumettes ❦
## (MEAT)
*Yield: 24 drumettes (2 drumettes = 1 serving)*

1½ pounds chicken wing drumettes, skinned
3 tablespoons fresh lemon juice
1½ tablespoons sodium-reduced soy sauce
2 large cloves garlic, smashed and minced
2 teaspoons minced fresh gingerroot
2 tablespoons dry sherry
2 tablespoons hoisin sauce or plum sauce
1 tablespoon sesame seeds (optional)

1. Sprinkle the drumettes with the lemon juice.

2. Place the chicken in a plastic bag, combine the remaining ingredients, add to the chicken, and coat thoroughly.

3. Marinate overnight in the refrigerator, turning the bag from time to time to distribute the marinade.

4. Place the marinated drumettes in a 13 × 9 × 2-inch glass baking dish. Bake in the upper third of a preheated 400° oven for 30 to 35 minutes, turning to brown on both sides. If desired, sprinkle with sesame seeds after 25 minutes. When done, the drumettes should be browned and glazed.

*To Serve:* Place the drumettes in a warmed casserole or a chafing dish so that they stay hot. Accompany with plenty of cocktail napkins.

| PER SERVING | | | |
|---|---|---|---|
| 2.0 gm total fat | .54 gm saturated fat | .2 gm fiber | 59 calories |
| 20 mg cholesterol | 30.5% fat | 379 mg sodium | 18 calories from fat |

### HARRIET'S HINTS

*To clean knives, scrub with a moistened cork dipped in cleanser. This method is quick, effective, and safe.*

# SOUPS

My Mother's Chicken Soup    138
Turkey Broth    140
Vegetable Broth    141
Fish Stock    142
Egg Drop Soup (Einlauf)    143

Cold Cucumber Soup    143
Blender Beet Borscht    145
My Mother's Green Bean and Potato Borscht    145
Schav Borscht (Sorrel Soup)    147
Carrot Vichyssoise    148
Chilled Tomato Soup    149

Green Pea Soup    150
Barbara Bernstein's Fresh Asparagus Soup    151
Quick Tomato Soup    152
French Onion Soup    153
Minestrone    154
Sarah's Lima Bean and Barley Soup with Mushrooms    155
My Mother's Potato Soup    156
Turkey, Rice, and Vegetable Soup    157
Vegetarian Lentil Soup    158
Mollie Roth's Quick Soup    159
Vegetarian Vegetable Soup    160
Yellow Split Pea Soup with Matzo Balls    162
Green Split Pea Soup    163
Caraway Soup    164
Chicken Soup in the Microwave    165
Connie Reif's Vegetable and Bean Soup (How to Make Lemonade Out of Lemons)    166
Carrot Soup    168
Hungarian Sauerkraut Soup    169
Nanette Nathanson's Corn Soup    170
Harriet Friedman's Mother's Cabbage Borscht    171
Low-Calorie Cabbage Borscht    172
Shurba (Sephardic Tomato Rice Soup)    173

Soup, whether served first or as a main course, is nutritionally useful in several ways. Since soup is so filling, a low-calorie soup can be a helpful part of a weight-control eating plan. Soup can be an easy way to add fiber to our diets. Soups have infinite possibilities.

But most important, soup tastes good—whether it's a hearty hot borscht or lima bean and barley soup to add warmth to those wintry days or nights, or an ice-cold beet borscht or cucumber soup to cool us inside and out on a warm summer day.

Most of us think of soup as a first course, but soups make a terrific main course when accompanied by a salad and some good bread. My oldest brother, Herb, frequently starts and ends his meal with a bowl of soup. Maybe this isn't a bad idea—at eighty-seven, he's got the health and longevity to substantiate his practice.

Here are some basic rules in soup making:

- Broths should never be boiled or cooked completely covered or they will become cloudy.

- To defat broths use a gravy separator or chill in the refrigerator until the fat solidifies.

- When you freeze soups, always leave 1 inch of space for expansion.

- Most soups taste even better the second day, after flavors have had a chance to marry or blend.

- Meat-based soups that have been refrigerated for 3 or more days should be brought to a boil before serving.

- A bouquet garni—a small package of Italian flat-leaf parsley, bay leaves, peppercorns, and thyme—makes it convenient to remove the seasonings at the end of cooking. The bouquet may be secured in a piece of cheesecloth or a stainless tea ball or infuser, then lowered into the soup or stew.

- If you use salt in a soup, it should be added just before serving. In this way, you can use less salt, and the taste will be more vibrant.

## ❧ My Mother's Chicken Soup ❧
### (MEAT)
*Serves: 10 to 12 (1 cup = 1 serving)*

Whether it's to cure a cold or comfort a broken heart, good old-fashioned chicken soup has assumed importance as "Jewish penicillin." A pot of chicken soup simmering on the stove and served with noodles or matzo balls, rice or kreplach, has never been replaced as the number-one Jewish soul food.

Because of the sheer number of people served at each meal when I was growing up, an all-chicken (and therefore expensive) soup was only served on special occasions and holidays. Most days, the chicken broth was enriched with a flavorful piece of beef *flanken* and the boiled chicken and beef were eaten together, as in the classic French *pot-au-feu!*

> 1 (5-pound) stewing hen or chicken, cut into 8 pieces, fat removed
>   Giblets, excluding liver, and cleaned chicken feet if possible
> 2 pounds chicken backs or wings, or 3 pounds lean beef *flanken*
> 4 quarts *cold* water
> 3 medium onions, peeled (cut an X in the root end)
> 2 leeks, split lengthwise, washed, and tied with string
> 1 parsnip or parsley root, scrubbed, trimmed, and cut in half
> 5 celery ribs with leaves, cut in 2-inch pieces
> 6 carrots, cut in quarters, or 16 packaged peeled baby carrots
>   Bouquet garni (in cheesecloth or tea ball): 1 bay leaf, sprigs Italian flat-leaf parsley, 6 peppercorns
> ½ bunch Italian flat-leaf parsley, tied with string
> ½ teaspoon ground white pepper
>   Salt to taste

1. Wash the chicken and parts in cold running water. Place in a large stockpot and cover with the cold water. Bring to a boil; reduce the heat to low, and skim off

the scum carefully for about 20 minutes, using a perforated flat spoon (*schomleffel*) or triple-mesh strainer.

2. Add the onions, leeks, parsnip, celery, carrots, and bouquet garni. Simmer, partially covered, for 2 hours.

3. Add the ½ bunch parsley and the pepper and simmer, uncovered, for 30 minutes more, or until the chicken is tender.

4. Discard the leek, onion, parsley, and bouquet garni. Remove the chicken parts with a slotted spoon. Remove the skin from the chicken (and save for the dog—they don't have to be concerned about cholesterol). The chicken may be boned and saved for chicken salad, chicken pâté, chicken hash, or chicken sandwiches. It may also be returned to the soup and served as boiled chicken.

5. Taste and adjust seasonings with salt and pepper.

6. Let the soup cool, then refrigerate. It's even better the next day.

7. *Remove* and *discard* the *fat* that has congealed on the top. Bring the soup to a simmer with added fresh parsley or dill.

*To Serve:* Pour in heated soup bowls with no-yolk noodles, farfel, rice, matzo balls, or kreplach.

*To Freeze:* Place in freezer containers after the fat has been removed and allow 1 inch head space for expansion. You may also freeze individual portions in small freezer bags and reheat in the microwave.

VARIATION: All soup vegetables, with the exception of the parsley and green part of leek, may be puréed in a food processor or blender with ½ cup broth. Then add as much additional chicken broth as you need to give the soup the consistency that pleases you. (I guess I'm a purist, but I prefer my soup the old-fashioned way: clear.)

--- PER SERVING ---

| | | | |
|---|---|---|---|
| 0 gm total fat | 0 gm saturated fat | 0 gm fiber | 22 calories |
| 0 mg cholesterol | 0% fat | 3 mg sodium | 0 calories from fat |

--- ❧ HARRIET'S HINTS ❧ ---

**W**hen cooking whole onions, cut an X in the root end to prevent it from slipping apart in cooking.

# ❧ Turkey Broth ❧

## (MEAT)

*Yield: 10 to 12 cups (1 cup = 1 serving)*

If you are left with a turkey carcass after a holiday meal, you can break it up to make this broth. Meat may be removed from the carcass after cooking to add to the soup.

> Carcass and skin of roasted turkey
> Any leftover giblets (except liver)
> 3½ quarts cold water
> 2 onions, with skin, washed and quartered
> 6 ribs celery with leaves, chopped coarse
> 3 carrots, peeled and chopped coarse
> 1 parsnip, peeled and chopped coarse
> 1 leek, split and washed
> Bouquet garni (in cheesecloth or tea ball): 2 bay leaves, 10 peppercorns, 1 teaspoon dried thyme, ½ cup Italian flat-leaf parsley

1. Break up the carcass and place it in a large stockpot. Add the giblets, water, and remaining ingredients.

2. Bring to a boil, reduce the heat, and simmer partially covered for 2½ to 3 hours. Skim from time to time with a perforated flat spoon (*schomleffel*).

3. Strain the broth through a triple-mesh strainer. Discard solids, allow to cool, and refrigerate or freeze for future use. Remove any visible fat before using as a base for soup, such as the Turkey, Rice, and Vegetable Soup on page 157.

--- PER SERVING ---

| | | | |
|---|---|---|---|
| 0 gm total fat | 0 gm saturated fat | 0 gm fiber | 22 calories |
| 0 mg cholesterol | 0% fat | 5 mg sodium | 0 calories from fat |

# ❧ Vegetable Broth ❧

## (PAREVE)

*Yield: 8 to 9 cups (1 cup = 1 serving)*

With vegetarian cooking gaining more flavor and popularity all the time, a good vegetarian broth is an indispensable addition to any Jewish cook's recipe collection and provides a good basis for any soup. This broth will be cloudy when finished.

1 large onion, peeled
1 large leek, split and washed
1 celery root, scrubbed and peeled
6 carrots, peeled
8 ribs celery with leaves
1 Idaho potato, peeled
1 parsnip, peeled
1 turnip, peeled
4 ripe Italian plum tomatoes
1 cup fresh mushrooms or 1 ounce dried mushrooms, soaked
2 zucchini
2 cups shredded green cabbage (optional)
2 teaspoons olive oil
¼ cup green lentils, washed
12 cups cold water
Bouquet garni (in cheesecloth or tea ball): 8 sprigs Italian flat-leaf parsley, 4 crushed cloves garlic, 3 bay leaves, ½ teaspoon dried thyme or basil or 8 sprigs fresh thyme, 10 peppercorns, ½ teaspoon ground red pepper (cayenne) (optional)

1. Coarsely chop all the vegetables into about 1-inch chunks.
2. Heat the oil in a large stockpot. Add the onion, leek, celery root, carrot, and celery and sauté over medium-low heat for 10 minutes, or until soft. Stir frequently to sweat down the vegetables. Add the remaining vegetables (except cabbage), lentils, ½ cup water, and bouquet garni, and stew for 10 minutes.
3. Add the remaining cold water and bring to a boil. Reduce to a simmer and cook, partially covered, for 1 hour. Skim if necessary. (Cabbage may be added at this time if you like.)
4. Remove the cover and simmer 30 minutes, or until the broth is flavorful.

5. Strain through a sieve, pressing the vegetables with a spoon to release flavors and as much liquid as possible. Discard the solids.

6. Reduce the liquid by simmering over medium heat to enrich flavor. Taste and adjust seasonings.

| PER SERVING | | | |
|---|---|---|---|
| 1 gm total fat | 0 gm saturated fat | 0 gm fiber | 30 calories |
| 0 mg cholesterol | 33% fat | 5 mg sodium | 9 calories from fat |

## ❧ Fish Stock ❧
(PAREVE)
*Yield: 1 quart (1 cup = 1 serving)*

A great base for a fish soup or chowder, as a bouillon for poaching fish, or as a stock for heating gefilte fish from jars or frozen gefilte fish.

2 pounds white-fleshed fish bones with heads (rinsed thoroughly to remove any blood) (see Note)
4 cups cold water
¾ cup dry white wine
2 large onions, chopped, or 2 leeks, white part only, split, washed, and chopped
2 cloves garlic, smashed and peeled
2 ribs celery with leaves, sliced
2 carrots, sliced
1 parsnip, quartered
6 sprigs Italian flat-leaf parsley
1 bay leaf
6 peppercorns

1. Place all the ingredients in a saucepan and bring to a boil.
2. Reduce the heat and skim off any scum that comes to the top.
3. Cover partially and simmer for 1 hour.
4. Strain through a fine sieve, discarding the solids. Store in a *tightly* covered

container in the refrigerator for up to 1 week or freeze for up to 4 months. NOTE: Do not use bones of salmon or sturgeon. They are too strongly flavored.

PER SERVING

| | | | |
|---|---|---|---|
| 0 gm total fat | 0 gm saturated fat | 0 gm fiber | 22 calories |
| 0 mg cholesterol | 0% fat | 5 mg sodium | 0 calories from fat |

## ❦ Egg Drop Soup (Einlauf) ❦
### (PAREVE)
*Serves: 4 to 6*

2 extra-large egg whites
Dash of salt
Dash of ground white pepper
⅓ cup uncooked farina (cream of wheat)
Dash of water
4 cups defatted sodium-reduced chicken broth, boiling

1. Stir the egg whites, salt and pepper, and farina together with a fork until smooth, adding enough water to give a consistency of heavy cream.
2. Pour slowly into the boiling broth. Reduce the heat, cover, and simmer about 5 minutes. Serve immediately.

PER SERVING

| | | | |
|---|---|---|---|
| .1 gm total fat | 0 gm saturated fat | .3 gm fiber | 56 calories |
| 0 mg cholesterol | 2.7% fat | 77 mg sodium | 1 calorie from fat |

## ❦ Cold Cucumber Soup ❦
### (DAIRY)
*Serves: 6 (about ¾ cup = 1 serving)*

A chilled soup in hot weather is one of the most refreshing courses that you can serve. Accompanied by delicious crusty rye, whole wheat, or pumpernickel bread—what could be better?

2  teaspoons olive oil

3  cucumbers, peeled, seeded, and sliced, or 1 large European cucumber, peeled and sliced thin

1  leek, white part only, split, washed, and chopped

2  bay leaves

1  tablespoon unbleached all-purpose flour

3  cups Vegetable Broth (page 141)

½  cup evaporated skim milk

½  cup nonfat sour cream

Juice of ½ lemon

¼  cup chopped fresh dill

Kosher salt to taste

⅛  teaspoon ground white pepper

Nonfat sour cream or yogurt and additional chopped fresh dill, for garnish

1. Place the oil in a medium saucepan; add 2 of the sliced cucumbers, the leek, and the bay leaves, and sauté slowly until wilted but not brown.

2. Add the flour and mix well.

3. Discard the bay leaves and gradually stir in the vegetable broth. Simmer 25 minutes, stirring occasionally.

4. Purée in a food processor or blender. Chill the soup in the refrigerator for several hours.

5. Before serving, finely chop the remaining cucumber and add to the chilled soup with the milk, sour cream, lemon juice, and chopped dill. Taste and adjust seasonings with salt and pepper.

*To Serve:* Chill cups and serve the cold soup with dollops of nonfat sour cream or yogurt and a sprinkle of fresh dill.

--- PER SERVING ---

| | | | |
|---|---|---|---|
| 2.2 gm total fat | .28 gm saturated fat | .9 gm fiber | 83 calories |
| 1 mg cholesterol | 22.6% fat | 48 mg sodium | 20 calories from fat |

## ❧ Blender Beet Borscht ❧
### (DAIRY)
*Serves: 4 to 5*

I'm always interested in easy, creative recipes.

1 (15-ounce) can salt-free sliced or shredded beets
1 can water
1 (6-ounce) can frozen pink lemonade
¼ cup egg substitute or 1 whole egg
   Nonfat sour cream or nonfat plain yogurt, for garnish
2 tablespoons chopped fresh dill, for garnish

1. Place all the ingredients in a food processor or blender except ½ cup of the beets.
2. Blend until smooth.
3. Chill several hours or overnight.

*To Serve:* Place in chilled bowls or glasses. Garnish with a dollop of nonfat sour cream, shredded beets, and chopped fresh dill.

| PER SERVING | | | |
|---|---|---|---|
| .6 gm total fat | 0 gm saturated fat | .7 gm fiber | 117 calories |
| 0 mg cholesterol | 4.1% fat | 66 gm sodium | 5.4 calories from fat |

## ❧ My Mother's Green Bean ❧ and Potato Borscht
### (DAIRY)
*Serves: 12 to 14*

During the hot, sticky summer months in Pittsburgh, my mother used to prepare a borscht on Friday to be served icy cold for supper Saturday night. The liquid ingredients were always the same, but she varied the fresh vegetables, using either green beans, green cabbage, or spinach.

1 pound green beans, cut into 1-inch pieces
2 cups Idaho potatoes, peeled and cut into 1-inch cubes
6 cups boiling water with ½ teaspoon kosher salt
¾ teaspoon sour salt (citric acid)
1 extra-large egg
⅓ cup egg substitute
½ cup nonfat sour cream
¾ cup nonfat or skim milk or 1 percent low-fat milk
¼ teaspoon ground white pepper
  Chopped chives, for garnish

1. Cook the beans and potatoes in boiling salted water for 30 minutes or until quite tender.

2. Drain and reserve the cooking liquid. Set the potatoes and beans aside. Add the sour salt to the hot liquid; stir to dissolve. Allow the liquid to cool to room temperature.

3. Beat the egg and egg substitute with an electric hand beater until foamy. Add the sour cream and beat until mixed. Add the milk and pepper. Add the cooled bean liquid, beating constantly until incorporated.

4. Add the reserved beans and potatoes to the milk mixture and chill 3 to 4 hours or overnight. Before serving, taste and adjust seasonings. (This borscht will have a sour or piquant flavor.)

*To Serve:* Pour into chilled bowls and sprinkle with chopped chives and freshly ground pepper. Accompany with crisp radishes, green onions, and pumpernickel bread.

VARIATION: Either a 1¼-pound head of green cabbage, shredded, or 3 pounds of fresh leaf spinach, thoroughly washed, may be substituted for the beans and potatoes.

---

PER SERVING

| | | | |
|---|---|---|---|
| .8 gm total fat | .27 gm saturated fat | 1.0 gm fiber | 50 calories |
| 18 mg cholesterol | 13.6% fat | 197 mg sodium | 7 calories from fat |

# ❦ Schav Borscht (Sorrel Soup) ❦

## (DAIRY)

*Serves: 4 to 6*

Commonly served at Shavuot, schav is a cold soup made from sorrel, a deliciously sour herb. You may replace a 10-ounce package of frozen chopped spinach or a 16-ounce package of washed spinach for half the sorrel.

    1 pound fresh sorrel (tough stems removed)
    1 small onion, peeled (cut an X in the root end)
    4 cups water
    3 tablespoons sugar
    2 tablespoons fresh lemon juice or ¼ to ½ teaspoon sour salt (citric acid)
    ½ teaspoon kosher salt
    ⅛ teaspoon ground white pepper
    1 extra-large egg
    ¼ cup egg substitute
    ½ cup nonfat sour cream
4 to 6 hot boiled new potatoes, peeled
    4 scallions, sliced, for garnish

1. Wash the sorrel thoroughly in cold water. Drain and chop coarse.
2. Combine the sorrel, onion, water, and sugar in a medium nonaluminum saucepan.
3. Bring to a boil, lower the heat, and simmer for 20 minutes.
4. Remove from the heat; add the lemon juice, salt, and pepper.
5. Let the broth cool and discard the onion.
6. Beat the egg and egg substitute with an electric hand mixer. Add the sour cream and beat until combined.
7. Slowly add the *cooled* broth to the egg mixture while beating. Taste and adjust seasonings.
8. Chill several hours or overnight before serving.

*To Serve:* Pour the chilled soup in chilled bowls with hot potatoes and sprinkle with scallions.

VARIATION: Diced cucumber and a dollop of sour cream may be added instead of potatoes.

---

PER SERVING

| | | | |
|---|---|---|---|
| 1.9 gm total fat | .37 gm saturated fat | .9 gm fiber | 82 calories |
| 41 mg cholesterol | 19.1% fat | 240 mg sodium | 17 calories from fat |

---

## ❦ Carrot Vichyssoise ❦
### (DAIRY)
*Serves: 6 to 8 (¾ cup = 1 serving)*

This cold soup is especially tasty when prepared with buttery Yukon Gold potatoes.

4 Idaho or Yukon Gold potatoes (about 1½ pounds), peeled and cubed
4 medium carrots, peeled and sliced
2 tablespoons dried onion flakes or 1 small leek, white part only, cleaned and sliced
3 cups Vegetable Broth (page 141)
1 cup nonfat sour cream or nonfat plain yogurt
    Ground white pepper to taste
    Nonfat sour cream, 1 carrot, shredded, and 2 scallions, sliced, for garnish

1. Place the potatoes, carrots, onion flakes, and broth in a saucepan and bring to a boil. Reduce the heat and simmer for 15 minutes, or until the vegetables are fork tender.
2. Purée the vegetables in a food processor or blender. Return to the liquid in the saucepan. Stir.
3. Add the sour cream and pepper; blend until smooth.
4. Chill several hours or overnight before serving.

*To Serve:* Place in chilled bowls and garnish with a dollop of sour cream sprinkled with shredded carrots and topped with a few scallions.

---

PER SERVING

| | | | |
|---|---|---|---|
| .6 gm total fat | .04 gm saturated fat | 3.0 gm fiber | 131 calories |
| 0 mg cholesterol | 3.7% fat | 39 mg sodium | 5 calories from fat |

# ❧ Chilled Tomato Soup ❧

(PAREVE)

*Yield: 10 servings (1 cup = 1 serving)*

All vegetables taste better in season, particularly tomatoes. Opt for July, August, or September as the time to prepare this refreshing soup.

 1 large (6 ounces) red onion, peeled and cubed
 2 large cloves garlic, smashed and peeled
 1 shallot, peeled and quartered
 ¼ cup fresh basil leaves
 3 pounds ripe tomatoes (preferably plum), halved crosswise, seeded, and cubed
 3 cups low-sodium V-8 juice
 1 teaspoon sugar
 ⅛ teaspoon ground white pepper
 1 teaspoon ground cumin
3 to 4 tablespoons balsamic vinegar or Aquavit
 1½ cups diced cucumber
 ½ cup sliced toasted almonds, for garnish
   Nonfat plain yogurt or nonfat sour cream, for garnish (optional)

1. Place the onion, garlic, and shallot in a food processor and process until minced.

2. Add the basil and 3 cups of the tomatoes and purée. Transfer to a mixing bowl; purée another 3 cups of tomatoes and repeat until all the tomatoes are puréed.

3. Add the juice, sugar, pepper, cumin, and 3 tablespoons of vinegar. Stir to blend well. Taste and adjust seasonings. Add the cucumbers.

4. Refrigerate overnight or at least for 3 to 4 hours.

*To Serve:* Pour into chilled mugs or bowls and sprinkle with toasted almonds. If served with a dairy meal, garnish with a dollop of nonfat yogurt or sour cream and fresh basil.

VARIATION: To serve hot, add 2 cups of defatted sodium-reduced chicken or vegetable broth, bring to a boil, simmer 5 minutes, and garnish with toasted croutons. You may also add 1 cup of cooked rice to the soup when served hot.

---

——— P E R   S E R V I N G ———

| | | | |
|---|---|---|---|
| .6 gm total fat | .06 gm saturated fat | 2.1 gm fiber | 55 calories |
| 0 mg cholesterol | 8.7% fat | 28 mg sodium | 5 calories from fat |

---

# ❧ Green Pea Soup ❧
## (PAREVE)
### Yield: 7 cups (1 cup = 1 serving)

4 cups hot Vegetable Broth (page 141) or 3 tablespoons vegetable broth base with 4 cups hot water
1 (16-ounce) package salt-free frozen peas
⅔ cup thinly sliced leeks or scallions, white part only
2 teaspoons onion powder
⅛ teaspoon ground white pepper
1 teaspoon dried chervil or 1 tablespoon chopped fresh chervil
Salt to taste

1. Place 1 cup of the broth in a medium saucepan and bring to a boil.
2. Add the peas, leeks, and onion powder. Bring to a boil; reduce the heat to a simmer, and cook until soft—about 20 minutes.
3. Purée the pea mixture in a food processor or blender until smooth.
4. Combine the puréed peas with the remaining 3 cups of hot vegetable broth. Add the pepper and chervil.
5. Simmer over medium heat for 10 minutes to blend flavors. Taste and adjust seasonings with salt and freshly ground pepper.

---

——— P E R   S E R V I N G ———

| | | | |
|---|---|---|---|
| .8 gm total fat | .05 gm saturated fat | 3.1 gm fiber | 68 calories |
| 0 mg cholesterol | 10.6% fat | 78 mg sodium | 7.2 calories from fat |

# Barbara Bernstein's Fresh Asparagus Soup

(MEAT OR PAREVE)

*Yield: 6 cups (1 cup = 1 serving)*

When our neighbors Barbara and Arthur discovered that their cholesterol levels were higher than they should be, they gave judicious attention to changing their lifestyle. They cut the fat and animal protein and upped the vegetables and grains. They still enjoy eating, but it's with their health in mind. Barbara gets special pleasure out of making soups. Using fresh vegetables as a base always gives a vibrant, uncomplicated taste to a light soup.

2 teaspoons olive oil
1 shallot, peeled and sliced
2 large leeks, white part only, split, washed, and chopped
1 medium Idaho potato, peeled and sliced
2 pounds asparagus, tough ends removed, cut into 2-inch lengths
2 (14-ounce) cans (1¾ cups) defatted sodium-reduced chicken broth
    or vegetable broth
Juice of half a lemon
Ground white pepper to taste
Chopped chives, for garnish
Croutons, for garnish

1. Heat the oil in a large nonstick saucepan. Add the shallot, leeks, potato, and asparagus and sauté 3 to 5 minutes.

2. Add the broth, bring to a boil, and reduce the heat. Cover and simmer until fork tender, about 20 minutes.

3. Drain, returning the liquid to the saucepan, and purée the solids in a blender or food processor. Add 1 cup of liquid to smooth the mixture.

4. Return the purée to the remaining liquid in the saucepan. Stir to blend. Add the lemon juice and white pepper.

5. Heat and serve in warm bowls with a garnish of chopped chives and/or a few croutons.

---

PER SERVING

| | | | |
|---|---|---|---|
| 1.7 gm total fat | .24 gm saturated fat | 1.6 gm fiber | 78 calories |
| 0 mg cholesterol | 20.4% fat | 13 mg sodium | 16 calories from fat |

# ❦ Quick Tomato Soup ❦

### (MEAT OR PAREVE)

*Serves: 8 (1 cup = 1 serving)*

Another quick recipe that can be prepared from foods you usually have stocked in your pantry.

    2 teaspoons olive oil
    ½ small onion, peeled and chopped fine
    1 rib celery with leaves, cut into ¼-inch slices
    2 carrots, peeled and cut into ½-inch slices
    2 cloves garlic, smashed, peeled, and minced (optional)
    1 (14-ounce) can sodium-reduced stewed tomatoes
    4 cups defatted sodium-reduced chicken broth or vegetable broth
    ½ cup dry white wine or vermouth
       Freshly ground pepper
       Croutons and chopped Italian flat-leaf parsley or cilantro, for garnish

1. Heat the oil in a medium saucepan; add the onion, celery, carrots, and garlic, and sauté 5 minutes, stirring occasionally. *Do not brown.*

2. Add the tomatoes and broth, bring to a boil, and lower the heat. Simmer for 20 minutes, or until the vegetables are fork tender.

3. Purée, in batches if necessary, in a food processor or blender.

4. Return to the saucepan, add the wine, season to taste, and heat to the boiling point.

*To Serve:* Ladle into warm cups or soup bowls and garnish with croutons and chopped parsley or cilantro.

VARIATION: This soup may be served without being puréed.

| ——— PER SERVING ——— | | | |
|---|---|---|---|
| 1.3 gm total fat | .18 gm saturated fat | 1.1 gm fiber | 43 calories |
| 0 mg cholesterol | 29.2% fat | 21 gm sodium | 12 calories from fat |

# 🌱 French Onion Soup 🌱

## (MEAT)

*Serves: 10 to 12 (1 cup = 1 serving)*

This is certainly not a traditional Jewish soup; however, you don't have to be French to enjoy sautéed onions steeped in a good broth.

2 pounds onions, peeled and sliced thin, or 2 cups Onion Helper (page 254)
1 tablespoon olive oil
1 teaspoon packed brown sugar
1 teaspoon salt-free vegetable seasoning
3 tablespoons unbleached all-purpose flour
½ cup dry white wine
8 cups defatted sodium-reduced beef and/or chicken broth
   Ground white pepper to taste
2 tablespoons Cognac (optional)
   Toasted crouton slices rubbed with garlic, for garnish

1. Cook the sliced onions with the oil in a large covered saucepan over medium heat for 15 minutes. Stir occasionally. If using Onion Helper, heat briefly.

2. Add the brown sugar and vegetable seasoning and cook, uncovered, over medium heat for 30 to 40 minutes. Stir frequently—the onions should be golden brown.

3. Sprinkle with the flour. Stir and cook several minutes so the flour loses its raw taste.

4. Gradually add the wine, then stir in the broth. Season with freshly ground pepper.

5. Simmer, partially covered, for 20 to 30 minutes. (May be prepared a day in advance to this point or frozen for future use.)

6. Add the Cognac just before serving.

*To Serve:* Ladle the soup into warmed individual soup bowls or crocks and top with toasted crouton slices or homemade challah rubbed with garlic. Of course, a good sourdough or crusty baguette is a must with this soup.

---
PER SERVING
---

| 1.3 gm total fat | .18 gm saturated fat | 1.5 gm fiber | 62 calories |
| 0 mg cholesterol | 20.4% fat | 8 mg sodium | 11 calories from fat |

HARRIET'S HINTS

*To remove garlic or onion odor from your hands, rub the hands on a piece of stainless steel, such as a pot or a bowl, under cold running water.*

## Minestrone

(PAREVE)

*Yield: 16 to 18 cups (1 cup = 1 serving)*

Hearty soups like this add much-needed fiber as well as flavor to a low-fat diet.

**1 tablespoon olive oil**
**2 large brown-skinned onions, peeled and chopped coarse**
**6 large cloves garlic, smashed, peeled, and minced**
**4 carrots, peeled and cut into 2-inch slices**
**4 ribs celery with leaves, cut into 2-inch slices**
**1 head green cabbage (about 1 pound), coarsely shredded**
**10 leaves Swiss chard, cut up**
**12 cups water**
**1 (28-ounce) can salt-free diced tomatoes in juice**
**1 (16-ounce) can sodium-reduced garbanzo beans (chick-peas) with liquid**
**1 (16-ounce) can sodium-reduced red kidney beans with liquid**
**Bouquet garni (in cheesecloth or tea ball): ¼ bunch Italian flat-leaf parsley, 1 teaspoon dried thyme, 2 bay leaves, and 10 peppercorns**
**1 cup small elbow macaroni or pasta shells**

1. Heat the olive oil in a large stockpot. Add the onions and garlic. Sauté 2 to 3 minutes, stirring constantly. Add the carrots and celery and cook over low heat for 10 minutes, until the onions are limp.

2. Add the cabbage, Swiss chard, water, tomatoes, and beans. Bring to a boil, reduce the heat to a simmer, and add the bouquet garni. Cover and simmer for about 45 minutes.

3. Add the pasta and cook uncovered for an additional 15 minutes. Remove the bouquet garni and serve hot.

NOTE: This may be served with Parmesan cheese alternative with a dairy meal.

```
————————————————— PER SERVING —————————————————
| 2.5 gm total fat    .32 gm saturated fat    4.4 gm fiber       186 calories          |
| 0 mg cholesterol    11.5% fat               202 mg sodium      22 calories from fat   |
```

# ❧ Sarah's Lima Bean and Barley Soup ❧ with Mushrooms

## (MEAT)

### *Yield: 16 servings (1½ cups = 1 serving as entrée)*

If I had to name one soup as my favorite, I guess this would be the one. Valuable soluble fiber is supplied by both beans and barley. On a cold winter night, a large bowl of this soup accompanied by hearty whole wheat, corn rye, or pumpernickel bread and ending with fresh fruit or a baked apple or pear for dessert makes for more than a satisfying supper.

 1 cup dried large lima beans
12 cups defatted sodium-reduced chicken broth
 2 cups water
   Bouquet garni (in cheesecloth or tea ball): ¼ bunch Italian flat-leaf parsley, 2 bay leaves, 10 peppercorns, and 2 teaspoons dried thyme
 1 cup barley, washed and drained
 1 ounce dried mushrooms
 4 cups diced peeled carrots
 4 cups diced celery with leaves
 8 ounces fresh mushrooms, cleaned and sliced
 1 cup chopped Italian flat-leaf parsley
 ½ teaspoon ground white pepper
 1 teaspoon Hungarian paprika

1. Soak the beans overnight in water to cover; drain (see Note) and rinse. Or cover with 4 cups of water and microwave on High for 8 minutes; drain and rinse.

2. Place the beans, broth, water, bouquet garni, and barley in a large kettle. Bring to a boil, reduce the heat, and simmer over medium heat, partially covered, for 1 hour. Stir occasionally.

3. Meanwhile, soak the dried mushrooms in 1 cup of hot water for 30 minutes.

Drain off the liquid through a fine strainer and reserve. Squeeze the mushrooms dry (rinse several times) and slice.

4. Add the diced carrots, celery, and fresh and dried mushrooms to the bean mixture, along with the mushroom liquid. Simmer an additional 30 minutes.

5. Add the chopped parsley and seasonings to the soup 5 minutes before serving, or use as a garnish on top of each bowl.

NOTE: Draining beans after soaking or precooking eliminates their gas-producing quality.

--- PER SERVING ---

| | | | |
|---|---|---|---|
| .6 gm total fat | .12 gm saturated fat | 4.6 gm fiber | 100 calories |
| 0 mg cholesterol | 5.5% fat | 47 mg sodium | 5 calories from fat |

# ❦ My Mother's Potato Soup ❦
## (PAREVE)
### Yield: 14 to 15 cups (1 cup = 1 serving)

When my husband started junior high school he was "privileged" to eat lunch in a school cafeteria for the first time. Passing through the line, he saw potato soup listed as a choice and immediately ordered some. The milky white purée served up was one of his first culinary disappointments outside of his mother's kitchen.

    1 tablespoon olive oil or Onion-flavored Olive Oil (page 255)
    ½ cup unbleached all-purpose flour
    1 medium onion, peeled and grated
    1 leek, white part washed and diced, green part well washed and
      tied with string
   10 cups water
    1 teaspoon dried thyme or 3 sprigs fresh thyme
    1 bay leaf
    2 teaspoons salt-free vegetable seasoning
      Ground white pepper to taste
    2 parsley roots, scrubbed, trimmed, and diced
    6 carrots, peeled and cut into ½-inch slices
    4 ribs celery with leaves, cut into ½-inch slices
    3 large Idaho potatoes, peeled and cut into ¾-inch cubes (4 cups)
    ¼ bunch Italian flat-leaf parsley, tied with string
      Kosher salt to taste

1. Heat the oil in a large saucepan; add the flour and stir constantly with a wooden spoon over medium heat until the mixture is caramel-colored. Do not scorch.

2. Add the grated onion and stir for about 1 minute. Add the diced leek and stir an additional minute.

3. Gradually stir in the water. Add the green part of leek and the seasonings. Bring to a boil.

4. Add the parsley roots, carrots, celery, and potatoes; bring to a second boil. Reduce the heat and simmer, partially covered, for about 1 hour or until the vegetables are very tender. Add the parsley about 15 minutes before the end of cooking. Taste and adjust seasonings with salt and pepper. Remove the green part of leek, bay leaf, and parsley before serving.

VARIATION: As an alternative the soup may be puréed in a food processor or blender after the green parts of leek and parsley are removed. Garnish with chopped fresh chives before serving.

---

PER SERVING

| | | | |
|---|---|---|---|
| 1.1 gm total fat | .16 gm saturated fat | 2.3 gm fiber | 83 calories |
| 0 mg cholesterol | 11.8% fat | 25 mg sodium | 10 calories from fat |

# ❧ Turkey, Rice, and Vegetable Soup ❧
## (MEAT)
### Yield: 1½ quarts (1 cup = 1 serving)

It's always convenient to have a homemade broth available to make a quick soup. Any leftover roast turkey or chicken that you may have on hand can be added.

    4 cups Turkey Broth (page 140), defatted
    ½ cup uncooked converted white rice
    1 rib celery, cut into ½-inch slices
    1½ cups frozen mixed vegetables
    ½ cup chopped Italian flat-leaf parsley
      Salt and freshly ground pepper to taste

1. Bring the broth to a boil in a medium saucepan. Add the rice and celery; simmer 20 minutes.

2. Add the frozen vegetables and parsley and simmer 5 to 10 minutes. Taste and adjust seasonings.

─────────────────── PER SERVING ───────────────────

| .4 gm total fat | .08 gm saturated fat | 2.4 gm fiber | 107 calories |
| 0 mg cholesterol | 3.4% fat | 132 mg sodium | 3 calories from fat |

# ❧ Vegetarian Lentil Soup ❧
## (PAREVE)
*Yield: About 18 cups (1 cup = 1 serving)*

    2  teaspoons extra-virgin olive oil
    1  large onion, peeled and fine chopped
    2  ribs celery with leaves, chopped fine
    3  carrots, peeled and chopped fine
    1  parsnip, peeled and chopped fine
    4  large cloves garlic, smashed, peeled, and minced
    2  teaspoons Italian herb blend, crushed
    1  teaspoon dried rosemary, crushed
       Pinch of hot red pepper flakes
    2  teaspoons lemon-herb seasoning
    2  bay leaves
    1  pound (2 cups) lentils, washed and drained
   10  cups hot water
    1  (28-ounce) can salt-free diced tomatoes in juice or crushed tomatoes
       Nonfat plain yogurt or nonfat sour cream and sliced scallions, for garnish (optional)

1. Heat the oil in a large kettle. Add the onion, celery, carrots, parsnip, and garlic; sauté about 5 minutes.

2. Add the herb blend, rosemary, hot pepper, lemon-herb seasoning, bay leaves, and lentils and stir to combine.

3. Add the hot water; bring to a boil. Reduce the heat to low, cover, and simmer for 45 to 60 minutes, stirring occasionally.

4. Remove 3 cups of the lentils, purée in a blender, and return to the soup mixture with the tomatoes. Cook 30 more minutes, stirring occasionally. Remove the bay leaves. Taste and adjust seasonings.

*To Serve:* Place in warm bowls and, if desired, garnish with a dollop of nonfat yogurt or nonfat sour cream, topped with sliced scallions.

---

PER SERVING

| | | | |
|---|---|---|---|
| .9 gm total fat | .14 gm saturated fat | 4.1 gm fiber | 116 calories |
| 0 mg cholesterol | 6.9% fat | 18 mg sodium | 8 calories from fat |

## ❦ Mollie Roth's Quick Soup ❦
(DAIRY OR PAREVE)
*Serves: 6 to 8*

A quick vegetarian soup that can be pulled together quickly; the ingredients are always on hand in my kitchen.

    2 teaspoons light margarine
    ½ cup minced onion
    1 cup sliced fresh mushrooms (optional)
    1 cup julienned carrots
    1 cup thinly sliced celery
    2½ cups water
    ⅛ teaspoon ground white pepper
    ½ cup fine no-yolk noodles or 3 tablespoons orzo
    1 (15-ounce) can green peas, with liquid

1. Melt the margarine in a saucepan. Add the onion and sauté 3 to 5 minutes; stir frequently but do not brown.

2. Add the mushrooms and sauté 2 to 3 minutes.

3. Add the carrots, celery, water, and pepper. Bring to a boil and simmer 5 minutes.

4. Add the noodles or orzo, and simmer 7 to 10 additional minutes. Add the peas with their liquid; heat and serve.

---

PER SERVING

| .8 gm total fat | .14 gm saturated fat | 2.2 gm fiber | 70 calories |
| 0 mg cholesterol | 10.3% fat | 175 mg sodium | 7 calories from fat |

---

꿩 HARRIET'S HINTS 꿩

*For a quick low-fat soup, heat Manischewitz beet borscht and serve with diced boiled potatoes and a dollop of nonfat sour cream or yogurt.*

---

# 꿩 Vegetarian Vegetable Soup 꿩
## (PAREVE)

*Yield: 18 cups (1½ cups = 1 serving as entrée; ¾ cup = 1 serving as first course)*

This soup tastes even better the next day. I don't think it freezes as well as some soups since the vegetables get a little mushy. But if you purée it, it freezes and reheats beautifully.

    1 large onion, peeled and minced
    1 leek, white part only, split, washed, and minced
    2 shallots, peeled and minced
    1 tablespoon olive oil
    4 carrots, peeled and diced
    4 ribs celery, diced
    1 cup shredded green cabbage
    1 cup diced green beans
    1 cup whole-kernel corn, fresh, frozen, or canned
    1 parsley root, scrubbed, trimmed, and diced
    1 parsnip, peeled and diced
    1 kohlrabi, peeled and diced
    1 turnip, peeled and diced

  1 cup fresh or frozen peas
 10 fresh mushrooms, sliced thin
1½ cups diced potatoes
1½ cups canned salt-free tomatoes with juice, diced
  8 cups Vegetable Broth (page 141) or boiling water
  1 teaspoon sugar
  2 teaspoons salt-free vegetable seasoning
  3 tablespoons chopped Italian flat-leaf parsley
  4 sprigs fresh thyme or 1 teaspoon dried thyme
 ⅛ teaspoon ground white pepper


1. Sauté the onion, leek, and shallots in the olive oil in a large stockpot until transparent, about 5 minutes.

2. Add the remaining vegetables except the potatoes and tomatoes and cook 10 minutes, stirring constantly.

3. Stir in the potatoes, tomatoes, broth, and seasonings; simmer until the vegetables are tender.


VARIATION: If desired, you may purée the vegetables in a food processor before serving. Cooked mini matzo balls (page 76) or schliskas (page 243) may be added to the soup at the end of the cooking time and simmered 5 additional minutes.

--- PER SERVING ---

| .9 gm total fat | .13 gm saturated fat | 2.1 gm fiber | 54 calories |
| 0 mg cholesterol | 13.2% fat | 27 mg sodium | 8 calories from fat |

# ❧ Yellow Split Pea Soup with Matzo Balls ❧
## (PAREVE)

*Serves: 10 to 12 (¾ cup = 1 serving as first course; 1½ cups = 1 serving as entrée)*

This yellow split pea soup tastes quite different from green split pea soup. And the addition of small matzo balls gives it a personality of its own.

2 teaspoons extra-virgin olive oil
1 onion, peeled and diced
1 leek, white part only, split, washed, and diced
2 large cloves garlic, smashed, peeled, and chopped
1 parsley root, scrubbed, trimmed, and chopped
1 pound (2 cups) yellow split peas, sorted and washed
5 carrots, peeled and chopped
5 ribs celery with leaves, chopped
   Bouquet garni (in cheesecloth or tea ball): 6 sprigs Italian flat-leaf parsley, 1 teaspoon dried thyme, 2 bay leaves, pinch of hot red pepper flakes
8 cups cold water
   Matzo balls (page 76), made half the regular size (optional)

1. Heat the oil in a medium-large saucepan. Add the onion, leek, and garlic, and sauté until wilted, 3 to 4 minutes, stirring from time to time.
2. Add the parsley root and split peas. Sauté 2 to 3 minutes.
3. Add the carrots, celery, bouquet garni, and water. Bring to a boil and simmer, partially covered, for 1½ hours.
4. Purée, in batches if necessary, in a food processor or blender.
5. Add matzo balls and simmer 5 minutes.

VARIATIONS: If you like a thinner soup, add enough water to reach the desired consistency. One cup of frozen mixed vegetables may be added for a change. One half cup of Minute Rice may also be added.

---

### PER SERVING

| | | | |
|---|---|---|---|
| 1.4 gm total fat | .18 gm saturated fat | 3.4 gm fiber | 148 calories |
| 0 mg cholesterol | 8.1% fat | 33 mg sodium | 12 calories from fat |

# ❦ Green Split Pea Soup ❦
### (PAREVE)
*Yield: 14 cups (1 cup = 1 serving)*

I sometimes add ⅔ cup farfel to this beautiful green puréed soup, and simmer for about 15 minutes before serving.

- 1 tablespoon olive oil
- 1 onion, peeled and chopped
- 2 large cloves garlic, smashed, peeled, and chopped
- 2 leeks, white part only, split, washed, and chopped (green part washed, tied with string, and reserved)
- 1 pound (2 cups) green split peas, rinsed and drained
- 5 carrots, peeled and chopped
- 1 parsnip, peeled and chopped
- 5 ribs celery with leaves, sliced
- 10 cups water
  Bouquet garni (in cheesecloth or tea ball): 6 sprigs Italian flat-leaf parsley, 2 bay leaves, ½ teaspoon dried thyme, pinch of hot red pepper flakes
  Salt and freshly ground pepper to taste

1. Heat the oil in a kettle and sauté the onion, garlic, and white part of leek for 5 minutes.
2. Add the split peas, carrots, parsnip, and celery; stir.
3. Add the water, bouquet garni, and green part of leek.
4. Bring to a boil, reduce the heat to a simmer, cover partially, and cook about 1½ hours, or until the peas are very soft.
5. Remove the leek green and bouquet garni and purée the remainder of the soup in a food processor or blender. Taste and adjust seasonings with salt and pepper. Serve hot.

NOTE: This may be frozen for future use.

| PER SERVING | | | |
|---|---|---|---|
| 1.5 gm total fat | .21 gm saturated fat | 3.5 gm fiber | 156 calories |
| 0 mg cholesterol | 8.4% fat | 73 mg sodium | 14 calories from fat |

# ❧ Caraway Soup ❧
## (PAREVE)
### Serves: 6

According to my Hungarian grandmother, Fannie Lebovitz, this soup, in addition to chicken soup, was guaranteed to cure all ills—particularly a queasy stomach. She used butter, but I love my low-fat version even more!

½ cup peeled and diced carrots
½ cup peeled and diced onion
½ cup diced celery
1 tablespoon canola oil or extra-virgin olive oil
1 tablespoon caraway seeds
2 tablespoons all-purpose flour
6 cups Vegetable Broth (page 141) or cold water
   Salt and freshly ground pepper to taste
   Chopped fresh parsley, for garnish

1. Chop the carrots, onion, and celery in a food processor. Sauté them in a non-stick skillet coated with olive oil cooking spray for about 5 minutes, or until lightly browned. Stir frequently to keep from sticking.

2. Meanwhile, heat the oil in a saucepan, add the caraway seeds, and cook for 1 minute, or until they start to pop. Add the flour to make a roux (einbrenne), stirring until caramel colored. Make sure it does not burn.

3. Gradually add the broth and whisk until blended; add the vegetables, bring to a boil, lower the heat, and simmer for 20 minutes or until smoothed and slightly thickened.

4. Strain and discard the vegetables and caraway seeds. Bring to a simmer. Taste and adjust seasonings with salt and pepper. Garnish with parsley.

*To Serve:* Serve hot with melba toast, matzos, or garlic toast made by toasting rye bread and rubbing with a peeled clove of garlic. Or cut the garlic-flavored toast into croutons and serve with the soup.

---

PER SERVING

| | | | |
|---|---|---|---|
| 2.5 gm total fat | .18 gm saturated fat | 1.0 gm fiber | 45 calories |
| 0 mg cholesterol | 48% fat | 13 mg sodium | 23 calories from fat |

---

# ❧ Chicken Soup in the Microwave ❧
## (MEAT)
### *Yield: 8 cups (1 cup = 1 serving)*

1 (3-pound) chicken (with giblets, except liver), cut into 10 pieces, fat removed, or 3 pounds chicken backs or trimmings, or 3 pounds halved chicken breasts
1 medium onion, peeled and chopped coarse
2 ribs celery with leaves, chopped coarse
2 carrots, peeled and chopped coarse
1 whole leek split, washed, and sliced, or 4 whole scallions, sliced
1 parsnip, peeled and quartered
Bouquet garni (in cheesecloth or tea ball): 6 sprigs Italian flat-leaf parsley, 1 bay leaf, 3 sprigs fresh dill, 6 peppercorns, and 1 teaspoon dried thyme
8 cups cold water
Kosher salt (optional)
Ground white pepper to taste

1. Place the chicken, onion, celery, carrots, leek, parsnip, bouquet garni, and 1 cup of the water in a large microwave casserole. Cover and cook on High for 5 minutes.

2. Stir, add the remaining 7 cups of cold water, cover, and continue cooking on High for 40 minutes. Stir once during cooking.

3. Remove the chicken, cool slightly, and remove and discard the skin and bones. Refrigerate or freeze the meat for future use.

4. Strain, chill, and defat the broth. It can be stored in the refrigerator for up to 3 days, or frozen for future use. Season if desired before using.

*To Freeze Broth:* Divide it among several small airtight containers (1 cup is a useful size), leaving an inch of head space for expansion, and cover tightly.

Variation: To make microwave chicken in the pot, skin the chicken but leave the bones in. Return the chicken and vegetables to the strained and defatted broth and add a bit of salt, white pepper, and cooked rice.

| PER SERVING | | | |
|---|---|---|---|
| 0 gm total fat | 0 gm saturated fat | 0 gm fiber | 22 calories |
| 0 mg cholesterol | 0% fat | 3 mg sodium | 0 calories from fat |

# ❦ Connie Reif's Vegetable and Bean Soup ❦ (How to Make Lemonade Out of Lemons)
## (PAREVE OR MEAT)
*Yield: 20 servings (1 cup = 1 serving)*

After the earthquake of 1994 in Los Angeles, my friend Connie found herself still quaking with the aftershocks. Then her creative juices started to flow. She prepared this most delicious soup with what she had in what was left of her home; as you'll see, she keeps a well-stocked kitchen! You may vary it with your favorite ingredients, but I suggest that you make it according to this recipe the first time, and then make any variations to suit your taste.

    1 tablespoon olive oil
    2 large onions, peeled and chopped fine or sliced thin
    3 large cloves garlic, smashed, peeled, and minced, or 2 heads
      garlic, minced
    8 carrots, peeled and cut into ¾-inch slices, or ½ pound packaged peeled
      baby carrots, halved crosswise
   10 cups defatted sodium-reduced chicken broth or vegetable broth
    2 cups water
    1 medium cauliflower (1½ pounds), cored and cut into small florets
    5 red potatoes (1½ pounds), peeled and cut into ¾-inch cubes
    1 (32-ounce) can peeled Italian tomatoes, with juice, crushed
    1 (10-ounce) can salt-free, sugar-free whole-kernel corn

2 (15-ounce) cans sodium-reduced cannellini or white kidney beans, rinsed and drained
3 bay leaves
½ teaspoon crushed herbes de Provence
½ teaspoon crushed dried basil
¼ teaspoon ground white pepper
1 cup uncooked arborio or converted white rice
Chopped Italian flat-leaf parsley or fresh basil, for garnish

1. In a large stockpot, heat the olive oil and add the onions, garlic, and carrots. Place over moderate heat, cover, and let the vegetables sweat for 10 to 12 minutes, stirring occasionally.

2. Add the chicken broth and water; bring to a boil.

3. Add the cauliflower, potatoes, tomatoes, corn, beans, bay leaves, herbes de Provence, basil, and pepper. Simmer, partially covered, for 45 minutes. Stir occasionally.

4. Add the rice and simmer another 20 minutes, stirring several times.

5. Taste and adjust seasonings. Remove the bay leaves.

*To Serve:* Ladle into hot bowls, sprinkle with chopped parsley or basil, and serve immediately with a hearty whole wheat or rye bread.

NOTE: As with most recipes, this soup tastes better the next day, but it also gets thicker. If it is too thick for your taste, add water, vegetable broth, or chicken broth to suit your palate, tasting and adjusting the seasonings.

VARIATIONS: Substitute broccoli florets for cauliflower. Two ribs of celery, diced, and/or two leeks (white part only), minced, may also be added.

| ——— PER SERVING ——— | | | |
|---|---|---|---|
| 1.2 gm total fat | .18 gm saturated fat | 3.6 gm fiber | 167 calories |
| 0 mg cholesterol | 6.4% fat | 131 mg sodium | 11 calories from fat |

# ❧ Carrot Soup ❧
## (PAREVE OR MEAT)
### *Serves: 8 to 10*

A puréed soup made with carrots, onions, and potatoes. It's high in vitamin A and beta-carotene. Try using carrots with fresh green tops instead of packaged carrots. They are fresher and sweeter.

2 teaspoons olive oil
2 large onions, peeled and sliced
2 pounds carrots, peeled and sliced
2 Idaho potatoes (about 1 pound), peeled and cut into 1-inch cubes
1 bay leaf
⅛ teaspoon ground white pepper
¼ teaspoon freshly grated nutmeg or 1 teaspoon grated fresh gingerroot
6 cups defatted sodium-reduced vegetable or chicken broth
  Chopped chives or fresh chervil leaves, for garnish

1. Place the oil in a heavy-bottomed saucepan over medium heat. Add the onions and carrots; stir, cover, and allow to wilt for about 8 to 10 minutes. Stir occasionally.

2. Add the potatoes, bay leaf, pepper, nutmeg, and broth. Cook about 50 minutes or until the carrots are fork-tender. Discard the bay leaf.

3. Remove the vegetables with a slotted spoon to a food processor or blender. Add 1 cup of liquid and process until a smooth purée results.

4. Return to the saucepan and stir until blended and smooth. Taste and adjust seasonings.

*To Serve:* Heat for 5 minutes, serve in warm bowls, and sprinkle with either chopped chives or fresh chervil leaves. This light soup is nice to serve as a first course with broiled fish as an entrée.

---

PER SERVING

| | | | |
|---|---|---|---|
| 1.1 gm total fat | .18 gm saturated fat | 3.2 gm fiber | 95 calories |
| 0 mg cholesterol | 11.1% fat | 27 mg sodium | 10 calories from fat |

# ❧ Hungarian Sauerkraut Soup ❧

## (MEAT)

*Yield: 12 to 14 cups (1 cup = 1 serving)*

This sour soup is for eaters who love strong flavors. Those whose tastes dictate a milder flavor can add sugar; the soup will still be uniquely delicious!

2 pounds beef marrow bones, sawed in 2-inch pieces
8 cups cold water
1 medium onion with skin (cut an X in the root end)
2 bay leaves
1 tablespoon olive oil
⅓ cup unbleached all-purpose flour
1 small onion, peeled and grated
2 cups low-sodium tomato juice
1 (28-ounce) can salt-free diced tomatoes in juice
1 (16-ounce) jar low-sodium sauerkraut
½ teaspoon ground white pepper
1½ teaspoons sour salt (citric acid), or to taste

1. Put the bones in a stockpot and add the cold water. Bring to a boil; skim off the foam, add the unpeeled onion and bay leaves, and reduce the heat. Simmer for 1 hour while partially covered.

2. In a 2-quart nonstick saucepan, heat the oil; sprinkle the flour over the oil, and prepare a roux, or *einbrenne*, by stirring with a wooden spoon until the flour is golden brown. Add the grated onion and stir 1 minute.

3. Gradually add the tomato juice and the liquid from the diced tomatoes and whisk until smooth.

4. Add the tomatoes, sauerkraut, and white pepper; stir to combine. Add this mixture to the broth.

5. Add the sour salt, stir, and cook for 30 minutes.

6. Taste and adjust seasonings.

*To Serve:* Serve the soup *hot* in warmed bowls with boiled or steamed potatoes and dark pumpernickel or corn rye bread.

Note: If you want to make this soup nonfat, brown the flour without oil in a non-stick skillet and continue as in the recipe directions.

— PER SERVING —

| | | | |
|---|---|---|---|
| 1.6 gm total fat | .33 gm saturated fat | 1.4 gm fiber | 58 calories |
| 1 mg cholesterol | 23.3% fat | 272 mg sodium | 15 calories from fat |

## ❧ Nanette Nathanson's Corn Soup ❧
### (dairy)
*Serves: 8*

This is an easy soup that can be prepared from your pantry and refrigerator shelves. Although the fat content is a bit higher than in other soups, it comes from the tofu, a soybean product that is low in saturated fat.

10½ ounces low-fat soft tofu, drained
  1 cup nonfat milk
  ½ cup chopped onion
  ½ red bell pepper, seeded and diced
  1 (14½-ounce) can defatted sodium-reduced chicken broth
  1 (17-ounce) can cream-style corn
  1 (12-ounce) can sugar-free, salt-free whole-kernel corn or 1 (10-ounce) package frozen Green Giant white peg kernel corn
  1 teaspoon dried basil, crushed, or 1 tablespoon chopped fresh basil
  ½ teaspoon ground white pepper
  2 tablespoons sliced scallions or chopped Italian flat-leaf parsley or fresh cilantro, for garnish

1. Purée the tofu with the milk in a food processor or blender.
2. Sauté the chopped onion in a nonstick saucepan coated with vegetable oil cooking spray until wilted. (Place a lid over the onion to speed the sweating process.)
3. Add the bell pepper, chicken broth, cream-style corn and corn kernels, basil, ground pepper, and puréed tofu mixture. Stir and bring to a simmer; *do not boil.*

*To Serve:* Serve in warm soup bowls and sprinkle with sliced scallions or chopped parsley or cilantro.

| ──────── P E R  S E R V I N G ──────── | | | |
|---|---|---|---|
| 2.3 gm total fat | .38 gm saturated fat | 1.9 gm fiber | 122 calories |
| 1 mg cholesterol | 15.9% fat | 23 mg sodium | 21 calories from fat |

# ❦ Harriet Friedman's Mother's ❦ Cabbage Borscht
## (PAREVE OR MEAT)
### *Yield: 15 to 16 cups (1 cup = 1 serving)*

Harriet Friedman says, "My Yiddishe Mama added a dollop of sour cream to the hot soup when it was prepared without meat—but then, sour cream was added to just about everything when I was growing up." That's a common remark among my friends! You can top this savory soup with nonfat sour cream if you like.

    1 pound ground turkey (optional)
    1 teaspoon garlic powder
    1 medium head (about 1½ pounds) green cabbage, shredded or chopped
    1 large onion, peeled, halved, and sliced thin
    2 (16-ounce) cans salt-free diced tomatoes in juice
    3 cups low-sodium tomato juice
    1 cup water or vegetable broth
    ½ teaspoon sour salt (citric acid)
 8 to 10 gingersnaps, crushed in a food processor
    2 teaspoons caraway seeds
      Grated zest and juice of 2 lemons
    ½ pound dried apricots, chopped
    3 carrots, peeled and sliced thin

1. In a nonstick stockpot, or one coated with vegetable oil cooking spray, sauté the ground turkey until lightly browned. Sprinkle with garlic powder.

2. Add the cabbage, onion, tomatoes with juice, tomato juice, water, sour salt, gingersnaps, caraway seeds, lemon zest and juice, apricots, and carrots. Stir to blend.

3. Cook over a low flame, partially covered, for 2 hours.

4. After 2 hours, taste and adjust seasonings until you have achieved the precise blend of sweet and sour flavors that you like. If it is too thick, add broth, tomato juice, or water.

-------- PER SERVING --------

| | | | |
|---|---|---|---|
| 1.0 gm total fat | .21 gm saturated fat | 3.3 gm fiber | 99 calories |
| 1 mg cholesterol | 8.3% fat | 231 mg sodium | 9 calories from fat |

## ❦ Low-Calorie Cabbage Borscht ❦
### (PAREVE OR DAIRY)
*Serves: 12*

This soup may be prepared ahead and reheated.

    1 medium head (1½ pounds) green cabbage, shredded
    8 cups Vegetable Broth (page 141) or water
    3 shallots, minced
    2 onions, peeled and sliced thin
    2 fresh or salt-free canned plum tomatoes, peeled, seeded, and chopped
    1 rib celery, diced fine
    ¼ cup chopped Italian flat-leaf parsley
    ⅛ teaspoon ground white pepper
    1 teaspoon salt
    1 bay leaf
    5 large beets, cooked, peeled, and cut into julienne
      Juice of ½ lemon
    ½ cup dry white wine or vermouth
    1 teaspoon sugar
    3 tablespoons chopped fresh dill or 1 teaspoon dried dill weed
      Nonfat sour cream and chopped fresh dill or sliced scallions,
      for garnish

1. In a large saucepan, combine the cabbage, broth, shallots, onions, tomatoes, celery, parsley, pepper, salt, and bay leaf. Bring to a boil, reduce the heat, and cover. Simmer for 1½ hours.

2. Remove the bay leaf. Add the beets, lemon juice, wine, sugar, and dill. Cover and simmer 30 to 40 minutes. Taste and adjust seasonings.

*To Serve:* Ladle the hot borscht into soup bowls, top with a dollop of nonfat sour cream, and sprinkle with chopped fresh dill or sliced scallions.

---

PER SERVING

| | | | |
|---|---|---|---|
| .2 gm total fat | .04 gm saturated fat | 2.4 gm fiber | 41 calories |
| 0 mg cholesterol | 5% fat | 223 mg sodium | 2 calories from fat |

---

# ❦ Shurba (Sephardic Tomato Rice Soup) ❦
## (MEAT)
### *Serves: 8*

This soup has a rather thick consistency. If you prefer, thin it with chicken broth.

3 (8-ounce) chicken breast halves, skinned
4 cups water
½ (6-ounce) can salt-free tomato paste
1 medium onion, peeled and diced
1 carrot, peeled and diced
1 rib celery with leaves, sliced thin
1 clove garlic, smashed, peeled, and minced
1 potato, peeled and cubed
½ cup uncooked white rice
   Salt and freshly ground pepper to taste

1. Poach the chicken breasts in 4 cups of simmering water until tender, about 20 minutes.

2. Add the tomato paste, onion, carrot, celery, garlic, and potato. Bring to a boil and simmer, partially covered, for 30 minutes.

3. Add the rice, cover, and cook until the rice is tender, about 20 minutes.

4. Remove the chicken from the bone, dice, and return to the soup. Taste and adjust seasonings with salt and pepper. Serve hot.

--- PER SERVING ---

| | | | |
|---|---|---|---|
| 2.4 gm total fat | .66 gm saturated fat | 1.3 gm fiber | 173 calories |
| 42 mg cholesterol | 12.8% fat | 126 mg sodium | 22 calories from fat |

# SALADS

Marinated Cucumbers     178
Two-Pea Salad     179
Cucumber Salad     179
Mixed Fresh Vegetable Salad     180
Crunchy Cauliflower and Pea Salad     181
Apple Date Salad     182
Marinated Bean Salad     183
Israeli Vegetable Salad     184
Chopped Salad     185
Red and Green Chopped Salad     186
Radish, Celery, and Cucumber Salad     187
Gingered Cucumbers     188
Parsley and Minced Celery Salad Vinaigrette     189
Farfel Salad     190
Hungarian Caraway Slaw     191
Hungarian Wilted Lettuce and Tomato Salad     191
Apple Cabbage Salad     192
Hungarian Vegetable Salad     193
Syrian-Style Potato Salad     194
"Egg Salad" Spread     195

Ranch-Style Dressing     196
Low-Cal Tomato Dressing     197
Lemony Tahini Dressing     198
Creamy Tofu Dressing     198
Russian Dressing     199
Light Vinaigrette Dressing     200
Connie Reif's Light Asian Dressing     201

Salads are about the last dish to come to mind when we think of traditional Jewish cooking. Modern Jewish cooks should be aware of both the importance of the fiber in salads and the vitamins and minerals present in raw vegetables. Salads also fill us up without adding fat or empty calories, which is handy for weight control.

Here are some recipes to expand your repertoire beyond the old lettuce-and-tomato grind. I've also supplied some favorite dressings for maximum flavor without the fat, sodium, and sugar of most bottled dressings.

# ❦ Marinated Cucumbers ❦
## (PAREVE)
### Serves: 6

This salad's fresh, tangy flavor is a great complement for either fish or fowl. If you are avoiding sugar, you may substitute 3 tablespoons of frozen apple juice concentrate or 3 to 4 packets of artificial sweetener for the sugar.

    1 cucumber, peeled, halved, and seeded, or ½ European cucumber,
      unpeeled, sliced thin
      Salt (optional)
    ½ green bell pepper, seeded and diced
    ½ red bell pepper, seeded and diced
    3 scallions, sliced, or ½ small mild onion, sliced thin
    1 cup cold water
    3 tablespoons sugar
    ¼ cup distilled white vinegar or rice wine vinegar
    2 tablespoons chopped fresh dill or 2 teaspoons dried dill weed

1. Place the sliced cucumber in a bowl and, if desired, sprinkle with salt. Allow to stand for at least 30 minutes.

2. Drain and squeeze the liquid from the cucumber. Return to the bowl and add the diced peppers and scallions.

3. Make a mixture of the water, sugar, vinegar, and dill, stirring until the sugar is dissolved. Add to the cucumber mixture and let stand in the refrigerator for several hours or overnight. Taste and adjust seasonings before serving.

--- PER SERVING ---

| | | | |
|---|---|---|---|
| .1 gm total fat | .02 gm saturated fat | .5 gm fiber | 36 calories |
| 0 mg cholesterol | 2.5% fat | 4 mg sodium | 1 calorie from fat |

# ❧ Two-Pea Salad ❧
### (PAREVE)
*Serves: 4*

½ pound fresh snow peas
1 cup salt-free frozen peas, thawed
1 medium red or white onion, peeled and sliced thin
½ cup Light Vinaigrette Dressing (page 200)
  Freshly ground pepper
  Radicchio lettuce or red cabbage, for lining bowl

1. Wash the snow peas, string, and remove the ends.
2. Place in a bowl with the thawed peas, onion, dressing, and pepper to taste. Toss lightly to combine.
3. Chill in the refrigerator several hours before serving.

*To Serve:* Spoon chilled salad onto a leaf of radicchio or red cabbage. Great with chicken or turkey.

| PER SERVING | | | |
|---|---|---|---|
| .2 gm total fat | .04 gm saturated fat | 2.2 gm fiber | 72 calories |
| 0 mg cholesterol | 2.2% fat | 118 mg sodium | 2 calories from fat |

# ❧ Cucumber Salad ❧
### (DAIRY)
*Serves: 10*

This salad is delicious as an accompaniment to poached salmon or with gefilte fish when served as an entrée.

1 European cucumber, unpeeled, halved lengthwise and sliced thin
1 small white or red onion, peeled and diced
½ red bell pepper, seeded and diced
1 cup nonfat sour cream
  Freshly ground pepper
3 tablespoons chopped fresh dill or 1 tablespoon dried dill weed
1 tablespoon sugar (optional)

1. Combine the cucumber, onion, bell pepper, and sour cream in a bowl. Mix to blend.
2. Add the ground pepper, dill, and sugar. Taste and adjust seasonings.
3. Chill at least 30 minutes before serving so that flavors can blend.

---

PER SERVING

| | | | |
|---|---|---|---|
| .1 gm total fat | .02 gm saturated fat | .5 gm fiber | 22 calories |
| 0 mg cholesterol | 2.5% fat | 14 mg sodium | 1 calorie from fat |

---

## ❦ Mixed Fresh Vegetable Salad ❦
### (DAIRY)
*Serves: 8*

Use only the best fresh raw vegetables in this salad; omit those that don't appeal or add any that you like. This is particularly tasty with fish.

1 cup diced peeled jicama
1 cup diced peeled carrots
1 cup diced zucchini
1 cup small cauliflowerets
1 cup small broccoli florets
3 scallions, sliced
½ red bell pepper, seeded and diced
½ green bell pepper, seeded and diced

*Salad Dressing:*
¼ cup dry white wine or dry vermouth
½ cup nonfat plain yogurt
½ cup nonfat sour cream
1 teaspoon sugar
2 cloves garlic, smashed, peeled, and minced
½ teaspoon each dried oregano, marjoram, and basil, crushed, or 2 teaspoons each fresh herbs, chopped
⅛ teaspoon ground red pepper (cayenne) (optional)

1. Combine all the vegetables in a bowl; toss to mix.

2. Mix the ingredients for the salad dressing and pour over the vegetables. Stir lightly with a fork and chill at least 1 hour before serving.

---

PER SERVING

| | | | |
|---|---|---|---|
| .2 gm total fat | .06 gm saturated fat | 1.6 gm fiber | 49 calories |
| 0 mg cholesterol | 4.1% fat | 32 mg sodium | 2 calories from fat |

---

# ❦ Crunchy Cauliflower and Pea Salad ❦
## (DAIRY)
### *Serves: 6*

1¼ cups chopped cauliflower
1 (10-ounce) package salt-free frozen peas, thawed
1¼ cups diced celery
½ red bell pepper, seeded and diced
½ cup diced scallions
½ cup nonfat sour cream
¾ cup Ranch-Style Dressing (page 196)
½ cup chopped toasted almonds, for garnish

1. In a mixing bowl, combine the cauliflower, peas, celery, diced pepper, and scallions.

2. Combine the sour cream and dressing in a separate bowl. Add to the vegetables; toss and chill. Garnish with toasted almonds just before serving.

---

PER SERVING

| | | | |
|---|---|---|---|
| 6.2 gm total fat | .73 gm saturated fat | 4.7 gm fiber | 137 calories |
| 1 mg cholesterol | 38.4% fat | 133 mg sodium | 56 calories from fat |

# ❦ Apple Date Salad ❦

## (DAIRY)

### Serves: 6

If you can find Medjool dates, use them for this dish; they are particularly flavorful.

2 large red apples, washed, cored, and diced
1 tablespoon fresh orange juice
8 dates, pitted and chopped (see Note)
1 rib celery, diced
½ cup nonfat lemon or vanilla yogurt
1 tablespoon chopped toasted almonds
2 carrots, peeled and coarsely shredded, for garnish

1. Combine the apples, juice, dates, and celery in a bowl; toss lightly.
2. Stir the yogurt, add to the apple mixture, and blend with a fork.

*To Serve:* Place on a chilled platter, sprinkle with almonds, and surround with shredded carrot.

NOTE: Use kitchen shears for cutting dates; it's immeasurably easier than trying to slice or chop them with a knife.

———— PER SERVING ————

| | | | |
|---|---|---|---|
| 1.0 gm total fat | .11 gm saturated fat | 2.6 gm fiber | 86 calories |
| 1 mg cholesterol | 9.4% fat | 19 mg sodium | 9 calories from fat |

———— ❦ Harriet's Hints ❦ ————

*To chop dates or any dried fruit: coat kitchen shears with vegetable oil cooking spray or cold water, then snip to desired size.*

# ❦ Marinated Bean Salad ❦

## (PAREVE)

*Yield: About 12 cups (1½ cups = 1 serving as entrée; ½ cup = 1 serving as side dish)*

Current nutrition research cites the value of beans as a good vegetarian source of protein as well as of soluble fiber. I've used canned beans for convenience in the recipe. You, of course, may cook your own—refer to the chart on page 235.

This salad is very popular as part of a buffet, barbecue, or picnic.

1 (15½-ounce) can sodium-reduced red kidney beans, drained
1 (15½-ounce) can sodium-reduced garbanzo beans, drained
1 (15½-ounce) can black beans, drained
1 (15½-ounce) can cannellini or small white beans, drained
2 ribs celery, diced
1 cup salt-free frozen peas, thawed
1 cup salt-free, sugar-free whole-kernel corn
1 cup steamed green beans, cut into ½-inch pieces
4 ounces chopped pimiento, drained, or 1 cup diced red bell pepper
1 (10¾-ounce) can quartered artichoke hearts, drained
⅓ cup Light Vinaigrette Dressing (page 200) or ½ cup fat-free, low-calorie
    Italian dressing mixed with 1 tablespoon balsamic vinegar
    Freshly ground pepper to taste
    Kale or radicchio or bronze lettuce leaves, to line bowl or platter
3 tablespoons chopped fresh oregano or dill, for garnish
    Cherry tomatoes, for garnish

1. Place all the canned beans in a colander, rinse thoroughly under cold running water, and drain.

2. When well drained, put the beans in a mixing bowl with the celery, peas, corn, green beans, pimiento, and artichokes. Toss lightly with the vinaigrette to combine. Taste and adjust seasonings with pepper. Cover and chill several hours before serving.

*To Serve:* Place in chilled serving bowl lined with kale or mound on a platter lined with radicchio or bronze lettuce leaves. Sprinkle with fresh oregano or dill and surround with cherry tomatoes.

| PER SERVING | | | |
|---|---|---|---|
| 6.3 gm total fat | .09 gm saturated fat | 2.7 gm fiber | 90 calories |
| 0 mg cholesterol | 6.3% fat | 35 mg sodium | 6 calories from fat |

# ❦ Israeli Vegetable Salad ❦
## (PAREVE)
### *Serves: 6*

The vegetables in this salad are those most readily available in Israel. When combined and dressed just before serving, they provide a fresh, delicate crunch to your meal. This mixed vegetable salad is frequently served at breakfast.

      2 small cucumbers, peeled, seeded, and diced
      1 medium red or green bell pepper, seeded and diced
      4 red radishes, diced
      2 scallions, sliced
      ¼ head lettuce, shredded
      2 carrots, peeled and grated
      2 tablespoons chopped Italian flat-leaf parsley
      3 ripe Italian plum tomatoes, diced
      1 tablespoon extra-virgin olive oil
 1 to 2 tablespoons fresh lemon juice, or to taste
        Freshly ground pepper to taste
        Nonfat sour cream, for garnish (optional)

1. Place all the vegetables except the tomatoes in a salad bowl. Toss to combine. Add the tomatoes, reserving a few dice for garnish, and stir gently with a fork.

2. Sprinkle the vegetables with the olive oil and toss lightly to coat.

3. Add lemon juice and freshly ground pepper. Toss again.

4. Garnish, if desired, with several dollops of sour cream and scatter a few diced tomatoes on top.

*To Serve:* This salad should be served as soon as it is dressed with the olive oil and lemon juice. It is very refreshing with fish or a dairy dinner.

```
──────── PER SERVING ────────
2.6 gm total fat    .36 gm saturated fat    2.0 gm fiber     53 calories
0 mg cholesterol    39.9% fat               43 mg sodium     23 calories from fat
```

# ❧ Chopped Salad ❧
## (MEAT, DAIRY, OR PAREVE)
*Serves: 6*

Chopped salads provide a welcome change from the usual mixed green salad. If you have any fresh basil, oregano, chives, or thyme leaves on hand, toss them in to add another dimension to an already tasty first course.

1 head romaine lettuce, washed, dried, and chopped fine
½ small sweet onion, chopped fine
1 (4-ounce) jar chopped pimientos, drained
1 (15½-ounce) can sodium-reduced garbanzo beans (chick-peas), rinsed, drained, and chopped
4 canned artichoke bottoms or hearts, drained and diced
3 ripe Italian plum tomatoes, cored and diced
4 ounces diced cooked chicken or turkey, 1 (3-ounce) can tuna in water, drained, or 2 ounces feta or low-fat cheese (optional)
Freshly ground pepper
3 tablespoons fat-free low-calorie Italian dressing or 2 tablespoons extra-virgin olive oil
1 tablespoon balsamic vinegar or rice vinegar

1. Put the lettuce in a salad bowl and add the onion, pimientos, garbanzos, diced artichoke, tomatoes, and meat, fish, or cheese if desired. Toss to combine the ingredients, cover, and chill in the refrigerator until serving time.

2. Just before serving, add freshly ground pepper and sprinkle the salad with salad dressing or olive oil. Toss and add vinegar. Toss again and serve immediately.

---

PER SERVING

| | | | |
|---|---|---|---|
| 3.1 gm total fat | .59 gm saturated fat | 3.7 gm fiber | 157 calories |
| 17 mg cholesterol | 17.4% fat | 113 mg sodium | 28 calories from fat |

---

# ❧ Red and Green Chopped Salad ❧
## (PAREVE OR DAIRY)
### *Serves: 8*

You can mix and match these ingredients to suit your taste.

   ½ medium head radicchio, chopped fine
   1 Belgian endive, cored and sliced
   1 bunch arugula, sliced thin
   1 bulb fennel, feathery greens removed, diced fine
   1 bunch watercress, leaves only, chopped fine
     Juice of ½ lemon
3 to 4 tablespoons fat-free, low-calorie Italian dressing
   3 tablespoons soy-based Parmesan cheese alternative or 1 ounce crumbled
     blue cheese (optional)

1. Combine the radicchio, endive, arugula, fennel, and watercress in a salad bowl.
2. Sprinkle with lemon juice and salad dressing; toss lightly.
3. Sprinkle with cheese if desired, toss lightly, and serve immediately.

NOTE: All vegetables for the salad except the watercress and arugula may be chopped 4 to 6 hours earlier in the day and stored in a plastic bag till serving time.

---

PER SERVING

| | | | |
|---|---|---|---|
| .2 gm total fat | .01 gm saturated fat | .4 gm fiber | 21 calories |
| 0 mg cholesterol | 9.4% fat | 99 mg sodium | 2 calories from fat |

# ❦ Radish, Celery, and Cucumber Salad ❦

## (DAIRY)

*Serves: 6*

This salad is particularly delicious with a fish entrée. I like to serve this with gefilte fish (page 71 or 289) as a main course.

2 cups sliced red radishes
1 cup diced black radishes (optional)
3 ribs celery, diced (1½ cups)
2 cups sliced European cucumber
   Freshly ground pepper
1 tablespoon chopped fresh dill
   Red lettuce leaves, for lining bowl
   Whole red radish roses, for garnish

*Dressing:*
   ½ cup nonfat sour cream or nonfat plain yogurt
   2 tablespoons rice vinegar
2 to 3 teaspoons sugar
   2 tablespoons chopped fresh dill or 2 teaspoons dried dill weed
   ¼ teaspoon dried mustard (optional)

1. Combine the sliced radishes, celery, and cucumber in a bowl. Sprinkle with pepper and dill; toss lightly.
2. Blend the dressing ingredients and toss with the radish mixture.

*To Serve:* Line a bowl with lettuce leaves and mound the salad mixture on top. Garnish with radish roses and additional chopped dill.

---
PER SERVING
---

| | | | |
|---|---|---|---|
| .3 gm total fat | .03 gm saturated fat | .8 gm fiber | 35 calories |
| 0 mg cholesterol | 6.6% fat | 40 mg sodium | 3 calories from fat |

---
#### ❧❧  HARRIET'S HINTS  ❧❧

*For added fiber and food value, in a mixed green salad sprinkle thawed frozen mixed vegetables over salad greens before adding vinaigrette dressing.*
---

# ❧ Gingered Cucumbers ❧
## (PAREVE)
### *Serves: 8 (½ cup = 1 serving)*

½ cup rice vinegar
¼ cup water
1 tablespoon sodium-reduced soy sauce
1½ to 2 teaspoons grated fresh gingerroot
2 tablespoons frozen unsweetened apple juice concentrate or 1 tablespoon sugar
1 European cucumber, sliced thin
1 large carrot, peeled and grated
3 scallions, sliced thin
2 tablespoons chopped Italian flat-leaf parsley

1. Combine the vinegar, water, soy sauce, ginger, and apple juice concentrate in a serving bowl. Blend well.

2. Add the cucumber, carrot, scallions, and parsley. Toss to combine.

3. Cover and refrigerate 1 to 2 hours. Taste and adjust seasonings. Toss again before serving.

---
#### PER SERVING

| | | | |
|---|---|---|---|
| .1 gm total fat | .02 gm saturated fat | .7 gm fiber | 19 calories |
| 0 mg cholesterol | 3.7% fat | 69 mg sodium | 1 calorie from fat |
---

# ❦ Parsley and Minced Celery ❦ Salad Vinaigrette

## (PAREVE)

### Serves: 4

We all have the habit of chopping a bit of parsley and then sprinkling it over a platter of food, or using clumps of parsley as a garnish and then disposing of it after the meal, as though it were inedible. What a loss! Parsley, whether curly or flat-leaf, is high in both vitamins A and C and is also a natural diuretic. It's great in soups and holds up well when cooked in sauces—although adding a little chopped fresh parsley just before serving lends bright flavor and color. I love parsley as a tasty salad herb mixed with other greens or, as in the recipe below, served by itself.

> 2 large bunches curly parsley, washed and thoroughly dried, stems removed
> 1 rib celery, diced fine
> 2 extra-large hard-cooked egg whites, chopped, for garnish

**Salad Dressing:**

> ⅓ cup fat-free, low-calorie Italian dressing
> 1 to 2 tablespoons fresh lemon juice
> 1 large clove garlic, smashed, peeled, and minced
> Freshly ground pepper to taste

1. Chop 1 bunch of parsley and separate the other bunch into sprigs. Put all the parsley in a serving bowl.

2. Add the diced celery and toss. (The salad may be refrigerated at this point until serving time.)

3. Combine the salad dressing ingredients in a jar and shake to blend; taste and adjust seasonings with pepper.

4. Pour the dressing over the greens; toss to blend.

*To Serve:* Serve the salad on chilled plates. Sprinkle chopped egg whites over each serving.

Variation: Eight halved cherry tomatoes may be added with the celery, or 2 tablespoons of sliced sun-dried tomatoes may be marinated for 30 minutes in the salad dressing before serving.

| ──── PER SERVING ──── | | | |
|---|---|---|---|
| .3 gm total fat | .05 gm saturated fat | 1.9 gm fiber | 32 calories |
| 0 mg cholesterol | .4% fat | 250 mg sodium | 3 calories from fat |

## ❧ Farfel Salad ❧
### (PAREVE)

*Yield: 3 cups (½ cup = 1 serving)*

3 cups cooked no-yolk toasted farfel (see Note) or orzo
1 large shallot, peeled and chopped fine
¼ cup chopped fresh dill or basil
3 tablespoons chopped Italian flat-leaf parsley
1 tablespoon extra-virgin olive oil
1 tablespoon fresh lemon juice
¾ teaspoon kosher salt
  Freshly ground pepper to taste

1. Combine the cooked farfel or orzo in a mixing bowl with the shallot, dill, and parsley.
2. Add the oil, lemon juice, salt, and pepper and mix with a fork until combined.
3. Chill and serve cold or allow to stand at room temperature for several hours. Taste and adjust seasonings before serving.

Note: This is an Israeli product by Osem, available at many supermarkets or kosher food stores.

Variation: Blanched broccoli florets and diced red bell pepper may be added to the salad if desired.

| ──── PER SERVING ──── | | | |
|---|---|---|---|
| 3.6 gm total fat | .87 gm saturated fat | 1.4 gm fiber | 333 calories |
| 48 mg cholesterol | 10.9% fat | 316 mg sodium | 32.4 calories from fat |

## ❦ Hungarian Caraway Slaw ❦
### (PAREVE)
*Serves: 8 to 10*

1 large head (about 1½ pounds) red cabbage, shredded
1 small red bell pepper, seeded and diced
¼ cup caraway seeds
¼ cup distilled white vinegar
1 tablespoon sugar or 2 packets sweetener
1½ tablespoons canola oil

Combine all the ingredients in a large bowl; toss to blend. Chill in the refrigerator for several hours before serving.

--- PER SERVING ---

| | | | |
|---|---|---|---|
| 2.7 gm total fat | .19 gm saturated fat | 2.2 gm fiber | 58 calories |
| 0 mg cholesterol | 36.7% fat | 11 mg sodium | 24 calories from fat |

## ❦ Hungarian Wilted Lettuce ❦ and Tomato Salad
### (PAREVE)
*Serves: 6*

My mother served this unusual salad frequently. Hungarian wilted salad requires no oil, and the usual crispness of greens is replaced by soft, savory lettuce leaves.

½ cup distilled white vinegar
½ cup cold water
1 tablespoon minced white onion
2 to 3 teaspoons sugar, or to taste
Salt to taste
⅛ teaspoon ground white pepper
2 small heads iceberg or butter lettuce
2 Italian plum tomatoes, diced
Chopped chives, for garnish

1. Mix the vinegar, water, onion, sugar, salt, and pepper together and let stand at room temperature for 30 to 40 minutes. Taste and adjust seasonings.

2. Separate the heads of lettuce into leaves and place in a large serving bowl. Scatter diced tomatoes over the lettuce.

3. Sprinkle the dressing over the leaves and toss to coat them. Cover and allow to stand in the refrigerator 15 to 20 minutes before serving.

*To Serve:* Sprinkle the salad with chopped chives and freshly ground pepper.

| PER SERVING | | | |
|---|---|---|---|
| .4 gm total fat | .06 gm saturated fat | 1.8 gm fiber | 35 calories |
| 0 mg cholesterol | 8.7% fat | 40 mg sodium | 3 calories from fat |

# ❦ Apple Cabbage Salad ❦
## (DAIRY)
### *Serves: 6*

Cabbage, cooked and raw, has always been a staple vegetable in Eastern European countries. American Waldorf salad could have originated from this Hungarian classic.

1 small head (about 1 pound) savoy cabbage
3 tablespoons nonfat sour cream
1 teaspoon mustard
2 teaspoons sugar
⅛ teaspoon ground white pepper
3 red-skinned apples (Delicious, Cortland, or Spartan)
1½ tablespoons fresh lemon juice
4 fresh mint leaves, minced (optional)

1. Core and finely shred the cabbage.

2. Mix together the sour cream, mustard, sugar, and pepper.

3. Peel, core, and slice the apples thin. Sprinkle with lemon juice to prevent discoloration.

4. Combine the apples with the cabbage and salad dressing. Toss to coat thoroughly.

*To Serve:* Place in a salad bowl and sprinkle, if desired, with chopped fresh mint.

---
PER SERVING
---

| .3 gm total fat | .05 gm saturated fat | 2.8 gm fiber | 69 calories |
| 0 mg cholesterol | 4.0% fat | 36 mg sodium | 3 calories from fat |

## ❧ Hungarian Vegetable Salad ❧
### (PAREVE)
*Serves: 6*

A few years ago, at the celebrated Gundel Restaurant in Budapest, my husband and I were served a delicious salad. This is as close to duplicating its taste as I could come.

    1 head Boston lettuce
    4 cups sliced fresh mushrooms
    1 tablespoon canola oil
      Ground white pepper
  ¼ cup chopped Italian flat-leaf parsley
    1 cup tender green beans, cut up and steamed
   12 asparagus tips, steamed
    2 tomatoes, peeled and diced
 1½ cups diced roasted green bell pepper (page 246)
    1 cucumber, peeled, seeded, and sliced thin
    1 tablespoon sugar
  ¼ cup fresh lemon juice
      Salt and Hungarian paprika to taste

1. Chill all the vegetables.
2. Reserve 6 outer leaves from the lettuce; shred the remainder.
3. Sauté the mushrooms in a nonstick skillet in oil with ¼ teaspoon of pepper and the parsley. Stir over medium-high heat for about 3 minutes, or until lightly browned.
4. In a large bowl, combine the shredded lettuce with the green beans, asparagus, tomatoes, diced pepper, cucumber, and mushrooms. Season with the sugar, lemon juice, salt, paprika, and additional pepper.
5. Chill in the refrigerator for 1 hour before serving.

*To Serve:* Place the reserved lettuce leaves on chilled salad plates and mound with the marinated vegetable mixture. Serve as an appetizer or with a main course.

—————— PER SERVING ——————

| | | | |
|---|---|---|---|
| 2.8 gm total fat | .25 gm saturated fat | 2.5 gm fiber | 74 calories |
| 0 mg cholesterol | 30.5% fat | 37 mg sodium | 26 calories from fat |

# ❧ Syrian-Style Potato Salad ❧
## (PAREVE)
*Serves: 8*

6 medium potatoes (about 2 pounds), unpeeled
3 tablespoons canola oil or olive oil
   Juice of 1½ lemons
¾ teaspoon kosher salt
½ teaspoon ground allspice
3 tablespoons chopped Italian flat-leaf parsley
½ cup chopped scallions

1. Place the potatoes in a saucepan and cover with cold water. Bring to a boil and simmer until tender when pierced with a fork, about 30 minutes.
2. As soon as they are cool enough to handle, peel and cut into ¼-inch slices.
3. Place the potatoes in a shallow bowl and pour on the oil and lemon juice. Sprinkle with salt, allspice, parsley, and scallions. Toss gently. Serve at room temperature.

—————— PER SERVING ——————

| | | | |
|---|---|---|---|
| 5.2 gm total fat | .40 gm saturated fat | 1.8 gm fiber | 137 calories |
| 0 mg cholesterol | 5.2% fat | 227 mg sodium | 47 calories from fat |

# ❦ "Egg Salad" Spread ❦

## (PAREVE)
### *Serves: 4*

This is a wonderfully satisfying substitute for high-fat, high-cholesterol traditional egg salad. You may add sweet pickle relish, finely chopped scallions, celery, or parsley to make it taste like the one your Mama used to make.

    10½ ounces low-fat soft tofu, drained
      2 tablespoons reduced-fat cholesterol-free mayonnaise
1 to 1½ teaspoons Dijon mustard
      2 teaspoons apple cider vinegar or rice vinegar
     ¼ teaspoon ground turmeric
     ⅛ teaspoon ground white pepper

1. Press out excess water from the tofu with paper towels. Crumble the tofu into bowl.

2. Add the mayonnaise, mustard, vinegar, turmeric, and pepper and blend well with a fork.

3. Taste and adjust seasonings, adding whatever flavorings you desire.

*To Serve:* This may be served as an appetizer on lettuce with sliced tomatoes, as a main dish salad, as a sandwich in pita bread with shredded lettuce and chopped tomato, or as a sandwich spread on pumpernickel, rye bread, or toasted challah.

---

### PER SERVING

| | | | |
|---|---|---|---|
| 3.8 gm total fat | .52 gm saturated fat | .9 gm fiber | 69 calories |
| 0 mg cholesterol | 47.2% fat | 212 mg sodium | 34 calories from fat |

# ❦ Ranch-Style Dressing ❦
## (DAIRY)

*Yield: 1¼ cups (1 tablespoon = 1 serving)*

This is a pleasant change from vinaigrette. It's low in fat, and far superior to many "fat-free" supermarket dressings that have so much added sugar or corn syrup that the calorie count goes sky-high.

1 cup low-fat buttermilk, strained to remove fat globules
2 tablespoons cold water
2 tablespoons nonfat sour cream
1 tablespoon fresh lemon juice
1 tablespoon snipped fresh chives
1 teaspoon Dijon mustard
1 clove garlic, smashed, peeled, and minced, or ½ teaspoon garlic powder
  Dash of Tabasco and/or Worcestershire sauce
⅛ teaspoon ground white pepper, or to taste
2 teaspoons honey (optional)

Shake all the ingredients together in a jar until blended. Store in the refrigerator until serving time. This salad dressing will keep for 3 to 4 days.

VARIATIONS: You may add ½ cup grated peeled and seeded cucumber for a cucumber dressing. One to 2 tablespoons of low-sodium V-8 juice or 1 tablespoon of rinsed capers may be added for variety.

--- PER SERVING ---

| | | | |
|---|---|---|---|
| .1 gm total fat | .07 gm saturated fat | 0 gm fiber | 6 calories |
| 0 mg cholesterol | 17.4% fat | 21 mg sodium | 1 calorie from fat |

# 🌱 Low-Cal Tomato Dressing 🌱

## (PAREVE)

*Yield: 2¼ cups (1 tablespoon = 1 serving)*

12 ounces low-sodium V-8 juice
 3 tablespoons fresh lemon juice
 2 tablespoons red wine vinegar
 1 tablespoon finely chopped shallot
 1 tablespoon chopped Italian flat-leaf parsley
 1 large clove garlic, smashed, peeled, and minced
 ½ teaspoon frozen unsweetened apple juice concentrate
 ¼ teaspoon celery seed
 ½ teaspoon dried basil, crushed
   Freshly ground pepper to taste
 1 teaspoon arrowroot
   Few drops Tabasco sauce

1. Combine all the ingredients in a jar and shake to blend.
2. Place in a saucepan, bring to a boil, and simmer 3 minutes.
3. Cool and return to the jar, cover tightly, and store in the refrigerator. The dressing will keep up to 3 weeks.

---

### PER SERVING

| | | | |
|---|---|---|---|
| 0 gm total fat | 0 gm saturated fat | 0 gm fiber | 3 calories |
| 0 mg cholesterol | 4.1% fat | 2 mg sodium | 0 calories from fat |

## ❧ Lemony Tahini Dressing ❧
### (PAREVE)

*Yield: 1 cup (1 tablespoon = 1 serving)*

This is particularly tasty spooned over chopped vegetables or over flaked tuna in pita bread.

    3 tablespoons tahini (sesame paste)
    ¼ cup fresh lemon juice
      Freshly ground pepper to taste
    ⅓ cup cold water
    1 teaspoon Worcestershire sauce or ¼ teaspoon ground cumin
    3 tablespoons chopped Italian flat-leaf parsley or fresh dill

1. Using a blender, food processor, or small bowl and a whisk, mix together all the ingredients except the parsley until smooth and creamy.

2. Add the parsley or dill; taste and adjust seasonings. Store in the refrigerator in a covered container.

| PER SERVING | | | |
|---|---|---|---|
| 1.5 gm total fat | .20 gm saturated fat | .3 gm fiber | 18 calories |
| 0 mg cholesterol | 68.7% fat | 7 mg sodium | 14 calories from fat |

## ❧ Creamy Tofu Dressing ❧
### (PAREVE)

*Yield: About 1 cup (1 tablespoon = 1 serving)*

Tofu was first produced over 2,000 years ago. It is a "cheese" made from the milk of soy beans. There are 2 types of tofu: firm, which retains its shape and can be used cut up in cooking, and silken or soft tofu, which lends creamy texture to dips, dressings, soups, and sauces.

8 ounces low-fat soft tofu

2 tablespoons apple cider vinegar or rice vinegar

1 tablespoon fresh lemon juice

¼ teaspoon dry mustard

⅛ teaspoon ground white pepper

2 teaspoons Worcestershire sauce

2 tablespoons chopped Italian flat-leaf parsley

2 tablespoons canola oil

⅓ cup water

1 tablespoon toasted sesame seeds or tahini (optional)

1. Put the tofu in a blender or food processor and add the vinegar, lemon juice, mustard, pepper, Worcestershire, and parsley.

2. Purée until smooth. Add the oil and water gradually while the machine is in motion. Taste and adjust seasonings. Store in the refrigerator in a tightly covered container. Stir in the toasted sesame seeds before serving.

--- PER SERVING ---

| | | | |
|---|---|---|---|
| 1.5 gm total fat | .22 gm saturated fat | .2 gm fiber | 21 calories |
| 0 mg cholesterol | 62% fat | 7 mg sodium | 13 calories from fat |

## ❦ Russian Dressing ❦
### (DAIRY)
*Yield: 1 cup (1 tablespoon = 1 serving)*

¼ cup nonfat mayonnaise

½ cup nonfat plain yogurt

⅛ teaspoon garlic powder or onion powder

⅛ teaspoon ground white pepper

3 tablespoons sodium-reduced ketchup

2 tablespoons minced black olives or olive paste (tapenade)

2 tablespoons minced red bell pepper or pimiento

Blend all the ingredients except the olives and red pepper until smooth. Add the olives and red pepper, blend, and store in a covered container in the refrigerator until needed.

--- PER SERVING ---

| | | | |
|---|---|---|---|
| .1 gm total fat | .03 gm saturated fat | .1 gm fiber | 12 calories |
| 0 mg cholesterol | 10.5% fat | 63 mg sodium | 1 calorie from fat |

## ❦ Light Vinaigrette Dressing ❦
### (PAREVE)
*Yield: ⅔ cup (1 tablespoon = 1 serving)*

If you can find or happen to have Japanese rice vinegar on hand, it lends a special dimension to this salad dressing.

¼ cup rice vinegar or white wine vinegar
1 teaspoon sugar
2 tablespoons extra-virgin olive oil
2 tablespoons cold water
¼ teaspoon kosher salt
   Freshly ground pepper to taste
1 bunch scallions (white part only), sliced thin

Combine all the ingredients in a jar and shake well to blend before serving.

--- PER SERVING ---

| | | | |
|---|---|---|---|
| 1.4 gm total fat | .37 gm saturated fat | .3 gm fiber | 17 calories |
| 0 mg cholesterol | 76% fat | 61 mg sodium | 13 calories from fat |

# ❦ Connie Reif's Light Asian Dressing ❦
## (PAREVE)
### *Yield: 12 servings (1 tablespoon = 1 serving)*

Steamed snow peas with julienned carrots and cucumbers, seasoned with this dressing, make a perfect combination of flavors to precede a Chinese meal.

- 2 tablespoons cold water
- 2 tablespoons canola oil
- 1 tablespoon minced fresh garlic
- 2 tablespoons sodium-reduced soy sauce
- 3 tablespoons white wine vinegar
- 2 tablespoons dry sherry
- 1 tablespoon sugar
- Toasted sesame seeds (optional)

Combine all the ingredients in a jar and shake well to blend.

---

PER SERVING

| | | | |
|---|---|---|---|
| 2.3 gm total fat | .16 gm saturated fat | .1 gm fiber | 30 calories |
| 0 mg cholesterol | 72.9% fat | 81 mg sodium | 21 calories from fat |

# NOODLES AND GRAINS

*From Kasha to Kugels*

Brown and Wild Rice Pilaf     206
Bulgur and Beans     207
Kreplach     208
No-Cholesterol Pineapple Upside-Down Kugel     210
Pasta with Eggplant     211
Cabbage and Noodles (Kraut Pletzlach)     212
Spinach Noodle Casserole     213
Barley and Red Pepper Pilaf     214
Pasta and Beans     215
Kasha     217
Kasha Varnishkes     218
Sarah's Rice Kugel     218
Broccoli Noodle Kugel     219
Ruth Litt's Lokshen Kugel     220
Rice with Lentils and Currants     221
Phyllis's Special Kugel     222
Atlanta Pilaf with Pine Nuts, Pinto Beans, and Scallions     224
Connie Reif's Hot Cold Noodles     225
Vegetarian Fried Brown Rice     226
Mamaliga (Yellow Cornmeal Mush)     227
Blintz Sandwich     228

Pasta and grains are high in complex carbohydrates and fiber and naturally low in fat. Often, we add unnecessary fat in cooking them. With the help of modern food technology, which has given us more low-fat and no-fat, low-cholesterol and no-cholesterol products, combined with creative cooking, we can adjust recipes so that they are healthful but still have *tam* (good taste).

## BASIC DIRECTIONS FOR PREPARING GRAINS

Cereal grains comprise the principal source of food for most of the world's people. Grains are easily digested and rich in complex carbohydrates, B complex vitamins, and iron. They are low in fat and of course contain no cholesterol. Here is the basic recipe for cooking them:

1. Rinse the uncooked grain in cold water; drain.

2. Refer to the chart on the next page for the amount of cooking water needed. Bring the water to a boil in a saucepan over medium-high heat.

3. Add the grain and stir. Return to a boil, reduce the heat to low, cover, and cook according to the time on the chart.

4. Fluff with a fork and serve or use in your favorite recipe. (If the grain is not soft enough, add a small amount of hot water and cook a little longer. If the liquid remains

and the grain is tender, remove the lid, raise the heat, and continue cooking until the liquid evaporates.)

## COOKING TIMES AND MEASURES FOR GRAINS

| Grain | Number of Servings | Uncooked Amount | Amount of Water | Cooking Time | Cooked Amount |
|---|---|---|---|---|---|
| Barley | 4 | ½ cup (4 oz) | 3 cups | 50–60 min. | 2 cups |
| Buckwheat groats (kasha) | 4 | ⅔ cup (4 oz) | 1⅓ cups | 20 min. | 2 cups |
| Bulgur (cracked wheat) | 4 | ¾ cup (4 oz) | 1½ cups | 15–20 min. | 2 cups |
| Brown rice | 4 | ⅔ cup (4 oz) | 1⅔ cups | 40–50 min. | 2 cups |
| White rice | 4 | ⅔ cup (4 oz) | 1⅔ cups | 20 min. | 2 cups |
| Converted rice | 4 | ⅔ cup (4 oz) | 1⅔ cups | 20 min. | 2 cups |
| Quinoa | 5 | 1 cup (6 oz) | 2 cups | 10–15 min. | 2½ cups |

# ❧ Brown and Wild Rice Pilaf ❧
## (PAREVE)
### Serves: 5 to 6

  2 teaspoons extra-virgin olive oil
½ medium onion, peeled and chopped fine
  1 shallot, peeled and chopped fine
  1 cup packaged brown and wild rice mixture, washed
1½ cups sliced fresh mushrooms
2¼ cups boiling water, or defatted sodium-reduced vegetable or chicken broth
¼ cup chopped Italian flat-leaf parsley
  3 tablespoons toasted pine nuts (optional)

1. Heat the oil in a nonstick saucepan and sauté the onion and shallot for 3 to 5 minutes, until soft.

2. Add the rice and stir until coated and shiny.

3. Add the sliced mushrooms and sauté for 3 minutes.

4. Add the boiling water and bring to a boil. Reduce to a simmer, cover, and cook for 40 minutes.

5. Remove the cover. If there is still liquid that has not been absorbed, raise the heat and continue simmering with the lid off. When all the liquid has been absorbed, add the chopped parsley and pine nuts and fluff with a fork. Cover to keep warm or serve immediately.

PINEAPPLE VARIATION: Using 1 cup of wild rice, cook as above, omitting mushrooms, and add ½ cup dark raisins, plumped in warm pineapple juice, and ½ cup drained unsweetened crushed pineapple just before serving.

---

#### —— PER SERVING ——

| | | | |
|---|---|---|---|
| 2.5 gm total fat | .40 gm saturated fat | 1.7 gm fiber | 139 calories |
| 0 mg cholesterol | 16.1% fat | 5 mg sodium | 23 calories from fat |

---

# ❦ Bulgur and Beans ❦
## (PAREVE)
### Serves: 4

Whether served as an accompaniment to chicken or as the main course of a vegetarian meal, this easy Sephardic recipe provides flavor as well as soluble fiber from the beans and insoluble fiber from the bulgur wheat, both of which help lower cholesterol.

1 medium onion, peeled and chopped
2 teaspoons extra-virgin olive oil (see Note)
2 cups water
2 tablespoons tomato sauce
1 cup bulgur wheat
1 small can (1 cup) sodium-reduced garbanzo beans (chick-peas), rinsed and drained
2 tablespoons chopped Italian flat-leaf parsley (optional)

1. In a small saucepan, sauté the onion in the oil until transparent, about 5 minutes.
2. Add the water and tomato sauce. Bring to a boil.

3. Add the bulgur and beans and bring to a second boil. Reduce the heat, cover, and simmer for 20 minutes.

Note: Two tablespoons of sodium-reduced vegetable or chicken broth may be used instead of oil.

---

PER SERVING

| | | | |
|---|---|---|---|
| 3.8 gm total fat | .51 gm saturated fat | 8.6 gm fiber | 223 calories |
| 0 mg cholesterol | 14.8% fat | 56 mg sodium | 35 calories from fat |

---

# ❦ Kreplach ❦
## (MEAT)
### Yield: 24 kreplach (1 kreplach = 1 serving)

This is one of my husband's favorite traditional Jewish dishes. Kreplach work along the same lines as Chinese wonton. In this recipe, you can substitute wonton wrappers for the homemade dough.

### Filling:
    2 teaspoons canola oil
    ½ medium onion, chopped fine (about 1 cup)
    8 ounces ground raw turkey breast or 1 cup finely chopped leftover roast chicken or brisket, chopped fine
    1 tablespoon chopped Italian flat-leaf parsley
      Salt and freshly ground pepper to taste
    1 extra-large egg white or 3 tablespoons egg substitute

### Dough:
    1 cup unbleached all-purpose flour
    ⅛ teaspoon kosher salt
    1 extra-large egg, slightly beaten
    1 tablespoon water

1. Make the filling: Heat the oil in a nonstick skillet and sauté the onion over medium heat until golden brown, 5 to 7 minutes.

2. Add the turkey; stir to break up lumps and cook until no longer pink. Cool. Add the parsley, salt, and pepper; stir in the egg white. Set aside.

3. Make the dough: Place the flour in a food processor and add the salt. Add the egg and water and process until the dough forms a ball.

4. Turn out onto a lightly floured board and knead with the heel of your hand until the dough is smooth and elastic, adding flour as needed.

5. Make the kreplach: Divide the dough in half and roll out one half on a lightly floured surface until about 1/16 of an inch thick. Cover the other half and set aside.

6. Cut the dough into 2½-inch squares. Place 1 teaspoon of filling in the center of each square.

7. Moisten the edges of the dough with water; fold over to form a triangle and pinch the edges with fingers or fork tines. Repeat with the remaining dough and filling.

8. Bring a large pot of water to a boil. Drop in the kreplach, 8 at a time, and cook 15 to 20 minutes.

9. Remove with a slotted spoon, drain well, and allow to cool. Serve immediately, store in a covered container, or flash-freeze and place in a plastic bag.

*To Serve:* Warm in chicken soup for 20 minutes before serving.

VARIATION: Use ⅔ cup of Mashed Potatoes with Onions and Garlic (page 242) for the filling. Sauté the cooked dumplings in a nonstick skillet coated with butter-flavored cooking spray and serve hot with nonfat sour cream. This is called *vereniki*.

---

P E R   S E R V I N G

| | | | |
|---|---|---|---|
| .7 gm total fat | .12 gm saturated fat | .2 gm fiber | 34 calories |
| 14 mg cholesterol | 19.4% fat | 20 mg sodium | 6 calories from fat |

# ❦ No-Cholesterol Pineapple ❦ Upside-Down Kugel

## (PAREVE)

*Serves: 10*

12 ounces no-yolk wide noodles
¼ cup granulated sugar
4 extra-large egg whites, slightly beaten
¼ cup egg substitute
1½ teaspoons ground cinnamon
1 tablespoon light margarine
¼ cup packed brown sugar
1 (20-ounce) can pineapple slices in natural juice, drained (save ¼ cup of juice)
½ cup sugar-free frozen whole Bing cherries

1. Coat an 11 × 7-inch baking pan with vegetable oil cooking spray. Preheat the oven to 350°.

2. Cook the noodles according to the package directions and drain.

3. In a large bowl, mix the granulated sugar with the egg whites, egg substitute, and cinnamon; add the cooked noodles and blend.

4. Put the margarine in the prepared baking pan and place in the oven to melt. Add the brown sugar and ¼ cup pineapple juice; return to the oven until the sugar is melted and blended with the margarine.

5. Arrange the drained pineapple slices over the sugar mixture. Place cherries in the center of and between the slices. Carefully pour the noodle mixture over the pineapple.

6. Bake for about 45 minutes or until lightly browned on top.

*To Serve:* Loosen the kugel around the sides with a spatula or knife, place a platter on top, and invert.

| PER SERVING | | | |
|---|---|---|---|
| 1.4 gm total fat | .22 gm saturated fat | 1.3 gm fiber | 229 calories |
| 0 mg cholesterol | 5.3% fat | 49 mg sodium | 12 calories from fat |

# ❦ Pasta with Eggplant ❦

(PAREVE)

*Serves: 4 to 5*

Start your meal with a crisp, cold green salad and/or Carrot Soup (page 168). Serve this hearty pasta with slices of crunchy, warm baguette. If you like, pass some fragrant herbed olive oil for dipping the bread.

- 10 ounces bowtie pasta
- 1 tablespoon olive oil
- 2 medium-sized eggplants (about 1 pound each), peeled and diced
- 1 small onion, peeled and minced
- 4 large cloves garlic, smashed, peeled, and chopped fine
- 1 pound *ripe* plum tomatoes, peeled and diced
- 1 tablespoon finely chopped fresh oregano or 1 teaspoon dried oregano, crushed
- ¼ cup finely chopped Italian flat-leaf parsley or fresh basil
  Salt and freshly ground pepper to taste
  Grated Parmesan cheese alternative

1. Bring 2 quarts of water to a boil in a large saucepan. Add the pasta and cook about 12 minutes or according to package directions. Pasta should be al dente: tender but still firm.

2. Meanwhile, heat the oil in a large nonstick skillet over medium-high heat. Add the eggplant and stir with a wooden spoon until lightly browned. Remove the eggplant from the skillet.

3. Put the onion and garlic in the skillet and sauté 2 to 3 minutes. Add the tomatoes; sauté 1 minute. Return the eggplant with its juices to the skillet. Sprinkle with the oregano.

4. Remove and reserve ½ cup cooking liquid and drain the pasta. Do not rinse. Add the reserved liquid and pasta to the eggplant mixture, stir, and cook about 2 minutes over medium heat.

5. Add the parsley and mix well. Taste and adjust seasonings with salt and pepper. Serve immediately.

*To Serve:* Spoon hot pasta onto warmed plates or into soup bowls and pass grated Parmesan cheese alternative.

| PER SERVING | | | |
|---|---|---|---|
| 4.1 gm total fat | .58 gm saturated fat | 5.3 gm fiber | 304 calories |
| 0 mg cholesterol | 11.9% fat | 82 mg sodium | 37 calories from fat |

# ❦ Cabbage and Noodles (Kraut Pletzlach) ❦
## (PAREVE)

*Serves: 8 as a main course; 12 as an accompaniment*

My brother Irv would walk to the next county if he could be guaranteed a plate of *kraut pletzlach* at the end of his journey.

2 heads (4 pounds) green cabbage, cored and cut into 2-inch chunks
2 small brown-skinned onions, peeled and quartered
3 tablespoons olive oil or canola oil
1 teaspoon kosher salt (optional)
⅛ teaspoon ground white pepper
1 pound no-yolk noodles or 1 pound egg-free bowtie pasta
1 tablespoon caraway seeds (see Note) (optional)

1. Place the steel blade in a food processor. Add the cabbage and onions, working in batches if necessary. Process until chopped fine.

2. Coat a large nonstick skillet with olive oil cooking spray. Add the oil and cabbage mixture; season with salt and pepper. Stir to blend, cover, and sauté over medium heat for 3 to 5 minutes.

3. Remove the cover, lower the heat, and cook for about 45 minutes or until lightly browned. Be careful to stir from time to time in order to prevent the cabbage from sticking. The cabbage may be prepared ahead to this point, cooled, and frozen in an airtight plastic bag for future use.

4. Cook the pasta following package directions, drain, and add to the sautéed cabbage along with the caraway seeds. Stir to blend. Serve at once or refrigerate and reheat in the microwave the next day.

*To Serve:* Serve in a heated bowl as a main course or as an accompaniment to chicken, veal, brisket, or turkey.

NOTE: But that's not the way my mother used to serve it!

---
**——— PER SERVING AS MAIN COURSE ———**

| | | | |
|---|---|---|---|
| 6.4 gm total fat | .86 gm saturated fat | 7.3 gm fiber | 320 calories |
| 0 mg cholesterol | 17.7% fat | 46 mg sodium | 58 calories from fat |

---
**——— PER SERVING AS ACCOMPANIMENT ———**

| | | | |
|---|---|---|---|
| 4.3 gm total fat | .57 gm saturated fat | 4.9 gm fiber | 213 calories |
| 0 mg cholesterol | 17.7% fat | 30 mg sodium | 38 calories from fat |

---

# ❦ Spinach Noodle Casserole ❦
## (DAIRY)
### *Serves: 8*

This vegetarian casserole is a delicious accompaniment to Salmon Croquettes (page 104) or it can be served as part of a vegetarian dinner with grilled mixed vegetables.

¼ cup unbleached all-purpose flour
2 tablespoons nonfat dried milk powder
2 cups nonfat or skim milk
2 slices onion or 1 slice shallot
1 bay leaf
¼ teaspoon ground white pepper
¼ teaspoon freshly grated nutmeg
2 (10-ounce) packages frozen chopped spinach, thawed and squeezed dry
1 (10-ounce) package frozen mixed vegetables
¼ cup grated Parmesan cheese alternative
8 ounces no-yolk wide noodles
   Hungarian paprika (optional)

1. Mix the flour and powdered milk together in a large nonstick saucepan.

2. Gradually add the fresh milk while stirring with a wire whisk. Add the onion, bay leaf, pepper, and nutmeg.

3. Place over low heat and stir constantly until the mixture coats a whisk or wooden spoon. Remove from the heat and remove the onion and bay leaf.

4. Mix the drained spinach and frozen vegetables. Stir gently into the sauce. Add 3 tablespoons Parmesan cheese alternative.

5. Cook the noodles in boiling water until *barely tender*. Meanwhile, spray a 13 × 9 × 2-inch glass baking dish with vegetable oil cooking spray and preheat the oven to 350°.

6. Gently combine the noodles with the vegetable mixture in the saucepan. Transfer the mixture to the prepared baking dish.

7. Sprinkle with 1 tablespoon Parmesan cheese alternative and/or paprika. Bake uncovered for 35 to 40 minutes or until bubbly.

VARIATION: *For a Spinach Noodle Ring:* Add ½ cup egg substitute to the hot sauce made with spinach only. Cook 1 additional minute. Add the cheese and gently mix with the noodles. Turn into a 9-inch ring mold coated with butter-flavored cooking spray. Set the mold in a pan of hot water and bake uncovered at 350° for 45 to 50 minutes, or until a knife inserted comes out clean. Let cool a few minutes. Loosen the edge with a knife and unmold on a warm platter. Fill the center with the cooked mixed vegetables or a vegetable of your choice.

—————— PER SERVING ——————

| | | | |
|---|---|---|---|
| 1.0 gm total fat | .25 gm saturated fat | 4.5 gm fiber | 192 calories |
| 2 mg cholesterol | 4.9% fat | 113 mg sodium | 9 calories from fat |

# ❦ Barley and Red Pepper Pilaf ❦
## (PAREVE OR MEAT)
### *Serves: 8*

In European countries, barley is eaten much more frequently than here in the United States. It lends itself to many preparations, and is high in soluble fiber. We mostly think of it in association with mushroom-barley soup, but here is a savory and colorful change.

2 pounds red bell peppers, seeded, and cut into eighths
4 teaspoons olive oil
1 cup barley, washed and drained
2 cups sliced fresh mushrooms
3 large cloves garlic, smashed, peeled, and minced
⅛ teaspoon ground white pepper
4 cups defatted sodium-reduced vegetable or chicken broth

1. Place the peppers in a medium casserole.
2. Coat with 2 teaspoons of the oil and roast in a 400° oven for 20 minutes.
3. In a small skillet, sauté the barley and mushrooms in the remaining oil for about 3 minutes. Add the garlic and pepper and sauté 2 minutes more.
4. Add to the peppers and stir. Heat the broth and stir into the peppers.
5. Bake covered at 350° for 1 hour, or until the liquid is absorbed. *Do not stir while cooking.*

*To Serve:* I particularly like this pilaf served with roast chicken or as part of a vegetable plate.

| PER SERVING | | | |
|---|---|---|---|
| 3.3 gm total fat | .50 gm saturated fat | 5.8 gm fiber | 142 calories |
| 0 mg cholesterol | 20.6% fat | 9 mg sodium | 29 calories from fat |

# ❧ Pasta and Beans ❧
## (PAREVE)
### Serves: 6

Although not a traditional Jewish dish, this updated vegetarian entrée combines the best of all worlds: complex carbohydrates from pasta, soluble fiber from beans, and an addictive taste from the combination of herbs and seasonings.

8 ounces small pasta shells
1 large shallot, peeled and minced, or ¼ cup minced onion
3 large cloves garlic, smashed, peeled, and minced
2 teaspoons olive oil
¼ cup dry white wine or vermouth
4 ripe plum tomatoes, seeded and diced
4 kalamata olives, sliced (optional)
1 (15½-ounce) can sodium-reduced cannellini or white kidney beans, rinsed and drained
⅛ teaspoon ground white pepper
1 tablespoon grated Parmesan cheese alternative (optional)
½ cup chopped fresh basil leaves, for garnish

1. Cook the shells according to package directions. Drain and reserve ⅔ cup of the cooking liquid.

2. Add the shallot and garlic to the oil in a medium saucepan and sauté 1 minute. Add the wine, stir, and simmer 3 minutes.

3. Add the tomatoes, olives, and reserved cooking liquid; sauté 2 minutes.

4. Add the drained beans and hot drained pasta to the tomato mixture. Mix gently to combine. If the mixture seems dry, add some vegetable broth, or hot water mixed with tomato paste.

5. Taste and adjust seasoning with pepper.

*To Serve:* Place in a warm bowl, sprinkle with Parmesan cheese alternative, if desired, and top with chopped basil leaves. Accompany with a crisp Chopped Salad (page 185) and a hot crunchy sourdough baguette. A sorbet garnished with sliced strawberries and perhaps some fresh strawberry sauce makes a light but happy ending.

VARIATION: If you are lucky enough to have some left over, it may be served cold as a salad. Enhance it with any leftover cooked vegetables you may have.

| PER SERVING | | | |
|---|---|---|---|
| 2.8 gm total fat | .51 gm saturated fat | 3.4 gm fiber | 242 calories |
| 1 mg cholesterol | 2.8% fat | 25 mg sodium | 25 calories from fat |

## ❦ Kasha ❦

(PAREVE OR MEAT)

*Serves: 6*

Kasha is made from buckwheat, an oft-neglected whole grain. It's easy and quick to prepare, and its nutty flavor combines well with pastas.

1 extra-large egg white
1 cup buckwheat groats
2 cups boiling water, or reduced-sodium vegetable or chicken broth
¼ teaspoon ground white pepper

1. Beat egg white in bowl with a fork; add kasha, stir to coat kernels.
2. Add to 8- to 10-inch nonstick skillet; cook over high heat 3 minutes or until egg has dried on kasha and kernels separate.
3. Reduce heat to low and add boiling liquid. Cover and simmer 5 minutes or until liquid is absorbed and kernels are tender. Taste and adjust seasoning with pepper.

*To Serve:* Kasha may be served hot as is; with sautéed onions, diced peppers, and mushrooms; or as kasha varnishkes (recipe below).

| PER SERVING | | | |
|---|---|---|---|
| .7 gm total fat | .16 gm saturated fat | 4.5 gm fiber | 98 calories |
| 0 mg cholesterol | 6.4% fat | 12 mg sodium | 7 calories from fat |

## ❦ Kasha Varnishkes ❦

(PAREVE OR MEAT)

*Serves: 10*

1 cup chopped onion
1 tablespoon olive oil
1 cup sliced fresh mushrooms
  Kasha (recipe above)
6 ounces egg-free bowtie or no-yolk square pasta, cooked according to package directions
¼ cup defatted sodium-reduced chicken broth or leftover gravy, optional
  Salt and freshly ground pepper to taste
  Hungarian paprika, for garnish

1. Sauté the onion in the olive oil until golden.

2. Add the mushrooms; sauté several minutes.

3. Add the kasha and the cooked bowties to the onion mixture. One-quarter cup chicken broth or leftover brisket gravy may be added to moisten. Taste and adjust seasoning with salt and pepper.

4. Spoon into a casserole, sprinkle with paprika, and place under the broiler to brown.

---

PER SERVING

| | | | |
|---|---|---|---|
| 2.7 gm total fat | .40 gm saturated fat | 5.3 gm fiber | 177 calories |
| 0 mg cholesterol | 14% fat | 48 mg sodium | 14 calories from fat |

---

## ❧ Sarah's Rice Kugel ❧
### (PAREVE)
*Serves: 8 (1 square = 1 serving)*

This versatile kugel recipe may be served with roast chicken, as part of a vegetarian meal, or for dessert.

1 cup uncooked converted white rice
2 cups boiling water
1 tablespoon canola oil
⅓ cup confectioners' or granulated sugar
½ cup egg substitute
2 extra-large egg whites
1 teaspoon ground cinnamon
2 teaspoons grated lemon zest
½ cup dark raisins

*Topping:*

   1 tablespoon granulated sugar mixed with ¼ cup chopped walnuts
      and ½ teaspoon cinnamon (optional)

   1. Add the rice to the boiling water, cover, and simmer 20 minutes or until the rice is tender and water is absorbed. Remove from the heat.
   2. Coat an 8-inch square glass baking dish with vegetable oil cooking spray. Preheat the oven to 350°.
   3. Combine the oil, sugar, egg substitute, egg whites, cinnamon, and lemon zest. Beat thoroughly.
   4. Add the rice and mix well. Stir in the raisins.
   5. Pour into the prepared baking dish and sprinkle with topping if desired.
   6. Bake uncovered for 45 to 50 minutes or until lightly browned. Cut into squares and serve hot.

---

——————— P E R   S E R V I N G ———————

| | | | |
|---|---|---|---|
| 4.1 gm total fat | .40 gm saturated fat | 1.0 gm fiber | 180 calories |
| 0 mg cholesterol | 20.4% fat | 81 mg sodium | 37 calories from fat |

# ❦ Broccoli Noodle Kugel ❦
## (DAIRY)
### *Serves: 12 to 14*

This recipe is from my friend Bootsie Segal of Atlanta, Georgia. It's great for entertaining because of its ease of preparation. Plus, it can be prepared ahead of time, kept in the refrigerator, and then baked just before serving.

   16 ounces no-yolk fine noodles, cooked according to package directions and
      drained
    2 packages onion soup mix
    2 tablespoons canola oil
    2 cups nonfat evaporated milk
    2 (10-ounce) packages chopped broccoli, thawed and patted dry
    5 extra-large egg whites or 1 cup egg substitute plus 1 extra-large egg white
    2 tablespoons soy-based Parmesan cheese alternative (optional)

1. Preheat the oven to 350°. Coat a 3-quart casserole with vegetable oil cooking spray.

2. Combine the cooked and drained noodles in their saucepan with the soup mix, oil, evaporated milk, broccoli, and egg mixture. Sprinkle with Parmesan if desired.

3. Pour into the prepared casserole and bake for 50 to 60 minutes.

―――――――――――――― PER SERVING ――――――――――――――

| 3.0 gm total fat | .27 gm saturated fat | 2.0 gm fiber | 198 calories |
| 2 mg cholesterol | 13.4% fat | 559 mg sodium | 27 calories from fat |

## ❦ Ruth Litt's Lokshen Kugel ❦
### (DAIRY)
*Yield: 12 servings (1 square = 1 serving)*

When Sholem Aleichem wrote, "You should taste her noodle pudding. Then you would know what heaven on earth would be," he could have been talking about my sister Ruth's kugel. Every Jewish cook has her favorite recipe for kugel. Unfortunately, most call for egg noodles, and are loaded with sour cream, whole eggs, and lots of butter or margarine. With my sister's permission, I have adjusted this recipe so that you can enjoy it often.

12 ounces no-yolk wide noodles
 2 cups (16 ounces) nonfat cottage cheese
 2 cups (16 ounces) nonfat sour cream, plus additional for garnish (optional)
½ cup sugar or frozen unsweetened apple juice concentrate
 3 extra-large egg whites, slightly beaten
½ cup egg substitute
 1 tablespoon pure vanilla extract
 1 (28-ounce) can crushed pineapple in natural juice
 2 teaspoons ground cinnamon
 2 tablespoons melted light margarine (optional)

1. Coat a 13 × 9 × 2-inch glass baking dish with butter-flavored cooking spray. Preheat the oven to 350°.

2. Bring 5 quarts water to a boil in a large saucepan. Add the noodles gradually, return to a boil, reduce the heat, and simmer 10 minutes.

3. Meanwhile, in a food processor or blender, combine the cottage cheese, sour cream, sugar, egg whites, egg substitute, and vanilla. Process until smooth. (If no blender or food processor is convenient, just whisk all the ingredients together.)

4. Drain the noodles, return to the pot, and add the cheese mixture and crushed pineapple with juice. Blend with a slotted spoon.

5. Pour the noodle mixture into the prepared baking dish and sprinkle with cinnamon and then with melted margarine if desired.

6. Bake in the upper third of the oven for about 1 hour or until lightly browned.

*To Serve:* Cut the pudding into 12 squares and serve with dollops of nonfat sour cream as a topping if desired.

VARIATION: Mix 1 cup fresh or frozen unsweetened blueberries with 1 cup blueberry pie filling. Spoon on top of the kugel for the last 10 minutes of cooking time.

—————— P E R  S E R V I N G ——————

| | | | |
|---|---|---|---|
| .8 gm total fat | .14 gm saturated fat | 1.3 gm fiber | 238 calories |
| 2 mg cholesterol | 3.2% fat | 194 mg sodium | 8 calories from fat |

# ❦ Rice with Lentils and Currants ❦
## (PAREVE OR MEAT)
### *Serves: 8*

Lentils are a staple in cooking from India westward through Europe. They are high in incomplete protein (which becomes complete when combined with rice) and are a favorite in vegetarian cooking.

2 teaspoons olive oil
½ small onion, peeled and chopped fine
1 teaspoon minced garlic
1 cup uncooked converted white rice
1 cup dried currants or raisins
½ cup red or orange lentils, washed (parboiled if using green or brown)
2¼ cups water, or defatted sodium-reduced vegetable or chicken broth
¼ teaspoon ground white pepper

1. Heat the oil in a medium saucepan. Add the onion and garlic and cook over medium heat, stirring, until wilted, 3 to 4 minutes.

2. Add the rice, currants, and lentils; stir.

3. Add the water and pepper, bring to a boil, and stir.

4. Reduce the heat, cover, and simmer for 20 to 25 minutes. When the rice is done, the liquid will be absorbed.

5. Fluff the rice with a fork before serving.

NOTE: Lentils and other dried legumes or beans are often old when you buy them, and sometimes require additional cooking time. You can parboil them (1 cup lentils to 4 cups water) by covering with double plastic wrap and cooking on High in the microwave for about 15 minutes. Red, yellow, and orange lentils require less cooking time than brown or green.

---

**———— PER SERVING ————**

| | | | |
|---|---|---|---|
| 1.5 gm total fat | .22 gm saturated fat | 2.0 gm fiber | 188 calories |
| 0 mg cholesterol | 6.8% fat | 4 mg sodium | 13 calories from fat |

---

# ❧ Phyllis's Special Kugel ❧
## (DAIRY)
### Serves: 12

Whether you call it noodle kugel, kigel, or pudding, this is a great buffet dish. The original recipe called for ½ pound of butter and 6 whole eggs. I've modified its fat and cholesterol content by using canola oil, egg substitute, and egg whites.

16 ounces no-yolk medium-width noodles
⅔ cup egg substitute
6 extra-large egg whites
2 cups (16 ounces) nonfat cottage cheese
2 cups (16 ounces) nonfat sour cream
¾ cup sugar
1 teaspoon ground cinnamon
1 tablespoon canola oil
1 (16-ounce) jar sugar-free apricot or peach preserves

⅓ **cup cornflakes**

**2 tablespoons sugar mixed with 1 teaspoon cinnamon (optional)**

1. Preheat the oven to 350°. Coat a 3-quart oval or rectangular casserole with butter-flavored cooking spray.

2. Cook the noodles in a large kettle of boiling water for *half* the time called for in the package directions.

3. Beat the egg substitute and egg whites with a whisk or in a food processor; add the cottage cheese, sour cream, sugar, and cinnamon. Beat until smooth.

4. Drain the noodles. Return to the saucepan, add the oil and preserves, and stir over medium heat until the preserves are melted.

5. Add the sweetened noodles to the egg and cottage cheese mixture.

6. Pour the kugel into the prepared casserole.

7. Crumble the cornflakes on top of the noodles and sprinkle the mixture with cinnamon-sugar topping if desired.

8. Bake uncovered for 1 hour or until the top is very crisp.

*Serving Suggestion:* Use as a side dish with fish or as a very yummy dessert.

| PER SERVING | | | |
|---|---|---|---|
| 2.3 gm total fat | .34 gm saturated fat | 1.0 gm fiber | 361 calories |
| 2 mg cholesterol | 8.3% fat | 273 mg sodium | 21 calories from fat |

# ❧ Atlanta Pilaf with Pine Nuts, ❧ Pinto Beans, and Scallions
### (MEAT OR PAREVE)
*Serves: 8*

This pilaf is delicious as part of a vegetarian meal or as a nutritious accompaniment to broiled chicken.

    2  teaspoons canola oil
 1½  cups uncooked converted rice
    3  cups defatted sodium-reduced chicken broth or Vegetable Broth (page 141)
    1  (16-ounce) can sodium-reduced pinto beans, rinsed and drained
    1  cup chopped scallions
  ½  cup pine nuts, lightly toasted
      Salt and freshly ground pepper to taste

1. In a heavy saucepan, heat the oil over moderately low heat. Add the rice and stir for about 1 minute, or until the rice is opaque.

2. Add the chicken broth, bring to a boil, and lower the heat. Cover and simmer for 18 minutes or until the liquid is absorbed.

3. Add the beans and scallions; fluff the rice with a fork.

4. Let the pilaf stand, covered, off the heat for 5 minutes. Stir in the pine nuts; taste and adjust seasonings with salt and pepper.

---

###### PER SERVING

| | | | |
|---|---|---|---|
| 10.2 gm total fat | 1.51 gm saturated fat | 3.9 gm fiber | 308 calories |
| 0 mg cholesterol | 29.0% fat | 17 mg sodium | 92 calories from fat |

# ❦ Connie Reif's Hot Cold Noodles ❦

## (PAREVE)

### *Serves: 8 to 10*

If you make these noodles a day in advance, remember to toss frequently while they marinate in the refrigerator, and bring to room temperature before serving.

1 pound spaghettini
1 bunch scallions, trimmed and sliced thin
½ cup chopped fresh cilantro (optional)
1 cup fresh bean sprouts (optional)
Fresh-cut scallion rings and chopped cilantro or cilantro sprigs, for garnish

*Sauce Ingredients:*

1 tablespoon Chinese or Japanese toasted sesame oil
3 tablespoons sodium-reduced soy sauce
1 tablespoon grated fresh ginger root
1½ tablespoons rice vinegar or balsamic vinegar
2 tablespoons sugar
3 to 4 teaspoons hot chili oil or less, to taste
1 large clove garlic, smashed, peeled, and minced (optional)

1. Cook the pasta as directed on the package, until tender but still firm. Drain and rinse under cold water. Transfer the well-drained pasta to a bowl.

2. Combine all the sauce ingredients in a jar. Shake to blend.

3. Pour the sauce evenly over the pasta, using some of the pasta to wipe the bowl or jar clean of sugar, which very frequently settles at the bottom. Add the scallions, cilantro, and bean sprouts.

4. Serve at once, or cover the bowl and store overnight in the refrigerator. Serve at room temperature or just slightly chilled.

*To Serve:* Garnish with sliced scallions and sprigs of cilantro. This is a lovely buffet dish that presents well with steamed fish or barbecued salmon.

NOTE: The noodles should have a sweet and hot flavor. Chili heat becomes more intense as it stands, so if you prefer it not too spicy, add half the oil to start—you can always add more.

VARIATION: Add ½ pound shredded roast chicken and 2 cups blanched snow peas to the pasta after adding the sauce ingredients; toss, chill, and serve as an entrée.

---

PER SERVING

| | | | |
|---|---|---|---|
| 3.9 gm total fat | .62 gm saturated fat | 1.4 gm fiber | 213 calories |
| 0 mg cholesterol | 16.7% fat | 150 mg sodium | 35 calories from fat |

# ❦ Vegetarian Fried Brown Rice ❦
## (PAREVE)
### Serves: 6 to 8

When I was interviewed on *Good Morning, Hong Kong*, I asked what they do with all the rice bran, since I saw only white rice being served. "Oh, we feed it to the pigs," my host replied. Well, I prefer serving the brown rice, with all its fiber and minerals, to my family. Fried rice is a great way to use up leftovers, and because of the ease of preparation, it lends itself to last-minute cooking.

4 dried Chinese or shiitake mushrooms, covered with boiling water for 15 minutes
1 tablespoon canola oil
6 stalks bok choy, cut into ¼-inch diagonal slices, or 2 cups fresh bean sprouts
1 large carrot, peeled and sliced very thin
¼ cup sliced water chestnuts
6 cups cooked brown rice (page 206)
1 cup salt-free frozen peas, thawed, or fresh snow peas, cut in half lengthwise
1 tablespoon hoisin sauce
2 tablespoons sodium-reduced soy sauce
4 extra-large egg whites, slightly beaten
4 whole scallions, sliced thin, for garnish

1. Discard the stems from the drained mushrooms and slice the mushrooms thin.
2. Coat a wok or nonstick skillet with vegetable oil cooking spray. Add the 1 tablespoon of oil and heat.

3. Add the bok choy and carrot. Stir constantly for 1 minute. Add the mushrooms and water chestnuts and stir for ½ minute.
4. Add the rice and peas and stir-fry until hot.
5. Blend the hoisin and soy sauces and add to the hot rice.
6. Pour the egg whites on top of the rice and stir thoroughly to cook the whites.

*To Serve:* Heap in a warmed bowl or platter; garnish with sliced scallions.

VARIATION: Two cups shredded leftover roast or soup chicken may be added with or instead of the egg whites.

---

PER SERVING

| | | | |
|---|---|---|---|
| 3.2 gm total fat | .41 gm saturated fat | 4.2 gm fiber | 225 calories |
| 0 mg cholesterol | 12.7% fat | 229 mg sodium | 29 calories from fat |

---

# ꬱ Mamaliga (Yellow Cornmeal Mush) ꬱ
## (PAREVE)
*Serves: 6 to 7 (2 slices = 1 serving)*

Cooked cornmeal can be a different and a delicious hot cereal. This favorite Rumanian dish may be served plain with milk or with cottage cheese and applesauce.

½ teaspoon kosher salt
2½ cups boiling water
½ cup yellow cornmeal
½ cup cold water
   Flour or additional cornmeal for coating
1 tablespoon vegetable oil

1. Add the salt to boiling water in a small saucepan.
2. Mix the cornmeal with the cold water; slowly add to the boiling water.
3. Cook, stirring constantly, until thick, about 5 minutes.

4. Cover and cook ½ hour longer, stirring occasionally. Serve, or:

5. Turn the cooked cornmeal mush into a mold, such as a 7-inch loaf pan, coated with butter-flavored cooking spray. Cover with plastic wrap and chill overnight.

6. Turn out of the mold. Cut into ½-inch slices and dip in flour or cornmeal. Heat a nonstick skillet coated with cooking spray; add the oil. When the oil is hot, add the floured mush; sauté and lower to medium heat if you desire crisp, dry slices.

7. Brown on both sides; remove to ovenproof plate and keep warm in a 200° oven. Serve hot with cold maple syrup, nonfat sour cream, or sugar-free preserves.

---

PER SERVING

| | | | |
|---|---|---|---|
| .2 gm total fat | .02 gm saturated fat | .5 gm fiber | 36 calories |
| 0 mg cholesterol | 4.1% fat | 168 mg sodium | 1 calorie from fat |

---

# ❦ Blintz Sandwich ❦
## (DAIRY)
### Serves: 6

Great for breakfast, lunch, or dinner!

**12 slices challah or whole wheat bread**

*Filling:*
   1½ cups nonfat small-curd cottage cheese
   2 tablespoons nonfat whipped cream cheese
   1 tablespoon sugar or sugar-free apricot preserves

*Batter:*
   ½ cup egg substitute beaten with 1 extra-large egg white, or 6 extra-large egg whites
   ⅔ cup nonfat evaporated milk
   1 tablespoon frozen unsweetened apple juice concentrate
   1 teaspoon pure vanilla extract
   ½ teaspoon ground cinnamon (optional)

**Confectioners' sugar or nonfat sour cream or nonfat plain yogurt, for garnish**

1. Blend the filling ingredients.

2. Spread about ¼ cup filling on each of 6 slices of bread and top with the remaining slices.

3. Combine the batter ingredients in a shallow dish.

4. Dip the sandwiches into the batter on both sides.

5. Brown on both sides in a nonstick griddle coated with butter-flavored cooking spray.

6. Cut the sandwiches in half diagonally. If desired, sprinkle lightly with confectioners' sugar or a dollop of nonfat sour cream or yogurt.

VARIATION: Bake the batter-coated sandwiches in a preheated waffle iron coated with butter-flavored non-stick spray. The resulting product looks pretty and has a crunch to it.

---

 PER SERVING 

| | | | |
|---|---|---|---|
| 1.9 gm total fat | .36 gm saturated fat | 1.8 gm fiber | 206 calories |
| 6 mg cholesterol | 8% fat | 563 mg sodium | 17 calories from fat |

---

 ❦ HARRIET'S HINTS ❦ 

*Fresh berries make a delicious topping for blintzes, French toast, or pancakes instead of syrup or butter. Place berries in a saucepan, mash slightly, and add a bit of frozen unsweetened apple juice concentrate. Heat and stir until the juice is absorbed.*

# VEGETABLES

## From Beans to Greens

The Talmud suggests that "One should not live in a city that does not have a vegetable garden." The Jewish diet in past centuries was primarily vegetarian, with meat eaten only on Sabbath, holidays, and festive occasions. You'll see the richness of the Jewish vegetarian tradition on the following pages.

Jellied Beet Borscht Salad    236
Mrs. Rubenstein's Kosher Dill Pickles    237
Eggplant Parmesan    238
Marinated Vegetables    239
Ellen Batzdorf's Red Cabbage    240
Mashed Potatoes with Onions and Garlic    242
Schliskas (Potato Dumplings) from Aunt Ella Markell    243
Stuffed Peppers    245
Roasted Peppers    246
Carrot Ring    247
Vegetarian Stuffed Cabbage    248
Mushroom-Stuffed Tomatoes    250
A Little Tomato Sauce    251
A Lot of Tomato Sauce    252
Rosy Baked Onions with Raisins    253
Onion Helper    254
Onion-flavored Olive Oil    255
Potato Kugel    256
Vegetarian Stew    258
Sephardic Leeks and Beans    259
Tzimmes    260
Okra (Bamieh)    261
Creole Corn and Okra Casserole    262
Vegetarian Chili    263
Ratatouille    264
Corn Pudding    265
Dorothy Essick's Sweet and Sour Beets    266
Mustard Cabbage    267
Cousin Pearly from Pittsburgh's Lima Beans for a Crowd    268
Gisele Pollak's Hungarian Lecsó    269
Broccoli Kugel    270
Sweet Potato Ring    271
Carrot and Prune Tzimmes    272
My Mother's Sweet and Sour Green Beans    272
Chick-Peas (Nahit)    274
Prune and Rice Tzimmes    275
Chinese Cabbage with Mushrooms    276
Vegetarian Sandwich    276
Nita Williams' Stuffed Zucchini    277

In 1926, Mr. and Mrs. A. B. Mishulow coauthored *Vegetarian Cookbook for Rational Eating,* published by the "Better Health and Correct Eating Institute" in New York City. Published in Yiddish, it was described as "a book of knowledge for the right preparation and combination of natural vegetarian health foods, according to the latest scientific methods." This book belonged to my mother-in-law, Mollie Hollander Roth, and was recently resurrected by her daughter, Helen Kolatch. We have come full circle, with Nathan Pritikin's philosophy of more healthful eating and lifestyle, closely followed by Dr. Dean Ornish, who advocates a diet free of all animal protein and low in fat.

Mishulow writes, "Too much meat disturbs your health and causes sickness. Honest doctors recognize vegetarian food as being the most important cure for poor health." In reviewing the recipes, I found that they were full of eggs, butter, and cream. However, the importance of whole grains, fruits, and vegetables is very evident throughout the book. I've come to the conclusion that over the years, the more we change the more we are the same.

In traditional Jewish cooking, vegetables are thoroughly cooked, not simply boiled or steamed. Hungarians frequently stew their vegetables, usually with a sweet and sour sauce, and Sephardic cooks use complex combinations of spices and seasonings.

Vegetables are generally low in calories because of their high water and fiber content (we used to call it roughage) and low sugar content. They are a good source of energy-giving carbohydrates (as in potatoes, corn, peas, and lima beans) and provide a generous variety of nutrients. Dried peas, beans, and lentils are important sources of protein and soluble fiber that helps to lower cholesterol. Vegetables are rich in vitamin A and beta-carotene, especially carrots, sweet potatoes, red peppers, yellow squash, and green leafy vegetables. Vitamin C is found in potatoes, broccoli, cabbage, spinach, kale, and green peppers. In fact, the only vitamin not found in vegetables is $B_{12}$.

Most importantly, we should take note of the findings of scientists over the past twenty years. They have constantly pointed to evidence that people who eat greater amounts of vegetables and fruits have lower rates of most cancers. Cruciferous vegetables are particularly important in reducing the risk of colon cancer. They include all cabbages, brussels sprouts, radishes, horseradish, rutabaga, turnips, broccoli, cauliflower, and bok choy.

The current recommended daily allowance suggests that we consume a *minimum* of five servings of vegetables per day (1 cup raw, ½ cup cooked, and ¾ cup juice each equals 1 serving).

One of the main challenges in vegetable cookery is avoiding the repetition that comes from buying and preparing the same vegetables day after day. Try buying fresh vegetables in season; they are less expensive and certainly more flavorful at the height of their season. Fresh is best, but with present-day processing techniques frozen vegetables are often just as nourishing as the vegetables that are sold as fresh in the markets. There is little difference in food value between frozen and canned—except, of course, for the higher sodium content from added salt and often from preservatives, including sugar, in canned foods.

### A Few Guidelines for Optimum Nutrition from Vegetables:

• Don't cook it if you can eat it raw.

• Don't peel it if the skin can be thoroughly scrubbed and washed or is *not* waxed (cucumber, eggplant, and apples are frequently waxed).

• Steam, microwave, pressure cook, or use as little water as possible in cooking.

• Above all, choose the freshest vegetables you can find and avoid imported produce if possible. (If possible, find a local farmers market or food co-op where you can buy seasonal and organic fruits and vegetables.)

# Basic Directions for Preparing
# Dried Peas, Beans, and Lentils

Rich in protein, iron, complex carbohydrates, and other nutrients, dried beans were one of the earliest foods to be cultivated. You can cut way down on the preparation time if you use a microwave oven.

## In the Microwave:

### To Soak:

1. Place 1 to 2 cups washed and sorted beans in a 2-quart microwave-safe casserole with 3 cups water. (Small lima beans, lentils, and split peas do not require soaking before cooking.)
2. Cover with microwave plastic wrap and cook on High for 15 minutes. Remove from oven.
3. Let stand 5 minutes, uncover, and add 2 cups *hot* water.
4. Re-cover and let stand 1 hour. Drain.

### To Cook:

1. Place 1 cup presoaked beans in a microwave-safe casserole.
2. Add 4 cups water, cover with 2 sheets of microwave plastic wrap, and microwave on High for about 35 minutes.
3. Let stand 20 minutes before using.

NOTE: Navy beans and white beans require 40 minutes of cooking time and 30 minutes of standing time.

## On the Stove:

### To Soak:

1. Sort the beans, removing any broken beans and bits of stone. Rinse the beans thoroughly in cold water and drain. (Small lima beans, lentils, and split peas do not require soaking before cooking.)
2. Bring about 2½ quarts water to a boil in a large casserole or saucepan, add the beans, and bring to a boil. Boil 2 minutes, remove from the heat, cover, and let stand 1 hour.

3. Pour off the soaking water, rinse, and drain. (Flatulence is less of a problem if the soaking water is not used to cook the beans.)

## TO COOK:

1. Return the beans to the soaking pan and cover with water 2 to 3 times their volume.

2. Bring to a boil, reduce the heat to a slow simmer, and cook until just tender, referring to the chart below for cooking time.

NOTE: To freeze, cool, drain, and freeze in airtight plastic bags.

| COOKING TIMES FOR DRIED PEAS, BEANS, AND LENTILS* | |
| --- | --- |
| 1 Lb. Dried Beans | Cooking Time after Soaking |
| Soybeans | 3 to 3½ hours |
| Chick-peas (garbanzo beans) | 2 to 3 hours |
| Black beans or turtle beans | 1½ to 2 hours |
| Kidney or pinto beans | 1½ to 2 hours |
| Black-eyed peas | 1½ hours |
| Great Northern beans or navy beans | 1½ hours |
| Fordhook lima beans | 50 minutes to 1½ hours |
| Baby lima beans (do not soak) | 45 minutes to 1½ hours |
| Split peas or lentils (do not soak) | 45 minutes |

*1 cup uncooked dried beans, or 6 to 8 ounces (depending on the size) = about 2½ to 3 cups cooked beans.

# ❦ Jellied Beet Borscht Salad ❦
## (DAIRY)
*Serves: 8*

 2 (16-ounce) cans salt-free diced or julienned beets, drained (reserve the juice)
½ cup water
⅔ cup red wine vinegar
 1 3-ounce envelope Streit's dessert gel, raspberry flavor (see Note)
 2 tablespoons minced red onion

**1 cup nonfat sour cream**
**Sliced European cucumbers and 2 tablespoons chopped fresh dill, for garnish**

1. Pour the beet juice into a saucepan. Add the water and vinegar, and bring to a boil.
2. Pour the liquid into a mixing bowl; add the dessert gel and stir with a fork until dissolved.
3. Chill in the refrigerator for about 15 minutes or until syrupy.
4. Stir in the drained beets and the onion.
5. Pour into a 6-cup mold and chill until firm.

*To Serve:* Unmold on a chilled platter and place a bowl of nonfat sour cream sprinkled with dill in the center of the mold. Surround the mold with thin slices of cucumber.

NOTE: Any brand that does not contain gelatin is acceptable.

VARIATION: Diced cucumbers, scallions, green bell peppers, tomatoes, and/or radishes may be added to the sour cream and served with the borscht.

| PER SERVING | | | |
|---|---|---|---|
| .6 gm total fat | .01 gm saturated fat | 1.2 gm fiber | 94 calories |
| 0 mg cholesterol | 5% fat | 98 mg sodium | 5 calories from fat |

# ❦ Mrs. Rubenstein's Kosher Dill Pickles ❦
## (PAREVE)
### *Yield: About 12 pickles (1 pickle = 1 serving)*

Nothing tastes better than a cold, crisp, half-sour homemade pickle. Many years ago, in the early summer months, when Mrs. Rubenstein would babysit with our children, she used to come carrying these delicious pickles for us to enjoy. If somebody you know and love makes something that you especially appreciate, ask for the recipe—before it's too late.

12 cucumbers (3 inches long)
 1 teaspoon whole pickling spices
 1 scant tablespoon kosher salt
2 to 3 large cloves garlic, smashed
 4 sprigs fresh dill
 1 (2-inch) rye bread heel (optional)
   Boiling water to cover

1. Pack the cucumbers tightly into a clean quart mason jar.
2. Add the spices, salt, garlic, and dill. If you have the heel of a rye bread, place a 2-inch piece on top of the cucumbers.
3. Pour boiling water over the cucumbers to cover.
4. Adjust the rubber ring and cover but do not seal tightly.
5. Keep the jar at room temperature until the liquid becomes cloudy.
6. Cover tightly and store in the refrigerator.
7. Pickles are ready to eat in 7 to 10 days.

───── PER SERVING ─────

| .2 gm total fat | .05 gm saturated fat | 1.6 gm fiber | 22 calories |
| 0 mg cholesterol | 6.9% fat | 592 mg sodium | 2 calories from fat |

## ❦ Eggplant Parmesan ❦
### (DAIRY)
*Yield: 4 servings (4 slices = 1 serving as entrée)*

It used to be thought essential to salt eggplant before using to remove the bitter taste. But I rarely find that eggplants have a bitter taste, and we certainly don't need the additional sodium from the salt. However, most eggplants at the market are waxed, so I do peel them before cooking.

1 medium eggplant (1½ pounds), peeled, cut into 16 (½-inch) slices
½ cup egg substitute, slightly beaten with 1 extra-large egg white
¾ cup dried bread crumbs mixed with 2 tablespoons grated Parmesan cheese
2 cups Tomato Sauce (page 251)
⅓ cup shredded light mozzarella cheese

1. Dip the eggplant slices into the egg substitute mixture, then press on both sides into the bread crumb mixture.

2. Place the breaded eggplant slices on a nonstick baking sheet coated with olive oil cooking spray. Bake in the upper third of a preheated 450° oven for about 20 to 25 minutes, until lightly browned. Remove the baking sheet from the oven and reduce the oven heat to 425°.

3. Lightly coat the bottom of a 3-quart rectangular glass baking dish with olive oil spray.

4. Arrange 8 slices of baked eggplant in one layer in the baking dish.

5. Spread each slice with 2 tablespoons of tomato sauce and 2 teaspoons of shredded mozzarella. Top with another slice of baked eggplant and some of the remaining tomato sauce. Cover with foil and bake at 425° for 15 to 20 minutes or until piping hot.

*To Serve:* Serve with steamed broccoli spears and baked sweet potato.

TO MICROWAVE: Cover with wax paper and cook on High for 15 minutes.

---

#### ——— PER SERVING ———

| | | | |
|---|---|---|---|
| 3.8 gm total fat | 1.77 gm saturated fat | 4.4 gm fiber | 176 calories |
| 8 mg cholesterol | 18.7% fat | 382 mg sodium | 35 calories from fat |

---

## ❦ Marinated Vegetables ❦
### (PAREVE OR MEAT)
*Serves: 12 (½ cup = 1 serving)*

**Marinade:**

1½ cups canned vegetable broth or homemade Vegetable Broth (page 141)

⅓ cup dry white wine

6 peppercorns

6 large cloves garlic, smashed, peeled, and sliced

1 shallot, peeled and chopped

1 teaspoon salt-free vegetable seasoning

6 sprigs Italian flat-leaf parsley

1 bay leaf

3 tablespoons fresh lemon juice

2 teaspoons olive oil

2 teaspoons balsamic vinegar, optional

*Vegetables:*

- 2 small onions, peeled and quartered, or 12 red and white pearl onions, peeled
- 1 large zucchini, sliced diagonally ½ inch thick
- 2 yellow crookneck squash, sliced diagonally ½ inch thick
- 2 summer squash, sliced diagonally ½ inch thick
- 1 small green bell pepper, seeded and cut into 1-inch cubes
- 1 small red bell pepper, seeded and cut into 1-inch cubes
- 1 bulb fennel, feathery greens removed, sliced thin
- ¼ cup chopped Italian flat-leaf parsley and/or other fresh herbs, to taste

1. Combine all the marinade ingredients in a small saucepan. Bring to a boil, reduce the heat, cover, and simmer 30 minutes. Strain and discard the solids.

2. Prepare the vegetables: Place the onions in a large saucepan, add the strained marinade, cover, and cook 8 to 10 minutes or until tender.

3. Add the zucchini, crookneck and summer squash, peppers, and fennel. Bring to a boil, cover, and cook over medium heat 5 minutes. Allow to cool.

4. Pour into a shallow glass container, cover, and chill overnight. Sprinkle with chopped parsley and fresh herbs such as thyme and chives before serving.

| ——— PER SERVING ——— | | | |
|---|---|---|---|
| .8 gm total fat | .10 gm saturated fat | .1 gm fiber | 14 calories |
| 0 mg cholesterol | 50.3% fat | 2 mg sodium | 7 calories from fat |

# ❦ Ellen Batzdorf's Red Cabbage ❦
## (PAREVE)
### *Yield: 12 cups (½ cup = 1 serving)*

While traveling in Prague, we ate at a kosher restaurant and enjoyed the traditional red cabbage that we were served on a vegetarian plate. Jewish cooking from Eastern Europe often has both sweet and sour flavors. Ellen's easy, delicious recipe uses applesauce instead of apples, resulting in a flavor very similar to that of the red cabbage we had in Czechoslovakia.

    2 teaspoons canola oil
    1 medium onion, peeled and chopped fine
 1½ large heads (about 3 pounds) red cabbage, shredded (see Note)
    1 cup raspberry, red wine, or apple cider vinegar
    1 (23-ounce) jar unsweetened applesauce
   ⅓ cup water
    2 teaspoons ground cinnamon
    1 teaspoon freshly grated nutmeg
    1 teaspoon ground ginger
      Salt and freshly ground pepper to taste

1. Heat the oil in a large saucepan and sauté the onion 3 to 4 minutes, until wilted.

2. Add the cabbage, vinegar, applesauce, water, and seasonings. Stir with a slotted spoon to combine.

3. Cook, covered, over medium heat for 2 hours. Stir from time to time to prevent sticking.

*To Serve:* This is lovely as part of a vegetable plate. It also makes a flavorful accompaniment to roast or broiled chicken, or that occasional serving of brisket.

NOTE: Packaged shredded raw red cabbage is an easy, time-saving substitute for head cabbage.

—————————— PER SERVING ——————————

| | | | |
|---|---|---|---|
| .5 gm total fat | .07 gm saturated fat | 1.5 gm fiber | 29 calories |
| 0 mg cholesterol | 14.5% fat | 17 mg sodium | 5 calories from fat |

# ❦ Mashed Potatoes with Onions and Garlic ❦
## (PAREVE OR MEAT)
### Serves: 8

I'd have to say that potatoes are one of my family's favorite foods, whether just plain baked, sautéed, boiled, served as latkes, kugel, or mashed. What could be better than potatoes with onions and garlic?

1 large onion, or ¾ cup Onion Helper (page 254)
1 tablespoon plus 2 teaspoons olive oil
6 Idaho potatoes (about 3 pounds), peeled
6 large cloves garlic, smashed and peeled
1 teaspoon kosher salt
  Ground white pepper to taste
  About ⅓ cup defatted reduced-sodium vegetable broth or defatted chicken broth, heated
2 tablespoons finely chopped Italian flat-leaf parsley or chives, for garnish

1. Slice the onion and sauté in 2 teaspoons of olive oil until lightly browned. Set aside.

2. Cut the potatoes into quarters or sixths (2-inch cubes). Place in a saucepan with the garlic, salt, and hot water to barely cover.

3. Bring to a boil and simmer 20 minutes or until tender. Drain, return to the saucepan, and mash.

4. Add the remaining 1 tablespoon of oil, the sautéed onions, and pepper; blend well. Add warm broth while beating, a bit at a time, until the desired consistency has been reached. Taste and adjust seasonings with salt and pepper. Sprinkle with parsley and serve while hot.

VARIATION (DAIRY): One (10-ounce) package thawed and well-drained chopped spinach may be added in place of sautéed onions and garlic. Add 1 percent milk or nonfat sour cream instead of broth. One teaspoon of onion powder and a little freshly grated nutmeg add great flavor with the spinach.

---

PER SERVING

| | | | |
|---|---|---|---|
| 3.0 gm total fat | .42 gm saturated fat | 2.4 gm fiber | 147 calories |
| 0 mg cholesterol | 17.9% fat | 44 mg sodium | 27 calories from fat |

*To peel garlic quickly, smash the garlic clove with the flat side of a large knife. This will loosen the skin of the garlic so that it can be peeled easily.*

# ❧ Schliskas (Potato Dumplings) ❧ from Aunt Ella Markell
## (PAREVE)

*Yield: About 160 pieces*
*Serves: 12*

Italian cooks call potato-dough dumplings *gnocchi*. My aunt Ella, who lived with us, used to make *schliskas* from time to time. When she did, it was never a small amount, but then she never prepared anything except in king-size quantities. I have left out the egg she used to include; this eliminates the cholesterol and fat and also results in a lighter dumpling. She used to serve *schliskas* with buttered bread crumbs (*brazel*). They were delicious, and one of my childhood favorites. They stayed with you for days and days!

**2 pounds boiling potatoes, scrubbed**
  **About 1½ cups unbleached all-purpose flour**
**¾ teaspoon kosher salt**
  **Few grains ground white pepper**

1. Boil the potatoes in their jackets in water to cover until tender. Test after about 30 minutes of cooking with the tip of a paring knife. (Be careful, too frequent testing results in watery potatoes.)

2. Drain and peel the potatoes while still hot. (Use a towel or potholder to protect your hands.)

3. Purée in a food mill or potato ricer, or use a potato masher. (Do not use a food processor; it will turn the potatoes gummy and inedible.)

4. Add 1⅓ cups of the flour, the salt, and pepper, mixing until you have a smooth dough that is just slightly sticky.

5. Divide the dough into four portions. On a lightly floured surface, with lightly floured hands, roll into ropes about as thick as your index finger. Cut into 1-inch pieces.

6. Bring 5 quarts of salted water to a boil in a large pot. Drop in the dumplings, about 3 dozen at a time. Simmer uncovered 1½ to 2 minutes, or until the dumplings rise to the top of the water. Do not overcook.

7. Remove with a slotted spoon, drain, and transfer to a heated platter. Repeat with the remaining dumplings.

*To Serve:* Top with bread crumbs mixed with olive oil; a tasty tomato sauce; or a chicken, veal, or beef gravy that you may have on hand.

NOTE: *Schliskas* may be prepared through step 5, placed on lightly floured wax paper, and stored at room temperature for 1 hour or in the refrigerator for several hours or until mealtime.

VARIATION #1: *Sweet Potato Schliskas:* Two pounds of sweet potatoes boiled in their jackets may be substituted for white potatoes; proceed in the same manner as the above recipe.

VARIATION #2: *Krupen:* The white potato dough may be rolled out to about ¼ inch in thickness and cut into 3-inch circles. Fill with 1 heaping teaspoon of Lekvar (page 411), cover with a second circle, seal the edges with the tines of a fork, and boil gently for about 4 to 5 minutes.

Drain, then dip in bread crumbs mixed with canola oil and place on a nonstick baking sheet coated with butter-flavored cooking spray. Bake in a preheated 350° oven for about 20 minutes.

———————— PER SERVING ————————

| | | | |
|---|---|---|---|
| .2 gm total fat | .04 gm saturated fat | 1.6 gm fiber | 123 calories |
| 0 mg cholesterol | 1.7% fat | 150 mg sodium | 2 calories from fat |

# ❦ Stuffed Peppers ❦
## (PAREVE)

*Serves: 8 as a side dish (½ pepper = 1 serving)*

Red bell peppers are about six times higher in vitamin A than green peppers and are higher in vitamin C than oranges. These peppers are stuffed with a variety of vegetables and cooked brown rice, barley, kasha, or farfel. They may be prepared the day before and reheated.

    2  teaspoons extra-virgin olive oil
    1  small onion, peeled and chopped fine
    2  large cloves garlic, smashed, peeled, and minced
    1  rib celery with leaves, chopped fine
    1  cup sliced fresh mushrooms
    1  zucchini, coarsely grated
    1  carrot, peeled and grated
    2  teaspoons salt-free vegetable seasoning
    1  tablespoon chopped fresh thyme or ½ teaspoon dried thyme
       Ground white pepper to taste
    1  cup thawed frozen or salt-free, sugar-free canned corn kernels
    1  cup salt-free frozen peas, not thawed
 2½  cups cooked brown rice (page 206)
    ½  cup currants or raisins
    ¼  cup chopped Italian flat-leaf parsley
    ½  cup chopped scallions
    2  red and 2 green bell peppers, halved lengthwise, seeds and ribs discarded

*Sauce:*
 1½  tablespoons unbleached all-purpose flour
    1  (28-ounce) can salt-free diced tomatoes in juice
    1  cup low-sodium V-8 juice
    1  bay leaf
       Freshly ground pepper to taste

1. Heat the oil in a large nonstick skillet. Add the onion and garlic; sauté until wilted. Add the celery and mushrooms; sauté 2 minutes. Add the zucchini and carrot; sauté 1 minute.

2. Season with vegetable seasoning, thyme, and pepper. Add the corn, peas, rice, currants, parsley, and scallions and mix with a fork. Remove from the heat and fill the hollowed peppers with the mixture.

3. Make the sauce: Brown the flour in a sauté pan or casserole until golden brown, stirring constantly. Gradually add the tomatoes and V-8 juice, stirring to blend in the flour. Add the bay leaf and pepper. Bring to a boil. Reduce the heat to a simmer.

4. Arrange the stuffed peppers in the pan and spoon the tomato sauce over them. Cover with a lid and cook over low heat 40 to 45 minutes, basting occasionally.

5. Taste the sauce and adjust seasonings. Remove the bay leaf before serving.

---

PER SERVING

| | | | |
|---|---|---|---|
| 2.4 gm total fat | .38 gm saturated fat | 5.0 gm fiber | 194 calories |
| 0 mg cholesterol | 10.4% fat | 57 mg sodium | 21 calories from fat |

---

## ❦ Roasted Peppers ❦
### (PAREVE)
*Yield: Serves 12*
*(¼ red pepper + ¼ green pepper = 1 serving)*

A bright red bell pepper is a fully matured, ripened green bell pepper. Unfortunately, it's not always available, is quite perishable, and because of its late harvest, is more expensive. Try using these peppers raw in salads, or stuffed; for a delicious change, roast them before using.

**3 red bell peppers**
**3 green bell peppers**

1. Lay the peppers on their sides on a broiling pan close to the heat and scorch black on all sides. Watch closely so the peppers do not get too burned.

2. Remove the roasted peppers to a brown paper bag or plastic bag and allow to steam for 10 to 15 minutes.

3. Scrape off the charred skins and remove the stems, seeds, and liquid. Roasted peppers should be used within a day or so (unless marinated), or they will deteriorate.

Uses for Roasted Peppers: Peppers may be sliced and marinated in a vinaigrette dressing, to be used as a delicious addition to a green salad or as part of a relish tray or antipasto.

To marinate roasted pepper slices, sprinkle them with 1 tablespoon of olive oil, 2 tablespoons of red wine vinegar, and 1 minced clove of garlic. Store, covered, in the refrigerator. They will keep this way for a week.

---

**PER SERVING**

| | | | |
|---|---|---|---|
| .2 gm total fat | .03 gm saturated fat | .6 gm fiber | 9 calories |
| 0 mg cholesterol | 15.6% fat | 1 mg sodium | 2 calories from fat |

---

# ❧ Carrot Ring ❧
## (PAREVE)
### Serves: 12 to 14

You don't have to be a carrot lover to enjoy this recipe. This longtime favorite is a delicious company dish and makes a colorful addition to a buffet service. In addition, it's high in beta-carotene.

⅓ cup fine dried bread crumbs
⅓ cup canola oil
¾ cup packed brown sugar
½ cup egg substitute or 3 extra-large egg whites
3 cups grated peeled raw carrots (1 pound)
2 tablespoons water
2 teaspoons pure vanilla extract
3 tablespoons fresh lemon juice
  Grated zest of 1 lemon
2 cups unbleached all-purpose flour
1 teaspoon baking soda
2 teaspoons baking powder
½ teaspoon ground cinnamon
½ teaspoon freshly grated nutmeg
4 extra-large egg whites

1. Preheat the oven to 350°. Coat a 3-quart ring mold with butter-flavored cooking spray and dust with bread crumbs.

2. In a food processor, blend the oil and brown sugar. Add the egg substitute and blend well.

3. Add the carrots, water, vanilla, lemon juice and zest, flour, baking soda, baking powder, cinnamon, and nutmeg. Blend with pulsing action 3 or 4 seconds, just to combine. Pour the batter into a bowl.

4. In a separate bowl, beat the egg whites until stiff but not dry; glossy soft peaks will form.

5. Fold the beaten egg whites into the carrot mixture.

6. Transfer the batter to the prepared ring mold and bake for 1 hour. Remove from the oven and allow to cool for 3 to 5 minutes. Loosen the edges carefully with a knife, place a serving platter over the mold and invert.

*To Serve:* Fill the center with a combination of baby carrots and green peas, or green peas and steamed snow peas.

---

PER SERVING

| | | | |
|---|---|---|---|
| 5.9 gm total fat | .52 gm saturated fat | 1.4 gm fiber | 191 calories |
| 0 mg cholesterol | 27.6% fat | 156 mg sodium | 53 calories from fat |

# ❧ Vegetarian Stuffed Cabbage ❧
## (PAREVE OR DAIRY)

*Yield: 12 cabbage rolls*
*(2 rolls = 1 serving as entrée; 1 roll = 1 serving as side dish)*

Stuffed cabbage lovers who are also vegetarians will enjoy this variation on the traditional stuffed cabbage.

1 tablespoon extra-virgin olive oil
1 large onion, peeled and chopped fine
1 large shallot, peeled and chopped fine
1 pound fresh mushrooms, cleaned, trimmed, and sliced
2 carrots, peeled and grated
1 small rutabaga (yellow turnip), peeled and grated (about 1 cup)
2 (10-ounce) packages frozen chopped spinach, thawed and squeezed dry

    2 zucchini, trimmed and diced
 1½ cups cooked brown rice, barley, or kasha (page 206)
    2 teaspoons salt-free vegetable seasoning
      Freshly ground pepper
  ½ cup chopped Italian flat-leaf parsley
 12 large savoy cabbage leaves
    3 cups shredded savoy cabbage
    2 cups Vegetable Broth (page 141)

*Sauce:*

    6 fresh ripe or canned plum tomatoes, cored and diced
    2 teaspoons extra-virgin olive oil

*Garnish:*

  ⅓ cup nonfat plain yogurt or nonfat sour cream
    3 tablespoons chopped fresh dill or chives, for garnish

1. Add the oil to a large nonstick skillet. Sauté the onion and shallot 3 to 5 minutes. Add the mushrooms, carrots, and rutabaga and sauté for about 3 minutes.

2. Stir in the spinach and zucchini; add the rice, seasonings, and parsley. Taste and adjust seasonings.

3. Place about ⅓ cup of the vegetable mixture on each of 12 cabbage leaves at the stem end. Roll up, tucking in the sides.

4. Sprinkle the shredded cabbage on the bottom of a 3-quart casserole and top with the cabbage rolls, placing seam side down. Pour the broth over.

5. Cover with foil and bake in a 350° oven for about 1½ hours or until cooked through.

6. Prepare a sauce by sautéing the tomatoes in the oil for about 3 to 5 minutes; set aside.

*To Serve:* Spoon the hot tomato sauce over the cabbage rolls; add a dollop of yogurt and sprinkle with chopped fresh dill or chives. Serve with mashed or boiled potatoes and Strawberry Rhubarb Jumble (page 402) for dessert.

| PER SERVING | | | |
|---|---|---|---|
| 5.3 gm total fat | .76 mg saturated fat | 8.7 gm fiber | 208 calories |
| 0 mg cholesterol | 21.1% fat | 145 mg sodium | 48 calories from fat |

# ❧ Mushroom-Stuffed Tomatoes ❧
## (DAIRY)
*Serves: 6 (1 tomato = 1 serving)*

Prepare this dish when tomatoes are in season and at the height of their flavor.

6 medium ripe tomatoes
  Salt-free vegetable seasoning to taste
  Freshly ground pepper to taste
1 pound fresh cremini, white, or portobello mushrooms, cleaned and chopped
1 shallot, peeled and chopped fine
2 tablespoons light margarine
½ teaspoon dried thyme, crushed
½ cup nonfat sour cream or nonfat plain yogurt
1 extra-large egg white, slightly beaten
¼ cup fine dried bread crumbs
2 tablespoons grated Parmesan cheese alternative mixed with 2 tablespoons dried bread crumbs
  Hungarian paprika

1. Cut a slice from the stem end of each tomato and scoop out the seeds and pulp. Season the tomato shells with no-salt vegetable seasoning and freshly ground pepper. Turn the shells upside down to drain.

2. Chop the tomato pulp fine; measure 1 cup.

3. In a medium saucepan, sauté the mushrooms and shallot in the margarine until tender, about 5 minutes. Add the thyme and pepper.

4. Combine the sour cream and egg white. Add to the mushroom mixture with the tomato pulp and bread crumbs. Cook and stir until the mixture thickens.

5. Arrange the tomato shells in a baking dish. Spoon the mushroom mixture into the tomatoes.

6. Top with the cheese mixture, sprinkle with paprika, and bake at 375° for about 25 minutes. Serve with broiled fish and steamed broccoli.

―――――――――― PER SERVING ――――――――――

| | | | |
|---|---|---|---|
| 2.4 gm total fat | .64 gm saturated fat | 2.5 gm fiber | 94 calories |
| 1 mg cholesterol | 21.2% fat | 144 mg sodium | 21 calories from fat |

# ❦ A Little Tomato Sauce ❦

## (PAREVE)

*Yield: 18 servings (⅔ cup = 1 serving)*

This quick tomato sauce has a fresh tomato taste that enhances any pasta. I particularly enjoy it with ziti, penne, fusilli, or schliskas (page 243), but it also combines well with spaghetti.

2 cups finely chopped peeled carrots
2 cups finely chopped celery with leaves
2 cups finely chopped red or yellow onions
2 (28-ounce) cans crushed plum tomatoes in purée
1 teaspoon sugar
1 tablespoon olive oil (optional)
Freshly ground pepper to taste

1. Put the chopped vegetables, tomatoes, and sugar in a large nonaluminum saucepan and simmer uncovered for 40 minutes. Stir occasionally.

2. Purée, in batches if necessary, in a food processor, blender, or food mill until your preferred consistency is reached.

3. Return to the saucepan and simmer uncovered for 15 additional minutes. (If desired, olive oil may be added at this time.)

4. Taste and adjust seasonings with freshly ground pepper. This will keep in the refrigerator for several days or it may be frozen for future use.

VARIATION: For a meat meal, serve with turkey meatballs (page 128) that have been heated in the sauce for 15 minutes. For a dairy meal, add ½ cup skimmed evaporated milk and proceed as in step 3.

—— PER SERVING ——

| | | | |
|---|---|---|---|
| .3 gm total fat | .05 gm saturated fat | 1.7 gm fiber | 35 calories |
| 0 mg cholesterol | 6.1% fat | 170 mg sodium | 2 calories from fat |

# ❦ A Lot of Tomato Sauce ❦

## (MEAT OR PAREVE)

*Yield: 8 pints (½ cup = 1 serving)*

This is a convenient staple to have on hand, as well as a clever way to get the last goodness out of a roast chicken. When you have the time to prepare it, this delicious sauce freezes well and is a flavorful sauce for pasta, eggplant, or meatballs (page 128).

- 2 large onions, peeled and quartered
- 6 large cloves garlic, smashed and peeled
- 1 tablespoon olive oil
- 3 pounds ripe plum tomatoes, peeled, seeded, and diced
- 4 (28-ounce) cans crushed tomatoes in purée
- 4 (6-ounce) cans salt-free tomato paste
- 1 teaspoon ground white pepper
- 3 tablespoons chopped fresh oregano or 1½ tablespoons dried oregano, crushed
- 3 tablespoons diced fresh basil or 1 tablespoon dried basil, crushed
- ¾ cup chopped Italian flat-leaf parsley
- 2 bay leaves
- 1 leftover roast chicken carcass
- 1 cup dry red or white wine

1. Chop the onions and garlic in a food processor or blender.
2. Heat the oil in a large saucepan; add the onion mixture. Sauté until tender, about 5 minutes.
3. Add the fresh tomatoes, canned crushed tomatoes, tomato paste, pepper, oregano, basil, parsley, and bay leaves. Bring to a boil.
4. Add the chicken carcass and bring to a second boil. Reduce the heat and simmer partially covered for 2 hours.
5. Discard the chicken bones; add the wine and simmer uncovered for 15 minutes.
6. Cool and store in the refrigerator or freeze in pint-sized containers for future use.

| PER SERVING | | | |
|---|---|---|---|
| 1 gm total fat | .15 gm saturated fat | 2.3 gm fiber | 54 calories |
| 0 mg cholesterol | 14.2% fat | 187 mg sodium | 9 calories from fat |

— ❧ Harriet's Hints ❧ —

*To quickly peel ripe tomatoes: Run the blade of a table knife over the entire surface of the tomato without cutting or piercing the skin. Remove the core with a paring knife and use the sharp end of the knife to lift off the skin.*

# ❧ Rosy Baked Onions with Raisins ❧
## (PAREVE)
### Serves: 8 to 10 (4 onions = 1 serving)

This is a savory accompaniment to any poultry dish. Eight small red-, white-, or yellow-skinned onions, halved crosswise, may be substituted for pearl onions.

  3 dozen assorted pearl onions (red-, white-, and yellow-skinned), peeled (see Note), or 1 (16-ounce) package frozen onions
⅓ cup low-sodium V-8 juice
  1 tablespoon Hungarian paprika
  1 tablespoon olive oil
  2 tablespoons honey
⅛ teaspoon ground white pepper
  1 teaspoon salt-free vegetable seasoning
½ cup dark raisins
  6 leaves fresh sage (optional)

1. Place the peeled onions in a shallow casserole coated with olive oil cooking spray.

2. Combine the juice, paprika, oil, honey, pepper, vegetable seasoning, raisins, and sage. Pour over the onions.

3. Cover with foil and bake in the upper third of a 300° oven for about 45 minutes (or 1 hour for 4 large onion halves) or until the onions are tender. Baste the onions several times during cooking. Remove the sage leaves before serving.

NOTE: For easy peeling, plunge the onions into boiling water for 2 to 3 minutes. Drain and cut off the root ends, and the skins will slide right off.

---

### PER SERVING

| | | | |
|---|---|---|---|
| 1.5 gm total fat | .21 gm saturated fat | 1.0 gm fiber | 46 calories |
| 0 mg cholesterol | 27.7% fat | 4 mg sodium | 14 calories from fat |

---

# ❦ Onion Helper ❦
## (PAREVE OR MEAT)
*Yield: 5½ cups (1 tablespoon = 1 serving)*

If I had to choose only one essential ingredient in Jewish cooking, it would be onions. Whether used in roasts, fricassees, goulash, soups, knishes, verenikis, with eggs or with potatoes, their flavor enhances every dish. It's certainly a help not to have to peel, slice, and sauté these tasty roots every time. Why not cook up a batch and freeze them in plastic bags for future use?

  1 tablespoon olive oil
6 to 8 (4 pounds) medium yellow onions, peeled, halved, and sliced thin (see Note)
  1 tablespoon salt-free vegetable seasoning
  ½ teaspoon ground white pepper
  ¼ cup defatted sodium-reduced chicken broth or vegetable broth, or dry white wine
  3 large cloves garlic, peeled and minced
  1 tablespoon Hungarian paprika (optional)

1. Heat the oil in a nonstick sauté pan; add the onions, vegetable seasoning, and pepper. Cover and sweat over medium heat for 4 to 5 minutes, stirring frequently.

2. Uncover, add the broth, garlic, and paprika, and cook until the onions are wilted and transparent, about 15 minutes. Stir occasionally while cooking. *Do not brown*.

NOTE: If you have a food processor, the slicing takes only seconds.

To freeze for future use, measure into ½- to 1-cup portions and place in freezer bags or containers. Before using, remove from the bag and thaw in a microwave oven or in a covered sauté pan.

---

PER SERVING

| | | | |
|---|---|---|---|
| .2 gm total fat | .03 gm saturated fat | .3 gm fiber | 7 calories |
| 0 mg cholesterol | 21.9% fat | 1 mg sodium | 2 calories from fat |

---

## ❦ Onion-flavored Olive Oil ❦
### (PAREVE)
*Yield: About 2¾ cups (1 tablespoon = 1 serving)*

We have a friend who misses the "Jewish popcorn" (*griebenes*, or chicken cracklings) his mother used to make when cooking rendered chicken fat (*schmaltz*). Now, his wife uses olive oil instead. I stopped cooking with schmaltz years ago. However, in certain traditional recipes, I used to miss the chicken fat to develop flavor. Dishes such as chopped eggs and onions, vegetarian chopped liver, fricassee, goulash, and mashed potatoes all benefit from a small amount of this oil or its onions instead of schmaltz. The oil may be refrigerated or frozen and used directly out of the freezer, for it never quite gets solid. Olive oil is high in monosaturated fat that helps to raise your HDLs (the good cholesterol); however, it is *still a fat*, to be used judiciously and in limited amounts.

    3 cups olive oil
    1 large onion, peeled and chopped (about 2 cups)
    1 teaspoon Hungarian paprika, mild or spicy (optional)
    ⅛ teaspoon ground white pepper (optional)

1. Place the oil and onion in a heavy-bottomed medium saucepan.
2. Bring to a boil and reduce the heat to a simmer. Add spices if desired. Stir occasionally to prevent sticking.

3. Cook uncovered until the onions are golden brown. Remove from the heat.

4. Strain the onions and oil through a fine triple-mesh strainer and press the onions to drain off all the fat. Remove the remaining grease from the onions with paper towels.

5. Store the oil in a jar or a tightly covered container in the refrigerator or freezer. The onions may be used in making mashed potatoes, knishes, chopped eggs and onions, or vegetarian chopped liver; or they may be frozen for future use.

―――――――――― PER SERVING ――――――――――

| | | | |
|---|---|---|---|
| 14.7 gm total fat | 1.99 gm saturated fat | .1 gm fiber | 132 calories |
| 0 mg cholesterol | 98.8% fat | 0 mg sodium | 132 calories from fat |

## ❧ Potato Kugel ❧
### (PAREVE)
*Yield: 8 slices (1 slice = 1 serving)*

When I prepare potato kugel, I always use a glass pie plate for two reasons. It comes out wonderfully crispy and crusty, and there are no arguments about who gets the crispy corner pieces.

1½ tablespoons canola oil
4 cups peeled and cubed Idaho potatoes
½ small onion, peeled and cubed
3 extra-large egg whites
⅓ cup dried bread crumbs, white flour, or matzo meal
1 teaspoon baking powder
¼ teaspoon ground white pepper
½ teaspoon salt or to taste

1. Preheat the oven to 425°. Coat a 10-inch glass pie plate with vegetable oil cooking spray.

2. Pour the oil into the pie plate and heat for 2 to 3 minutes in the oven.

3. Place 1 cup of the potatoes, the onion, and the egg whites in a food processor or blender. Using the steel blade, process with pulsing action for 1 minute or until chopped.

4. Add the remaining potatoes and process just until finely minced. (*Be careful not to purée.*)

5. Pour the mixture into a bowl. Add the bread crumbs, baking powder, and seasonings, and stir to blend. Add the heated oil, stir, and pour the mixture into the hot pie plate.

6. Bake in the upper third of the 425° oven for 45 to 50 minutes or until brown and crispy.

*To Serve:* Cut into pie-shaped wedges and accompany with applesauce and/or nonfat sour cream.

VARIATION: *Individual Potato Kugel:* This can be prepared by using the same kugel recipe and pouring it into hot muffin tins coated with vegetable oil cooking spray. Bake for 30 to 40 minutes in a preheated 425° oven until browned. These may be frozen and heated in a 425° oven for 5 to 10 minutes before serving.

---

PER SERVING

| | | | |
|---|---|---|---|
| 2.9 gm total fat | .26 gm saturated fat | 1.5 gm fiber | 116 calories |
| 0 mg cholesterol | 22.0% fat | 208 mg sodium | 26 calories from fat |

---

HARRIET'S HINTS

*For sodium-reduced bouillon cubes, freeze a can of defatted sodium-reduced chicken broth in an ice cube tray. When solid, place individual cubes in tightly sealed plastic bags and use when enrichment or a bit of broth is needed in sautéing.*

# ❦ Vegetarian Stew ❦

## (DAIRY)

*Serves: 6 as an entrée; 10 as an accompaniment*

1 small eggplant (1 pound), peeled and cut into ½-inch slices
1 teaspoon olive oil
½ cup chopped onion
2 large shallots, peeled and chopped
3 large cloves garlic, smashed, peeled, and minced
½ green bell pepper, seeded and cut into 1-inch pieces
½ red bell pepper, seeded and cut into 1-inch pieces
2 carrots, peeled and cut into ½-inch diagonal slices
2 medium zucchini, cut into ½-inch diagonal slices
3 crookneck squash, cut into ½-inch diagonal slices
  Freshly ground pepper
1 teaspoon ground cumin
1½ teaspoons curry powder (optional)
¼ teaspoon hot red pepper flakes
2 (14½-ounce) cans salt-free diced tomatoes in juice
1 (6-ounce) can salt-free tomato paste
½ cup Vegetable Broth (page 141) or dry white wine
1 (15-ounce) can sodium-reduced Great Northern, kidney, cannellini
  or garbanzo beans (chick-peas), rinsed and drained
¼ cup chopped Italian flat-leaf parsley or fresh cilantro
1 tablespoon soy-based Parmesan cheese alternative

1. Lightly coat a nonstick baking sheet with olive oil cooking spray. Lay the peeled eggplant slices in one layer on the sheet. Broil until lightly browned; turn and repeat on the other side.

2. Heat the oil in a large nonstick sauté pan and cook the onion, shallots, and garlic over medium heat for 5 minutes, stirring occasionally.

3. Add the bell peppers, carrots, zucchini, squash, and ground pepper. Cook 2 to 3 minutes. Add the cumin, curry, and hot pepper flakes.

4. Stir in the tomatoes, tomato paste, and vegetable broth. Bring to a boil. Reduce the heat and simmer for 10 minutes.

5. Add the beans and stir.

6. Layer 6 eggplant slices on the bottom of a large casserole. Top with half the vegetable mixture. Repeat. Sprinkle with the parsley and Parmesan alternative.

7. Cover and bake in a preheated 350° oven for 30 minutes.

*To Serve:* Serve hot as an entrée over kasha or steamed wild and brown rice; serve hot or cold as an accompaniment.

NOTE: This dish may be prepared one day ahead.

--- PER SERVING AS ENTRÉE ---

| | | | |
|---|---|---|---|
| 2.0 gm total fat | .35 gm saturated fat | 5.0 gm fiber | 199 calories |
| 0 mg cholesterol | 8.5% fat | 60 mg sodium | 18 calories from fat |

--- PER SERVING AS ACCOMPANIMENT ---

| | | | |
|---|---|---|---|
| 1.2 gm total fat | .21 gm saturated fat | 3.0 gm fiber | 119 calories |
| 0 mg cholesterol | 8.5% fat | 36 mg sodium | 11 calories from fat |

# ❧ Sephardic Leeks and Beans ❧
## (PAREVE)
### *Serves: 4 to 6*

Sephardic culinary tradition includes many vegetarian dishes. This is one of my favorites.

2 leeks, white part only
1 large onion, peeled and chopped coarse
1 cup defatted sodium-reduced vegetable or chicken broth
2 teaspoons olive oil
1 cup no-salt diced tomatoes in juice
1 teaspoon sugar
  Juice of 1 lemon or to taste
1 (14-ounce) can sodium-reduced Great Northern or cannellini beans, drained and rinsed

1. Split and wash the leeks thoroughly. Cut into 1-inch pieces.

2. Place in a saucepan with the remaining ingredients except the beans, cover, and cook over medium heat till tender, about 30 minutes.

3. Add the beans and cook 15 minutes more.

——— PER SERVING ———

| | | | |
|---|---|---|---|
| 2.0 gm total fat | .32 gm saturated fat | 1.0 gm fiber | 133 calories |
| 0 mg cholesterol | 12.9% fat | 11 mg sodium | 18 calories from fat |

## ❧ Tzimmes ❧
### (PAREVE)
*Serves: 10 to 12*

Tzimmes is one of the recipes that has its own spin in every Jewish kitchen. It is a popular dish, a casserole of fruits and/or vegetables, usually served on the Sabbath or holidays.

         3 pounds carrots, peeled and sliced diagonally into 1-inch pieces
         2 pounds yams, peeled and sliced into 2-inch circles
        16 large pitted prunes, cut into thirds
    ½ to ⅔ cup honey
         1 tablespoon ground cinnamon
           Freshly grated nutmeg to taste

1. Preheat the oven to 350°. Coat a large covered casserole with vegetable oil cooking spray.

2. Layer the carrots, yams, and prunes alternately in the prepared pan, drizzling with honey to taste and sprinkling with the spices. Add water to cover the ingredients. Cover and bake 30 minutes.

3. Uncover and bake 30 additional minutes, or until the carrots and yams are soft and the liquid is reduced to a thick and slightly sticky consistency.

——— PER SERVING ———

| | | | |
|---|---|---|---|
| .5 gm total fat | .09 gm saturated fat | 5.5 gm fiber | 267 calories |
| 0 mg cholesterol | 1.5% fat | 57 mg sodium | 4 calories from fat |

# ❧ Okra (Bamieh) ❧

## (PAREVE)

*Serves: 6 to 8*

Okra is a very popular vegetable in the Middle East, in Israel, and in the southern United States. Okra has a sweet, somewhat nutty taste and a gluey quality when cooked. Look for plump green pods, no larger than 3 inches. Avoid shriveled, blemished, or soft pods. Sliced okra added to soup is a natural thickener. In this recipe, okra is cooked in a seasoned tomato sauce that can be prepared a day ahead or on the same day that you're going to serve it.

1 tablespoon olive oil
1 medium onion, peeled and chopped fine
2 packages frozen okra, partially thawed, or 2 pounds fresh whole okra, washed
1 (8-ounce) can salt-free tomato sauce
2 ripe plum tomatoes, diced
Juice of ½ lemon
2 large cloves garlic, smashed, peeled, and minced, or 1 teaspoon garlic powder
¼ teaspoon ground white pepper
Vegetable Broth (page 141) or water (optional)

1. Heat the oil in a large saucepan. Add the chopped onion and sauté until transparent, 3 to 4 minutes.

2. Add the okra, tomato sauce, tomatoes, lemon, garlic, and pepper. Mix well, cover, and cook for about 30 minutes on low heat. Stir occasionally to avoid scorching. If necessary, add a little vegetable broth or water.

*To Serve:* This dish can be served hot as a vegetable or cold as an appetizer with pita bread.

---

PER SERVING

| | | | |
|---|---|---|---|
| 2.1 gm total fat | .30 gm saturated fat | 1.8 gm fiber | 61 calories |
| 0 mg cholesterol | 27% fat | 191 mg sodium | 18 calories from fat |

# ❧ Creole Corn and Okra Casserole ❧
(PAREVE)
*Serves: 6*

2 teaspoons canola oil
1 pound whole okra, preferably small (see Note)
1 small onion, peeled and chopped
2 cloves garlic, smashed, peeled, and minced
1 green bell pepper, seeded and sliced
1½ cups fresh corn kernels or 1 (12-ounce) can salt-free, sugar-free corn
    kernels, drained
1 (15 ½-ounce) can sodium-reduced stewed or whole tomatoes, chopped (save
    the juice)
⅔ cup fine fresh whole wheat bread crumbs or matzo meal
2 teaspoons salt-free vegetable seasoning
2 tablespoons chopped Italian flat-leaf parsley or fresh cilantro
    Dash of ground red pepper (cayenne)

1. Heat the oil in a nonstick skillet; add the okra, onion, and garlic and sauté 3 to 5 minutes.

2. Add the green pepper, corn, tomatoes with their juice, bread crumbs, vegetable seasoning, parsley, and red pepper. Toss to combine.

3. Transfer the mixture to a medium baking dish, cover, and bake at 375° for 30 minutes. Or cover with plastic and microwave on High for 6 minutes.

NOTE: If okra pods are large, remove the stem ends and cut the pods into 1-inch slices.

| PER SERVING | | | |
|---|---|---|---|
| 2.5 gm total fat | .30 gm saturated fat | 3.2 gm fiber | 113 calories |
| 0 mg cholesterol | 18.2% fat | 51 mg sodium | 22 calories from fat |

# ❦ Vegetarian Chili ❦
## (PAREVE)
### *Yield: 14 cups (1 cup = 1 serving)*

Whether you're a vegetarian or not, you will love this chili. For great entertaining that's quick and easy, serve a steaming bowl of chili with a large green salad and end with a basket of seasonal fresh fruit and My Favorite Mandelbrot (page 385) for dessert.

    1 large onion, peeled and cut into eighths
    4 cloves garlic, smashed and peeled
    4 ribs celery with leaves, quartered
    1 green bell pepper, seeded and quartered
    1 red bell pepper, seeded and quartered
    3 carrots, peeled and quartered
    2 zucchini, quartered
    1 small eggplant (1 pound), peeled and cubed
    ½ cup dry white or red wine
 1½ to 2 tablespoons chili powder
    2 teaspoons ground cumin
    2 teaspoons dried oregano, crushed
    1 teaspoon dried basil, crushed
    1 teaspoon garlic powder
    ½ cup chopped Italian flat-leaf parsley
    2 (28-ounce) cans crushed tomatoes in purée (see Note)
    1 (27-ounce) can sodium-reduced kidney beans, rinsed and drained,
       or 3 cups cooked (page 235)
    1 (15½-ounce) can sodium-reduced garbanzo beans (chick-peas), rinsed
       and drained, or 2 cups cooked (page 235)
    1 (15½-ounce) can sodium-reduced black beans, rinsed and drained,
       or 2 cups cooked (page 235)

1. Place the onion, garlic, celery, green and red pepper, carrots, and zucchini in a food processor. Using the steel blade, process just until chopped. (Do not purée.)

2. Heat a large nonstick saucepan and coat with olive oil cooking spray. Add the chopped vegetables and stir over medium heat for about 5 minutes.

3. Add the eggplant, wine, and seasonings. Sauté 3 to 5 minutes. Add the parsley.

**4.** Add the tomatoes and beans. Stir, bring to a simmer, and cook uncovered for 25 minutes. Taste and adjust seasonings.

*To Serve:* Ladle the hot chili into soup bowls or individual ramekins. Accompany with crisp sourdough rolls and pass nonfat sour cream and diced sweet red or white onion.

NOTE: Or you may use an equal amount of diced fresh tomatoes and juice, and add ¼ cup of tomato paste.

——— P E R   S E R V I N G ———

| | | | |
|---|---|---|---|
| 1.5 gm total fat | .23 gm saturated fat | 6.1 gm fiber | 174 calories |
| 0 mg cholesterol | 7.3% fat | 212 mg sodium | 14 calories from fat |

# ❧ Ratatouille ❧
## (PAREVE)
### Serves: 8

2 tablespoons extra-virgin olive oil
1 large onion, peeled and chopped fine
2 small eggplants (1 pound each), peeled and diced
1 red bell pepper, seeded and sliced thin
1 green bell pepper, seeded and sliced thin
3 large cloves garlic, smashed, peeled, and minced
  Ground white pepper to taste
1 tablespoon chopped fresh thyme leaves or 2 teaspoons dried thyme, plus additional for topping
1 tablespoon chopped fresh basil leaves or 1 teaspoon dried basil
1 teaspoon chopped fresh oregano or ½ teaspoon dried oregano
3 large ripe tomatoes, sliced
3 medium zucchini, sliced diagonally into ½-inch slices
  Salt to taste

1. Heat the oil in a large nonstick sauté pan. Add the onion and eggplants; mix thoroughly. Cook about 10 minutes, stirring occasionally.

2. Add the bell peppers, garlic, ½ teaspoon white pepper, thyme, basil, and oregano. Cover and simmer 40 minutes.

3. Remove the cover and cook 20 to 30 minutes, or until excess liquid has evaporated. Taste and adjust seasonings.

4. Place the vegetable mixture in a 2-quart-size oval casserole and arrange the tomatoes and zucchini slices in diagonal rows on top of the vegetable mixture.

5. Coat the vegetables with olive oil cooking spray; season with salt, pepper, and thyme.

6. Bake in a preheated 375° oven for 15 to 20 minutes or until the vegetables are fork-tender.

--- PER SERVING ---

| | | | |
|---|---|---|---|
| 3.8 gm total fat | .53 gm saturated fat | 2.8 gm fiber | 81 calories |
| 0 mg cholesterol | 38.3% fat | 11 mg sodium | 35 calories from fat |

# ❦ Corn Pudding ❦
## (DAIRY)
### Serves: 8 to 10

2 (16-ounce) cans cream-style corn
1 (10-ounce) can salt-free, sugar-free whole-kernel corn, drained
1 cup chopped celery with leaves
½ red bell pepper, seeded and diced
½ cup minced onion
½ cup low-fat shredded cheese
¾ cup egg substitute mixed with 2 extra-large egg whites
2 cups nonfat or skim milk
2 cups nonfat cracker crumbs or matzo meal
1 teaspoon Hungarian paprika

1. Preheat the oven to 350°. Coat a 13 × 9 × 2-inch glass baking dish with vegetable oil cooking spray.

2. In a large mixing bowl, combine the cream-style corn and corn kernels with the celery, bell pepper, onion, and cheese. Add the egg substitute mixture and stir to combine. Add the milk and cracker crumbs and mix well.

3. Transfer the mixture to the prepared baking dish and sprinkle with paprika. Bake for 50 to 60 minutes, or until lightly browned.

| PER SERVING | | | |
|---|---|---|---|
| 2.9 gm total fat | 1 gm saturated fat | 2.4 gm fiber | 277 calories |
| 6 mg cholesterol | 8.9% fat | 158 mg sodium | 26 calories from fat |

## ❧ Dorothy Essick's Sweet and Sour Beets ❧
### (PAREVE)
*Serves: 6*

This is a wonderful accompaniment to broiled whitefish. Choose beets 2 to 3 inches in diameter with fresh green leaves. Save the leaves to add to a vegetable broth. Large beets or those without leaves are more mature and more likely to be fibrous and tough.

2 bunches small beets (about 2 pounds)
½ cup diced red onion and 2 tablespoons chopped fresh dill, for garnish

*Sauce:*
1 cup cider vinegar or red wine vinegar
2 tablespoons cornstarch
¼ cup sugar, or to taste
Fresh orange juice or water as needed

1. Preheat oven to 450°.

2. Cut off all but ½ inch of the beet tops and leave the tails on. Scrub the beets with a vegetable brush, being careful not to break the skin.

3. Place in a covered casserole and bake for 45 to 55 minutes, or until tender (test with the point of a paring knife). Or the beets may be wrapped individually in foil and baked at 325° for about 2½ hours. They tend to be juicier baked in foil at a lower tem-

perature. For microwave cooking, place in a covered container with 1 cup water and cook on High for about 20 minutes or until tender.

4. When the beets are cool enough to handle, cut off the tops, slip off the skins, and slice.

5. Combine the vinegar, cornstarch, and sugar in a saucepan and stir over moderate heat until clear and thickened. Add orange juice or water to thin the sauce if necessary.

6. Stir the beets into the sauce; taste and adjust seasonings.

*To Serve:* Place in a warm vegetable dish and sprinkle with diced onion and chopped fresh dill.

| PER SERVING | | | |
|---|---|---|---|
| 0 gm total fat | .01 gm saturated fat | .5 gm fiber | 76 calories |
| 0 mg cholesterol | .4% fat | 28 mg sodium | 0 calories from fat |

## ❦ Mustard Cabbage ❦
### (DAIRY)
*Serves: 4*

Cabbage is a common-looking vegetable that is believed to have special healthful qualities, along with its cruciferous cousins broccoli and cauliflower. It is easily available throughout the year.

    1½ cups nonfat or skim milk
     4 cups shredded green cabbage
       Few grains of ground red pepper (cayenne)
     2 teaspoons Dijon mustard
     2 tablespoons unbleached all-purpose flour
     2 tablespoons chopped Italian flat-leaf parsley, for garnish

1. Put 1¼ cups of the milk in a large saucepan and bring to a boil. Add the shredded cabbage and a few grains of cayenne and cook 5 minutes over medium heat.

2. In a small bowl, combine the mustard, flour, and the remaining ¼ cup of milk.

Mix thoroughly and stir into the cooked cabbage. Return to a boil and simmer several minutes, until the sauce is thickened.

*To Serve:* Place in a serving bowl and sprinkle with parsley.

---

PER SERVING

| | | | |
|---|---|---|---|
| .5 gm total fat | .13 gm saturated fat | 1.9 gm fiber | 67 calories |
| 2 mg cholesterol | 6.6% fat | 136 mg sodium | 4 calories from fat |

---

# ❦ Cousin Pearly from Pittsburgh's ❦ Lima Beans for a Crowd
## (MEAT)
### *Serves: 12*

Everybody has a favorite cousin—Pearly was mine. She is gone, but not forgotten, and all who taste her limas will remember her fondly. An easy favorite buffet dish.

½ pound lean beef flanken or veal brisket, cut into 2-inch pieces, or 1 pound marrow bones

1 (16-ounce) package dried large lima beans, picked over and soaked (page 235)

1 large onion, peeled and grated

2 tablespoons dark corn syrup

2 bay leaves

¼ teaspoon hot red pepper flakes
Freshly ground black pepper

3 tablespoons packed brown sugar

2 teaspoons Hungarian paprika

1 cup sodium-reduced ketchup

1. Combine all the ingredients in a large stockpot. Add water to cover.
2. Bring to a boil, reduce the heat, and simmer, covered, for 1 hour.
3. Carefully empty into a large roaster, cover, and cook for 2 hours in a 300° oven.

NOTE: *Do not stir.* Shake the pan so the limas don't stick. Add boiling water, additional ketchup, or brown sugar as needed and wanted.

*To Serve:* Transfer to a heated casserole.

---

――――――――――――― P E R   S E R V I N G ―――――――――――――

| | | | |
|---|---|---|---|
| 2.1 gm total fat | .82 gm saturated fat | 2.7 gm fiber | 121 calories |
| 9 mg cholesterol | 14.9% fat | 35 mg sodium | 19 calories from fat |

---

# ✿ Gisele Pollak's Hungarian Lecsó ✿
## (PAREVE)
### *Serves: 3 to 4*

The onions may be sautéed 2 to 3 minutes in 2 teaspoons of olive oil before the tomatoes are added, or they may be prepared as directed, with no fat. In Hungary, this popular vegetable conserve is purchased in jars.

1½ cups onions, peeled and chopped or sliced thinly
2 medium ripe tomatoes, chopped
2 teaspoons hot Hungarian paprika
4 long green Italian frying peppers or banana peppers, seeded,
  and cut into ¼-inch circles
  Salt and chili powder to taste (optional)

1. Combine the onions and tomatoes in a saucepan and cook over low heat, covered, for 5 minutes.

2. Add the paprika and peppers and stew together about 15 to 20 minutes, stirring occasionally.

3. Taste and adjust seasonings with salt and chili powder if desired.

*To Serve:* Spoon over steamed brown rice.

---

――――――――――――― P E R   S E R V I N G ―――――――――――――

| | | | |
|---|---|---|---|
| .5 gm total fat | .07 gm saturated fat | 2.8 gm fiber | 54 calories |
| 0 mg cholesterol | 7.5% fat | 11 mg sodium | 5 calories from fat |

# ❧ Broccoli Kugel ❧
## (PAREVE)
### Serves: 8

1 tablespoon matzo meal
3 (10-ounce) packages frozen chopped broccoli, thawed
1 cup chopped leek, white part only
1 cup chopped onion
1 clove garlic, smashed, peeled, and minced
1 tablespoon olive oil
½ cup egg substitute
2 cups defatted sodium-reduced vegetable broth or chicken broth
1 tablespoon chopped fresh dill
1 tablespoon chopped Italian flat-leaf parsley
  Salt and freshly ground pepper to taste
3 cups matzo farfel or 6 ounces no-yolk noodles, cooked
5 extra-large egg whites
1 teaspoon Hungarian paprika

1. Preheat the oven to 350°. Coat a 10- or 11-inch glass pie plate with olive oil cooking spray and dust with the matzo meal.

2. Drain the broccoli and place in a large bowl.

3. Sauté the leek, onion, and garlic in the oil until soft, about 5 minutes. Add to the broccoli.

4. Mix the egg substitute with the broth, dill, and parsley; add to the broccoli mixture, along with salt and pepper to taste.

5. Mix in the uncooked matzo farfel. The farfel will soften in baking.

6. In a separate bowl, beat the egg whites until they are shiny and form soft peaks. Fold into the broccoli mixture.

7. Pour the mixture into the prepared pie plate and sprinkle with Hungarian paprika. Bake for about 45 minutes.

8. Cut into wedges and serve hot.

| PER SERVING | | | |
|---|---|---|---|
| 2.4 gm total fat | .37 gm saturated fat | 2.5 gm fiber | 210 calories |
| 0 mg cholesterol | 10.2% fat | 118 mg sodium | 22 calories from fat |

# ❧ Sweet Potato Ring ❧

## (PAREVE)

*Serves: 12 to 14*

This is a beautiful way to serve sweet potatoes at a holiday dinner, particularly Thanksgiving.

   3 pounds sweet potatoes
 ½ cup toasted walnut halves
 ¼ cup packed brown sugar
 ½ cup egg substitute, well beaten
   1 tablespoon canola oil
   1 cup nonfat non-dairy coffee creamer or nonfat mocha blend
   1 teaspoon ground cinnamon
 ¼ teaspoon freshly grated nutmeg
   3 extra-large egg whites
   2 tablespoons granulated sugar

1. Scrub the sweet potatoes, cut off the stem ends, and boil in their jackets until tender, 35 to 40 minutes. When cool enough to handle, peel and mash.

2. Coat a 2½-quart ring mold with butter-flavored cooking spray. Arrange the walnut halves around it and sprinkle with the brown sugar. Preheat the oven to 350°.

3. Blend the well-beaten egg substitute, oil, non-dairy creamer, cinnamon, and nutmeg into the potatoes.

4. Beat the egg whites. When slightly thickened, add the granulated sugar gradually and beat until soft peaks form. Fold into the sweet potato mixture.

5. Turn the sweet potato mixture into the mold and bake for 45 minutes.

*To Serve:* Place a serving platter over the mold, invert, and let stand 5 minutes, then remove the mold. Fill the ring with green peas or baby lima beans.

| — PER SERVING — | | | |
|---|---|---|---|
| 4.5 gm total fat | .60 gm saturated fat | 2.4 gm fiber | 149 calories |
| 0 mg cholesterol | 26.6% fat | 44 mg sodium | 41 calories from fat |

## ❦ Carrot and Prune Tzimmes ❦

*Serves: 6 to 8*

I'm told that people in Atlanta, Georgia, really do make a *tzimmes* over Bootsie Segal's tzimmes!

  2 pounds carrots, peeled and sliced, or 2 pounds mini carrots, peeled
  ½ cup honey
  ⅓ cup frozen orange juice concentrate, thawed (not diluted)
  1 (8-ounce) package pitted prunes
  1 tablespoon cornstarch mixed with ¼ cup water

1. Boil the carrots in enough water to just cover until tender but still crisp, about 10 minutes.
2. Add the honey and orange juice. Stir and simmer about 15 minutes or until thickened.
3. Add the prunes and simmer until the prunes are soft, about 20 to 30 minutes.
4. Add the diluted cornstarch and stir until the mixture is clear and thickened.

─── PER SERVING ───

| .5 gm total fat | .04 gm saturated fat | 5.4 gm fiber | 215 calories |
|---|---|---|---|
| 0 mg cholesterol | 1.8% fat | 39 mg sodium | 4 calories from fat |

## ❦ My Mother's Sweet and Sour ❦ Green Beans

(PAREVE)

*Serves: 6 (½ cup = 1 serving)*

When I was a child, my mother frequently prepared vegetables with a simple sweet and sour sauce and served them as a separate course after the entrée. This was called a *tushspeise*.

1 pound fresh green beans, cut in 1-inch pieces
  Pinch of kosher salt
5 cups boiling defatted sodium-reduced vegetable broth or water
2 teaspoons canola oil
¼ cup unbleached all-purpose flour
¼ cup frozen unsweetened apple juice concentrate or 3 tablespoons
  granulated sugar
3 tablespoons distilled white vinegar

1. Add the green beans and salt to the boiling broth or water. Lower the heat, cover, and simmer 30 minutes or until the beans are tender.

2. Heat the oil in a heavy nonstick skillet and add the flour. Stir constantly with a wooden spoon over medium-low heat until the roux is golden brown. *Be careful not to burn.*

3. Remove the roux from the heat. Stir in ½ to 1 cup of liquid from the cooked beans. Return the mixture to the cooked beans and blend.

4. Add the apple juice and vinegar and stir over low heat until a smooth sauce results. Simmer for 15 to 20 minutes. Taste and adjust seasonings. This may be prepared the day before and reheated for serving.

*To Serve:* Serve in individual sauce dishes and as an accompaniment to simply prepared entrées like boiled or roast chicken, turkey, or flanken.

NOTE: If you have any leftover sauce, it can be frozen and saved for future use with some other vegetables.

VARIATION: Any one of the following vegetables may be substituted for the green beans: 1 pound rutabaga, peeled and cubed; 1 cup (8 ounces) dried large lima beans, brought to a boil and soaked 1 hour; 16 ounces White Rose or Yukon Gold potatoes, peeled and diced.

| PER SERVING | | | |
|---|---|---|---|
| 1.8 gm total fat | .17 gm saturated fat | 3.4 gm fiber | 153 calories |
| 0 mg cholesterol | 10.5% fat | 57 mg sodium | 16 calories from fat |

# ❧ Chick-Peas (Nahit) ❧
## (PAREVE)

*Serves: 6 to 8 (⅓ cup = 1 serving)*

Chick-peas (garbanzo beans) are traditionally served very simply on Purim—just cooked, seasoned with salt and pepper, and chilled.

> 2 cups dried chick-peas, cooked and drained (page 235), or 2 (14-ounce) cans sodium-reduced garbanzo beans, rinsed and drained
> ¼ cup nonfat mayonnaise
> 1 clove garlic, smashed, peeled, and minced
> 1 tablespoon finely chopped scallion
> 1 tablespoon finely chopped shallot
> 2 tablespoons finely chopped Italian flat-leaf parsley
> 1 tablespoon capers, rinsed and drained
> Freshly ground pepper and fresh lemon juice to taste

1. While the chick-peas are draining, combine the remaining ingredients in a bowl. Taste and adjust seasonings.
2. Add the drained chick-peas, mix, and refrigerate.

VARIATION: Chick-peas may also be seasoned with spices of your choice—whether allspice and cumin or garlic, onion powder, and spicy paprika. They can be placed on a baking sheet and toasted in a 375° oven until crisp and served as a snack.

---

#### PER SERVING

| | | | |
|---|---|---|---|
| 3.0 gm total fat | .32 gm saturated fat | 3.3 gm fiber | 191 calories |
| 0 mg cholesterol | 13.9% fat | 192 mg sodium | 27 calories from fat |

# ❦ Prune and Rice Tzimmes ❦
## (MEAT)
### *Serves: 4 to 6*

This is a relatively unsweetened tzimmes. For a dairy meal, omit the bones and add a few tablespoons of honey.

3 marrow bones, sawed in 2-inch pieces
8 ounces large pitted prunes
¼ cup frozen unsweetened apple juice concentrate
1 cup uncooked rice (brown or converted)
4 cups boiling water
¼ teaspoon ground cinnamon
2 teaspoons grated lemon zest
3 tablespoons fresh lemon juice

1. Combine all the ingredients in a heavy nonaluminum saucepan; bring to a boil, lower the heat, cover, and simmer 30 to 40 minutes or until the rice is tender. (Brown rice will take about 50 minutes to cook.)

2. Taste and adjust seasonings. Remove the bones before serving.

| PER SERVING | | | |
|---|---|---|---|
| .9 gm total fat | .15 gm saturated fat | 2.9 gm fiber | 170 calories |
| 0 mg cholesterol | 4.3% fat | 5 mg sodium | 8 calories from fat |

## ❦ Chinese Cabbage with Mushrooms ❦
### (PAREVE)
*Serves: 4 to 6*

1 pound Chinese greens (bok choy, Chinese cabbage, and/or broccoli)
4 dried wild mushrooms, stems removed, soaked in hot water 45 minutes or overnight and drained
1 tablespoon canola oil
¼ cup defatted sodium-reduced chicken broth
1 tablespoon sodium-reduced soy sauce
½ teaspoon sugar

1. Wash and dry the greens and cut into 1-inch pieces.
2. Cut the soaked mushrooms into quarters.
3. Heat the oil in a nonstick skillet or wok over a high flame. Add the greens and stir-fry 3 to 4 minutes. Add the mushrooms.
4. Add the chicken broth and bring to a boil. Add the soy sauce and sugar, stir-fry for 2 to 3 minutes, and serve immediately.

--- PER SERVING ---

| | | | |
|---|---|---|---|
| 2.4 gm total fat | .19 gm saturated fat | 1.0 gm fiber | 43 calories |
| 0 mg cholesterol | 49.9% fat | 188 mg sodium | 22 calories from fat |

## ❦ Vegetarian Sandwich ❦
### (PAREVE)
*Serves: 4 (1 sandwich = 1 serving)*

I don't know about you, but I am constantly inundated by information about the importance of eating vegetables and fruits. This recipe helps me carry out the guidelines. Plus, with both partners in many families working, this is a simple meal that children can make by themselves.

4 kaiser rolls, onion bialys, or pita bread, or 8 slices pumpernickel bread
1⅓ cups shredded romaine or mixed salad greens
4 ounces low-fat, sodium-reduced Swiss cheese or ½ cup Marinated
    Bean Salad (page 183) (see Note below)
8 slices ripe tomato
1 cup sliced artichoke hearts, frozen, canned, or fresh cooked
4 thin slices red or white onion
    Freshly ground pepper to taste
4 tablespoons fat-free, low-calorie Italian dressing or spread bread
    with nonfat mayonnaise

1. Place the bread of choice on a plate. Layer with romaine, cheese or beans, to-mato, artichoke, and onion; season with pepper.

2. Sprinkle with 1 tablespoon of dressing (or spread with mayonnaise) and top with remaining slice of bread or roll.

3. Cut in half and serve or wrap in plastic for a packed lunch.

*To Serve:* In summer, start with chilled beet borscht; in winter, a hearty split pea soup. End with fresh fruit.

NOTE: Hummus (page 123), Baba Ghanouj (page 107), Middle Eastern Chopped Eggplant (page 121), Israeli Vegetable Salad (page 184), or "Egg Salad" Spread (page 195) may be added or substituted according to your taste.

—————————— P E R  S E R V I N G ——————————

| 8.3 gm total fat | 3.04 gm saturated fat | 1.6 gm fiber | 289 calories |
| 20 mg cholesterol | 25.6% fat | 582 mg sodium | 75 calories from fat |

# ❦ Nita Williams' Stuffed Zucchini ❦
## (DAIRY)
*Serves: 16 (1 piece = 1 serving)*

Nita has that special touch in cooking. When she brings this zucchini as her contribution to a pot luck dinner, all the guests are pleased.

8 small zucchini (2 pounds), halved lengthwise and hollowed (see Note)
3 tablespoons lemon juice
2 teaspoons canola oil
1 bay leaf
1 tablespoon minced Italian flat-leaf parsley
¼ teaspoon freshly ground black pepper

*Filling:*
½ cup chopped onion
1 tablespoon olive oil
3 cups grated peeled carrots
½ cup chopped water chestnuts
¾ cup nonfat sour cream
¼ teaspoon freshly grated nutmeg
1 teaspoon dried dill weed
⅛ teaspoon ground white pepper
½ cup chopped toasted walnuts
2 teaspoons grated Parmesan cheese alternative

1. Combine the zucchini in a pot with the lemon juice, oil, bay leaf, parsley, and ground pepper. Add enough water to barely cover and bring to a boil. Boil 2 minutes.

2. Remove the zucchini to a paper towel, placing them face down to drain.

*Prepare the filling:*

1. Sauté the onion in the oil until golden, about 5 minutes.

2. Add the carrots and water chestnuts; sauté 2 minutes.

3. Add the sour cream, nutmeg, dill, pepper, and walnuts and stir to combine.

4. Preheat oven to 400°. Fill the zucchini halves with the filling and sprinkle with Parmesan cheese.

5. Bake for 15 to 18 minutes.

NOTE: Use a serrated grapefruit spoon or knife to hollow the zucchini, leaving a ¼-inch-thick base. Use the centers for the vegetable mixture or for soup.

| PER SERVING | | | |
|---|---|---|---|
| 3.9 gm total fat | .44 gm saturated fat | 1.3 gm fiber | 67 calories |
| 0 mg cholesterol | 48.9% fat | 29 mg sodium | 35 calories from fat |

# FISH

Fish Paprikash    284

Broiled Salmon with Mustard Sauce    285

Salmon Mousse Metz    286

Baked Salmon with Carrot-Zucchini Stuffing    288

Gefilte Fish Roll    289

Glazed Salmon Fillets    290

Oven-fried Flounder    291

Fish Fillets with Tomato and Garlic Concasse    292

Annette's Fillet of Sole with Banana    293

Baked Fish Hungarian Style    294

Poached Salmon    295

Green Sauce    296

Jellied Sweet and Sour Fish    297

Smoked Salmon Omelet
(or, What to Do with Leftover Salmon)    298

Fish is a highly nutritious food. It does contain cholesterol, as do all animal products, but most fish is no higher in cholesterol than chicken or beef. However, fish is low in saturated fat and also a good source of vitamin $B_{12}$, iodine, phosphorus, and selenium. It also contains a special polyunsaturated fatty acid known as omega-3, which has anticlotting properties and thus may protect against heart attacks, strokes, and high blood pressure. However, it is a good idea *not to eat the fatty portion of the fish itself and the skin*, because that is where contaminants settle.

Any fish may carry bacteria, viruses, and chemical pollutants. Fish is among the most perishable of foods—even when properly refrigerated, it doesn't last as long as poultry or meat. The U.S. Government does inspect fish (both canned and fresh), and makes rules about where it may be caught or harvested. However, government funds are short. The National Academy of Science's position is that fish, if cooked, is safe and wholesome when eaten in reasonable amounts, no more than three times a week, and *if you vary your choices*.

When making gefilte fish, it is advisable not to sample it until it is cooked, because raw fish is the most common source of parasitic infection in this country. If you do eat raw fish, it should first be frozen three days at below 0° Fahrenheit.

# HOW TO BUY FRESH FISH

- Let your nose be your guide. Fresh fish has a clean, pleasant odor like the ocean—never a fishy, ammonialike smell. Strong odors indicate bacterial presence and spoilage.

- Buy refrigerated fish that is displayed on thick layers of ice, not packaged. Be cautious about fish displayed under hot lights and piled high.

- Look for red gills, bright eyes, moist flesh, and a translucent sheen when buying whole fish.

- Avoid fillets that look bruised or brown.

# TIPS FOR STORING AND HANDLING FISH

- Buy fish just before going home and store it immediately in the coldest part of the refrigerator. Cook and eat it that day if possible, or the next. If that's not possible, wrap carefully and freeze for future use.

- The same rules apply when handling fish as when handling poultry. Wash hands, counters, utensils, etc., with hot soapy water after handling fish so as not to spread bacteria. Because fish contain a small amount of blood they need not be koshered.

- Store frozen raw fish at 0° and thaw in the refrigerator. Cook and serve as soon as possible after thawing.

# TIPS FOR COOKING FISH

- Marinate fish in the refrigerator, not at room temperature.

- Prepare fish stock or soup with smaller fish, as they are less likely to contain pollutants.

- Cook fish until opaque, and it flakes when tested with a fork. The rule of thumb, when cooking fish, is 8 minutes cooking time per inch of thickness.

- Quick cooking in a preheated oven or on a grill preserves flavor and texture. Broiling, pan broiling, or cooking in a microwave are easy ways to cook fish.

# FAT CONTENT OF FISH

The fat content of fish varies from under 1 percent to over 15 percent. If you are counting grams of fat, choose from among those fish considered lean or containing less than 3 percent fat.

Here is a list of some of the acceptable fishes that may be used in a kosher kitchen.

### THE FOLLOWING ARE CONSIDERED LEAN FISH (3% FAT):
Cod or scrod
Haddock
Hake
Pollock
Flatfish, such as sole, flounder, turbot, and halibut
Red snapper
Sea bass
Brook trout
Tilefish, such as yellow pike and yellow snapper
St. Peter's fish

### THE FOLLOWING ARE CONSIDERED MODERATELY FAT FISH:
Bluefish
Striped bass
Carp
Tuna
Pink salmon

### THE FOLLOWING ARE CONSIDERED FAT FISH (15% FAT):
Butterfish (called sable when smoked)
Chilean sea bass
Lake trout
Mullet
Mackerel
Lake whitefish
Pompano
Salmon (Coho, Chinook, Sockeye)
Sardines

Swordfish, sturgeon, and shark are not considered kosher because their scales are not removable from their skin.

# ❦ Fish Paprikash ❦
## (DAIRY)
### *Serves: 4*

A tasty dairy dinner.

    1  cup nonfat plain yogurt
    2  teaspoons olive oil
1⅓  pounds halibut or sea bass, cut into 1-inch chunks
    2  teaspoons Hungarian paprika
    ⅛  teaspoon ground white pepper
    1  medium green bell pepper, seeded and cut into ¾-inch pieces
    1  medium red bell pepper, seeded and cut into ¾-inch pieces
    1  tablespoon minced shallot
    2  large cloves garlic, smashed, peeled, and minced
    1  tablespoon cornstarch
    ¼  cup nonfat sour cream
    ⅓  cup chopped Italian flat-leaf parsley or fresh cilantro

1. Early in the day, or several hours before serving, set the yogurt to drain in a paper coffee filter.

2. Heat the oil in a 10-inch nonstick skillet. Add the fish and sprinkle with the paprika and ground pepper. Stir with a wooden spoon until the fish is opaque, about 3 or 4 minutes.

3. Remove the fish to a plate, leaving the juices in the pan. Add the bell peppers, shallot, and garlic to the juices. Cook, stirring, 3 minutes over medium-high heat.

4. Mix the drained yogurt with the cornstarch and sour cream.

5. Return the fish with its juices to the skillet and stir in the yogurt mixture. Cook over *low* heat for 2 to 3 minutes. *Do not boil.* Add the chopped parsley and cook just long enough to heat through. Serve immediately.

*To Serve:* Serve with boiled potatoes or rice and garnish with mounds of broccoli.

---

#### PER SERVING

| | | | |
|---|---|---|---|
| 6.2 gm total fat | .91 gm saturated fat | 1.1 gm fiber | 237 calories |
| 72 mg cholesterol | 24.1% fat | 130 mg sodium | 56 calories from fat |

# ❧ Broiled Salmon with Mustard Sauce ❧

(PAREVE)

*Serves: 4*

You can pick up the simple ingredients for this tasty dinner on the way home and have it on the table ready to eat within one hour.

4 pink skinned (5-ounce) salmon fillets
Juice of 1 lemon
Salt-free lemon vegetable seasoning
Hungarian paprika

*Mustard Sauce:*

¼ cup dry white wine
1 tablespoon frozen unsweetened apple juice concentrate
2 to 3 tablespoons Dijon mustard
2 tablespoons chopped fresh dill or 2 teaspoons dried dill weed

1. Preheat a broiler or grill.
2. Brush the salmon with the lemon juice and seasonings. Broil on an oiled grill about 4 minutes, basting with lemon juice.
3. Mix the ingredients for the mustard sauce. Brush the broiling salmon with mustard sauce 1 minute before it's finished, or serve the sauce on the side.

*To Serve:* Place on a heated platter on top of steamed spinach. A great meal with baked potatoes and Gingered Cucumbers (page 188).

———— PER SERVING ————

| | | | |
|---|---|---|---|
| 6 gm total fat | .82 gm saturated fat | .1 gm fiber | 198 calories |
| 70 mg cholesterol | 29% fat | 98 mg sodium | 54 calories from fat |

# ❧ Salmon Mousse Metz ❧
## (DAIRY)
*Serves: 8 as an entrée, 16 to 20 as an appetizer*

This mousse has its roots in Pittsburgh! My old friend Velma Friedman shared it with me. Salmon mousse always makes an attractive luncheon dish. It is also well received when served with *schwarzbrot* (black bread) as an appetizer.

2 to 2½  pounds fresh salmon steaks
Court bouillon (see below)
½ cup nonfat mayonnaise
½ cup nonfat sour cream
4 ounces nonfat whipped cream cheese
¼ teaspoon freshly ground pepper
3 tablespoons chopped Italian flat-leaf parsley
2 tablespoons finely chopped scallions
2 tablespoons chopped fresh chives
1 tablespoon chopped fresh tarragon
3 tablespoons fresh lemon juice or to taste
2 teaspoons Dijon mustard
¼ cup kosher lemon gelatin
Chopped fresh dill and cherry tomatoes, for garnish

1. Poach the salmon, covered, in the court bouillon until the fish flakes, about 20 to 25 minutes.

2. Cool the fish in the broth; remove the skin and bones, and flake roughly.

3. Strain the broth, reserving ½ cup liquid.

4. Place half the fish and half the mayonnaise, sour cream, and cream cheese in a food processor or blender. Blend until smooth. Pour into a mixing bowl. Repeat.

5. Add the pepper, parsley, scallions, chives, tarragon, lemon juice, and mustard. Stir to mix.

6. Soak the gelatin in the reserved ½ cup of fish stock. When the liquid is absorbed, dissolve the gelatin over low heat. Stir into the salmon mixture.

7. Pour the mousse into a 6-cup ring or fish-shaped mold lightly coated with vegetable oil cooking spray and chill several hours or overnight.

*To Serve:* Unmold on a bed of greens, sprinkle with chopped dill, and serve with Cucumber Salad (page 179).

VARIATION: Poach the salmon as in steps 1 and 2. Serve warm or chilled with Green Sauce (page 296).

─────── P E R   S E R V I N G   A S   E N T R É E ───────

| | | | |
|---|---|---|---|
| 9.8 gm total fat | 1.71 gm saturated fat | .1 gm fiber | 231 calories |
| 73 mg cholesterol | 39.7% fat | 376 mg sodium | 88 calories from fat |

─────── P E R   S E R V I N G   A S   A P P E T I Z E R ───────

| | | | |
|---|---|---|---|
| 3.9 gm total fat | .68 gm saturated fat | .1 gm fiber | 92 calories |
| 29 mg cholesterol | 39.7% fat | 150 mg sodium | 35 calories from fat |

## Court Bouillon

2 quarts water
1 cup dry white wine or vermouth
1 small onion, peeled and sliced
1 rib celery with leaves, sliced
1 scallion
6 sprigs fresh dill
6 peppercorns
1 bay leaf

Place all the ingredients in a large skillet (not aluminum or cast iron) and bring to a boil. Reduce the heat and simmer for 20 minutes before adding the salmon.

# ❦ Baked Salmon with ❦ Carrot-Zucchini Stuffing
### (PAREVE)
*Serves: 8 to 10*

A whole fish makes a spectacular, moist, and flavorful entrée. If a whole fish is not available, use fillets and top them with stuffing. This reduces your baking time by a little more than half.

> 1 pink salmon (3 to 4 pounds), eviscerated, head and tail left on, washed thoroughly with cold water
> Juice of ½ lemon
> 2 teaspoons salt-free vegetable seasoning
> Freshly ground pepper

**Carrot-Zucchini Stuffing:**

> 2 teaspoons olive oil
> 1 small onion, peeled and chopped fine
> 1 shallot, peeled and chopped fine
> 3 cups grated zucchini
> 1 cup grated peeled carrot
> ¼ cup minced Italian flat-leaf parsley
> 1 tablespoon minced fresh basil or tarragon
> ¼ cup fine dried bread crumbs or matzo meal (optional)

1. Preheat the oven to 350°.
2. Season the cavity of the salmon with lemon juice, vegetable seasoning, and pepper.
3. To make the stuffing: Heat the olive oil and sauté the onion and shallot until wilted, about 5 minutes. Add all the other ingredients and mix lightly.
4. Fill the cavity with the stuffing. Use toothpicks to close the cavity, placing any stuffing that will not fit on the bottom of the baking pan.
5. Lay the whole fish in the baking pan. Spray the top of the fish with olive oil cooking spray.
6. Cover with foil and bake for 30 minutes. Uncover and continue baking for 20 minutes or until the fish flakes easily.

*To Serve:* A fish-shaped platter is particularly attractive; you may cover it with either a bed of watercress or fresh dill before carefully transferring the salmon. Gently remove the skin before surrounding with lemon or lime slices and mounds of extra stuffing.

---

### PER SERVING

| | | | |
|---|---|---|---|
| 11 gm total fat | 1.85 gm saturated fat | .1 gm fiber | 236 calories |
| 76 mg cholesterol | 41.5% fat | 62 mg sodium | 99 calories from fat |

# ❦ Gefilte Fish Roll ❦
## (PAREVE)
*Serves: 8 to 10 (1 slice = 1 serving)*

Many Jewish cooks are both glad and sorry that the preparation of gefilte fish has become a lost art. Here is a quick, easy, and flavorful way out. It tastes more home-made than fish in the jar and makes a beautiful presentation. If you find quality fish in the freezer of a kosher market, try it. Then you can be the final judge.

⅔ cup dry white wine
2½ quarts water
2 or 3 large carrots, peeled and sliced diagonally in 1-inch pieces
3 ribs celery with leaves, sliced diagonally in 1-inch pieces
1 parsnip, chopped
1 large onion, peeled and chopped
1 bay leaf
½ bunch Italian flat-leaf parsley or fresh dill, tied with string
½ teaspoon peppercorns
1 teaspoon salt
1½ pounds frozen, ready-to-cook gefilte fish (made from whitefish and pike, no sugar added) (see Note)
1 large Idaho potato, peeled and cut into ½-inch-thick slices

1. In a 4-quart Dutch oven, combine the wine, water, carrots, celery, parsnip, onion, bay leaf, parsley, peppercorns, and salt (see Note). Bring to a boil. Reduce the heat and simmer 30 minutes uncovered.

2. Add the frozen fish roll in its paper wrapping and simmer for 1 hour, basting with the broth from time to time.

3. After 1 hour, add the potato slices and continue cooking 30 minutes.

4. Remove from the heat and allow to cool in the cooking liquid.

5. Remove the fish roll and peel off the paper. Place on a rack and allow to drain.

6. Wrap in plastic wrap, then foil, and chill at least overnight before serving.

*To Serve:* Cut in ¾-inch slices and top with a cooked carrot slice and a potato slice, if desired. Serve with chilled Homemade Beet Horseradish (page 73) and matzo or challah.

NOTE: Raskin's and a few other brands of frozen gefilte fish are acceptable; however, most of the others seem to have sugar, matzo meal, or potato starch added.

To make a richer stock, ask your fishmonger for some fish bones or heads to put in with the vegetables when making your court bouillon. (Do not use salmon bones or heads.)

| PER SERVING | | | |
|---|---|---|---|
| 2.5 gm total fat | .02 gm saturated fat | 1.3 gm fiber | 100 calories |
| 53 mg cholesterol | 22.2% fat | 570 mg sodium | 23 calories from fat |

# ❦ Glazed Salmon Fillets ❦
## (PAREVE)
### Serves: 4

This quick and easy fish preparation has a hint of Asia in its seasonings.

    2 tablespoons frozen unsweetened apple juice concentrate
    2 teaspoons Dijon mustard
1½ tablespoons minced fresh gingerroot or 1 teaspoon ground ginger
    2 teaspoons sodium-reduced soy sauce or 1 tablespoon hoisin sauce
    2 teaspoons fresh lemon juice
    4 (5-ounce) skinned Chinook salmon fillets, about ¾ inch thick, rinsed and
       dried

1. Preheat oven to 450°.

2. Combine the first 5 ingredients in a small jar or dish. (Keep refrigerated if not used that day.)

3. Arrange the fillets in a foil-lined baking dish and coat with the glaze.

4. Bake for 5 minutes.

5. Turn up the heat and glaze under the broiler for 1 to 2 minutes.

*To Serve:* Serve with steamed rice and a generous serving of stir-fried vegetables of your choice. A fresh fruit compote with Harriet Greenwald's Dessert Wafers (page 389) would be a perfect ending.

---

**——— PER SERVING ———**

| | | | |
|---|---|---|---|
| 12.3 gm total fat | 2.13 gm saturated fat | 0 gm fiber | 248 calories |
| 88 mg cholesterol | 46.3% fat | 222 mg sodium | 111 calories from fat |

---

# ❦ Oven-fried Flounder ❦
### (PAREVE)
*Serves: 4 (4 ounces cooked fish = 1 serving)*

The words "fried" or "crispy" automatically suggest a dish high in fat. But not these baked fillets! They are breaded with a no-yolk egg batter and baked without added fat.

> 4 (5-ounce) skinned flounder fillets
> ½ cup egg substitute mixed with 1 extra-large egg white and ⅛ teaspoon ground white pepper
> ½ to ⅔ cup fine dried bread crumbs
> 2 tablespoons chopped Italian flat-leaf parsley
> 1 teaspoon Hungarian paprika
> 4 lemon wedges, for garnish

1. Preheat the oven to 450°. Coat a nonstick baking sheet with butter-flavored cooking spray.

2. Dip the fillets in the egg substitute mixture.

3. Combine the bread crumbs, parsley, and paprika. Press the mixture onto both sides of the fish and lay on the baking sheet.

4. Bake for 10 to 12 minutes, or until the fish is lightly browned and flakes easily when tested with a fork.

*To Serve:* Place the fish, garnished with lemon wedges, on a warmed serving platter. Surround with baked potatoes topped with nonfat sour cream and chives and steamed broccoli and carrots. Start with a glass of Cold Cucumber Soup (page 143) and end with fresh fruit cup and My Favorite Mandelbrot (page 385).

| ── PER SERVING ── | | | |
|---|---|---|---|
| 3.5 gm total fat | .79 gm saturated fat | .8 gm fiber | 215 calories |
| 68 mg cholesterol | 15.3% fat | 301 mg sodium | 32 calories from fat |

# ❧ Fish Fillets with Tomato ❧ and Garlic Concasse
## (PAREVE)
*Serves: 4 (4 ounces cooked fish = 1 serving)*

⅔ cup peeled, seeded ripe plum tomatoes, chopped fine
½ teaspoon chopped garlic
1 teaspoon extra-virgin olive oil
4 (5-ounce) skinned fish fillets (red snapper or whitefish)
1 tablespoon fresh lemon juice
1 teaspoon salt-free vegetable seasoning
  Freshly ground pepper to taste
  Hungarian paprika to taste
  Lemon wedges, for garnish

1. Combine the tomatoes, garlic, and oil in a small bowl and stir to mix. Set aside.
2. Line a broiler pan with foil and coat with olive oil cooking spray; preheat in the broiler for about 2 minutes.
3. Arrange the fish on the preheated pan; sprinkle with lemon juice, vegetable seasoning, pepper, and paprika.
4. Broil 3 inches from the heat for 5 minutes. Top with the tomato mixture and broil 2 to 3 minutes longer or until the fish flakes easily when tested with a fork.

*To Serve:* Place the fillets on a warm serving platter, garnish with lemon wedges, and surround with stir-fried mixed squash and peas. Accompany with no-yolk noodles mixed with nonfat cottage cheese.

---

**PER SERVING**

| | | | |
|---|---|---|---|
| 3.2 gm total fat | .56 gm saturated fat | .4 gm fiber | 164 calories |
| 52 mg cholesterol | 18% fat | 95 mg sodium | 28 calories from fat |

---

# ❦ Annette's Fillet of Sole with Banana ❦
## (PAREVE)
### *Serves: 4*

4 (5-ounce) fillets of sole or flounder
½ cup unbleached all-purpose flour mixed with salt, pepper, and paprika
1 tablespoon canola oil
2 ripe (yet firm) bananas, cut in half lengthwise and quartered

**Sauce:**
¾ cup dry sherry
3 tablespoons fresh lemon juice
1 teaspoon ground ginger
3 tablespoons packed brown sugar

1. Dredge the sole on both sides in the seasoned flour.
2. Heat the oil in a nonstick frying pan; place the fillets in the hot pan, in batches if necessary, and brown on each side 3 to 5 minutes (depending on the thickness of the fish). Turn only once, it may break apart. When flaky, remove to a heated platter.
3. Combine the sauce ingredients in the skillet; simmer 2 to 4 minutes, until the sauce begins to caramelize.
4. Heat the bananas in the sauce for ½ minute, turning once. Be very careful not to overcook them.

*To Serve:* Place the bananas atop the fillets and coat each piece with 2 to 3 tablespoons of sauce. Serve immediately. Accompany with steamed brown and wild rice and peas.

---

PER SERVING
| | | | |
|---|---|---|---|
| 5.6 gm total fat | .80 gm saturated fat | 2.3 gm fiber | 305 calories |
| 68 mg cholesterol | 16.5% fat | 196 mg sodium | 51 calories from fat |

---

# ❦ Baked Fish Hungarian Style ❦
## (DAIRY)
### *Serves: 4*

4 (5-ounce) flounder fillets
  Salt-free vegetable seasoning to taste
  Ground white pepper to taste
1 cup nonfat plain yogurt
1 teaspoon hot Hungarian paprika
1 teaspoon caraway seeds
1 tablespoon grated onion

1. Coat a shallow baking dish or casserole with vegetable oil cooking spray. Preheat the oven to 400°.
2. Season the fillets with vegetable seasoning and pepper.
3. Combine the yogurt, paprika, caraway, and onion and blend thoroughly. Spread the yogurt mixture over the fish fillets.
4. Bake the fish in the upper third of the oven for 10 minutes, or until it flakes easily when tested with a fork.

*To Serve:* Serve immediately, surrounded with parsleyed new potatoes and steamed green beans.

---

PER SERVING
| | | | |
|---|---|---|---|
| 1.6 gm total fat | .40 gm saturated fat | .3 gm fiber | 141 calories |
| 56 mg cholesterol | 10.7% fat | 136 mg sodium | 15 calories from fat |

# ❦ Poached Salmon ❦

(PAREVE)

*Serves: 16 to 20*

Very few spring or summer dishes can rival a moist, fresh, delicately flavored salmon poached to perfection and served with a simple green sauce. Whether for a bris, bar mitzvah, or baby-naming brunch, this salmon is a consistent winner. It may be prepared the day before, covered with plastic wrap, and chilled until serving time.

1 small onion, peeled and sliced
2 ribs celery, sliced
2 carrots, peeled and sliced
  Bouquet garni (in cheesecloth or teaball): ½ bunch Italian parsley or dill, bay leaf, thyme, and peppercorns
1 cup red or white wine vinegar
1 whole 8- to 10-pound salmon, with head and tail, gutted and cleaned

1. Make a court bouillon: In a fish poacher or large oval kettle, combine the onion, celery, carrots, bouquet garni, vinegar, and 2 quarts of water. Simmer uncovered for 30 minutes.

2. Wash and wrap the whole salmon in a double thickness of cheesecloth, leaving 2 to 3 inches of cheesecloth at each end. Lower the fish into the simmering bouillon; add boiling water, if necessary, to cover the fish.

3. Cover and poach the fish at just below a simmer for about 45 minutes—the liquid should not boil.

4. Remove the pan from the heat and let the fish cool in the poaching liquid.

5. When cool, carefully lift the fish using the ends of the cheesecloth. Unwrap and discard the cheesecloth.

6. Discard the head and tail of the salmon (if desired). Carefully peel off the skin; turn and peel the skin from the underside. Trim off any small bones along the spine.

*To Serve:* Place the salmon on a fish-shaped or oval platter. Garnish with fluted lemon halves sprinkled with chopped fresh dill or parsley, crisp sliced cucumbers arranged to simulate fresh scales, and cherry tomatoes. Accompany with Green Sauce (recipe follows).

When serving, start with the top layer until finished, then carefully lift and discard the center bone, continuing on the bottom layer.

---

**———— P E R   S E R V I N G ————**

| | | | |
|---|---|---|---|
| 5.4 gm total fat | .95 gm saturated fat | .1 gm fiber | 107 calories |
| 39 mg cholesterol | 47.5% fat | 30 mg sodium | 49 calories from fat |

---

# ❦ Green Sauce ❦
### (PAREVE OR DAIRY)
*Yield: About 3 cups (1 tablespoon = 1 serving)*

½ cup Italian flat-leaf or curly parsley sprigs, washed and thoroughly dried
½ bunch watercress, washed and thoroughly dried, stems removed
2½ cups nonfat or cholesterol-free fat-reduced mayonnaise or nonfat plain yogurt
½ cup fresh dill, leaves only
1½ teaspoons mild mustard
1½ teaspoons Dijon mustard
1 tablespoon fresh lemon juice
½ teaspoon white wine vinegar
Dash of ground white pepper
Fresh herbs (optional)

1. Place the parsley and watercress in a food processor; chop till finely minced.
2. Add the mayonnaise, dill, mustards, lemon juice, vinegar, pepper, and herbs. Process briefly until well combined. Taste and adjust seasonings.
3. Remove to a bowl, cover, and refrigerate until serving time.

---

**———— P E R   S E R V I N G ————**

| | | | |
|---|---|---|---|
| 0 gm total fat | 0 gm saturated fat | .1 gm fiber | 11 calories |
| 0 mg cholesterol | 2% fat | 166 mg sodium | 0 calories from fat |

# ❧ Jellied Sweet and Sour Fish ❧

## (PAREVE)

*Serves: 8 to 10*

This easy make-ahead dish goes well with a buffet or makes a nice summer supper.

  3 pounds fish steaks (salmon or carp)
    Juice of ½ lemon
½ cup red wine vinegar or rice wine vinegar
1⅔ cups water
  1 tablespoon frozen unsweetened apple juice concentrate
  1 bay leaf
  3 whole cloves
    Pinch of hot red pepper flakes
¼ teaspoon ground cinnamon
⅓ cup packed brown sugar
  1 small onion, peeled, halved, and sliced thin
  3 carrots, peeled and cut diagonally into ½-inch slices
¼ cup dark raisins
¼ cup sliced almonds
¼ cup chopped Italian flat-leaf parsley, for garnish

1. Wash the fish in bowl of cold water acidulated with the lemon juice. Drain.

2. In a 4-quart saucepan, combine the vinegar, water, apple juice concentrate, bay leaf, cloves, hot pepper, cinnamon, brown sugar, and onion. Bring to a boil, reduce the heat, and simmer for 5 minutes.

3. Add the fish and the carrots. The liquid should cover about ⅔ of the fish; add water if necessary.

4. Cover and simmer for 30 minutes.

5. Remove the fish with a slotted spoon to a shallow serving casserole. Sprinkle with the raisins and almonds.

6. Boil the remaining liquid until it is reduced by half.

7. Pour the sauce through a strainer over the fish. Allow to cool. Cover and refrigerate overnight to jell. Garnish with parsley.

─────────── PER SERVING ───────────

| | | | |
|---|---|---|---|
| 13.0 gm total fat | 2.18 gm saturated fat | 1.4 gm fiber | 296 calories |
| 84 mg cholesterol | 39.9% fat | 77 mg sodium | 117 calories from fat |

# ❧ Smoked Salmon Omelet ❧
# (or, What to Do with Leftover Salmon)
(PAREVE)

*Serves: 2*

    4 extra-large egg whites
    ½ cup egg substitute
      Freshly ground pepper to taste
    2 ounces smoked salmon (tails are fine)
    ¼ cup chopped fresh chives

1. Break the egg whites into a bowl and beat lightly with a fork.
2. Add the egg substitute and freshly ground pepper and blend.
3. Cut the smoked salmon into strips.
4. Coat a medium-size nonstick skillet with butter-flavored cooking spray and heat. Pour in the egg mixture and cook over low heat by lifting up the cooked portion with a wooden spoon or spatula and allowing the uncooked portion to spread.
5. When the eggs are firm, top with the salmon strips and chives.

*To Serve:* Remove from the heat and fold over onto warm plates with sliced tomatoes and onion rolls, toasted bagels, or bialys. Potato pancakes with sour cream or applesauce are always a welcome addition.

--- PER SERVING ---

| | | | |
|---|---|---|---|
| 3.3 gm total fat | .69 gm saturated fat | .2 gm fiber | 112 calories |
| 7 mg cholesterol | 27.8% fat | 412 mg sodium | 30 calories from fat |

--- ❧ HARRIET'S HINTS ❧ ---

*Frozen fish is frequently processed by dipping it into a brine prior to freezing. If you are on a low-sodium diet, avoid frozen fish and use fresh fish only.*

# POULTRY

My Mother's Roast Stuffed Chicken   303

Gefilte Helzel (Stuffed Neck)   305

Baked Chicken with Bing Cherries   306

"Jewish" Chicken   307

Bombay Chicken Breasts   308

Oven-fried Chicken   309

Gayle Kohl's Garlic Chicken   310

Ten Easy Pieces of Chicken Breast   311

Cyrus Faridi's Apricot Chicken   312

Middle Eastern Chicken Breasts   313

Lemon Chicken for a Crowd   314

Honey Glazed Chicken   315

Indoor Barbecued Chicken   317

My Favorite Chicken Paprikash with Rice   318

Chicken in Sauerkraut with Caraway Seeds   319

Chicken with Potatoes and Red Peppers   320

Hungarian Stuffed Cabbage   321

Stuffed Grape Leaves (Dolmas, Yaprakis de Oja, Yebra)   323

Syrian Stuffed Eggplant (Specha)   324

My Family's Favorite Turkey Meat Loaf   326

Carnatzlach (Rumanian Broiled Hamburgers)   327

Turkey Cutlets or Schnitzel   328

Cornish Hen with Sweet and Sour Glaze   329

Cornish Hens with Ginger Plum Sauce   331

With ever-greater public awareness about nutrition and our attendant quest for healthful cooking and eating, consumption of poultry is at an all-time high. Poultry is lower in fat and cholesterol than most red meats, and it can be prepared in myriad ways. That's the good news. The bad news is that not all chicken and turkey—or parts thereof—is created equal.

1. Some poultry is higher in fat than others. The highest is turkey thigh, followed closely by chicken backs, then chicken thighs, turkey drumsticks, chicken drumsticks, chicken breast, and finally the lowest: turkey breast. Chicken thighs have almost twice the fat of chicken drumsticks.

2. All poultry should be eaten without the skin and with fat trimmed and discarded. Save the skin, wing tips (including double portions, and giblets except liver), and freeze for future stock or soup preparations. You can, in some cases, cook chicken with the skin; however, if you have not seasoned under the skin, the flavor will be lost when the skin is removed after cooking.

3. If you eat ground turkey or chicken, choose ground breast meat free of skin and visible fat. Turkey or chicken breast cutlets are a better choice than ground.

4. Some birds develop more fat than others, so for low-fat cooking, "start with a skinny chicken," meaning 2- to 2½-pound broilers, not fryers, roasters, or capons that are allowed to mature and fed to develop fat deposits in the muscles of the meat.

5. Try using a vertical roaster to cook a whole chicken upright. It cuts the cooking time and allows fat to drip away from the poultry.

6. When possible, make sure that your poultry has no antibiotics, hormones, pre-

servatives, or other chemicals added. Kosher poultry is far ahead of most commercial poultry products in this respect. In fact, many of my non-Jewish friends prefer the taste and healthful qualities of kosher poultry.

7. Remember to limit your consumption of animal protein. Whether chicken, Cornish hen, or turkey, a portion should be about the size and thickness of a deck of cards, or 4 ounces cooked. Choose one day a week—possibly Shabbat—to eat chicken. The other days, opt for turkey or fish or, best of all, low-fat vegetarian. I say, "Try not to eat anything that has a face (animal protein) more than 3 or 4 days per week."

### A Word About Sodium

Since most kosher poultry is koshered *with* the skin, which you will not be eating, the sodium content of the poultry meat is relatively unaffected by the koshering process.

### A Few Hints About Buying Poultry

- When purchasing prepackaged poultry, select a package with little or no liquid.
- If the poultry is not packaged, it should not have a strong odor. The skin color of chicken may vary, depending on what it has been fed.
- Frozen poultry packages should not be torn.
- Fresh poultry should be used within 2 days of purchasing. Store in the refrigerator, lightly wrapped, so that air can circulate.
- Frozen whole chickens and turkeys, properly wrapped, keep for up to one year in the freezer.
- Frozen chicken parts keep up to 9 months; frozen turkey parts keep up to 6 months.

### Safe Handling Instructions

In order to minimize the danger of bacteria that could cause illness, the following are some safe handling instructions for your protection:

1. Keep poultry refrigerated or frozen. Thaw in the refrigerator or microwave, not at room temperature.
2. Keep raw poultry separate from other foods.
3. Wash work surfaces and cutting boards, utensils, and hands with hot water and soap after touching raw meat or poultry.
4. Cook thoroughly.
5. Keep hot foods hot and cold foods cold, not at room temperature. Poultry should be kept in the refrigerator until you are ready to cook it. Once poultry is cooked, it

should not be left at room temperature for longer than 2 hours. Refrigerate leftovers as soon as possible.

6. To check poultry to see if it is done: A whole turkey should be 160° to 170° when it is adequately cooked. For small cuts of poultry, test with a sharp paring knife or skewer; the juices should run clear and the color of the meat should be white rather than pink.

7. If you have any questions about storing or handling poultry, call the USDA meat and poultry hotline at 1-800-535-4555.

# ✠ My Mother's Roast Stuffed Chicken ✠
## (MEAT)
*Serves: 4 (¼ chicken with stuffing = 1 serving)*

Preparing this makes me feel as though I'm back at my mother's house. I use a broiling chicken instead of a roaster (because it is leaner), with all visible fat removed, and I stuff the chicken under the skin (rather than in the body cavity) with my mother's bread stuffing. The skin keeps the stuffing and the chicken moist and may be removed before serving or eating.

1 (2-pound) broiler (or Empire Kosher Rock Cornish Broiler), split along backbone only and flattened; wing tips, excess skin, and all visible fat removed
  Juice of ½ lemon
1 teaspoon salt-free vegetable seasoning
1 small onion, peeled and minced
1 rib celery with leaves, minced
½ teaspoon garlic powder
1 teaspoon canola or olive oil
  Defatted sodium-reduced chicken broth or water (optional)
½ loaf stale water challah, crust removed
¼ teaspoon kosher salt
⅛ teaspoon ground white pepper
2 extra-large egg whites and ¼ cup egg substitute, slightly beaten
½ cup chopped Italian flat-leaf parsley
2 teaspoons baking powder
  Hungarian paprika
  Watercress and cherry tomatoes, for garnish

1. Using kitchen shears and your fingers, loosen the chicken skin, forming pockets to hold the stuffing.

2. Sprinkle the chicken under its skin with lemon juice and vegetable seasoning. Marinate in the refrigerator several hours or overnight.

3. To make stuffing: Sauté the onion, celery, and garlic powder in the oil in a nonstick skillet until transparent. If necessary, add some chicken broth to keep the vegetables from sticking.

4. Soak the bread briefly in warm water and squeeze dry. Crumble the bread into the sautéed onion and celery. Add salt and pepper; mix to blend. Add the egg mixture, parsley, and baking powder; blend thoroughly.

5. Stuff the pockets formed between the skin and body of the chicken with the bread mixture and secure with toothpicks or skewers.

6. Place the chicken, breast side up, in an attractive shallow roasting pan or casserole coated with olive oil cooking spray. Sprinkle with Hungarian paprika.

7. Roast in the upper third of a preheated 450° oven for 10 minutes; lower the heat to 375° and continue to roast for 45 to 60 minutes or until golden brown and done. (The chicken is cooked when the juices run clear.)

8. Cut the broiler into quarters. (Remove the skin if desired and sprinkle the stuffing with additional Hungarian paprika.)

*To Serve:* Garnish with watercress and fresh cherry tomatoes and serve immediately.

*My Mother's Bread Stuffing:* I often make a larger amount of this stuffing to stuff a turkey or serve in a casserole alongside a turkey breast. Make the stuffing as directed in steps 3 and 4 above, doubling or tripling all the ingredients except the baking powder (increase that by only 1 teaspoon if you're doubling or 2 if you're tripling). Spray a baking dish of the appropriate size with olive oil cooking spray. Spoon the stuffing mixture lightly into the dish and bake, covered, in the oven along with your bird for the last 45 minutes, uncovering toward the end to crisp the top.

NOTE: Store stuffing separately from chicken to avoid risk of salmonella.

| PER SERVING | | | |
|---|---|---|---|
| 9.3 gm total fat | 2.35 gm saturated fat | 2.9 gm fiber | 425 calories |
| 75 mg cholesterol | 20.4% fat | 720 mg sodium | 84 calories from fat |

# ᴡᴘ Gefilte Helzel (Stuffed Neck) ᴡᴘ

## (MEAT)

*Yield: 20 to 22 slices (1 slice = 1 serving)*

Helzel is a natural accompaniment to roast poultry. If you buy packaged chicken, the skin from the neck may be impossible to find. However, butchers in kosher poultry markets can be persuaded to keep the skin intact. When it comes to eating, savor the filling and scrap the skin!

**Skin of 1 chicken neck**
3 tablespoons grated onion
2 tablespoons olive oil
2 tablespoon finely diced celery
1 tablespoon chopped Italian flat-leaf parsley
1 cup unbleached all-purpose flour or matzo meal
⅛ teaspoon kosher salt
⅛ teaspoon ground white pepper
1½ teaspoons Hungarian paprika

1. Clean the skin thoroughly, removing any fat or pinfeathers.
2. To make the stuffing, sauté the onion in the oil for for 3 to 5 minutes, until transparent. Add the celery, parsley, flour, salt, pepper, and paprika.
3. Sew the small end of the chicken neck with a trussing needle and white thread or dental floss; or use skewers to close.
4. Fill the skin three-fourths full of stuffing; sew or skewer the other end closed.
5. Wash with cold water, then pour boiling water over the helzel. This will tighten and smooth the skin.
6. Place in a roasting pan with chicken, turkey, or brisket, or cook in tzimmes or cholent. The helzel may also be roasted separately with a little leftover gravy or on a bed of onions, carrots, celery, and chicken broth for about 1½ to 2 hours.
7. Remove the thread from both ends before slicing to serve.

---

**PER SERVING**

| | | | |
|---|---|---|---|
| 1.8 gm total fat | .18 gm saturated fat | .2 gm fiber | 37 calories |
| 2 mg cholesterol | 42.4% fat | 15 mg sodium | 16 calories from fat |

# ❧ Baked Chicken with Bing Cherries ❧
## (MEAT)
### Serves: 8

I first prepared this recipe forty years ago while living in Cleveland. It was a success with guests then and it still is today.

   2 (2-pound) broilers, skinned, defatted, and quartered
     Juice of 1½ lemons
   2 teaspoons salt-free vegetable seasoning
     Freshly ground pepper to taste
     Hungarian paprika to taste
   1 (16-ounce) can pitted Bing cherries
2½ teaspoons cornstarch
   2 tablespoons dry sherry
   1 tablespoon brandy
   ½ cup lightly toasted sliced almonds for garnish (optional)

1. Preheat the oven to 375°.
2. Arrange the chicken pieces in a shallow casserole. Sprinkle with the juice of 1 lemon and the seasonings.
3. Bake in the upper third of the oven for 50 to 60 minutes, or until tender and lightly browned.
4. Drain the juice from the cherries and combine with the cornstarch in a saucepan. Cook until the juice thickens and is shiny.
5. Add the remaining lemon juice (about 2 tablespoons), the sherry, and brandy; stir and bring to a boil. Add the drained cherries and heat 1 minute.

*To Serve:* Pour the hot cherry sauce over the chicken and serve over parsleyed steamed rice and with tender steamed green beans and baby carrots.

—————— PER SERVING ——————

| | | | |
|---|---|---|---|
| 6.2 gm total fat | 1.68 gm saturated fat | .3 gm fiber | 213 calories |
| 73 mg cholesterol | 26.3% fat | 73 mg sodium | 56 calories from fat |

# ❦ "Jewish" Chicken ❦
## (MEAT)

*Serves: 8 (1 piece chicken breast or 2 chicken legs = 1 serving)*

An old college friend (who isn't Jewish) makes delicious baked chicken that she refers to as her "Jewish" chicken—and it does have a traditional taste. She always uses fresh kosher chickens.

1 large onion, peeled, halved, and sliced
2 whole chicken breasts (about 2 pounds), skinned, defatted, and cut crosswise
8 chicken legs (about 2 pounds), skinned and defatted
2 teaspoons onion powder
2 teaspoons garlic powder
   Ground white pepper to taste
1 tablespoon Hungarian paprika
   Sodium-reduced defatted chicken broth, as needed

1. Preheat the oven to 350°.
2. Sprinkle the onion slices on the bottom of a roasting pan.
3. Sprinkle chicken with the seasonings on both sides; arrange the chicken pieces on top of the onions. Add chicken broth to a depth of ¼ inch.
4. Cover and bake for 30 minutes.
5. Uncover and continue to roast until tender and lightly browned, about 35 minutes. If desired, brown under the broiler before serving.

---

**PER SERVING**

| | | | |
|---|---|---|---|
| 5.7 gm total fat | 1.55 gm saturated fat | .5 gm fiber | 186 calories |
| 87 mg cholesterol | 28.5% fat | 81 mg sodium | 51 calories from fat |

---

❦ HARRIET'S HINTS ❦

*Always save leftover gravies from chicken, beef, or veal roasts; label and freeze sealed in little plastic bags. They can be used as enrichment in gravy, sauces, or soups.*

# ᭡ Bombay Chicken Breasts ᭡
## (MEAT)
### Serves: 6

Condiments that may be served with this curried chicken are sliced scallions, chutney, dark raisins, and toasted slivered almonds. The sliced oranges not only look pretty, but they add vitamin C and potassium to your diet.

> 6 (4-ounce) boned and skinned chicken breast halves
>   Juice of ½ lemon
> 1 teaspoon salt-free vegetable seasoning
> ⅛ teaspoon ground white pepper
> 1½ teaspoons curry powder, or to taste
> ½ cup fresh orange juice
> 3 tablespoons honey
> ¼ teaspoon Dijon mustard
> 2 navel oranges
>   Watercress, for garnish (optional)

1. Preheat the oven to 325°.
2. Sprinkle the chicken with lemon juice, vegetable seasoning, and pepper on both sides.
3. Heat the curry powder in a dry saucepan for about 1 minute, stirring constantly. Add the juice, honey, and mustard. Stir to blend.
4. Dip the chicken pieces in the marinade and place in a shallow nonstick baking dish. Pour any remaining marinade over the chicken.
5. Cover the dish with foil and place in the oven for 20 minutes. Remove the foil.
6. Turn the chicken over and bake uncovered until tender, 15 to 20 minutes.
7. While the chicken is baking, peel the oranges with a serrated knife, removing all the white portion. Cut into ¼-inch slices and halve if they are large.

*To Serve:* Remove the chicken to a warm serving platter. Add the orange slices to the juices in the pan and heat briefly. Pour the sauce over the chicken and arrange the orange slices around it. Garnish with a few sprigs of watercress. This is delicious served with the suggested condiments. Brown or white rice and steamed fresh broccoli are tasty accompaniments.

---

———— PER SERVING ————

| | | | |
|---|---|---|---|
| 3.2 gm total fat | .86 gm saturated fat | .3 gm fiber | 187 calories |
| 73 mg cholesterol | 15.5% fat | 71 mg sodium | 28 calories from fat |

---

# ❧ Oven-fried Chicken ❧
## (MEAT)
### *Serves: 6*

An old family favorite, particularly with children and for picnics. I use drumsticks instead of thighs because of their lower fat content and ease of handling for youngsters.

- 2 tablespoons olive oil or canola oil
- 2 tablespoons fresh lemon juice
- 3 pounds chicken breasts, halved, skinned, and defatted, or 12 drumsticks (3 pounds), skinned
- 1½ teaspoons garlic powder
- 1 teaspoon onion powder
- ⅛ teaspoon ground white pepper
- 1¼ cups crushed sugar-free cornflakes mixed with 1½ teaspoons salt-free vegetable seasoning
  Hungarian paprika to taste
  Watercress and red grapes, for garnish

1. Preheat the oven to 400°.
2. Mix the oil and lemon juice. Dip the chicken in the mixture.
3. Season the chicken with garlic and onion powder and the pepper.
4. Roll in cornflake crumbs and place on a nonstick baking sheet. Sprinkle with paprika.
5. Cover with foil and bake in the upper third of the oven for 15 minutes. Uncover and bake 25 to 30 minutes more, or until browned, crisp, and tender.

*To Serve:* Place the chicken on a bed of watercress on a platter and garnish with 3 to 4 small bunches of red grapes.

---

PER SERVING

| | | | |
|---|---|---|---|
| 6.5 gm total fat | 1.33 gm saturated fat | .3 gm fiber | 247 calories |
| 73 mg cholesterol | 24.6% fat | 284 mg sodium | 59 calories from fat |

---

# ❦ Gayle Kohl's Garlic Chicken ❦
## (MEAT)
### *Serves: 4*

2 whole boneless chicken breasts (about 2 pounds)
1 teaspoon sake or dry vermouth
1 teaspoon sesame oil
1 extra-large egg white, slightly beaten
2 teaspoons canola oil
3 carrots, peeled and sliced diagonally into 1-inch pieces
½ cup canned bamboo shoots, drained, rinsed, and sliced thin
½ cup canned water chestnuts, drained, rinsed, and sliced thin
8 large cloves garlic, smashed, peeled, and minced
1 cup defatted sodium-reduced chicken broth
1 tablespoon rice vinegar
1 tablespoon arrowroot

1. Cut the chicken into 2-inch pieces. Combine the sake, sesame oil, and egg white; pour over the chicken. Marinate 30 minutes.

2. In a wok or nonstick skillet coated with vegetable oil cooking spray, heat the canola oil over medium heat. Add the chicken and sauté 15 minutes, stirring frequently. Add the carrots and bamboo shoots; stir-fry 5 minutes or until the carrots are crisp-tender. Add the water chestnuts and garlic; stir-fry 2 to 3 minutes.

3. In a saucepan, heat ¾ cup of the stock to boiling; add the rice vinegar. Combine the remaining ¼ cup of stock with the arrowroot and gradually add to the boiling broth, stirring constantly until the broth begins to thicken.

4. Pour the sauce over the chicken and cook several minutes.

*To Serve:* Spoon over hot steamed rice or kasha, and accompany with steamed fresh snow peas and red bell pepper strips.

---

### PER SERVING

| | | | |
|---|---|---|---|
| 6.6 gm total fat | 1.21 gm saturated fat | 2.1 gm fiber | 239 calories |
| 73 mg cholesterol | 25.8% fat | 101 mg sodium | 60 calories from fat |

## ❧ Ten Easy Pieces of Chicken Breast ❧
### (MEAT)
*Serves: 10*

This recipe was shared with me by a woman I met on a plane while traveling to Detroit, Michigan. What a lucky seat assignment!

½ cup fresh orange juice
  Grated zest of ½ orange
2 large shallots, peeled and chopped fine
2 tablespoons Worcestershire sauce
½ cup red currant jelly
2 teaspoons olive oil
1 tablespoon grated fresh gingerroot
3 large cloves garlic, smashed, peeled, and minced, or 1 teaspoon
  garlic powder
  Few drops of Tabasco
5 boneless chicken breasts, halved (about 2½ to 3 pounds)
  Orange slices and watercress or parsley, for garnish

1. In a small saucepan, combine the orange juice and zest, shallots, Worcestershire, currant jelly, oil, ginger, garlic, and Tabasco. Heat until the jelly dissolves. Remove from the heat and cool.
2. Arrange the chicken breasts in a nonaluminum roasting pan and pour the cooled mixture over them.
3. Cover and marinate in the roasting pan overnight in the refrigerator.
4. Bake, covered, in a preheated 375° oven for 30 minutes.
5. Uncover and bake 15 minutes more.

*Serving Suggestion:* Place the chicken breasts napped with sauce on a heated platter. Garnish with orange slices and watercress or parsley. A wild rice pilaf (page 206) and steamed cauliflower and broccoli make perfect accompaniments.

---
**PER SERVING**

| | | | |
|---|---|---|---|
| 4.0 gm total fat | .99 gm saturated fat | .2 gm fiber | 203 calories |
| 73 mg cholesterol | 18% fat | 100 mg sodium | 36 calories from fat |

---

# ❦ Cyrus Faridi's Apricot Chicken ❦
## (MEAT)
### *Serves: 4*

My husband and I frequent a delightful neighborhood restaurant in Los Angeles called The Primary Process, where the chef-owner is Cyrus Faridi. He prepares two succulent but simple chicken dishes that he has been kind enough to share with me.

    1 large shallot, chopped
    ⅛ teaspoon ground white pepper
    1 cup dry vermouth or white wine
    1 cup defatted sodium-reduced chicken broth
    3 tablespoons sugar-free apricot preserves
    2 teaspoons grated fresh gingerroot
    4 (4-ounce) boneless chicken breast halves
      Juice of ½ lemon
    ⅛ teaspoon Hungarian paprika

1. Preheat the oven to 375°.
2. Place the shallot, white pepper, vermouth, and chicken broth in a small saucepan. Boil and reduce to 1 cup. Add the preserves and ginger and simmer 2 to 3 minutes. Pour through a strainer and reserve as sauce.
3. Sprinkle the chicken with lemon juice, more pepper, and paprika. Sear the chicken breasts *on one side only* in a nonstick skillet or on a grill that has been coated with cooking spray.
4. Turn the breasts, transfer to a baking pan, and place in the oven for 8 to 10 minutes. Serve immediately.

*To Serve:* Place the chicken breasts on individual plates and coat with sauce. Accompany with steamed rice, lentils, and currants and a vegetable medley of steamed peas, pea pods, and puréed banana squash.

VARIATION: *Chicken with Plum Sauce:* Prepare the chicken breasts as in the above recipe. After reducing the shallot, vermouth, and chicken broth to 1 cup, add 3 tablespoons plum preserves, stir, simmer 2 minutes, and strain. Add 1 to 2 teaspoons of Dijon mustard just before serving.

---
PER SERVING
---

| | | | |
|---|---|---|---|
| 3.1 gm total fat | .87 gm saturated fat | .1 gm fiber | 179 calories |
| 73 mg cholesterol | 16.2% fat | 82 mg sodium | 28 calories from fat |

# ❦ Middle Eastern Chicken Breasts ❦
## (MEAT)
### *Serves: 8*

  3 large onions, peeled and chopped
    Freshly ground pepper to taste
  4 whole chicken breasts (about 4 pounds), halved, skinned, and defatted
¼ teaspoon saffron dissolved in ½ cup hot water
  1 teaspoon ground ginger
  1 cinnamon stick, halved
  2 cups defatted sodium-reduced chicken broth or water
  2 large sweet potatoes, baked until barely soft, peeled, and cut into 1-inch cubes
  2 cups moist pitted prunes
⅓ cup honey

1. Spray a large nonstick sauté pan or casserole with olive oil cooking spray. Heat over medium heat.

2. Add the onions and freshly ground pepper, cover, and allow to sweat for about 10 minutes.

3. Add the chicken in one layer, cover, and cook on low heat for about 20 minutes. Stir and turn the chicken from time to time.

4. Combine the saffron mixture with the ginger and cinnamon; add to the

chicken. Add the broth. Bring to a boil, reduce to a simmer, and cook covered for about 25 to 30 minutes or until tender.

5. Remove the chicken and keep warm. Add the cubed sweet potatoes, prunes, and honey and cook uncovered about 15 minutes. Remove the cinnamon stick and return the chicken to the pan. Coat with sauce and heat 5 to 10 minutes before serving.

*To Serve:* Spoon the chicken pieces on a warmed platter. Surround with a border of couscous, brown rice, or kasha. Spoon the onion sauce with sweet potatoes and prunes over the chicken.

NOTE: Cover and chill in the refrigerator if the chicken is to be served the next day. The flavor will be even more intense. Reheat over low heat, covered.

—————————————— P E R   S E R V I N G ——————————————

| | | | |
|---|---|---|---|
| 3.4 gm total fat | .91 gm saturated fat | 5.2 gm fiber | 348 calories |
| 73 mg cholesterol | 8.7% fat | 73 mg sodium | 31 calories from fat |

## ❧ Lemon Chicken for a Crowd ❧
### (MEAT)
*Serves: 24 (one-quarter 2-pound broiler = 1 serving)*

An easy, tasty entrée to serve guests. I suggest serving one fourth of a 2-pound broiler per person and encourage second helpings of noodles, grains, and vegetables instead of chicken.

  1½ cups fresh lemon juice
   ⅓ cup olive oil
    1 large onion, peeled and minced
    1 tablespoon hot Hungarian paprika
    2 tablespoons sweet Hungarian paprika
  1½ teaspoons ground white pepper
    1 teaspoon freshly ground black pepper
    2 tablespoons salt-free garlic-flavored seasoning
    6 (2-pound) broilers, quartered, skinned, and defatted

1. In a medium bowl, combine the lemon juice, olive oil, onion, paprikas, peppers, and garlic seasoning. Mix well.

2. In two 17 × 11-inch roasting pans, arrange the quartered chickens in one layer. Pour the lemon mixture over the chicken. Place in the refrigerator to marinate for several hours before baking.

3. Bake uncovered in a preheated 375° oven for 1½ hours, or until the chicken is fork-tender, spooning pan juices over the chicken 2 or 3 times while cooking.

4. If the chicken is not browned to your liking at this time, cook briefly under the broiler.

*To Serve:* Accompany chicken with individual Potato Kugels (page 256), puréed banana squash, and steamed asparagus.

---

| PER SERVING | | | |
|---|---|---|---|
| 9.1 gm total fat | 2.08 gm saturated fat | .5 gm fiber | 194 calories |
| 73 mg cholesterol | 43.1% fat | 71 mg sodium | 82 calories from fat |

---

# ⚜ Honey Glazed Chicken ⚜
## (MEAT)
### *Serves: 8 to 10*

A sweetly simple chicken dish that can be prepared Sunday afternoon for Tuesday night's dinner.

**2 (2-pound) broilers, quartered, skinned, and defatted**

### Marinade:

⅓ cup honey
½ cup hoisin sauce
½ cup sodium-reduced soy sauce
1 tablespoon packed brown sugar
Juice of 1 lemon
3 tablespoons grated fresh gingerroot
Chopped scallion, for garnish

1. Separate the wings from the breast quarters and the thighs from the drumsticks.
2. Combine all the marinade ingredients in an ovenproof glass dish (see Note).
3. Add the chicken pieces and turn to coat thoroughly. Cover with plastic wrap and refrigerate 2 days before baking. Several times a day, turn the pieces of chicken in the marinade to distribute seasonings.
4. Remove the chicken from the marinade and arrange in one layer in a shallow roasting pan that has been lined with foil.
5. Place in the upper third of a preheated 400° oven and bake for 1 hour (turn and baste after 30 minutes), until browned and crisp. Chop the chicken into smaller serving portions with a Chinese cleaver or heavy knife.

*To Serve:* Place the chicken pieces on a warm platter and garnish with chopped scallions. Serve with either steamed or vegetarian fried rice, and Chinese cabbage with mushrooms.

NOTE: Or use a large zip-lock plastic bag for marinating. Add the chicken and marinade, seal, and turn to coat. Turn the bag several times a day until ready to cook.

---

**PER SERVING**

| | | | |
|---|---|---|---|
| 4.9 gm total fat | 1.33 gm saturated fat | .1 gm fiber | 175 calories |
| 58 mg cholesterol | 25.3% fat | 441 mg sodium | 44 calories from fat |

---

**HARRIET'S HINTS**

**N**ever *place cooked meat, poultry, or fish back into uncooked marinade. If you use the marinade for a sauce, boil it for several minutes before serving in order to destroy bacteria from raw meat.*

# ❧ Indoor Barbecued Chicken ❧

## (MEAT)

*Serves: 8*

This savory dish can be prepared in winter or summer.

2 (2-pound) broilers, quartered, skinned, and defatted, wings removed (see Note)
2 teaspoons canola oil
2 cups chopped onion
⅔ cup sodium-reduced ketchup
3 tablespoons distilled white vinegar
2 tablespoons packed brown sugar
⅓ to ½ cup water
2 teaspoons Dijon mustard
2 teaspoons Worcestershire sauce
Freshly ground pepper to taste

1. Preheat the oven to 350°.
2. Arrange the chicken pieces in a 13 × 9 × 2-inch glass baking dish lined with aluminum foil.
3. Heat the oil in a nonstick saucepan over medium heat. Add the onion and sauté 5 minutes. Stir, cover with a lid, and wilt about 5 minutes.
4. Add the remaining ingredients; bring to a boil and reduce the heat. Simmer uncovered for 15 minutes, stirring occasionally. Pour the hot barbecue sauce over the chicken.
5. Bake for 50 to 60 minutes or until tender, basting occasionally with the sauce.

*To Serve:* In the summer, serve with fresh corn on the cob, a crisp coleslaw, and toast rubbed with garlic and olive oil. For dessert try Jackie Keller's Pear Cranberry Strudel (page 366) or a platter of fresh fruit.

NOTE: Save the wings and giblets (except liver) in the freezer for broth.

---

| PER SERVING | | | |
|---|---|---|---|
| 7.4 gm total fat | 1.77 gm saturated fat | 1.2 gm fiber | 217 calories |
| 73 mg cholesterol | 31.1% fat | 106 mg sodium | 67 calories from fat |

# ❦ My Favorite Chicken Paprikash ❦ with Rice

## (MEAT)

*Serves: 4 (4 ounces cooked chicken = 1 serving)*

When I want to prepare a dinner that's deliciously simple as well as healthy, this one fills the bill. I always try to keep quartered, skinned broilers in my freezer so that they are ready to cook. If I forget to defrost them in the refrigerator the night before, I can always defrost them in my microwave.

    1 (2-pound) broiler, skinned, quartered, and defatted
    ½ lemon
    1 tablespoon salt-free vegetable seasoning
      Freshly ground pepper to taste
    1 teaspoon garlic powder
    1 teaspoon onion powder
    2 tablespoons Hungarian paprika
    1 small onion, peeled and diced
    3 cups defatted reduced-sodium chicken broth or water
 1½ cups uncooked white rice

1. Wash the chicken under cold running water. Drain, dry with paper towels, and separate the wings from the breast quarters and the thighs from the drumsticks.

2. Sprinkle with lemon juice then shake in a plastic bag with the vegetable seasoning, pepper, garlic powder, onion powder, and paprika.

3. Coat a heavy nonstick casserole or sauté pan with olive oil cooking spray; heat the pan over medium-high heat.

4. Add the seasoned chicken and brown on one side. Turn the chicken pieces with tongs, add the diced onion, and finish browning on the second side. Add about ½ cup broth to keep the meat from sticking. Lower the heat, cover, and cook 15 minutes.

5. Add the rice, mix, and add the remaining broth. Cover and cook 20 minutes, or until the rice is tender.

*To Serve:* Place on a heated platter or serve directly from the casserole. Accompany with steamed brussels sprouts and applesauce.

---

**PER SERVING**

| | | | |
|---|---|---|---|
| 7.0 gm total fat | 1.84 gm saturated fat | 2.7 gm fiber | 458 calories |
| 73 mg cholesterol | 14.4% fat | 81 mg sodium | 63 calories from fat |

---

# ❦ Chicken in Sauerkraut ❦ with Caraway Seeds
## (MEAT)
### Serves: 4

The combination of chicken steeped in onions, sauerkraut, and caraway seeds results in a dish with Old World flavor. This is family fare that company will love.

> 1 (2-pound) broiler, quartered, skinned, and defatted
> 2 teaspoons salt-free lemon pepper seasoning
> 1 teaspoon garlic powder
> Hungarian paprika to taste
> 1 large onion, peeled and sliced thin
> 12 red pearl onions, peeled (see page 253)
> 1 large ripe tomato, cored and cut into 1-inch dice
> 1 red bell pepper, seeded and cut into 1-inch dice
> 1 (28-ounce) jar low-sodium sauerkraut with juice
> 1 (4-ounce) can low-sodium V-8 juice
> 1 tablespoon caraway seeds
> Freshly ground pepper to taste

1. Preheat the oven to 350°.
2. Wash the chicken under cold running water and pat dry. Place it in a roaster or casserole coated with olive oil cooking spray. Season with the lemon pepper seasoning, garlic powder, and 2 teaspoons of paprika.

3. Coat a sauté pan with olive oil cooking spray. Place over medium heat and add the sliced onion. Cover and cook the onion until wilted.

4. Add the red onions, the tomato, and bell pepper and simmer 5 minutes.

5. Add the sauerkraut with its juice, V-8 juice, caraway seeds, freshly ground pepper, and 1 tablespoon of paprika.

6. Pour the mixture over the chicken, cover, and bake for about 1 hour to 1 hour and 15 minutes, or until cooked through.

*To Serve:* Start with a mixed green salad with vegetables and serve the chicken with a boiled or baked potato.

―――――――― PER SERVING ――――――――

| | | | |
|---|---|---|---|
| 7.2 gm total fat | 1.82 gm saturated fat | 4.8 gm fiber | 246 calories |
| 73 mg cholesterol | 25.6% fat | 439 mg sodium | 65 calories from fat |

## ⋎ Chicken with Potatoes and Red Peppers ⋎
### (MEAT)
*Serves: 2*

A quick meal for two that does a great job of using up cooked chicken.

2 teaspoons olive oil
½ red bell pepper, seeded and cut into 1-inch pieces
8 ounces peeled, cooked new potatoes, cut into 1-inch cubes
8 ounces skinned, cooked chicken cut into 1- to 2-inch cubes
1 medium clove garlic, smashed, peeled, and minced
1 cup salt-free tomato purée or sauce
½ teaspoon dried oregano, crushed, or 2 teaspoons minced fresh oregano
¼ teaspoon dried basil, crushed, or 2 teaspoons minced fresh basil
⅛ teaspoon dried thyme, crushed, or 1 teaspoon fresh thyme leaves

1. Preheat the oven to 350°.

2. Heat the oil in a small nonstick skillet. Add the bell pepper, cover, and cook over low heat about 5 minutes.

3. Combine the bell pepper, potatoes, and chicken in a small casserole.

4. In a small bowl, combine the garlic with the tomato purée, oregano, basil, and thyme; add to the casserole and stir to combine.

5. Cover and bake 25 to 30 minutes, until heated through.

─────────── P E R  S E R V I N G ───────────

| | | | |
|---|---|---|---|
| 7.6 gm total fat | 3 gm saturated fat | 4.0 gm fiber | 310 calories |
| 73 mg cholesterol | 22% fat | 105 mg sodium | 68 calories from fat |

# ❦ Hungarian Stuffed Cabbage ❦
## (MEAT)
### Yield: 12 rolls (2 rolls = 1 serving as entrée)

Hungary has probably invented more ways to prepare cabbage than any other nation. The most popular cabbage dish in Hungary is sauerkraut, and these Hungarian cabbage bundles are baked in it. They are sour but delicious. If you like a sweet and sour flavor, you may prefer the recipe on page 41. This happens to be a favorite of mine; perhaps because it's the way Mama used to make it.

1 large head (2 pounds) green cabbage, trimmed of bruised or withered leaves, cored, and *frozen 2 days* or blanched 3 minutes
2 extra-large egg whites
½ cup uncooked white or brown rice
½ medium onion, peeled and grated
½ teaspoon garlic powder
Freshly ground pepper to taste
¼ teaspoon kosher salt
1 pound ground turkey breast, no fat or skin (see Note)

*Sauce:*
1 tablespoon canola oil
⅓ cup unbleached all-purpose flour
½ small onion, peeled and grated
2 cups low-sodium tomato juice
1 (28-ounce) can salt-free diced tomatoes in juice
1 (16-ounce) jar low-sodium sauerkraut
¼ teaspoon ground white pepper
1 teaspoon sour salt

1. Defrost the cabbage for 24 hours in refrigerator the day before or for 5 to 7 minutes in the microwave on High. Separate 12 large outer leaves and reserve; shred the remaining cabbage.

2. Beat the egg whites in a mixing bowl slightly with a fork. Add the rice, grated onion, garlic powder, pepper, and salt. Add the turkey and combine, using a fork or clean hands. Set aside.

3. Make the sauce: In a saucepan, heat the oil; prepare a roux by sprinkling flour over the oil and stirring with a wooden spoon until the flour is golden brown, about 20 minutes; add the grated onion and stir 1 minute.

4. Gradually stir in the tomato juice and juice from the diced tomatoes; whisk until smooth.

5. Add the tomatoes, sauerkraut, and white pepper; stir to combine.

6. Add the sour salt and stir; taste and adjust seasonings.

7. Place about ½ cup of the turkey mixture at the stem end of each reserved cabbage leaf and roll up, tucking in the sides.

8. Place the shredded cabbage on the bottom of a large Dutch oven or heavy roaster or casserole. Arrange the cabbage rolls on top, seam side down. Add the sauce, cover, and simmer for 30 minutes on top of the stove. Meanwhile, preheat the oven to 325°.

9. Transfer to the oven and bake uncovered for 1½ hours or until the cabbage is tender.

NOTES: Half a pound of extra-lean ground beef or veal may be substituted for half the ground turkey.

This may be frozen before or after cooking or prepared the day before serving.

───────────────── PER SERVING ─────────────────

| | | | |
|---|---|---|---|
| 4.0 gm total fat | .53 gm saturated fat | 6.8 gm fiber | 288 calories |
| 50 mg cholesterol | 12% fat | 766 mg sodium | 36 calories from fat |

# ᴥ Stuffed Grape Leaves ᴥ
## (Dolmas, Yaprakis de Oja, Yebra)
### (MEAT)
*Yield: 48 rolls (1 roll = 1 serving)*

All Jewish stuffed grape leaves recipes are derived from the Sephardic tradition. Renée Holland's mother, Latifa, prepared these *yebra* many years ago in Syria. The following recipe is prepared with turkey; however, you may omit the turkey and just make it with rice, raisins, and pine nuts. It works well as an appetizer or part of a buffet.

1 (16-ounce) jar grape leaves in lemon juice, *not brine*
3 tablespoons olive oil
1 large onion, peeled and chopped fine
  Water
1 cup uncooked white or brown rice
¼ cup chopped Italian flat-leaf parsley
2 tablespoons dried mint leaves, crushed
1 teaspoon ground allspice
½ teaspoon ground cinnamon
½ teaspoon kosher salt
  Freshly ground pepper to taste
1 pound ground turkey breast, no fat or skin
36 dried apricot halves
6 tablespoons fresh lemon juice
1 tablespoon sugar
½ cup dark raisins or pine nuts (optional)

1. Wash the grape leaves in cold water. Pat dry, cut off the stems, and set aside.
2. Heat 1 tablespoon of olive oil in a sauté pan, add the onion, and cook over medium heat for 5 to 6 minutes, or until soft but not browned. Stir frequently.
3. Add 1 cup of water, the rice, parsley, mint, allspice, cinnamon, salt, and pepper. Stir, cover, and simmer about 10 to 15 minutes. Stir occasionally to prevent sticking. The rice will not be tender, just parboiled. (If you are using brown rice, add 10 minutes to the cooking time.) Cool.
4. Add the meat to the rice filling; mix well.

5. Spread a grape leaf on a work surface, vein side up. Put 1 tablespoon of filling in the center of the leaf. Fold the stem edge over the filling and fold both sides of the leaf toward the middle. Roll up like a small cigar. Repeat with the rest of the leaves. (The *yebra* may be frozen at this point on a wax paper–lined tray. When frozen solid, pack in tightly sealed plastic bags.)

6. Coat the bottom of a large heavy saucepan with olive oil spray. Line the bottom with half the apricots, cut side up. Top with the *yebra*, placing them together tightly, seam side down.

7. Combine the lemon juice, sugar, remaining 1 tablespoon of oil, and 1 cup of water, and add to the pan. Top with the remaining apricots, cut side down.

8. Place a heavy ovenproof plate (such as Pyrex) directly on top of the apricots to prevent the grape leaves from uncoiling. Cover the saucepan with a lid, bring to a boil, lower the heat, and simmer for 1 hour or until the grape leaves are tender.

9. Let the *yebra* cool in their liquid at room temperature or transfer carefully to a refrigerator container and chill.

*To Serve:* Place the stuffed grape leaves on a large platter in a sunburst pattern surrounded by a border of cooked apricots.

Note: The rice may be prepared as in steps 2 and 3, cooked until tender and served as a separate side dish.

---

| PER SERVING | | | |
|---|---|---|---|
| 1.5 gm total fat | .29 gm saturated fat | 1.6 gm fiber | 78 calories |
| 10 mg cholesterol | 16.5% fat | 381 mg sodium | 13 calories from fat |

---

# ❧ Syrian Stuffed Eggplant (Specha) ❧
## (MEAT)
### Serves: 12

When choosing an eggplant, look for those that are smooth, dark purple, and shiny, without bruises. Refrigerate and plan on using it within the next 3 to 4 days, since it is a fairly perishable vegetable. Eggplant lends itself to innumerable preparations. It can be served as an appetizer (page 121), as a vegetable (page 238), or as a Sephardic main dish as in this recipe. The meat and rice filling used to stuff the eggplant is called *hashu*. I have added the diced eggplant.

4 small (1 pound or less each) eggplants
1 medium onion, peeled and chopped fine
2 teaspoons olive oil
2 large cloves garlic, peeled and minced
½ cup canned sodium-reduced garbanzo beans (chick-peas), rinsed and drained
1½ pounds ground turkey breast, no fat or skin
⅓ cup uncooked white rice
1 teaspoon ground allspice
½ teaspoon ground cinnamon
⅓ cup finely chopped Italian flat-leaf parsley
   Salt to taste

1. Wash and dry the eggplants and remove the stem ends. Slice one of the eggplants into ½-inch-thick rounds and set aside.

2. Cut the remaining 3 eggplants in half lengthwise. Using a sharp knife or a grapefruit knife, scoop out the flesh, leaving a ½-inch shell. Dice the eggplant flesh into ½-inch cubes.

3. Coat the reserved eggplant slices lightly with olive oil cooking spray, arrange on a baking sheet, and brown under the broiler.

4. Sauté the onion in the oil in a large nonstick skillet until transparent. Add the garlic, garbanzo beans, and diced eggplant, and sauté an additional 3 minutes. Remove the skillet from the heat.

5. Add the turkey, rice, allspice, cinnamon, and parsley; mix well.

6. Layer half the broiled eggplant slices on the bottom of a flameproof casserole.

7. Fill the eggplant shells with the turkey mixture and place on top of the eggplant slices. Top with the remaining eggplant slices. Weight down with a plate, cover, and cook on top of the stove for 20 minutes. Meanwhile, preheat the oven to 300°.

8. Add enough water so that three fourths of the eggplant is covered. Taste and adjust seasonings with salt and allspice. Bring to a boil.

9. Transfer to the oven, cover, and bake for 2½ to 3 hours, or until the liquid has cooked down. (After 2½ hours check to see if the liquid is cooked down to sauce consistency; if not, remove the cover for the last 30 minutes of cooking.)

---
PER SERVING
---

| 3.2 gm total fat | .59 gm saturated fat | 5.1 gm fiber | 271 calories |
| 75 mg cholesterol | 10.3% fat | 61 mg sodium | 29 calories from fat |

# ❦ My Family's Favorite Turkey ❦ Meat Loaf

## (MEAT)

*Serves: 12 (2 slices = 1 serving)*

Meat loaf is enjoying a resurgence in popularity on many restaurant menus. Some people are reluctant to serve meat loaf as a meal for company, but I find that people really enjoy it. My family often requests this meat loaf, whether served hot or cold the next day in sandwiches.

    4 extra-large egg whites
    ¾ cup low-sodium V-8 juice or water
    1 cup fine dried bread crumbs, matzo meal, or quick-cooking rolled oats
    1½ tablespoons Worcestershire sauce
    1 tablespoon Dijon mustard
       Freshly ground pepper to taste
    2 teaspoons salt-free vegetable seasoning
    1 large onion, peeled and quartered
    4 large cloves garlic, smashed and peeled
    1 small green or red bell pepper, seeded and quartered
    2 carrots, peeled and quartered
    1 medium zucchini, trimmed and quartered
    1 pound ground turkey, no fat or skin
    1 pound ground turkey breast, no fat or skin
    ½ cup chopped Italian flat-leaf parsley

1. Preheat the oven to 375°. Coat a large shallow roasting pan with vegetable oil cooking spray.

2. In a mixing bowl, beat the egg whites lightly with a fork. Add the V-8 juice, bread crumbs, Worcestershire sauce, mustard, pepper, and vegetable seasoning. Beat together and let stand 5 to 10 minutes.

3. Meanwhile, place the onion, garlic, bell pepper, carrots, and zucchini in a food processor or blender and chop fine.

4. Add the vegetable mixture and ground turkey to the egg white mixture and toss lightly with a fork or clean hands to combine. Add the parsley and blend.

5. Divide the mixture in half and mound into two 8- or 9-inch loaf shapes in the prepared roasting pan. The mixture will be moist.

6. Bake in the upper third of the preheated oven for 55 to 60 minutes, or until browned. Remove from the oven and let stand 10 minutes before slicing.

*To Serve:* Place the sliced meat loaf on a platter and surround with parsleyed carrots. Serve with Mashed Potatoes with Onions and Garlic (page 242), and mounds of steamed spinach.

VARIATION #1: After 45 minutes of baking time, surround with quartered parboiled potatoes (sprinkled with freshly ground pepper, paprika, and onion powder) and bake for 20 additional minutes.

VARIATION #2: Surround with 8 sliced fresh mushrooms sprinkled with about 1 cup defatted reduced-sodium vegetable or chicken broth and bake for 20 additional minutes.

VARIATION #3: In a saucepan, combine 1 (15-ounce) can of salt-reduced stewed tomatoes, chopped, with 1 tablespoon of cornstarch or potato starch. Heat 2 to 3 minutes, stirring constantly, until shiny and thickened. Spoon over the meat loaf and bake 15 additional minutes or serve in a gravy boat with sliced meatloaf.

---

### PER SERVING

| | | | |
|---|---|---|---|
| 2.5 gm total fat | .73 gm saturated fat | 1.4 gm fiber | 162 calories |
| 48 mg cholesterol | 14.6% fat | 214 mg sodium | 23 calories from fat |

---

# ᏇᏊ Carnatzlach ᏇᏊ
# (Rumanian Broiled Hamburgers)
## (MEAT)

*Serves: 10 to 12 (1 carnatzlach = 1 serving)*

1½ pounds ground turkey (no fat or skin) or extra-lean ground beef
1 medium onion, peeled and grated
1 carrot, peeled and grated
1 large clove garlic, smashed, peeled, and minced
¼ cup egg substitute mixed with 1 extra-large egg white
2 teaspoons chopped fresh sage leaves or ½ teaspoon ground sage
⅛ teaspoon ground white pepper
3 tablespoons unbleached all-purpose flour mixed with 1 teaspoon Hungarian paprika and 1 teaspoon salt-free garlic-flavored seasoning

1. Combine all the ingredients except the flour mixture. Mix well.
2. Shape into 3-inch rolls 1 inch in diameter, tapering at the ends.
3. Roll in the flour mixture.
4. Place on a broiling pan and broil under moderate heat, turning to brown on all sides.

*To Serve:* Serve hot. If desired, you may serve these topped with sautéed and browned onions.

---

### PER SERVING

| | | | |
|---|---|---|---|
| .9 gm total fat | .24 gm saturated fat | .8 gm fiber | 125 calories |
| 57 mg cholesterol | 6.6% fat | 60 mg sodium | 8 calories from fat |

## ❦ Turkey Cutlets or Schnitzel ❦
### (MEAT)
*Serves: 8*

Because of our Thanksgiving menu, we're inclined to think that turkey is an exclusively American bird. But in Israel, I often found turkey schnitzel served in pita bread wrapped with wax paper and sold as fast food.

½ cup unbleached all-purpose flour mixed with 1 teaspoon no-salt vegetable seasoning
½ cup egg substitute and 1 extra-large egg white mixed with 2 tablespoons cold water
1 cup fine dried bread crumbs mixed with 1 teaspoon onion powder and freshly ground pepper to taste
8 thin slices raw turkey breast (about 2 pounds, cut ¼ inch thick)
Juice of ½ lemon
⅛ teaspoon ground white pepper
1 teaspoon garlic powder
1 tablespoon canola oil
Hungarian paprika
8 lemon slices, for garnish

1. Place the flour mixture, egg mixture, and bread crumbs on 3 separate flat plates or in pie plates.

2. Sprinkle the turkey cutlets with lemon juice, pepper, and garlic powder. Dip the slices into flour to coat thoroughly; shake off excess. Next coat with the beaten egg, then the seasoned bread crumbs.

3. Place the cutlets on a nonstick baking sheet that has been coated with olive oil cooking spray or brushed with olive oil. Lightly spray the cutlets with canola oil and sprinkle with paprika. Chill in the refrigerator for 1 hour.

4. Bake in the upper third of a preheated 400° oven for 8 to 10 minutes or until golden brown.

*To Serve:* Serve the warm schnitzel topped with lemon slices, accompanied by Mashed Potatoes with Onions and Garlic (page 242) or rice, and stir-fried zucchini slices topped with diced tomatoes.

VARIATION: For sandwiches, serve in warm pita bread with shredded lettuce and diced tomatoes.

―――――― PER SERVING ――――――

| | | | |
|---|---|---|---|
| 3.7 gm total fat | .63 gm saturated fat | .9 gm fiber | 238 calories |
| 75 mg cholesterol | 14.5% fat | 199 mg sodium | 33 calories from fat |

# ❦ Cornish Hen with Sweet and Sour Glaze ❦
## (MEAT)
*Serves: 4 (¼ hen = 1 serving)*

Cornish hens are a favorite for entertaining because of their attractive presentation and the relative ease of preparation (no carving or slicing required). They also can be conveniently stored in the freezer in case of unexpected guests.

1 (2-pound) Empire Kosher Cornish hen, quartered, defatted, and excess skin removed
1½ teaspoons onion powder
1½ teaspoons garlic powder
　Freshly ground pepper
　Hungarian paprika

*Basting Sauce:*

    ¼ cup red wine vinegar
    3 tablespoons packed brown sugar
    ¼ cup fresh orange juice
    1½ tablespoons sodium-reduced soy sauce

**Watercress and 2 oranges, peeled and sliced, for garnish**

1. Rinse the hen with cold running water; pat dry with paper towels.
2. Rub the onion and garlic powders and freshly ground pepper under the skin and over the surface of the hen. Sprinkle with paprika.
3. Preheat the broiler or oven to 450°.
4. Combine the basting sauce ingredients.
5. Place the seasoned hen skin side down in a broiling pan and place about 7 inches from the heat, or in a baking pan. Broil or bake 15 minutes or until golden.
6. Brush the hen with sauce and broil or bake 5 minutes longer.
7. Turn skin side up and broil or bake 20 minutes more or until browned and fork-tender, brushing frequently with the remaining sauce.

*To Serve:* Place on a warm serving platter; garnish with watercress and orange slices. Accompany with Brown and Wild Rice Pilaf (page 206) and steamed asparagus.

| PER SERVING | | | |
|---|---|---|---|
| 3.5 gm total fat | .84 gm saturated fat | .1 gm fiber | 175 calories |
| 87 mg cholesterol | 17.2% fat | 237 mg sodium | 30 calories from fat |

# ❦ Cornish Hens with Ginger Plum Sauce ❦

## (MEAT)

*Serves: 8 (¼ hen = 1 serving)*

2 (2-pound) Empire Kosher Cornish hens, halved, skinned, and defatted
Juice of 1 lemon
2 teaspoons garlic powder
2 teaspoons onion powder

*Ginger Plum Sauce:*

1 (17-ounce) can purple plums, drained, pitted, and puréed
1 (6-ounce) can frozen lemonade concentrate
⅓ cup sodium-reduced chili sauce
1 tablespoon sodium-reduced soy sauce
2 to 3 teaspoons grated fresh gingerroot
1 teaspoon Worcestershire sauce
2 teaspoons Dijon mustard
Tabasco to taste

Watercress, for garnish

1. Wash the hens under cold running water and pat dry with paper towels. Arrange them in a shallow roasting pan coated with vegetable oil cooking spray. Season on both sides and under the skin with lemon juice and the garlic and onion powders.

2. Roast in a preheated 350° oven for about 35 minutes on each side.

3. While the hens are roasting, combine the sauce ingredients in a saucepan and simmer for 10 to 15 minutes.

4. When the hens are browned and tender, brush generously with the ginger plum sauce and roast 15 minutes more.

*To Serve:* Cut the hens in quarters and arrange on a platter lined with watercress. Extra sauce may be served on the side. Serve with Kasha Varnishkes (page 218), puréed banana squash, and steamed green beans.

----------------- PER SERVING -----------------

| | | | |
|---|---|---|---|
| 3.3 gm total fat | .84 gm saturated fat | .4 gm fiber | 173 calories |
| 87 mg cholesterol | 17.1% fat | 294 mg sodium | 30 calories from fat |

# BEEF, LAMB, AND VEAL

Mrs. Rubenstein's Brisket    335

Edie Wahl's Brisket    337

Israeli Steak Sandwich    338

Potted Shoulder Steak with Onions    339

Hungarian Gulyás    340

My Family's Favorite Veal Roast    342

Savory Veal Brisket    343

Braised Lamb Shanks    344

Lamb Shanks and Beans    345

# ❧ Mrs. Rubenstein's Brisket ❧

(MEAT)

*Serves: 10*

One of the tried and true entrées in Jewish cooking is, of course, beef brisket. These days, I trim all visible fat before roasting, use only the first cut, defat the gravy or sauce, and serve smaller portions accompanied by larger portions of rice, kasha, noodles, potatoes, kugels, and vegetables. Meat has relinquished the spotlight to grains and vegetables. This is an old family recipe—not my family's, but Mrs. Rubenstein's, who was a beloved surrogate grandmother and babysitter for our two children.

3 to 3½ pounds first-cut brisket, visible fat removed
    1 teaspoon garlic powder
    1 teaspoon onion powder
    1 tablespoon Hungarian paprika
    Freshly ground pepper to taste
    1 large onion, peeled and chopped coarse
    2 slices corn rye bread, cubed
    2 teaspoons Worcestershire sauce
    1 cup sodium-reduced chili sauce
    1 bottle light beer or nonalcoholic beer
  24 baby carrots
    Defatted sodium-reduced chicken broth or water (optional)
    Chopped Italian flat-leaf parsley, for garnish

1. Season the brisket on both sides with garlic and onion powders, paprika, and pepper.

2. Make a bed of chopped onion and cubed rye bread in a roasting pan and place the meat on top.

3. Sprinkle the meat with Worcestershire sauce, chili sauce, and beer. Surround with the carrots topped with freshly ground pepper.

4. Cover with a tight-fitting lid and place in a preheated 350° oven for 1 hour.

5. Reduce the temperature to 300° and bake for another 1 to 1½ hours, or until fork-tender. During cooking, check to see if additional liquid (chicken broth or water) should be added.

6. When the meat is tender, remove it to a platter along with the carrots and cover with foil. Let stand at least 30 minutes before slicing. Meanwhile, prepare the gravy (see below).

7. Slice the meat against the grain, arrange in the roaster, and heat with the carrots about 20 to 30 minutes.

To prepare gravy: Place the bread and onion and half the liquid from the roasting pan in a food processor or blender and purée until smooth. Return the purée to the roasting pan and blend with the remaining liquid. Remove to a sauceboat.

*To Serve:* Arrange the meat on a warm serving platter; nap with some gravy. Surround with carrots. Sprinkle the carrots with chopped parsley and serve with additional gravy in a sauceboat.

NOTE: The meat may be prepared a day in advance, defatted, covered with foil, and refrigerated for serving the next day.

| PER SERVING | | | |
|---|---|---|---|
| 15.8 gm total fat | 6.22 gm saturated fat | .2 gm fiber | 300 calories |
| 90 mg cholesterol | 45.2% fat | 507 mg sodium | 142 calories from fat |

---

**— ❧ HARRIET'S HINTS ❧ —**

**A** *few words about meat:*

• *Keep raw meat refrigerated or frozen.*

• *Thaw frozen meat in the refrigerator or in a microwave oven.*

• *Keep raw meat and poultry separate from other foods.*

• *Wash hands and working surfaces, including cutting boards and utensils, with soap, after being in contact with raw meat or poultry.*

• *Refrigerate leftovers within 2 hours.*

---

# ❧ Edie Wahl's Brisket ❧
## (MEAT)
### *Serves: 8*

2½ pounds first-cut brisket
2 teaspoons onion powder
1 teaspoon garlic powder
2 teaspoons Hungarian paprika
   Freshly ground pepper to taste
1 (10½-ounce) can defatted sodium-reduced chicken broth

1. Preheat the oven to 325°.

2. Place the meat in a roasting pan with a tight-fitting lid. Combine the onion and garlic powders, paprika, and pepper. Rub the meat all over with the spices.

3. Cover and bake 1 hour. After 1 hour, pour off the drippings to defat and trim visible fat from the meat.

4. Return the meat to the roasting pan and raise the heat to 375°. Cook the brisket uncovered for ½ hour, or until the meat is browned and starts to stick to the pan. Remove the brisket and keep warm.

5. Add the chicken broth to deglaze the pan. Return the meat and defatted juices to the roaster and cook covered at 325° for 1 additional hour or until fork-tender.

*To Serve:* Start with Green Split Pea Soup (page 163). Slice and arrange the brisket in a shallow heated casserole. Surround with bundles of steamed carrot sticks and pour over the pan juices. Accompany with Cabbage and Noodles (Kraut Pletzlach) (page 212) and Hungarian Vegetable Salad (page 193).

---
PER SERVING
---

| | | | |
|---|---|---|---|
| 15.8 gm total fat | 6.22 gm saturated fat | .2 gm fiber | 266 calories |
| 90 mg cholesterol | 55% fat | 77 mg sodium | 142 calories from fat |

# ❦ Israeli Steak Sandwich ❦
## (MEAT)
### *Serves: 4*

When visiting Israel, I found that steak sandwiches were very popular, although beef is rarely served there. They are served in warm pita bread wrapped in paper napkins at snack bars called *steakias*—rather like our fast-food hamburgers.

    4 (4-ounce) beef shoulder steaks
    ½ teaspoon ground black pepper
    ¼ teaspoon ground coriander
    ¼ teaspoon ground cumin
    1 teaspoon hot Hungarian paprika
    2 pita breads, halved

1. Pound the steaks between 2 sheets of wax paper or plastic wrap, using a wooden board or kitchen mallet. Flatten till about ½ inch in thickness.
2. Make 3 diagonal slashes on each steak and season with a mixture of the pepper, coriander, cumin, and paprika.
3. Preheat the broiler or grill and broil the meat for about 4 to 5 minutes on each side.

*Serving Suggestion:* Tuck the steaks into warmed pita bread; add Israeli Vegetable Salad (page 184) and dill pickles. Lemony Tahini Dressing (page 198) is also an option.

---

——— PER SERVING ———

| | | | |
|---|---|---|---|
| 8.3 gm total fat | 2.90 gm saturated fat | 2.8 gm fiber | 252 calories |
| 77 mg cholesterol | 31% fat | 51 mg sodium | 74 calories from fat |

---

## ❧ Potted Shoulder Steak with Onions ❧
### (MEAT)
*Serves: 4 (4 ounces cooked meat = 1 serving)*

On the rare occasions when my husband eats beef, this shoulder steak smothered in onions and surrounded with mashed potatoes is his choice.

- 1 large onion, peeled, halved, and sliced
- 2 cloves garlic, smashed, peeled, and minced
- 1 teaspoon olive oil
- 2 tablespoons unbleached all-purpose flour
- 1 teaspoon kosher salt
- Freshly ground pepper to taste
- 1 teaspoon dried thyme leaves, crushed
- ½ teaspoon Hungarian paprika
- 1¼ pounds beef shoulder steak, cut into 4 portions
- ½ cup dry red wine
- ½ cup defatted sodium-reduced beef or vegetable broth
- Chopped Italian flat-leaf parsley, for garnish

1. Place the onion and garlic in a nonstick skillet with the oil. Cover and cook over low heat for 5 minutes. Remove the cover and continue to cook, stirring occasionally, until wilted and lightly browned.

2. In a measuring cup or small bowl, mix the flour with the salt, pepper, thyme, and paprika.

3. Sprinkle the meat with the seasoned flour. Pound in the flour with a mallet or the edge of a heavy plate.

4. Remove the onion mixture from the skillet and brown the meat on both sides.

5. Add the wine and broth, bring to a simmer, and return the onions to the pan with the meat.

6. Cover and simmer 45 minutes or until tender.

*To Serve:* Garnish with chopped parsley and serve with freshly cooked green beans and mashed potatoes, or noodles mixed with poppy seeds.

---

PER SERVING

| | | | |
|---|---|---|---|
| 8.3 gm total fat | 2.91 gm saturated fat | 1.1 gm fiber | 241 calories |
| 85 mg cholesterol | 32% fat | 393 mg sodium | 75 calories from fat |

---

# ❦ Hungarian Gulyás ❦
## (MEAT)
### *Serves: 9 to 10 as an entrée*

Hungarian Nobel laureate Professor Albert Szent-Györgyi proved that Hungarian paprika is a good source of vitamin C, which he named ascorbic acid. Its color should be bright red, and its unique flavor is slightly sweet or slightly hot (about as hot as black pepper). The kind to look for is *rózsa* (rose-red), and a good brand is Szeged. Above all, only buy Hungarian paprika and store it in the refrigerator to maintain freshness.

Paprika is the Hungarian national spice. It is an essential ingredient in the preparation of *paprikás* and *gulyás*, a souplike dish that contains beef or veal, onion, paprika, and cubed potatoes. Sometimes unbrowned farfel or dumplings are added. For a superior flavor, use beef, chicken, or vegetable broth instead of water.

1 tablespoon olive oil
2 medium onions, peeled and chopped fine (about 2 cups)
2 tablespoons Hungarian paprika
2¼ pounds boneless beef or veal (from shin or neck), cut into ¾-inch cubes
2 cloves garlic, smashed, peeled, and minced
½ teaspoon caraway seeds (optional)
½ teaspoon salt
½ teaspoon white pepper
2½ quarts warm defatted sodium-reduced broth or water (see Note)

> 1 green or yellow Hungarian long pepper or Italian frying pepper, seeded and
>   cut into rings
> 1 large ripe tomato, peeled, seeded, and cut into 1-inch dice
> 1½ pounds new potatoes, peeled and cut into ¾-inch cubes

1. Heat the oil in a large, heavy Dutch oven. Add the onions, stir, and sauté until golden yellow.

2. Add the paprika and stir. Add the meat, stir, and sauté about 10 minutes.

3. While the meat is browning, mix the garlic with the caraway seeds, salt, and pepper.

4. Add the garlic mixture to the meat, stirring rapidly with a wooden spoon.

5. Add the warm broth, bring to a boil, and reduce the heat. Simmer covered for about 45 minutes or until the meat is barely tender.

6. Add the pepper and tomato and simmer 15 minutes.

7. Add the potatoes and simmer, covered, for 30 to 45 minutes or until tender. Taste and adjust seasonings. If you feel additional broth is needed for a soupy consistency, add some now and cook an additional few minutes.

*To Serve:* This one-dish meal should be served in warm soup bowls. For a traditional Hungarian dinner, accompany with Hungarian Vegetable Salad (page 193), loaves of hearty Russian rye or whole grain bread, and a dessert of apple strudel and tea.

NOTE: Cold liquid toughens meat when added while cooking.

VARIATION: After the potatoes have cooked for about 15 minutes, add 1 pound savoy cabbage cut into 1-inch cubes; cook until the potatoes are tender. Taste and adjust seasonings.

---

PER SERVING

| | | | |
|---|---|---|---|
| 11 gm total fat | 3.36 gm saturated fat | 3.3 gm fiber | 378 calories |
| 102 mg cholesterol | 26.3% fat | 240 mg sodium | 99 calories from fat |

# ❦ My Family's Favorite Veal Roast ❦
## (MEAT)
### Serves: 10 to 12

Veal has little flavor of its own, so it needs to be well seasoned when cooking. Prepared the day before, this roast develops an even more delicious flavor, and is easier to slice. The recipe provides a generous amount of sauce to enjoy with homemade challah. My son Larry is one of the great dunkers of all time!

3½ to 4 pounds veal shoulder, fat trimmed
        2 teaspoons salt-free lemon pepper seasoning
        1 tablespoon Hungarian paprika
        ⅛ teaspoon ground white pepper
        1 medium onion, peeled and sliced
        1 leek, white part only, split, washed, and sliced
        2 carrots, peeled and sliced
        2 ribs celery, sliced
        3 large cloves garlic, smashed, peeled, and minced
     1½ cups dry white wine, vermouth, or defatted sodium-reduced chicken broth
        1 cup canned salt-free crushed plum tomatoes
        2 cups defatted sodium-reduced chicken broth or water
        1 bay leaf
        4 sprigs fresh thyme or 1½ teaspoons dried thyme

1. Preheat the broiler. Season the veal with lemon pepper seasoning, paprika, and pepper.

2. Place the veal in a roasting pan that has been coated with olive oil cooking spray and brown under the broiler on all sides.

3. Add the onion, leek, carrots, celery, and garlic. Broil an additional 5 to 10 minutes, stirring once or twice and being careful not to burn.

4. Remove the pan from the broiler, add the wine, and bring to a boil on top of the stove. Add the tomatoes, broth, bay leaf, and thyme. Bring to a simmer.

5. Cover and bake for 1½ to 2 hours, or until tender.

6. Remove the roast to a plate and let rest 15 to 20 minutes. Trim away any visible fat and cut the meat into ¼-inch slices. If desired, strain the sauce, discarding the bay

leaf, and purée the vegetables in a food processor or blender. Return to the sauce, mix to blend, and heat the vegetable-thickened gravy.

*To Serve:* Arrange slices of veal on a warm platter and nap with the gravy. Surround with green cabbage wedges steamed in chicken broth. Either potato pancakes with applesauce or a noodle raisin kugel would make a delicious accompaniment to this entrée.

---
PER SERVING
---

| | | | |
|---|---|---|---|
| 7.6 gm total fat | 2.80 gm saturated fat | 1.8 gm fiber | 226 calories |
| 125 mg cholesterol | 30.6% fat | 178 mg sodium | 68 calories from fat |

## ❧ Savory Veal Brisket ❧
### (MEAT)
*Serves: 6 to 8*

Veal is higher in cholesterol than beef, but lower in the saturated fat that raises cholesterol. Served in limited amounts, veal brisket is a welcome occasional change from the usual beef brisket. My Sally (is that one word?) loves this for Shabbat dinner or any other meal.

2 to 2½ pounds veal brisket, all visible fat removed
1 envelope low-sodium onion soup mix
½ cup dry white wine or defatted sodium-reduced chicken broth
2 cups water
2 teaspoons Hungarian paprika
1 teaspoon dried rosemary, crushed
1 teaspoon garlic powder
    Freshly ground pepper to taste
6 medium new potatoes, peeled and quartered
6 carrots, peeled and cut into 2-inch diagonal slices
    Paprika and freshly ground pepper
2 tablespoons unbleached all-purpose flour
¼ cup cold water

1. Preheat the broiler.

2. Place the veal in a medium roasting pan, top side up, and brown under the broiler until golden brown on both sides. Reduce the oven heat to 325°.

3. Drain off any fat from the roasting pan. Combine the onion soup mix, wine, and water and add to the pan. Stir to blend, and baste the meat.

4. In a cup or small bowl, mix the paprika, rosemary, garlic powder, and pepper. Sprinkle the brisket with the seasonings, cover, and return to the oven. Bake for 1 hour. Turn the roast over occasionally, basting with the juices.

5. Add the potatoes and carrots; sprinkle with additional paprika and pepper. Cook, covered, 30 to 45 additional minutes or until the meat and vegetables are tender.

6. Drain the juices from the roaster and defat. Pour into a saucepan. Blend the flour with ¼ cup cold water until smooth. Gradually stir into the pan juices, stirring constantly with a wooden spoon. Cook until the mixture thickens and coats the spoon.

*To Serve:* Before carving, cool 15 minutes and remove any visible fat from the meat. Carve into ¼- to ½-inch-thick slices, cutting diagonally against the grain of the meat. Return to the roaster and heat. Arrange on a heated platter; surround with potatoes, carrots, and steamed brussels sprouts. Nap the meat with gravy or pass a gravy boat separately.

---

**PER SERVING**

| | | | |
|---|---|---|---|
| 6.4 gm total fat | 2.27 gm saturated fat | 3.8 gm fiber | 302 calories |
| 101 mg cholesterol | 19.4% fat | 537 mg sodium | 58 calories from fat |

# ❧ Braised Lamb Shanks ❧
## (MEAT)
### Serves: 2

2 lamb shanks (about 2 pounds), trimmed of all visible fat
1 tablespoon flour
2 teaspoons salt-free lemon herb seasoning
  Freshly ground pepper to taste
2 teaspoons Hungarian paprika

1 large clove garlic, peeled and cut into 6 slivers
1 small onion, peeled and chopped fine
⅔ cup low-sodium V-8 juice
½ cup dry red wine
1 teaspoon dried rosemary, crushed

1. Rinse the lamb shanks and pat dry with paper towels.

2. In a cup or small bowl, combine the flour, herb seasoning, pepper, and paprika.

3. Make 2 slashes with a paring knife in each lamb shank. Insert a sliver of garlic in each. Chop the remaining garlic and reserve.

4. Coat the lamb shanks with seasoned flour. Coat a small heavy pan with olive oil cooking spray.

5. Brown the shanks on both sides in the pan over moderate heat.

6. Add the onion and reserved garlic, and cook 2 to 3 minutes, stirring constantly to avoid burning.

7. Add the juice, wine, and rosemary; cover and simmer over low heat for 1 to 1½ hours, or until tender, turning every ½ hour. This dish may be prepared 1 or 2 days ahead and reheated or frozen for future use.

*Serving Suggestion:* Reheat slowly and serve with parsleyed steamed new potatoes or on a bed of no-yolk broad noodles with heaps of broccoli and carrots. Either Marinated Cucumbers (page 178) or Onion Cabbage Slaw (page 108) is a good salad to serve with this dish.

—————————— PER SERVING ——————————

| | | | |
|---|---|---|---|
| 9.8 gm total fat | 3.36 gm saturated fat | 2.0 gm fiber | 289 calories |
| 106 mg cholesterol | 30.7% fat | 96 mg sodium | 88 calories from fat |

# ❧ Lamb Shanks and Beans ❧
## (MEAT)
### *Serves: 8*

I try to add beans to a dish whenever I can. They add protein, fiber, and flavor— and they help fill you up, so you can go easy on the meat! Have the butcher split the lamb shanks for you.

2 teaspoons canola oil
2 large onions, peeled and chopped coarse
2 large cloves garlic, smashed, peeled, and minced
6 ripe plum tomatoes, cored and cut into 1-inch dice
2 large red bell peppers, seeded and cut into 1-inch dice
2 large green bell peppers, seeded and cut into 1-inch dice
2 teaspoons salt-free vegetable seasoning
3 fresh rosemary sprigs or 1 teaspoon dried rosemary
Freshly ground pepper to taste
1 tablespoon Hungarian paprika
4 lamb shanks (about 4 pounds), cracked in half and visible fat removed
Juice of 1 lemon
1 to 1½ cups defatted sodium-reduced vegetable broth or water
4 (16-ounce) cans rinsed and drained sodium-reduced cannellini (white kidney) beans or vegetarian baked beans

1. Heat the oil in a Dutch oven or large sauté pan. Cook the onions and garlic until wilted but not brown, 5 to 7 minutes. Preheat the broiler.

2. Add the tomatoes, bell peppers, and seasonings.

3. Sprinkle the lamb shanks with lemon juice and brown under the broiler. Add to the mixture, cover, and simmer over low heat for 2 hours, or until tender. From time to time, add a small amount of broth or water to keep the meat from sticking.

4. When the meat is tender, add the beans and simmer an additional 30 minutes. Taste and adjust seasonings.

*To Serve:* Place on a heated platter or serve in a casserole. Start the meal with a crisp green salad and accompany with crusty whole wheat or rye rolls. Fresh seasonal fruit provides a light ending to this hearty main dish.

NOTE: Lamb shanks are a kosher cut, but leg of lamb usually is not. See page xxiv to learn why this is so.

| PER SERVING | | | |
|---|---|---|---|
| 12.1 gm total fat   3.74 gm saturated fat | | 21.9 gm fiber | 519 calories |
| 106 mg cholesterol   19.9% fat | | 1097 mg sodium | 109 calories from fat |

# OODLES OF STRUDELS

*Appetizers*

Chicken Strudel    350
Mini Knishes    351
Onion Cheese Roll    353
Ricotta and Artichoke Flowers    354
Ricotta and Sun-dried Tomato Phyllo Cups    355

*Entrées*

Chicken Breasts in Phyllo    356

*Vegetables*

Spinach Strudel    358
Potato Onion Strudel    360
Squash Strudel    361

*Desserts*

Almost Aunt Dora's Strudel    362
Gisele Pollak's No-Fat Apple Strudel    364
Mama's Apple Kugel (Schalet)    365
Jackie Keller's Pear Cranberry Strudel    366

M ost Jewish cooks today can't take the time to prepare strudel dough the way their mothers and grandmothers did. Fortunately, high-quality strudel leaves are now widely available. Whether you call it strudel dough, phyllo, or filo, these pastry leaves have unlimited possibilities in the Jewish kitchen. Phyllo is easy to work with and endlessly adaptable for appealing dishes ranging from appetizers to desserts. It is virtually fat- and cholesterol-free, and is readily available in most markets, fresh or frozen. I prefer fresh, but frozen is also good and often convenient. Don't be intimidated by the delicacy of the tissuelike dough; you'll find it's really quite easy to use if you follow certain precautions:

- If you use frozen strudel leaves, thaw in the refrigerator overnight before using.

- Keep the dough covered with plastic in an airtight container, except when actually using the sheets; otherwise, it becomes dry and brittle. Unused sheets may be stored in the refrigerator for several months.

- You may find holes, tears, or partial sheets in the phyllo, but don't worry: since you use several layers, these imperfections will eventually be covered.

- Avoid contact with moisture (wet towels or wet hands), as it causes strudel leaves to stick.

- Many strudel recipes can be prepared well ahead of time and frozen. Once the strudel is filled, freeze uncovered on a cookie sheet. When frozen solid, wrap tightly in plastic and then foil. When ready to bake, unwrap and transfer the frozen strudel directly into a preheated oven on a jelly roll pan. Do not thaw, as it tends to make the strudel soggy.

- Do not roll strudel leaves too tightly, as the cooked filling expands, and will tear leaves as it bakes.

- Above all, have all recipe ingredients ready before starting—*and work quickly* to assemble!

# ❦ Chicken Strudel ❦
## (MEAT)
*Yield: About 32 slices (1 slice = 1 serving)*

This is a wonderful way to use up leftover roast chicken, turkey, brisket, or veal—or 2 cups Vegetarian Chopped Liver (page 7) may be substituted. For freezing instructions, see the Spinach Strudel recipe on page 358.

      1 tablespoon olive or canola oil
      1 medium onion, peeled and chopped fine
      1 large clove garlic, smashed, peeled, and chopped fine
      ½ cup chopped scallions
      2 cups finely chopped cooked chicken or turkey
        Chicken or turkey gravy (optional)
      1 extra-large egg white, slightly beaten
 2 to 3 tablespoons defatted sodium-reduced chicken broth (optional)
      1 teaspoon Hungarian paprika
      2 teaspoons chopped fresh thyme or ½ teaspoon dried thyme, crushed
      ¼ cup chopped Italian flat-leaf parsley
      ¼ cup snipped chives
        Salt and freshly ground pepper to taste
      2 sheets phyllo
      6 tablespoons fine dried bread crumbs mixed with 1 tablespoon olive oil

1. Heat the oil in a medium skillet and sauté the onion and garlic until wilted and yellow.

2. Add the scallions, stir, then add the chopped meat. (Two to three tablespoons of leftover gravy may be added at this time if available.)

3. Remove from the heat and add the slightly beaten egg white. If the mixture is dry, add a bit of chicken broth.

4. Stir in the paprika, thyme, parsley, and chives; taste and adjust seasonings with salt and pepper. Cool before using. You should have about 2½ to 3 cups of filling.

### To Prepare Strudel:

1. Place a phyllo sheet, with one short side facing you, on a clean kitchen towel. (Keep the remaining sheets covered.) Coat the sheet with olive oil cooking spray. Sprinkle with about 3 tablespoons of bread crumbs.

2. Leaving a 1-inch border on the bottom and both sides, spoon a ¾-inch-wide strip of chicken filling along the bottom of the phyllo.

3. Lift up the ends of the towel and roll the strudel and filling over onto itself to form a cylinder about 1½ inches in diameter.

4. Place on a shallow baking sheet coated with cooking spray and lightly spray the top of the strudel. Before baking, cut *halfway through* with a serrated knife into 1-inch pieces. (The strudel may be frozen at this point for future use.)

5. Repeat with the remaining phyllo and filling. You should have a total of four 8-inch strudels.

6. Bake in a preheated 375° oven for about 30 minutes, or until golden brown.

VARIATION: For an Asian touch, omit the thyme and add 1 teaspoon of grated fresh ginger and ½ teaspoon of Chinese five-spice seasoning; use 1 tablespoon of sodium-reduced soy sauce instead of salt. Sprinkle with sesame seeds before baking.

---

PER SERVING

| | | | |
|---|---|---|---|
| 1.2 gm total fat | .25 gm saturated fat | .2 gm fiber | 29 calories |
| 8 mg cholesterol | 37.5% fat | 27 mg sodium | 11 calories from fat |

---

## ❦ Mini Knishes ❦
### (DAIRY)
*Yield: 36 knishes (1 knish = 1 serving)*

This appetizer is easy to prepare, freezes well, and is always a crowd-pleaser. People love bite-sized morsels that they can pop in their mouths and savor. This is wonderful for large parties.

1 medium onion, peeled and chopped
1 teaspoon olive oil
2 cups (16 ounces) nonfat small-curd cottage cheese
2 tablespoons egg substitute mixed with 1 extra-large egg white
⅛ teaspoon ground white pepper
1 cup cooked and mashed Idaho or other baking potatoes
3 sheets phyllo pastry
⅓ cup fine dried bread crumbs

1. Sauté the onion in the olive oil until wilted and golden (see Note).
2. Mix the onion, cottage cheese, egg mixture, pepper, and potatoes in a bowl. Beat well by hand or with a hand mixer.
3. Coat 1 phyllo sheet with olive oil cooking spray. (Keep the rest of the phyllo dough covered.) Sprinkle with 1 tablespoon of bread crumbs and cut into 4-inch squares. (A pizza cutter does a good job.)
4. Place 1 scant tablespoon of filling in the center of each square.
5. Fold the top and bottom of the phyllo over the filling. Turn over and fold the 2 sides toward the center. There will be several thicknesses of dough on both the top and bottom of the knish. Place the second folded side down on a nonstick baking sheet coated with olive oil spray.
6. Repeat as above until all the mixture has been used.
7. Prick each knish once with a fork; coat lightly with olive oil spray.
8. Bake in a preheated 325° oven for about 30 minutes or until golden brown.

NOTE: 1 cup fried onions from Onion-flavored Olive Oil (page 255) may be substituted for fresh onion.

VARIATION: *Kasha Knishes:* Sauté ½ cup minced onion in 1 tablespoon of olive oil until wilted and lightly browned. Combine the onion with 2 cups of cooked kasha, add salt and pepper to taste, and proceed as in step 3, omitting bread crumbs.

——————————————— PER SERVING ———————————————

| | | | |
|---|---|---|---|
| .3 gm total fat | .05 mg saturated fat | .2 gm fiber | 23 calories |
| 1 mg cholesterol | 11.5% fat | 64 mg sodium | 3 calories from fat |

# ❦ Onion Cheese Roll ❦

## (DAIRY)

*Yield: 60 pieces (2 pieces = 1 serving)*

This bite-sized, flaky appetizer is easy to prepare, freezes well, and tastes delicious with chilled, sodium-reduced tomato juice.

> 1 tablespoon olive oil
> 3 large onions, peeled, halved and thinly sliced
> 4 ounces Neufchâtel cheese, at room temperature
> 1 cup shredded low-fat Jarlsberg or fat- and sodium-reduced Swiss cheese
> 1 teaspoon caraway seeds (optional)
> 9 sheets phyllo pastry

1. Heat the oil in a nonstick skillet; add the onions and cook, covered, over moderate heat for about 5 minutes. Remove the cover; cook and stir frequently for about 15 minutes, or until the onions are limp and pale gold but not browned.

2. Remove from the heat and let stand until lukewarm.

3. Mix the onions thoroughly with the cheeses and caraway seeds.

4. To make each cheese roll, stack 3 sheets of phyllo dough, coating very lightly between layers with olive oil cooking spray. (Keep the rest of the dough covered.) Spoon one third of the onion-cheese mixture in an even strip along the longest edge of the phyllo dough and roll the strudel over on itself to form a cylinder.

5. Cut the roll in half crosswise and place the halves seam side down, several inches apart, on a nonstick baking sheet coated with olive oil spray.

6. Coat the surface of the roll lightly with olive oil spray to prevent drying. Repeat to make 2 more large rolls. You may cover the rolls with plastic wrap and chill them overnight at this point, or they may be wrapped and frozen for future use.

7. Cut the rolls into 1-inch-long pieces almost to the bottom, leaving them in place.

8. Bake the rolls in a preheated 400° oven for about 12 minutes, or 17 minutes if they have been chilled overnight. Cool slightly and cut through into individual pieces before serving.

---

| PER SERVING | | | |
|---|---|---|---|
| 2.1 gm total fat | .90 gm saturated fat | .3 gm fiber | 48 calories |
| 5 mg cholesterol | 39.7% fat | 59 mg sodium | 19 calories from fat |

# ❦ Ricotta and Artichoke Flowers ❦
## (DAIRY)
### *Yield: 32 flowers (1 flower = 1 serving)*

A simply delicious appetizer that can be prepared quickly, covered with plastic, and refrigerated until time to bake and serve. You will need one or two mini muffin pans to make these.

8 ounces nonfat ricotta cheese or yogurt cheese (see page 355)
2 tablespoons grated Parmesan, low-fat goat cheese, or feta cheese
¼ cup snipped chives or 2 tablespoons chopped fresh basil leaves
1½ tablespoons slightly beaten egg white or 2 tablespoons egg substitute
Freshly ground pepper to taste
4 sheets phyllo pastry
2 (14-ounce) cans quartered artichoke hearts, rinsed and well drained (see Note)
Hot Hungarian paprika

1. To make the ricotta filling, combine the cheeses, chives, egg white, and pepper; stir until blended.

2. To assemble the flowers: Coat 4 sheets of phyllo with olive oil cooking spray and stack together. With a sharp knife, cut the phyllo into squares 4 inches wide and 4 inches long. You will need 1 square for each 1¾-inch mini muffin cup.

3. Gently press the phyllo into the muffin cups. Spoon about 1½ teaspoons of cheese in the center and top with ¼ artichoke heart. Coat with olive oil spray. Sprinkle lightly with paprika.

4. Repeat until all the ingredients are used.

5. Bake in a preheated 375° oven for 15 to 20 minutes, or until golden brown and crisp. Remove gently and serve immediately while warm.

NOTE: For a more pronounced flavor, the artichokes may first be marinated in a fat-free, low-calorie vinaigrette dressing; or marinated, well-drained artichokes may be used.

---

### PER SERVING

| | | | |
|---|---|---|---|
| .2 gm total fat | .08 gm saturated fat | .2 gm fiber | 20 calories |
| 1 mg cholesterol | 10% fat | 27 mg sodium | 2 calories from fat |

*T*o make nonfat yogurt cheese: Line a fine strainer with 2 layers of cheesecloth or a paper coffee filter. Spoon plain nonfat yogurt (made without gelatin) into the filter. Set the strainer over a bowl. Cover with plastic and drain in the refrigerator 24 hours. One pint nonfat yogurt makes ¾ to 1 cup cheese. Store the cheese in an airtight container for as long as 10 days.

# ❧ Ricotta and Sun-dried Tomato ❧ Phyllo Cups

## (DAIRY)

### Yield: 16 cups (1 cup = 1 serving)

These cups make lovely appetizers or a wonderful topping to a salad of mixed greens.

   4 sheets phyllo pastry, each coated with olive oil spray, layered, and cut into 5-inch squares
   1 recipe ricotta filling from Ricotta and Artichoke Flowers (page 354)
  16 whole sun-dried tomatoes in oil, well drained and dried with a paper towel (see Note)

1. Line each cup in a 16-cup standard-size muffin tin with 4 squares of phyllo, as in step 2 of previous recipe.

2. Put 1½ to 2 tablespoons filling in each cup and top with 1 whole sun-dried tomato.

3. Bake in a preheated 375° oven for 15 minutes or until golden brown.

4. Let cool for a few minutes, then gently remove from the tin with a metal spatula and serve warm.

NOTE: Dry (not oil-packed) sun-dried tomatoes may be marinated in fat-free vinaigrette for a lower fat content.

---

PER SERVING

| | | | |
|---|---|---|---|
| .8 gm total fat | .19 gm saturated fat | 0 gm fiber | 34 calories |
| 2 mg cholesterol | 21.1% fat | 50 mg sodium | 8 calories from fat |

---

## ❧ Chicken Breasts in Phyllo ❧
### (MEAT)
*Serves: 8 (1 packet = 1 serving)*

I used to teach a version of this elegant and delicious dish in my French cooking classes. Of course, then each leaf of phyllo was covered in butter. I have cut the fat and now am happy to rely on herbs and spices to lift the flavor. This dish is particularly convenient to have in the freezer for a quick meal.

**Stuffing:**
  1 large shallot, peeled and minced
  2 large cloves garlic, smashed, peeled, and minced
  1 cup finely chopped onion
  1 cup finely chopped celery
  2 cups chopped assorted fresh mushrooms
  2 tablespoons chopped fresh thyme or 2 teaspoons dried thyme
  2 teaspoons olive oil
  2 tablespoons defatted sodium-reduced chicken broth

  8 chicken breast halves, skinned, boned, and defatted (about 2 pounds)
  Juice of 1 lemon
  Freshly ground pepper

  4 sheets phyllo pastry
  Watercress, for garnish

1. Sauté all the stuffing ingredients in a nonstick pan in the oil and 2 tablespoons of chicken broth until wilted and the mixture is dry, about 5 to 7 minutes.

2. Cut a deep pocket in the thick portion of each chicken breast.

3. Season the chicken breasts with lemon juice and pepper.

4. Stuff each breast with about 1½ tablespoons of the stuffing mixture. Sear both sides quickly in a nonstick skillet coated with olive oil cooking spray. Cool.

5. Place 1 sheet of phyllo on a work surface, cut in half lengthwise, coat with olive oil spray, and fold each half in half lengthwise again. Coat lightly with cooking spray. Place a stuffed breast at one end of the phyllo, angled in the corner. Fold diagonally (as in a flag fold) into a triangular packet to use the entire strip of phyllo. (See Note.)

6. Place on a lightly greased baking sheet and refrigerate while preparing the remaining breasts. Preheat oven to 375°.

7. Lightly coat the top of each packet with olive oil spray.

8. Bake in the upper third of the oven for 25 to 30 minutes, or until golden brown.

*To Serve:* Arrange on a serving platter banked with watercress and accompany with sautéed diced zucchini, tomatoes, and garlic and Brown and Wild Rice Pilaf (page 206).

NOTE: The chicken packets may be prepared through step 5 and then frozen. Freeze on a baking sheet and wrap in plastic then foil. To bake, unwrap and bake frozen in a preheated 350° oven for 35 to 40 minutes or until golden brown.

VARIATION: *Fish Fillets in Phyllo:* Eight 4-ounce seasoned salmon or halibut fillets may be substituted for chicken. Sear each seasoned fillet quickly in a nonstick skillet, about 1 minute on each side. Top the fish with the mushroom mixture and proceed as in step 5.

| PER SERVING | | | |
| --- | --- | --- | --- |
| 4.9 gm total fat | 1.12 gm saturated fat | 1 gm fiber | 200 calories |
| 73 mg cholesterol | 22.5% fat | 125 mg sodium | 44 calories from fat |

# ❦ Spinach Strudel ❦
## (DAIRY)
### *Serves: 10 to 12 (1 slice = 1 serving)*

This may be served as an accompaniment to fish or as part of a vegetable plate. It is a different way to get your vegetables—and like them!

3 (10-ounce) packages frozen chopped spinach, thawed and squeezed dry
1 cup Onion Helper (page 254) or 1 large onion, chopped and sautéed in 2 teaspoons olive oil
1 bunch scallions, trimmed and sliced
1 teaspoon garlic powder
½ cup snipped fresh dill
1 cup (8 ounces) nonfat ricotta cheese mixed with 1 extra-large egg white, slightly beaten
2 tablespoons grated Parmesan cheese alternative
3 tablespoons nonfat sour cream (optional)
   Freshly ground pepper to taste
8 sheets phyllo pastry
¾ cup fine dried bread crumbs mixed with ¼ teaspoon freshly grated nutmeg
2 red bell peppers, roasted, quartered, and blotted dry (see page 246)
1 teaspoon extra-virgin olive oil
   Black and/or white seasame seeds, for garnish (optional)

1. In a bowl, combine the spinach, onions, scallions, garlic powder, dill, ricotta, Parmesan, sour cream, and freshly ground pepper. Blend well. Taste and adjust seasonings.

2. Arrange 1 phyllo sheet on a clean kitchen towel. (Keep the others covered.) Coat the sheet with olive oil cooking spray and sprinkle with 2 tablespoons of bread crumbs. Repeat 2 more times, stacking the phyllo layers.

3. Lightly coat the fourth layer with olive oil spray and arrange half the quartered red peppers across a long side of the dough, leaving a 2-inch border at each side. Top the peppers with half the spinach mixture. Preheat oven to 350°.

4. Fold in the flaps of dough at the sides of the filling. Coat lightly with olive oil spray. Lift up the ends of the towel nearest the filling; carefully roll the phyllo and filling over and onto itself to form a cylinder. Place on a nonstick baking sheet coated

with olive oil spray. Lightly brush the strudel with olive oil, using a goose feather or pastry brush. Cut into 2-inch slices, cutting only through the top 2 strudel leaves. Sprinkle with black and/or white sesame seeds. Repeat with the remaining ingredients to form a second strudel and place on the same baking sheet (see Note).

5. Bake 35 to 45 minutes or until golden brown.

*To Serve:* Arrange on a long rectangular platter, cut into serving portions with a serrated knife, and surround with steamed baby carrots and sugar snap peas.

Note: The strudel may be prepared through step 4 and then frozen. When frozen solid, wrap in plastic, then foil. To bake, put the *frozen* strudel on an oiled baking sheet and place in a preheated 350° oven. *Do not thaw first.* Bake for about 50 minutes, or until golden brown.

Variation: *Onion Leek Strudel:* Omit the spinach. For the onions in the above recipe, substitute 4 cups of thinly sliced onions, and 2 cups of thinly sliced leek (white part only). Sauté in 1 tablespoon of olive oil until wilted and lightly browned. Add 4 dried mushrooms soaked until soft, drained, and chopped. Sauté 2 minutes more. Add 1 cup of sliced scallions. Mix with cheeses and herbs and proceed.

---

PER SERVING

| | | | |
|---|---|---|---|
| 2.6 gm total fat | .53 gm saturated fat | 3.2 gm fiber | 119 calories |
| 3 mg cholesterol | 18.6% fat | 195 mg sodium | 24 calories from fat |

# ❦ Potato Onion Strudel ❦

## (PAREVE)

*Serves: 10 to 12 as a vegetable (1 piece = 1 serving)*

1 recipe Mashed Potatoes with Onions and Garlic (page 242)
¼ cup chopped fresh chervil, Italian flat-leaf parsley, or snipped chives
8 sheets phyllo pastry
¾ cup fine dried bread crumbs
1 tablespoon extra-virgin olive oil
  Black and/or white sesame seeds, for garnish
  Soy-based Parmesan cheese alternative, for garnish

1. Taste and adjust seasonings in the potato mixture. Add the fresh chervil, parsley, or chives and blend.

2. Arrange 1 phyllo sheet on a clean kitchen towel. (Keep the rest covered.) Coat with olive oil cooking spray and sprinkle with 2 tablespoons of bread crumbs. Repeat 2 more times, stacking the phyllo layers.

3. Coat the fourth layer of phyllo with olive oil spray and spoon half the potato-onion mixture across a long side of the dough, leaving a 2-inch border at each side.

4. Fold in the flaps of dough at the sides of the filling. Coat lightly with olive oil spray. Carefully lift up the ends of the towel nearest the filling; roll the phyllo and filling over and onto itself to form a cylinder. Preheat oven to 350°.

5. Place on a nonstick baking sheet coated with olive oil spray. Lightly brush the strudel with olive oil, using a goose feather or pastry brush. Cut into 2-inch slices, cutting through only the top 2 strudel leaves. Sprinkle with black and/or white sesame seeds and Parmesan cheese alternative.

6. Bake 35 to 40 minutes or until golden brown.

*To Serve:* Place on a long rectangular platter, cut into serving portions with a serrated knife, and surround with steamed string beans, sliced carrots, and assorted squashes.

*To Freeze:* See freezing directions for Spinach Strudel, page 359.

---

### PER SERVING

| | | | |
|---|---|---|---|
| 6.2 gm total fat | .9 gm saturated fat | 2.7 gm fiber | 246 calories |
| 0 mg cholesterol | 22.5% fat | 194 mg sodium | 56 calories from fat |

# ❦ Squash Strudel ❦

## (DAIRY)

*Serves: 8 to 10*

1 pound zucchini, ends trimmed, shredded coarse
1 pound yellow crookneck squash, ends trimmed, shredded coarse
2 teaspoons olive oil
1 medium onion, peeled and chopped fine
1 large clove garlic, smashed, peeled, and minced
1 tablespoon unbleached all-purpose flour
1 cup nonfat evaporated milk
1 tablespoon chopped fresh thyme leaves
2 teaspoons chopped fresh rosemary leaves
¼ cup chopped Italian flat-leaf parsley
2 tablespoons grated Parmesan cheese
¼ cup shredded low-fat mozzarella cheese
  Freshly ground pepper to taste
8 sheets phyllo pastry

1. Squeeze the shredded squash to remove excess liquid.

2. Heat the oil in a heavy saucepan and sauté the onion and garlic until soft, about 5 minutes. If necessary, cover with a lid to sweat and release juices.

3. Add the flour, stir to blend, and cook 1 minute.

4. Add the squash, mix, and sauté 3 minutes, stirring constantly.

5. Stir in the milk and simmer uncovered until the liquid is absorbed, stirring from time to time.

6. Remove from the heat and add the herbs, cheeses, and freshly ground pepper; stir to blend.

7. Cool the mixture and proceed as for Spinach Strudel (page 358).

VARIATION: *Banana Squash Strudel:* Cook 2 pounds banana squash in the microwave oven on High until soft. Remove from the skin and mash. Add 2 tablespoons orange marmalade and 2 teaspoons packed brown sugar. Blend well. Proceed as for Spinach Strudel, substituting crushed cornflakes for bread crumbs.

---

**PER SERVING**

| | | | |
|---|---|---|---|
| 1.8 gm total fat | .58 gm saturated fat | 1.4 gm fiber | 59 calories |
| 3 mg cholesterol | 25.5% fat | 66 mg sodium | 16 calories from fat |

---

# ❦ Almost Aunt Dora's Strudel ❦
## (PAREVE)
### *Yield: 30 slices (1 slice = 1 serving)*

This recipe comes from my friend Marilyn Steinberg from Atlanta. Her Aunt Dora Steinberg-Fleischman's strudel is famous from North Carolina to Georgia, and her recipe will be handed down for generations.

Unlike Aunt Dora, most contemporary cooks can use packaged phyllo leaves, and I have eliminated the pound of melted butter and ¾ cup sugar. However, the wonderful flavor and memories remain the same.

1½  cups Damson plum preserves
½  cup sugar-free strawberry preserves
⅓  cup crab apple jelly
1  cup chopped toasted pecans
1  cup dark raisins, plumped in hot orange juice or apricot brandy and drained
5  cups cornflakes, crushed
5  sheets phyllo pastry
¼  cup sugar mixed with 1 tablespoon ground cinnamon
1  tablespoon canola oil

1. Mix the plum and strawberry preserves, jelly, pecans, raisins, and ½ cup of crushed cornflakes. Set aside.

2. Place 1 sheet of phyllo on a large clean kitchen towel and coat with butter-flavored cooking spray. Sprinkle with 1 heaping tablespoon of cornflake crumbs. (Keep the remaining phyllo covered.)

3. Repeat with 2 more sheets of phyllo, stacking the layers. On the third sheet, sprinkle 1 heaping tablespoon of cinnamon sugar over the entire layer.

4. Spread one third of the preserve mixture evenly over half of the phyllo sheet, starting at one short edge. Roll up in jelly roll fashion, using the towel to help you roll the dough.

5. Place the roll on a nonstick cookie sheet or baking pan coated with butter-flavored spray. Pinch the ends of the roll closed.

6. Brush the top of the strudel lightly with oil. Sprinkle generously with cinnamon sugar, and make cuts 2 inches apart, but only through the top 2 layers. Cover with a damp towel and refrigerate while you are preparing the other 2 rolls. Preheat the oven to 375°.

7. Repeat the procedure, placing additional rolls on the baking sheet.

8. Bake for 10 minutes, then reduce the heat to 350° and bake 20 to 25 minutes more.

9. Remove from the oven, cool, and cut each roll into 10 serving pieces. (Using a sharp serrated knife makes it easier to cut slices without the strudel leaves crumbling.)

*To Freeze:* Place the baked strudel in a single layer in a freezer container or freezer foil and wrap airtight before placing in the freezer. Heat for 5 to 10 minutes in the oven before serving. Serve with a scoop of nonfat vanilla frozen yogurt if desired.

---

**PER SERVING**

| | | | |
|---|---|---|---|
| 3.7 gm total fat | .32 gm saturated fat | .8 gm fiber | 134 calories |
| 0 mg cholesterol | 23.3% fat | 58 mg sodium | 33 calories from fat |

---

❦ HARRIET'S HINTS ❦

Cool toasted nuts before chopping in a blender or food processor or they will become pasty when processing.

# ❦ Gisele Pollak's No-Fat Apple Strudel ❦
## (PAREVE)
### *Serves: 6 to 8*

Gisele Pollak is a friend of my husband's who grew up in Budapest. She uses a non-fat honey mixture to coat the leaves of her new classic Hungarian apple strudel instead of oil or butter.

6 green apples (preferably Granny Smith), peeled, cored, and sliced
2 tablespoons frozen unsweetened apple juice concentrate
½ cup golden raisins (see Note)
1 teaspoon ground cinnamon
4 sheets phyllo pastry
¼ cup honey mixed with ¼ cup hot water
1 egg white, slightly beaten

1. Stew the apple slices, juice, raisins, and cinnamon in a covered heavy saucepan, stirring occasionally, until the liquid disappears, or microwave on High for 5 minutes. Cool.

2. Place 1 sheet of phyllo on a clean kitchen towel with one short end facing you. (Keep the rest covered.) Using a pastry brush or goose feather brush, spread the phyllo lightly with the honey mixture. Repeat with the remaining phyllo, stacking the sheets. Preheat the oven to 350°.

3. Leaving a 2-inch margin at the top and both sides, layer a 3-inch strip of the cooled apple mixture on the end of the phyllo sheet closest to you. Fold over the side flaps of the dough and coat with the honey mixture.

4. Lift up the ends of the towel nearest the filling. Carefully roll the phyllo and filling over on itself to form a cylinder.

5. Spread the top of the strudel with egg white. Transfer to a nonstick baking sheet.

6. Bake for 35 to 40 minutes or until golden brown. Cool slightly before slicing.

NOTE: You may want to avoid using golden raisins because of the sulfites that are added to maintain the color. In that case, substitute dark raisins.

| ——————— PER SERVING ——————— | | | |
|---|---|---|---|
| .9 gm total fat | .15 gm saturated fat | 3.1 gm fiber | 160 calories |
| 0 mg cholesterol | 5% fat | 56 mg sodium | 8 calories from fat |

# ❦ Mama's Apple Kugel (Schalet) ❦
## (PAREVE)
### Serves: 6 to 8

A kugel is a sweet or savory baked pudding. When my mother prepared strudel, she often made a small apple kugel at the same time. I wish I had been smart enough to write the recipe down; however, here is the recipe as I remember it from watching and tasting. Most children do enjoy tasting their mothers' cooking. As Billy Crystal said, "I was thirteen years old before I realized my name wasn't *'Taste this.'* "

  1 tablespoon canola oil
  4 sheets phyllo pastry
  ¼ cup sugar-free apricot preserves heated with 1 tablespoon apricot brandy
  ¼ cup sugar mixed with 1 teaspoon ground cinnamon
  ⅓ cup ground walnuts or hazelnuts
  ¼ cup dried bread crumbs
  ½ cup dark raisins
  3 green apples, peeled and thinly sliced (about 4 cups)

1. Brush a medium-size 6-cup round Pyrex bowl or soufflé dish with oil. Preheat the oven to 400°.

2. Place 1 sheet of phyllo on a clean kitchen towel. Brush with the warmed preserves-brandy mixture.

3. Place a second layer of phyllo atop the first; coat with butter-flavored cooking spray. Sprinkle with 1 tablespoon of cinnamon-sugar, 1 tablespoon of ground nuts, and 1 tablespoon of bread crumbs.

4. Repeat step 3 with a third layer.

5. Brush the fourth layer of pastry with apricot glaze and sprinkle with half the re-

maining nuts, bread crumbs, and raisins. Layer apples over two thirds of the phyllo and sprinkle with the remaining nuts, bread crumbs, and raisins.

6. Lift up the ends of the towel nearest the filling and roll the phyllo lengthwise over on itself to form a cylinder. Coil into a snail shape. Place in the lightly oiled oven-proof bowl; press down lightly with your hand or a spoon. Sprinkle with any remaining cinnamon-sugar mixture, and drizzle with any remaining apricot glaze.

7. Cover with foil and place the bowl in a baking pan. Add about 1 inch of hot water to the baking pan. Bake for 15 minutes; uncover, raise the oven temperature to 425°, and bake 40 to 50 minutes more, or until golden brown.

*To Serve:* Unmold on a platter and sprinkle with more cinnamon sugar and ground nuts if desired. This kugel tastes best served warm.

NOTE: After rolling the dough into a cylinder in step 6, you may bake it as an apple strudel in a preheated 350° oven for 35 to 40 minutes.

| PER SERVING | | | |
|---|---|---|---|
| 5.7 gm total fat | .57 gm saturated fat | 2.2 gm fiber | 183 calories |
| 0 mg cholesterol | 26.9% fat | 85 mg sodium | 52 calories from fat |

# ❦ Jackie Keller's Pear Cranberry Strudel ❦
## (PAREVE)
### *Serves: 6*

Jackie Keller, a gifted cook of Hungarian descent, is the founder of Nutrific Foods, a Los Angeles-based company that makes delicious low-fat, low-cholesterol desserts. Her healthful goodies are a double treat for the busy cook!

½ cup frozen unsweetened apple juice concentrate or pear brandy
3 cups peeled, cored, coarsely chopped ripe Anjou or Bartlett pears
¼ cup dried cranberries
¼ teaspoon nutmeg, preferably freshly grated
3 sheets phyllo pastry
1 egg white, slightly beaten
 Confectioners' sugar, for garnish (optional)

1. Heat the apple juice in a saucepan; add the pears and simmer uncovered until tender, about 7 minutes. Add the cranberries and nutmeg and mix well. Cool. Preheat the oven to 400°.

2. Lay a phyllo sheet on a clean kitchen towel. Coat the sheet lightly with butter-flavored cooking spray. Repeat with the remaining sheets, stacking them as you go.

3. Spoon the drained pear mixture in a strip along a long edge of the phyllo and roll up tightly.

4. Place the roll on a nonstick baking sheet that has been lightly coated with cooking spray. Lightly coat the top of the strudel with egg white and score the top diagonally into 6 sections, using a serrated knife.

5. Bake for 15 to 20 minutes, or until golden brown.

*To Serve:* Serve the strudel warm, dusted with confectioners' sugar or with a scoop of cranberry sorbet.

## Variation: Pear Strudel Squares

*Serves: 12*

½ cup frozen unsweetened apple juice concentrate
1 tablespoon packed brown sugar (optional)
6 ripe but firm Anjou or Bartlett pears, peeled, cored, and sliced
⠀⠀½ inch thick (or 6 peeled, sliced cooking apples)
⅓ cup dried cranberries
½ teaspoon freshly grated nutmeg
6 sheets phyllo pastry
1 egg white, slightly beaten
⠀⠀Confectioners' sugar, for garnish

1. Using the apple juice concentrate and brown sugar, prepare the pear slices until barely tender as in step 1 of the above recipe.

2. Coat a 13 × 9 × 2-inch glass baking dish with butter-flavored cooking spray. Preheat the oven to 400°.

3. Place a sheet of phyllo crosswise in the pan and coat with butter-flavored cooking spray. Fold in half and coat the top with cooking spray. Repeat with a second and a third sheet of phyllo.

4. Spread the drained pears on the phyllo. Top with 3 additional sheets of phyllo

prepared as the first two were, coating each layer. Spread the top layer lightly with beaten egg white.

5. Cut into 12 squares, using a sharp serrated knife and just cutting through the top phyllo layers.

6. Bake for 20 to 30 minutes or until golden brown.

*To Serve:* Cut into 3-inch squares and dust lightly with confectioners' sugar before serving.

---

PER SERVING

| | | | |
|---|---|---|---|
| 1.1 gm total fat | .14 gm saturated fat | 2.6 gm fiber | 132 calories |
| 0 mg cholesterol | 7% fat | 52 mg sodium | 10 calories from fat |

# BAKING

## *From Muffins to Mandelbrot*

Sam Mackler's Water Bagels   373

Cinnamon Raisin Rolls   375

Mother's Date and Nut Bread   377

Orange-flavored Cream Cheese   378

No-Fat Honey Tea Loaf   379

Easy Bran Muffins   380

Hungarian Sour Cherry Muffins   382

Oat Nut Slices with Jam   383

Spiced Ginger Cookies   384

My Favorite Mandelbrot   385

Marbled Mandelbrot   386

Dorothy Essick's Poppy Seed Crisps   388

Harriet Greenwald's Dessert Wafers   389

Cream Cheese Squares   390

A Very Good Chocolate Cake   391

Dorothy Essick's Rhubarb Bars   392

Italian Prune Plum Crisp   394

Busy Day Chocolate Cake   395

The foods that many people miss most when trying to maintain a low-fat, low-cholesterol life style are sweets and desserts. This also seems to be the area where self-discipline is lacking! But try a water bagel or one of the low- or no-fat treats like Marbled Mandelbrot (page 386) or No-Fat Honey Tea Loaf (page 379) instead of your usual sweet selection, and remember to include ripe seasonal fruits. You won't feel deprived at all!

Occasionally, if you are craving rich buttery kuchen . . . enjoy one piece, then forget it and don't feel guilty. Just continue with your usual healthy lifestyle, and remember, it's the food choices you make day in and day out that affect your health, not the occasional indulgence.

People just love fresh-baked bread of all kinds. One of my fondest memories of my brother-in-law Jerry Litt was his weekly early Sunday morning trek to Beverlywood Bakery in Los Angeles and Charlie's Deli on Pico Boulevard. He would stop and fill his car with freshly baked bagels, breads, kaiser and onion rolls. Then there was lox with cream cheese and, of course, the whitefish he added because some of the children preferred that to smoked salmon. Each care package had its own special request filled. Off he would go, delivering these lovingly purchased bags of baked goods and delicatessen. He would deposit them on the doorsteps of each of his four children. Most times, it was so early in the morning that they were still asleep, but when, still half-asleep, they went to bring in the Sunday paper, there was this redolent treasure for them to savor and share with their families for Sunday morning brunch.

The food was special—but not nearly so special as the love and devotion this man showed to his family—and not just on Sundays.

Did you ever wish you were born with a knack for baking? It's my belief that baking skills are acquired. If your mother could toss things together and get delicious results, her secret ingredient was practice, practice, practice. Experience develops judgment. Conversely, a good recipe is the perfect substitute for experience. Follow these tips for perfect results:

1. Read the recipe carefully. *Assemble all the ingredients* and prepare your pans before you begin to mix.
2. Preheat the oven to the required temperature.
3. Measure flour correctly. The best method is to spoon it carefully into the measure and then level the top by scraping with a metal spatula or other straight edge. Sift the flour before measuring only if the recipe calls for it.
4. Scoop and level granulated white sugar. Pack brown sugar firmly.
5. Measure liquid ingredients in cups resting on a level surface.
6. Measure dry ingredients in plastic or metal measuring cups and liquids in glass measuring cups.
7. Have egg whites at room temperature before beating.

## SUBSTITUTIONS FOR LOW-FAT BAKING AND DESSERT MAKING

| *Instead of:* | *Use:* |
| --- | --- |
| Butter, margarine, or vegetable shortening | Canola oil, or substitute applesauce for part of fat in baking |
| Sugar | Frozen unsweetened apple juice concentrate, date sugar; or cut amount of sugar in recipe by ⅓ to ½ of the amount listed |
| Sour cream | Nonfat plain yogurt (no gelatin added), nonfat sour cream (or light), strained buttermilk, or plain low-fat yogurt |
| Cream cheese | Neufchâtel or nonfat cream cheese or ricotta |
| Whole milk | Nonfat milk or nonfat evaporated milk (also called skim), or 1% fat milk |

| | |
|---|---|
| 1 egg yolk | 1 tablespoon egg substitute |
| Egg yolks or whole eggs | Egg whites (2 extra-large egg whites equal 1 whole egg) or ¼ cup no-cholesterol egg substitute |
| Chocolate | Cocoa (3 tablespoons cocoa plus 1 tablespoon canola oil equal 1 ounce chocolate) |
| All white flour | Whole wheat or (sometimes) a combination of whole wheat and unbleached all-purpose flour in cookies, cakes, sweet breads, and plain breads |
| Melted butter or margarine | Butter-flavored cooking spray for coating pans |
| Nuts in cake or cookies | Crushed cereals, dried fruits (e.g., raisins and dates), apple juice concentrate, a few ground nuts, cinnamon |
| Pastry crust | Low-fat graham cracker or zwieback crumbs |
| ½ teaspoon baking powder | 1½ teaspoons low-sodium baking powder |
| 1 tablespoon flour (for thickening) | 1½ teaspoons cornstarch, potato starch, arrowroot |
| 1¼ cups sugar + ¼ cup liquid | 1 cup honey |

# ❦ Sam Mackler's Water Bagels ❦
## (PAREVE)
### Yield: 24 bagels (1 bagel = 1 serving)

Sam Mackler, now retired, had a Jewish-style bakery in Culver City, California, for twenty years. Sam is descended from generations of Jewish bakers, and his recipe for bagels was used by his father and grandfather from Poland before him, and now, I hope, it will be used by you. Sam has been kind enough to adapt his recipe for easy home preparation. These bagels are delicious, whether fresh or toasted with a smear of nonfat or light cream cheese, as a base for a bagel pizza, or made into bagel chips. A few hours in the kitchen will pay off with hours of your family's eating pleasure. This recipe produces delicious, crusty bagels that are chewy on the inside, low in fat, and low in calories.

3 cups warm water (about 120° to 130°)
4 packages active dry yeast
3 tablespoons sugar
1 tablespoon kosher salt
1 to 2 tablespoons canola oil (optional) (see Note)
9 to 10 cups unbleached white flour, or as needed
4 quarts boiling water with 1 tablespoon granulated sugar
Poppy seeds, sesame seeds, and caraway seeds as topping (optional)

1. Put the 3 cups of warm water in the bowl of a standing electric mixer. Sprinkle the yeast and sugar over the water and allow to stand until foamy, about 5 minutes.

2. Add the salt, oil (if desired), and 4 cups of the flour. Beat *with the dough hook* for 3 minutes; add enough of the remaining flour, ½ cup at a time, to form a very stiff dough. Knead with the dough hook for about 2 minutes, or until the dough is smooth.

3. Cover with a kitchen towel and allow to rise until doubled, about 1 hour. Punch down the dough and turn out onto a lightly floured board.

4. Divide the dough into 24 even portions. Roll into 6-inch lengths, ¾ inch thick but tapered at the ends. Form into circles, pinch tightly to close, and allow to stand just 10 minutes.

5. Preheat the oven to 400°. Coat a baking sheet with vegetable oil cooking spray.

6. Drop the bagels into the boiling sugared water, about 4 at a time. Bring to a boil again (about 1 minute). Turn and boil 1 minute on the other side. Remove with a slotted spoon and place on the prepared baking sheet. Sprinkle with seeds, if desired. Repeat with remaining bagels.

7. Bake for about 20 to 25 minutes, or until golden brown.

8. Remove from the oven, loosen from the baking sheet, and cool on a rack. Store in tightly sealed bags at room temperature or in the freezer.

Note: If you use oil in the recipe, it will result in a chewier bagel that keeps its fresh quality longer.

Variations:

*Bialys:* Bialys are made from the same dough as bagels; however, they are not boiled in a water bath or glazed before baking. Make rounds of dough and flatten into 3- to 4-inch circles ½ inch thick. Brush with water or flour, make a depression in the center with fingers, and sprinkle center with chopped red or white onions and poppy seeds.

Allow to rise for about 15 minutes on a nonstick baking sheet. Press down the center again and bake in a preheated 375° oven for about 20 to 25 minutes, or until the undercrust of the bialys is firm and lightly browned.

*Herbed Bagels:* Add ⅔ cup of your favorite chopped fresh herbs (such as rosemary, basil, oregano, or chives) with the flour and proceed as in the plain water bagel recipe.

*Raisin Bagels:* Add 1 cup dark raisins dusted with flour along with the flour.

*Twisted Bagels:* Many years ago, twisted bagels were very popular. They are prepared with the same dough, but the strip of dough is twisted before the ends are pinched together.

--- PER SERVING ---

| | | | |
|---|---|---|---|
| .6 gm total fat | .09 gm saturated fat | 1.7 gm fiber | 199 calories |
| 0 mg cholesterol | 2.6% fat | 294 mg sodium | 5 calories from fat |

## ❦ Cinnamon Raisin Rolls ❦
### (DAIRY)
*Yield: 24 rolls (1 roll = 1 serving)*

If you are intimidated by the multi-step preparation of yeast breads, try these. You'll get immediate gratification, because they are easy to make and delicious to eat. Bake them in two round pans: one to enjoy now and a second to freeze for the future, or coat a baking sheet with butter-flavored cooking spray and bake them flat on the sheet.

1 package plus 1 teaspoon rapid-rise yeast
1½ cups warm (115°) evaporated skim milk
1 teaspoon kosher salt
⅓ cup granulated sugar or honey
3½ cups unbleached all-purpose flour (see Note)
1½ cups sifted cake flour or whole wheat pastry flour
1 extra-large egg and 1 extra-large egg white, slightly beaten
¼ cup canola oil, 4 tablespoons (½ stick) light margarine, melted, or ⅓ cup unsweetened applesauce

*Filling:*

    ¾ cup chopped toasted walnuts
    ⅔ cup dark raisins, plumped in hot water or orange juice and drained
    ¼ cup packed brown sugar
    2 teaspoons unsweetened cocoa powder (optional)
    1 teaspoon ground cinnamon
    ¼ cup water

*or*

    ½ cup honey
    3 tablespoons frozen unsweetened apple juice concentrate
    ½ cup chopped nuts
    ½ cup dark raisins
    1 tablespoon ground cinnamon

    **Confectioners' sugar, for garnish**

1. Dissolve the yeast in 1 cup warm milk. Add the salt and 1 tablespoon of the sugar, and allow to proof till foamy.

2. Place the flours and remaining sugar in a mixing bowl. Stir with a whisk or slotted spoon to blend. Make a well in the flour and add the eggs, oil, and remaining ½ cup milk, stirring to mix thoroughly.

3. Turn the dough out onto a floured board and knead by hand for 8 to 10 minutes, until smooth and elastic, or blend with a dough hook and knead in an electric mixer about 4 minutes, until smooth and satiny.

4. Place the dough in a clean greased bowl. Cover with a towel; let rise in a warm place until double in bulk—about 35 to 40 minutes.

5. Punch the dough down and divide into two pieces. Remove one piece, knead lightly, and roll out the dough on a lightly floured board into a rectangle about 12 × 8 inches.

6. Combine the filling ingredients; spread half on the dough, leaving a ½-inch border on the short sides of the dough and about 1 inch on the long sides.

7. Starting with a long side, roll tightly jelly roll fashion and cut into twelve 1-inch slices.

8. Arrange the rolls, cut side up, about 1 inch apart in a 10-inch layer cake pan coated with butter-flavored cooking spray. Repeat with the remaining dough. Cover with a kitchen towel and let rise ½ hour or longer, until doubled in size.

9. Bake in a preheated 350° oven for about 20 minutes or until lightly browned on top. Turn out of the pans and allow the rolls to cool on a rack.

*To Serve:* When slightly cooled, sprinkle the top generously with confectioners' sugar.

NOTE: *Remember to scoop and level flour*—do not pack or tap the cup to level.

*To Freeze:* Wrap tightly in plastic. Reheat in a brown paper bag in a 200° oven or in a microwave.

VARIATION: You may frost with 1 cup confectioners' sugar mixed with 2 teaspoons lemon juice, 1 tablespoon hot milk, and ½ teaspoon pure vanilla extract. Mix until smooth and creamy and drizzle over warm cinnamon rolls, or cool the rolls before frosting if you prefer.

―――――― PER SERVING ――――――

| | | | |
|---|---|---|---|
| 5 gm total fat | .43 gm saturated fat | .9 gm fiber | 169 calories |
| 10 mg cholesterol | 26.4% fat | 73 mg sodium | 45 calories from fat |

## ❧ Mother's Date and Nut Bread ❧

*Yield: Four 20-ounce loaves (48 slices) (1 slice = 1 serving)*

My mother baked this bread in many sizes and shapes, depending upon the empty cans she had available. To standardize the recipe, I'm suggesting four 20-ounce lead-free cans, but you can be as flexible as you choose. Simply decrease the baking time for smaller cans and increase it for larger ones. The round slices make lovely little tea sandwiches with orange-flavored fat-free cream cheese (below).

  2 teaspoons baking soda
  1 cup boiling water
  1 cup fresh orange juice
 24 Medjool dates (8 ounces), cut up with scissors or sliced
  1 cup toasted chopped walnuts
  1 cup dark raisins
  3 extra-large egg whites
 ½ cup granulated sugar
 ½ cup packed brown sugar
  2 teaspoons pure vanilla extract
  3 tablespoons canola oil
  4 cups unbleached all-purpose flour
    Orange-flavored Cream Cheese (see below)

1. Dissolve the baking soda in the boiling water and pour immediately over the orange juice, dates, nuts, and raisins in a heatproof bowl. Let stand until cool.

2. Preheat the oven to 350°. Lightly coat four 20-ounce cans with butter-flavored cooking spray.

3. Beat the egg whites with a whisk until foamy. Add the sugars and vanilla; beat thoroughly. Add the oil and blend.

4. Add the cooled date mixture. Blend.

5. Add the flour one cup at a time, mixing with a wooden spoon until all the ingredients are moistened.

6. Fill the prepared cans half full of batter. Bake for 55 to 60 minutes, depending upon the size of the can.

*To Serve:* Let cool slightly in the cans, loosen with a spatula, and remove to cool on a rack.

*To Freeze:* Wrap the cooled loaves in plastic wrap and then foil. They will keep very successfully for several months in the freezer.

## Orange-flavored Cream Cheese

Mix ½ cup nonfat cream cheese with 2 tablespoons fresh orange juice, 1 tablespoon grated orange zest, and a pinch of freshly grated nutmeg. Use as a spread with slices of date-nut bread or to prepare tea sandwiches or lunch sandwiches.

─────────── PER SERVING ───────────

| | | | |
|---|---|---|---|
| 2.0 gm total fat | .15 gm saturated fat | .8 gm fiber | 81 calories |
| 0 mg cholesterol | 21.3% fat | 47 mg sodium | 18 calories from fat |

─── ❦ HARRIET'S HINTS ❦ ───

*Fresh eggs will sink to the bottom of cold water. The staler the egg, the higher it will rise. Eggs separate more easily when cold, but egg whites beat to a larger volume when at room temperature, with either a few grains of salt or cream of tartar added. When beating egg whites, use a glass or metal bowl, not plastic.*

# ❧ No-Fat Honey Tea Loaf ❧
## (PAREVE)

*Yield: 2 loaves cut into 36 slices and halved (½ slice = 1 serving)*

I have changed my traditional recipe by cutting the amount of sweetener in half, deleting the oil, using egg whites only, and substituting part whole wheat flour and part oat bran for some of the white flour. This no-cholesterol, no-fat loaf is lovely to serve with tea or as a light dessert with fresh fruit.

    1  cup honey
 1⅓  cups hot strong decaffeinated coffee
    2  cups unbleached all-purpose flour
    1  cup whole wheat pastry flour
  ½  cup oat bran
    1  tablespoon baking powder
    1  teaspoon baking soda
    2  teaspoons ground cinnamon
  ½  teaspoon ground allspice
  ½  cup egg substitute
    6  extra-large egg whites, at room temperature
    6  tablespoons sugar
  ¼  teaspoon cream of tartar
  ¼  cup sliced almonds

1. Preheat the oven to 350°. Lightly coat the bottoms of two 9 × 5 × 3-inch loaf pans with vegetable oil cooking spray and line with wax paper.
2. Dissolve the honey in the hot coffee and cool.
3. Combine the flours, oat bran, baking powder, baking soda, cinnamon, and allspice and mix together with a whisk or slotted spoon.
4. In the bowl of an electric mixer, beat the cooled coffee mixture, egg substitute, 2 of the egg whites, and 3 tablespoons of the sugar. Add the dry ingredients and mix on low speed until smooth.
5. In a separate bowl, beat the remaining 4 egg whites with the cream of tartar until slightly thick. Add the remaining 3 tablespoons sugar, 1 tablespoon at a time, while beating until stiff and shiny.
6. Fold the beaten egg whites into the cake mixture gently, just until blended.
7. Pour the batter into the prepared loaf pans, sprinkle the tops of the loaves with

the almonds, and bake for about 1 hour or until the cake starts to pull away from the sides of the pans.

8. Invert the pans onto a cake rack to cool completely.

9. Loosen the sides of the loaves with a spatula and remove from the pans. Remove the wax paper and slice.

*To Freeze:* Wrap the sliced loaf in plastic wrap and then in foil.

---

PER SERVING

| | | | |
|---|---|---|---|
| .2 gm total fat | .03 gm saturated fat | .2 gm fiber | 42 calories |
| 0 mg cholesterol | 3.2% fat | 25 mg sodium | 1 calorie from fat |

---

# ❧ Easy Bran Muffins ❧
## (DAIRY)
*Yield: 4 dozen (1 muffin = 1 serving)*

Isn't it nice to have the aroma of fresh muffins filling the house at breakfast or teatime? This high-fiber muffin batter keeps in the refrigerator for up to one month. I used to teach these muffins in my cooking classes. The recipe has been updated by cutting the sugar in half, the fat by three quarters, and the cholesterol entirely.

    1 (15-ounce) box bran flakes or raisin bran
    1 cup dark raisins, dried cranberries, or dried cherries
    ¼ cup wheat germ
    ½ cup granulated sugar
    ¾ cup packed brown sugar
    2½ cups unbleached all-purpose flour
    2½ cups whole wheat flour
    1 cup quick-cooking rolled oats or no-fat granola
    ½ teaspoon salt
    5 teaspoons baking soda
    ½ cup egg substitute
    3 extra-large egg whites
    1 quart low-fat buttermilk (strain out the fat globules)
    ⅓ cup canola oil
    ⅔ cup unsweetened applesauce

1. Preheat the oven to 400°. Coat two medium-size muffin tins with butter-flavored cooking spray.

2. In a large bowl, mix the bran flakes, dried fruit, wheat germ, sugars, flours, rolled oats, salt, and soda with a whisk or slotted spoon.

3. In another bowl, combine the egg substitute, egg whites, buttermilk, oil, and applesauce.

4. Add the liquid to the dry ingredients and stir until the dry ingredients are thoroughly moistened.

5. Fill the prepared muffin tins two-thirds full. Bake for 15 to 20 minutes; serve hot.

6. Store the remaining batter in a covered container in the refrigerator for up to 1 month.

VARIATION: Use some of the batter to make mini-muffins in 1½-inch tins. Place 1 teaspoon of batter in each cup, add ¼ teaspoon jelly or preserves, and cover with batter. Bake these muffins for about 12 minutes.

—— PER SERVING ——

| | | | |
|---|---|---|---|
| 2.2 gm total fat | .31 gm saturated fat | 1.9 gm fiber | 135 calories |
| 1 mg cholesterol | 14.3% fat | 269 mg sodium | 20 calories from fat |

—— ❧ HARRIET'S HINTS ❧ ——

*Pick up the flavor of canned unsweetened applesauce by adding lemon zest, orange zest, a sprinkling of freshly grated nutmeg, or a dash or two of cinnamon.*

# ❧ Hungarian Sour Cherry Muffins ❧
## (PAREVE)
*Yield: 12 muffins (1 muffin = 1 serving)*

If you have difficulty finding jars of Hungarian sour cherries, 1 cup of dried cherries reconstituted in ½ cup of boiling water may be substituted. It won't re-create the flavor of the sour cherries, but it certainly is more than acceptable!

     1 cup unbleached all-purpose flour
     1 cup cake flour or whole wheat pastry flour
     ⅔ cup sugar
     2 teaspoons baking powder
     1 teaspoon baking soda
       Pinch of salt
     ¼ cup canola oil
     3 extra-large egg whites, slightly beaten
     2 teaspoons grated lemon zest
     ½ teaspoon almond extract
   1¼ cups canned Hungarian sour cherries, drained

1. Preheat the oven to 375°. Coat muffin tins with butter-flavored cooking spray.

2. In a bowl, mix together the flours, sugar, baking powder, baking soda, and salt, using a slotted spoon or a whisk.

3. Combine the oil, egg whites, zest, extract, and cherries in a separate bowl.

4. Add the dry ingredients to the wet and stir just until blended and all the flour is moistened.

5. Fill each muffin cup two-thirds full of batter.

6. Bake for 18 to 20 minutes or until toothpick inserted in a muffin comes out clean.

7. Loosen the muffins and turn on their sides in the pan to cool slightly. These are delicious served warm, and they freeze beautifully for future use.

| ——— PER SERVING ——— | | | |
|---|---|---|---|
| 4.7 gm total fat | .36 gm saturated fat | .3 gm fiber | 178 calories |
| 0 mg cholesterol | 23.7% fat | 133 mg sodium | 43 calories from fat |

# ❦ Oat Nut Slices with Jam ❦

## (PAREVE)

*Yield: Thirty-two ½-inch slices (1 slice = 1 serving)*

This is a super-delicious, cholesterol-free sliced bar with jam that brings rave reviews. Caution: These cookies may be habit-forming. Remember, they still contain a bit of fat from the nuts.

¾ **cup ground toasted nuts (hazelnuts, walnuts, and/or almonds)**
¾ **cup rolled oats, finely chopped in the food processor**
¼ **cup oat bran**
¼ **cup sugar**
2 **extra-large egg whites and 1 teaspoon pure vanilla extract and/or almond extract, slightly beaten with a fork**
   **About 2 tablespoons sugar-free preserves (apricot, strawberry, or raspberry)**

1. Preheat the oven to 350° and coat a nonstick baking sheet with butter-flavored cooking spray.

2. Mix the nuts, oats, and oat bran with the sugar.

3. Add enough of the egg white and vanilla mixture to make a dough just firm enough so that the nuts, oats, and sugar all adhere.

4. Shape into two rolls 1½ inches in diameter and about 12 inches long and place on the prepared baking sheet.

5. Dip your finger in cold water and make a deep ridge down the center of each roll.

6. Bake for 15 to 20 minutes or until lightly browned.

7. Remove from the oven. When slightly cooled, spoon preserves down the length of each ridge and cool completely.

8. When cool, cut into diagonal ½-inch slices.

VARIATION: Use nonfat fudge topping instead of preserves.

| ——— PER SERVING ——— | | | |
|---|---|---|---|
| 1.8 gm total fat | .14 gm saturated fat | .5 gm fiber | 36 calories |
| 0 mg cholesterol | 42.7% fat | 4 mg sodium | 16 calories from fat |

# ❦ Spiced Ginger Cookies ❦
## (PAREVE)
*Yield: 48 cookies (1 cookie = 1 serving)*

We rarely had cookies as snacks when growing up, with one exception: these delicious, fragrantly spicy, crisp ginger cookies. They are a delight with cold milk or hot tea. If your child or grandchild likes working in the kitchen with you, they can use their hands to roll the dough before baking. I have substituted oat bran for some of the flour, and lowered the fat by using egg substitute, egg whites and a small amount of light margarine.

1⅔  cups unbleached all-purpose flour
⅔  cup oat bran
2  teaspoons baking soda
2  teaspoons ground cinnamon
2  teaspoons ground ginger
¼  teaspoon ground allspice
¼  teaspoon freshly grated nutmeg
5  tablespoons light margarine or ⅓ cup canola oil
1  cup packed brown sugar
3  tablespoons egg substitute mixed with 1 extra-large egg white
¼  cup dark molasses
   Grated zest of 1 lemon (optional)
   Ice water
½  cup granulated sugar

1. In a large bowl, mix the flour, oat bran, baking soda, and spices with a slotted spoon or whisk. Set aside.

2. Using a food processor or electric mixer, cream the margarine and brown sugar together.

3. Add the egg mixture, molasses, and lemon zest (if using) and process with a pulsing action until blended.

4. Mix in the dry ingredients until well blended. Remove the dough to a bowl, cover, and refrigerate for several hours or until firm.

5. When you are ready to begin baking, preheat the oven to 375°. Coat 2 or more baking sheets with vegetable oil cooking spray. Have ready a bowl of ice water and a small bowl of granulated sugar.

6. Pinch off pieces of the chilled dough and roll into 1-inch balls. Plunge quickly into the ice water, then roll in the sugar.

7. Place the sugared balls 2 inches apart on the prepared baking sheets. Bake for 10 to 12 minutes, or until the cookies have a crackled appearance and are firm to the touch.

8. Remove with a spatula to a wire rack; cool completely and store in airtight containers.

*To Freeze:* Place in airtight plastic bags.

| PER SERVING | | | |
|---|---|---|---|
| .8 gm total fat | .14 gm saturated fat | .4 gm fiber | 50 calories |
| 0 mg cholesterol | 13.7% fat | 73 mg sodium | 7 calories from fat |

# ✹ My Favorite Mandelbrot ✹
## (PAREVE)
*Yield: 60 slices (1 slice = 1 serving)*

Every Jewish cook has her favorite recipe for the crisp cookies known as *mandelbrot* (literally, almond bread). This one is cholesterol-free, and though not fat-free, it certainly is lower in fat than traditional recipes. It's easy to prepare and, if stored in an airtight container, the cookies stay crisp for weeks. When properly frozen the cookies will keep for up to 6 months.

1½ cups whole wheat pastry flour
1½ cups unbleached all-purpose flour
½ cup oat bran
¾ cup sugar
1 tablespoon baking powder
3 extra-large egg whites
¼ cup egg substitute
¼ cup canola oil
1 teaspoon pure vanilla extract
1 teaspoon pure almond extract
1 cup coarsely chopped salt-free dry-roasted almonds
3 tablespoons granulated sugar mixed with 1½ teaspoons ground cinnamon, for topping

1. Preheat the oven to 375°. Spray 2 baking sheets with butter-flavored cooking spray.

2. In a mixing bowl, combine the flours, oat bran, sugar, and baking powder. Blend well with a wooden spoon or whisk.

3. Combine the egg whites, egg substitute, oil, and extracts in a separate bowl.

4. Add the egg mixture to the dry ingredients and blend with a wooden spoon. Add the nuts and mix well.

5. Divide the dough into 4 portions; with lightly floured hands, shape into four 14-inch logs, about 1 inch in diameter.

6. Place the logs on the prepared baking sheets about 3 to 4 inches apart, as the dough will spread in baking. Bake for 30 minutes or until firm to the touch.

7. Remove the logs to a rack and cool slightly. Lower the oven heat to 300°. Cut the logs into ½-inch-thick diagonal slices. Arrange the slices on the baking sheets with cut sides down and sprinkle with half the cinnamon sugar. Return to the oven and bake for 10 minutes. Turn and sprinkle the second side with the remaining cinnamon sugar; bake for 10 additional minutes or until crisp and lightly browned.

8. Remove from the oven and cool before storing in airtight canisters or sealed plastic bags.

---

### PER SERVING

| | | | |
|---|---|---|---|
| 2.2 gm total fat | .2 gm saturated fat | .5 gm fiber | 57 calories |
| 0 mg cholesterol | 34.1% fat | 5 mg sodium | 20 calories from fat |

## ❦ Marbled Mandelbrot ❦
### (PAREVE)
*Yield: 48 slices (1 slice = 1 serving)*

Whether you call these *mandelbrot* or *biscotti*, they still taste great with a cup of tea.

1¼ cups unbleached all-purpose flour
¾ cup whole wheat pastry flour
1 teaspoon baking powder
½ teaspoon baking soda
1 cup sugar

4 extra-large egg whites

2 teaspoons pure vanilla extract

3 tablespoons unsweetened cocoa powder mixed with 3 tablespoons strong brewed coffee (2 teaspoons instant coffee powder mixed with 3 tablespoons hot water)

1 teaspoon almond extract

½ cup coarsely chopped salt-free dry-roasted almonds

1. Preheat the oven to 325°. Spray baking sheet with butter-flavored cooking spray.

2. Combine the flours, baking powder, baking soda, and sugar in a mixing bowl. Mix well with a wooden spoon or whisk.

3. In a separate bowl, whisk together the egg whites and vanilla. Add to the dry ingredients and mix until the flour is thoroughly moistened.

4. Divide the dough in half, leaving one half in the bowl. Add the coffee mixture, almond extract, and almonds to the bowl and mix just to combine.

5. Pat half the plain dough on a floured surface into a 10 × 5-inch rectangle. Pat half the chocolate dough on a floured surface into an 8 × 4-inch rectangle and place on top of the plain dough. Starting with a long side, roll tightly into a log about 12 inches long and place on the prepared baking sheet. Repeat with the remaining dough and place it well apart on the same baking sheet.

6. Bake for 20 to 25 minutes, or until firm to the touch. Remove from the oven and reduce the oven temperature to 300°.

7. Cool the logs on a rack for 10 minutes. Using a serrated knife, cut into ½-inch-thick *diagonal* slices. Stand the slices upright and bake at 300° for an additional 30 to 40 minutes.

8. Cool completely before storing in airtight containers or plastic bags.

| PER SERVING | | | |
|---|---|---|---|
| .7 gm total fat | .06 gm saturated fat | .2 gm fiber | 37 calories |
| 0 mg cholesterol | 16.2% fat | 14 mg sodium | 6 calories from fat |

# ❧ Dorothy Essick's Poppy Seed Crisps ❧
## (PAREVE)
### *Yield: About 120 pieces (1 piece = 1 serving)*

There is something especially *gemütlich* about sharing cookies and conversation. Neighbors and guests are always pleased to discover a platter of goodies gracing my friend Dorothy's kitchen counter.

⅓ cup canola oil
¾ cup sugar
 1 teaspoon pure vanilla extract plus ½ teaspoon almond extract, or 1 tablespoon fresh lemon juice
   Grated zest of 1 lemon
 4 extra-large egg whites, slightly beaten
¼ cup (2 ounces) poppy seeds or finely ground nuts
 2 cups unbleached all-purpose flour
 1 teaspoon baking powder
 1 teaspoon ground cinnamon

1. In the large bowl of an electric mixer, beat the oil and ½ cup of the sugar together until thick. Add the vanilla and almond extracts and zest. Blend.

2. Gradually add the 3 egg whites while beating. Continue to beat until thoroughly blended.

3. In a small bowl, mix the poppy seeds together with the flour and baking powder. Add one third of the flour mixture at a time to the oil and sugar mixture, beating after each addition until the flour is absorbed.

4. With floured hands, divide the dough into 4 pieces. Cover each in plastic wrap; flatten into a rectangular shape. Store in a plastic bag and chill in the refrigerator for 30 minutes before rolling (see Note).

5. Preheat the oven to 350°. Line a baking sheet with foil (shiny side up) and coat lightly with butter-flavored cooking spray.

6. Place a rectangle of dough between two pieces of wax paper lightly dusted with flour. Roll the dough into a rectangle ⅛ inch thick.

7. Remove the top sheet of wax paper and invert the dough directly on the foil, paper side up. Remove the second sheet of paper. Brush with egg white. Using a spatula or long dinner knife, cut through the dough in a geometric pattern: squares, diamonds, or triangles. Repeat with the remaining dough.

8. Mix the cinnamon with the remaining ¼ cup of sugar. Sprinkle 1 tablespoon of the cinnamon sugar over the dough and place the baking sheet in the oven. Bake for 8 to 10 minutes, or until lightly browned. (Check the cookies after about 6 minutes; if they seem to have baked together, cut apart on existing lines and separate slightly with a spatula.)

9. Using a metal spatula, transfer the cookies carefully to a rack.

*To Serve:* Serve with fresh or stewed fruit or with fresh fruit sorbet.

NOTE: This dough will keep for up to 4 days in the refrigerator or 4 weeks in the freezer.

| PER SERVING | | | |
|---|---|---|---|
| .8 gm total fat | .06 gm saturated fat | .1 gm fiber | 20 calories |
| 0 mg cholesterol | 33.9% fat | 1 mg sodium | 7 calories from fat |

# ❦ Harriet Greenwald's Dessert Wafers ❦
## (PAREVE)
### *Yield: 48 slices (1 slice = 1 serving)*

My smart-cooking friend Harriet Greenwald believes that prevention is better than a cure. Her recipe is low in fat, but has a crisp, satisfying taste. Try serving these wafers with fresh fruit or just a cup of hot tea.

 1 **cup plus 1 tablespoon unbleached all-purpose flour**
 3 **extra-large egg whites**
   **Few grains of salt**
⅓ **cup superfine sugar**
⅓ **cup chopped blanched or salt-free dry-roasted almonds**
½ **cup dark raisins plumped in 2 tablespoons fresh orange juice or apricot brandy, drained**
 1 **teaspoon pure orange or almond extract or rosewater**

1. Preheat the oven to 350°. Coat a 9 × 5 × 3-inch loaf pan with butter-flavored cooking spray. Sprinkle with 1 tablespoon of flour; invert the pan and tap to release excess flour.

2. Beat the egg whites and salt with an electric mixer until soft peaks form.

3. Add the sugar, 1 tablespoon at a time, while beating. Continue to beat until stiff and shiny.

4. Mix together the 1 cup of flour, nuts, and raisins. Fold into the egg white mixture along with the orange extract.

5. Pour and scrape into the prepared pan and bake for 35 to 40 minutes.

6. Invert the pan on a rack. Remove the loaf, cool, and wrap in foil. Refrigerate overnight.

7. Slice very thin (about 3/16 inch) with a serrated knife and place the slices on a baking sheet. Allow to dry out in a 250° oven for 15 minutes, and then for several hours in the oven *with no heat on.*

NOTE: Store in airtight containers, or freeze for future use.

---

**PER SERVING**

| | | | |
|---|---|---|---|
| .4 gm total fat | .04 gm saturated fat | .2 gm fiber | 24 calories |
| 0 mg cholesterol | 15.5% fat | 4 mg sodium | 4 calories from fat |

---

# ❦ Cream Cheese Squares ❦
## (DAIRY)
### Yield: 25 squares (1 square = 1 serving)

The original recipe for these bite-sized cheesecake squares came from my sister, Ruth Litt. I've adjusted the recipe to lower the fat and cholesterol. For even lower fat, try fat-free cream cheese.

       ¼ cup packed brown sugar
       ¾ cup unbleached all-purpose flour or graham cracker crumbs
       ½ cup chopped toasted pecans
2 to 3 tablespoons canola oil
       1 (8-ounce) package fat-reduced cream cheese
       ¼ cup granulated sugar
       ¼ cup egg substitute
       1 teaspoon pure vanilla extract
       2 tablespoons nonfat sour cream
       1 tablespoon fresh lemon juice

1. Preheat the oven to 350°.

2. In a bowl, mix the brown sugar, flour, and chopped nuts together. Stir in the oil, mixing with the hands until crumbly.

3. Remove ¾ cup of the mixture to be used as topping. Place the remainder in an 8-inch square pan, covering the bottom evenly, and press firmly. Bake 12 to 15 minutes.

4. Beat the cream cheese in a food processor or blender with the granulated sugar until smooth. Add the egg substitute, vanilla, sour cream, and lemon juice and blend.

5. Pour the filling into the baked crust and top with the reserved crumbs.

6. Return to the 350° oven for about 25 minutes.

7. Remove from the oven, allow to cool slightly, and cut into 1½-inch squares. When completely cool, cover with plastic wrap and refrigerate for future use. If you are going to use them shortly, they may be stored at room temperature.

---

——— PER SERVING ———

| | | | |
|---|---|---|---|
| 4.9 gm total fat | 1.19 gm saturated fat | .3 gm fiber | 87 calories |
| 5 mg cholesterol | 50.3% fat | 57 mg sodium | 44 calories from fat |

---

# ❧ A Very Good Chocolate Cake ❧
## (DAIRY)
### Serves: 20 (1 square = 1 serving)

This recipe is my children's favorite and mine, not only because it tastes good, but also because it's so easy to make.

¼ cup canola oil
1 cup minus 2 tablespoons sugar
1½ teaspoons pure vanilla extract
½ cup unsweetened cocoa powder
1¾ cups sifted cake flour or unbleached all-purpose flour
1 teaspoon baking soda
⅛ teaspoon salt
1 cup low-fat buttermilk, strained
Confectioners' sugar, for garnish

1. Preheat the oven to 350°. Lightly coat a 9-inch square nonstick baking pan with butter-flavored cooking spray.

2. In a mixing bowl, combine the oil and sugar; beat until well blended.

3. Add the vanilla and cocoa and blend.

4. Sift together the flour, baking soda, and salt in a separate bowl.

5. Add a third of the flour and half the buttermilk to the cocoa mixture and beat until smooth. Repeat; then beat in the final third of the flour.

6. Pour the batter into the prepared pan and bake for 30 minutes, or until the cake springs back when lightly touched and starts to pull away from the sides of the pan.

7. Cool on a rack and sprinkle with confectioners' sugar. If desired, the cake may be frosted with chocolate frosting.

─── PER SERVING ───

| | | | |
|---|---|---|---|
| 3.2 gm total fat | .43 gm saturated fat | 0 gm fiber | 104 calories |
| 1 mg cholesterol | 27.4% fat | 91 mg sodium | 28 calories from fat |

─── ❧ HARRIET'S HINTS ❧ ───

When baking with buttermilk, strain out the fat globules before using. Substitute soured milk for buttermilk in baking by measuring 1 tablespoon distilled white vinegar or lemon juice plus skim milk to equal 1 cup and allowing it to stand for 5 minutes.

# ❧ Dorothy Essick's Rhubarb Bars ❧
## (PAREVE)
### Yield: 24 bars (1 bar = 1 serving)

As with many recipes that are made with fruit, the sweetness, tartness, and moistness of these bars can vary. The rhubarb filling may be prepared the day before, to speed up the preparation. This confection may be cut into 3-inch squares and served with a scoop of nonfat vanilla yogurt alongside.

6 cups sliced fresh rhubarb (¼-inch slices) or 2 (20-ounce) packages frozen unsweetened rhubarb

¾ cup frozen unsweetened apple juice concentrate or fruit-sweetened cranberry-grape juice nectar

¼ cup fresh orange juice

1 tablespoon grated orange zest

2 tablespoons cornstarch

3 to 4 tablespoons sugar, or to taste

1 cup fresh strawberries, rinsed, hulled, and sliced (optional)

*Crumb Mixture:*

⅓ cup canola oil

⅓ cup packed brown sugar

½ teaspoon ground cinnamon

1½ cups chopped quick-cooking oats

⅓ cup toasted chopped almonds (optional)

1. Place the rhubarb, juices, and zest in a nonaluminum saucepan (see Note); simmer about 20 minutes or until softened, stirring occasionally.

2. Add the cornstarch, stir, and cook 5 minutes.

3. Add sugar to taste. (Strawberries may be added at this time if desired.) Cool and chill before using.

4. Preheat the oven to 375°.

5. Mix the crumb mixture ingredients. Reserve 1 cup of crumbs for the topping.

6. Press the remaining crumb mixture firmly on the bottom of an 11 × 7½-inch glass baking dish. Spread with the chilled rhubarb and sprinkle with the reserved topping and nuts, if desired.

7. Bake for about 35 minutes, or until browned.

*To Serve:* Allow to cool, cut into 2 × 1¼-inch bars, and dust lightly with confectioners' sugar before serving.

NOTE: The rhubarb-juice mixture may also be cooked in a microwave-safe dish on High for 6 minutes or until softened.

— PER SERVING —

| | | | |
|---|---|---|---|
| 3.5 gm total fat | .29 gm saturated fat | .8 gm fiber | 88 calories |
| 0 mg cholesterol | 34.1% fat | 5 mg sodium | 31 calories from fat |

# ❦ Italian Prune Plum Crisp ❦
(PAREVE)

*Serves: 8*

Italian prune plums are the small, purple ovals used in making plum butter (Lekvar, page 411). They are delicious either raw or cooked. They have a brief, early-fall (around September) season. I used to prepare a plum tart with a rich crust; however, I find this crisp topping makes a delicious alternative. The many people who request the recipe seem to like it, too!

Grated zest and juice of 1 lemon
3 pounds Italian prune plums, washed, quartered, and pitted, or peaches, peeled and sliced
½ to ¾ cup granulated sugar
1½ tablespoons cornstarch

*Topping:*

1 cup unbleached all-purpose flour
½ cup old-fashioned rolled oats
3 tablespoons packed brown sugar
2 tablespoons light margarine

1. Preheat the oven to 350°.
2. Sprinkle the lemon zest and juice over the plums. Add the sugar mixed with the cornstarch. Mix well and put in a medium oval baking dish.
3. Combine the flour, rolled oats, and brown sugar in a bowl. Rub in the margarine with clean fingers until the mixture is crumbly.
4. Sprinkle the topping over the plums and bake for about 50 to 60 minutes, or until the fruit is bubbly and the top brown.

*To Serve:* Serve warm on dessert plates with vanilla nonfat frozen yogurt.

| PER SERVING | | | |
|---|---|---|---|
| 2.9 gm total fat | .39 gm saturated fat | 4.3 gm fiber | 269 calories |
| 0 mg cholesterol | 9.2% fat | 37 mg sodium | 26 calories from fat |

# ❦ Busy Day Chocolate Cake ❦
## (PAREVE)
### *Serves: 16*

This recipe is "a piece of cake," and also cholesterol-free and very low in fat. You can prepare it the day before (actually, it tastes even better the second day) or freeze it. It can be mixed right in the baking pan or in a bowl and transferred to a pan (either an 8-inch square or 8-inch round springform pan) if you want to frost it on all sides. Of course, it is not calorie-free, so don't lose your head.

1½ cups unbleached all-purpose flour
1 cup granulated sugar or ½ cup granulated sugar plus ⅓ cup packed brown sugar
⅓ cup unsweetened cocoa powder
1 teaspoon baking soda
Pinch of kosher salt
1 cup cold water
½ cup canola oil
2 teaspoons pure vanilla extract
2 tablespoons distilled white vinegar

**Topping:**
**Fat-free fudge topping or chocolate frosting**

1. Preheat the oven to 375°.
2. Measure the flour, sugar, cocoa, baking soda, and salt into a mixing bowl or 8-inch square baking pan. Mix *thoroughly* with a slotted spoon.
3. Combine the cold water, oil, and vanilla. Add to the dry ingredients and mix with a slotted spoon until smooth.

4. Add the vinegar; stir quickly to blend and pour into the baking pan, if not already there.

5. Place the pan in the oven *immediately* and bake for 25 minutes or until the cake springs back when lightly touched.

NOTE: If you frost the cake in the pan, do it while the cake is hot so that the topping melts into the cake. Or cool and sprinkle with confectioner's sugar, or frost the entire top and sides of the cooled cake with Sea Foam Frosting (page 429).

VARIATION: *Chocolate Trifle (Dairy):* Place a layer of chocolate cake slices on the bottom of an attractive glass bowl. Spread the cake with sugar-free raspberry preserves that have been thinned with kirsch. Cover the preserves with vanilla, mocha, and chocolate nonfat frozen yogurt. Repeat the layers. Spoon a layer of nonfat fudge topping on top and sprinkle with toasted slivered almonds. Cover with 2 sheets of plastic wrap and freeze till serving time. Remove from the freezer 20 to 30 minutes before serving.

────────────── PER SERVING ──────────────

| 7.2 gm total fat | .65 gm saturated fat | .9 gm fiber | 146 calories |
| 0 mg cholesterol | 43.5% fat | 79 mg sodium | 65 calories from fat |

─────── ❧ HARRIET'S HINTS ❧ ───────

*H*oney that has crystallized can be made usable by heating it, in its jar, in hot water or briefly in a microwave oven.

# FRUIT
# DESSERTS

Sliced Oranges in Marmalade    399

Prune-Apricot Compote    400

Baked Apples Muscatel    401

Strawberry Rhubarb Jumble    402

Prune Whip    404

Spiced Baked Pears    404

Fresh Orange Sorbet    405

Spiced Fruit in Wine    406

Poached Apple Slices    407

Banana Pineapple Sherbet    408

Poached Pears with Raspberries    409

Phyllis's Hot Brandied Fruit    410

Lekvar (Plum Butter)    411

Rhubarb Sauce    412

We are primed from childhood to expect desserts to provide a special something sweet and sugary as a pleasant conclusion to a meal. With today's emphasis on no- or lowfat foods, fruit as a dessert gives us a healthful, tasty alternative.

Whether we are enjoying juicy, naturally sweet and succulent seasonal fruits or one of the fruit dishes in the following chapter, remember to make it special and keep it light.

NOTE: Remember to wash all fruits before eating or using in preparation. The presence of pesticides is always a concern unless the fruit is organically grown.

## ❦ Sliced Oranges in Marmalade ❦
### (PAREVE)
*Serves: 6 to 8*

An easy but elegant desert.

6 large navel oranges
1 cup sugar-free orange marmalade
¼ cup pine nuts, toasted for about 5 minutes in a 350° oven

1. Peel the oranges over a plate, using a sharp serrated knife and removing all of the white pith. Reserve the juices.

2. Cut the oranges into ¼-inch slices; arrange in a shallow serving dish.

3. Put the marmalade into a small saucepan and stir over low heat until melted. Add the reserved juices and blend.

4. Drizzle the marmalade over the orange slices and cover the dish with plastic wrap. Refrigerate until very cold, at least 2 to 3 hours.

*To Serve:* Remove plastic wrap; sprinkle with toasted pine nuts. Serve with a plain cookie such as My Favorite Mandelbrot (page 385) or Spicy Meringues (page 91).

VARIATION: 1 cup sweet Marsala or Sabra liqueur may be substituted for orange marmalade.

──────── PER SERVING ────────

| | | | |
|---|---|---|---|
| 4.4 gm total fat | .68 gm saturated fat | 5.7 gm fiber | 145 calories |
| 0 mg cholesterol | 25% fat | 5 mg sodium | 40 calories from fat |

## ❦ Prune-Apricot Compote ❦
### (PAREVE)
*Serves: 8 to 10*

When I was growing up, this was a favorite light dessert for Friday night. Leftover prunes and/or apricots can also be used to prepare a delicious Prune Whip (page 404).

    2 cups pitted prunes
    1 cup dried apricots
    5 cups water
    ⅓ cup frozen unsweetened apple juice concentrate
    2 strips orange zest or ½ orange, sliced and quartered
    ¼ lemon, with juice
    2 tablespoons Armagnac (optional)

1. Place all the ingredients in a 3-quart glass casserole, mix, cover, and microwave on High for 15 minutes, or until the prunes and apricots are plumped and soft.

2. Remove from the microwave oven and remove the lemon and orange zest. Cover and place in the refrigerator to chill before serving.

---

————————— P E R   S E R V I N G —————————

| | | | |
|---|---|---|---|
| .3 gm total fat | .02 gm saturated fat | 3.3 gm fiber | 124 calories |
| 0 mg cholesterol | 1.7% fat | 5 mg sodium | 2 calories from fat |

---

# ⊮ Baked Apples Muscatel ⊮
## (PAREVE)
### *Serves: 4 (1 apple = 1 serving)*

Apples prepared in a microwave oven have an incomparable taste and texture. I know there are still diehards who bake their apples in the oven for hours, but I prefer the fresh and delicate taste of apples or pears cooked in the microwave oven.

2 tablespoons dark raisins and/or chopped dates
3 tablespoons chopped walnuts
1 teaspoon ground cinnamon
  Juice of ½ orange or 2 tablespoons frozen unsweetened apple juice concentrate
4 apples (perferably Rome Beauty) (about 1½ pounds), cored, peeled halfway down from the stem end
4 tablespoons muscatel wine or frozen unsweetened apple juice concentrate
  Freshly grated nutmeg

1. Combine the raisins, 2 tablespoons of the nuts, the cinnamon, and orange juice.
2. Stuff the center of each apple with one quarter of the mixture. Top each apple with 1 tablespoon of wine and sprinkle with the remaining nuts and the nutmeg.
3. Place the apples in a round microwave-safe casserole with a cover, or cover with plastic wrap.
4. Microwave on High for 12 to 14 minutes. When finished baking, the apples will be tender but still retain their original shape.

*To Serve:* Serve the warm apples in glass compotes or dessert dishes and spoon the pan juices over.

VARIATION: Amaretto liqueur may be substituted for muscatel, and chopped almonds substituted for walnuts.

You can also just use apple juice, cinnamon, and nutmeg to prepare plain nonfat baked apples.

---
PER SERVING
---

| | | | |
|---|---|---|---|
| 4.0 gm total fat | .43 gm saturated fat | 5 gm fiber | 143 calories |
| 0 mg cholesterol | 23.2% fat | 3 mg sodium | 36 calories from fat |

# ❧ Strawberry Rhubarb Jumble ❧
## (PAREVE)
### Serves: 6

Strawberry and rhubarb are one of those flavor combinations that just seem to be made for one another.

### Fruit Filling:
- ½ pound strawberries (no white shoulders), washed, hulled, and quartered
- ¾ pound rhubarb, trimmed and cut into ¼-inch slices
- 2 firm bananas, peeled and cut into 1-inch slices
- ½ teaspoon ground cinnamon
  Grated zest and juice of 1 lemon
  Grated zest and juice of ½ orange
- 2 tablespoons granulated sugar
- ¼ cup packed brown sugar

### Topping:
- 1 cup unbleached all-purpose flour
- ¼ cup cornmeal or rolled oats
- 2 tablespoons light margarine, cubed
- 2 tablespoons packed brown sugar
- 2 tablespoons granulated sugar
- ¼ teaspoon ground cinnamon

1. Preheat the oven to 350°.

2. Place the fruit filling ingredients in a large bowl and combine thoroughly. Put the filling in an 8-inch square glass baking dish.

3. Combine all the topping ingredients in a bowl. Cut in the margarine until the mixture forms crumbs the size of peas, using your hands, a pastry blender, or two knives.

4. Sprinkle the topping over the fruit filling. Bake 45 to 50 minutes, or until golden brown and bubbly. Serve warm.

*To Serve:* Put a scoop of vanilla nonfat frozen yogurt on the side or allow 1 cup of yogurt to melt at room temperature and pour over warm jumble.

---

**PER SERVING**

| | | | |
|---|---|---|---|
| 2.6 gm total fat | .46 gm saturated fat | 3.5 gm fiber | 262 calories |
| 0 mg cholesterol | 8.7% fat | 55 mg sodium | 24 calories from fat |

---

**❦ HARRIET'S HINTS ❦**

*To buy the best berries: Remember that berries do not ripen after picking. Select strawberries with a rich red color, bright green leafy caps, and no white shoulders. Rinse the berries in cold water with caps still attached before stemming. Store unwashed berries in an airtight clean jar in the refrigerator. For the best flavor, berries should be allowed to reach room temperature before eating. (Try them with nonfat sour cream or a few drops of balsamic vinegar.)*

# ❦ Prune Whip ❦
## (PAREVE)
### Serves: 4

4 extra-large egg whites, at room temperature
2 to 3 tablespoons sugar
1 tablespoon fresh lemon juice
1¼ cups puréed stewed prunes and/or apricots (page 400)
Confectioners' sugar, for garnish

1. In the large bowl of an electric mixer, beat the egg whites until soft peaks form. Gradually add the sugar while continuing to beat until stiff and shiny.

2. Mix the lemon juice into the prune purée; fold into the egg whites. Serve chilled; or turn into a soufflé dish and bake in a preheated 350° oven for about 30 to 35 minutes.

*To Serve:* When done, sprinkle with confectioners' sugar. Serve at once with chilled nonfat non-dairy creamer.

If served cold, mound the chilled whip in sherbet cups, stemmed glasses, or custard cups.

---

PER SERVING

| .3 gm total fat | .02 gm saturated fat | 3.6 gm fiber | 161 calories |
| 0 mg cholesterol | 1.3% fat | 55 mg sodium | 2 calories from fat |

# ❦ Spiced Baked Pears ❦
## (PAREVE)
### Serves: 4 (2 halves = 1 serving)

4 pears, peeled, halved, and cored
3 tablespoons fresh lemon juice
2 tablespoons honey
1⅓ cups reduced-sugar cranberry juice
¼ teaspoon ground allspice
1 cinnamon stick
2 cardamom seeds

1. Place the prepared pear halves in a saucepan. Add the remaining ingredients and bring to a boil.

2. Reduce the heat, cover, and simmer gently for 15 to 20 minutes, or until fork-tender.

3. Cool in the syrup. Chill in the refrigerator for several hours or overnight before serving.

*To Serve:* Serve the chilled pear halves in dessert cups with some of the strained syrup. Accompany with Poppy Seed Komitzbrodt (page 65).

---

**PER SERVING**

| | | | |
|---|---|---|---|
| .7 gm total fat | .04 gm saturated fat | 4.3 gm fiber | 146 calories |
| 0 mg cholesterol | 3.8% fat | 9 mg sodium | 6 calories from fat |

---

## ❧ Fresh Orange Sorbet ❧
### (PAREVE)
*Serves: 6*

A refreshing finish to any meal.

Zest of 2 navel oranges (no white included)
⅓ cup sugar
4 cups freshly squeezed orange juice
2 tablespoons Grand Marnier liqueur
6 orange wedges and fresh mint leaves, for garnish

1. Place the orange zest and sugar in a food processor; using the steel blade, process until chopped fine.

2. Combine the sugar mixture, orange juice, and Grand Marnier and blend well.

3. Pour the juice mixture into ice cube trays and freeze several hours or overnight.

4. Just before serving, place the frozen cubes in a food processor fitted with the metal blade. Process the cubes by pulsing, then running continually until fine and smooth. Serve immediately.

*To Serve:* Ladle into chilled glass coupes and garnish with fresh mint leaves and an orange wedge. Pass a plate of Harriet Greenwald's Dessert Wafers (page 389).

| ─────── P E R   S E R V I N G ─────── | | | |
|---|---|---|---|
| .1 gm total fat | .02 gm saturated fat | .4 gm fiber | 127 calories |
| 0 mg cholesterol | .8% fat | 2 mg sodium | 1 calorie from fat |

# ❦ Spiced Fruit in Wine ❦
## (PAREVE)
### *Serves: 8*

You may eliminate any of the fresh fruits called for in this recipe and substitute a can of drained mandarin oranges, sliced Alberta peaches, Royal Anne cherries, or pears after the syrup is cooled.

## *Syrup Ingredients:*
½ cup sugar
   Juice and zest of 1 lemon
 1 cup water
 1 cup red wine
 6 whole cloves
 1 cinnamon stick
½ lemon, sliced thin

## *Fruit Mixture:*
 2 apples, peeled, cored, and quartered
 1 cup seedless grapes
 2 pears, peeled, cored, and halved
 3 peaches, peeled, pitted, and halved
 1 cup pitted cherries
 3 plums, pitted and halved
 3 apricots, pitted and halved

1. Make the syrup: Mix the sugar, juice, zest, and water. Bring to a boil, strain, and combine the remaining syrup ingredients. Cool.

2. Place the fruit in a saucepan and cover with the syrup mixture.

3. Bring to a boil; reduce the heat, and simmer 10 to 20 minutes, or until the fruit is barely tender. Refrigerate for several days, basting fruit with syrup from the bottom. Serve either hot or cold.

---

PER SERVING

| .8 gm total fat | .12 gm saturated fat | 4 gm fiber | 171 calories |
| 0 mg cholesterol | 3.8% fat | 3 mg sodium | 7 calories from fat |

---

# ❧ Poached Apple Slices ❧
## (DAIRY)
*Serves: 4 (1 apple with ¼ cup topping = 1 serving)*

Apples are high in soluble fiber that helps to lower cholesterol. This variation of baked apples using the microwave is a welcome and speedy change.

**4 cooking apples, such as Rome Beauty, McIntosh, or Granny Smith**
**½ cup unsweetened apple juice, fresh orange juice, or papaya nectar**
**½ teaspoon ground cinnamon**
**½ teaspoon freshly grated nutmeg**

## Topping:
**1 cup nonfat vanilla yogurt mixed with remaining warm cooking liquid**

1. Peel, core, and quarter the apples. Place in a microwave-safe dish.
2. Sprinkle with the juice, cinnamon, and nutmeg.
3. Cover and microwave on High for 4 minutes. Let stand for 5 minutes.
4. Spoon into dessert cups and drizzle each serving with about ¼ cup of the yogurt mixture.

---

PER SERVING

| 1.1 gm total fat | .15 gm saturated fat | 3.5 gm fiber | 141 calories |
| 3 mg cholesterol | 6.6% fat | 41 mg sodium | 10 calories from fat |

# ❧ Banana Pineapple Sherbet ❧
## (PAREVE)
### *Serves: 16 (⅓ cup = 1 serving)*

This refreshing *pareve* dessert takes a bit of time to make, but it can all be done in advance.

> 3 cups ripe pineapple (1 ripe pineapple, peeled, cored, and cut into 1-inch chunks), or 1 (16-ounce) package frozen pineapple chunks (or 3 cups frozen peaches, mangoes, or berries)
> 2 ripe bananas, peeled and cut into 1-inch chunks
> 2 tablespoons frozen unsweetened apple juice concentrate
> 1 cup frozen and partially defrosted nonfat non-dairy creamer (see Note)
> 1 to 2 teaspoons pure vanilla extract
> Scooped-out orange or lemon cups, for serving (optional)

1. Flash-freeze the pineapple and banana chunks on a baking sheet. When frozen solid, place the fruit in separate bags. Store in the freezer until ready to use.

2. Place half the frozen pineapple and banana in the chilled bowl of a food processor or blender. Add the apple juice concentrate and process until the mixture is puréed.

3. Add the remaining fruit and purée.

4. Add half the nonfat non-dairy creamer, process until a thick cream is formed, and continue adding creamer and vanilla while processing.

5. Freeze in a freezer container, parfait glasses, or hollowed lemon or orange cups for at least an hour before serving.

If you like, garnish with a lemon or camellia leaf before freezing or with mint leaves at time of serving. The sherbet keeps in the freezer for up to 2 months.

*To Serve:* Take from the freezer 15 minutes before serving. (Or if you forget, as I so frequently do, soften in the microwave oven on Low for just 10 seconds.) It's even more delicious with the following sauce.

A QUICK SAUCE: Purée 1 pint of fresh ripe raspberries or strawberries. (Raspberry sauce must be strained at this point to remove seeds.) Add 1 tablespoon of kirsch or

Grand Marnier. The sauce may be prepared ahead of time and stored in the refrigerator in an airtight container for up to 1 week. It also freezes quite well.

NOTE: 1 cup chilled evaporated skim milk may be used if served with a dairy meal.

---

**———— PER SERVING ————**

| | | | |
|---|---|---|---|
| .6 gm total fat | .22 gm saturated fat | .9 gm fiber | 41 calories |
| 0 mg cholesterol | 13.4% fat | 8 mg sodium | 6 calories from fat |

---

## ❧ Poached Pears with Raspberries ❧
### (PAREVE)
*Serves: 4 (½ pear = 1 serving)*

This readily available fruit lends itself to an easy and elegant dessert preparation.

   3 tablespoons fresh orange juice
   1 tablespoon frozen unsweetened apple juice concentrate
   ½ teaspoon ground cinnamon
   ½ teaspoon freshly grated nutmeg (optional)
   2 ripe pears, peeled, halved, and cored
   ½ cup fresh or frozen unsweetened raspberries

1. Mix the juices, cinnamon, and nutmeg (if using) together.
2. Place the pears in a microwave-safe dish. Sprinkle with the juices and cover with plastic wrap.
3. Microwave on High for 3 minutes. Remove from the oven and let stand 2 minutes. Serve warm.

*To Serve:* Place half a pear on a dessert plate with juice and sprinkle with raspberries.

---

**———— PER SERVING ————**

| | | | |
|---|---|---|---|
| .4 gm total fat | .03 gm saturated fat | 3.4 gm fiber | 70 calories |
| 0 mg cholesterol | 5.3% fat | 1 mg sodium | 4 calories from fat |

# ❧ Phyllis's Hot Brandied Fruit ❧

## (PAREVE)

*Serves: 20*

1 (28-ounce) can of each of the following *juice-sweetened* (i.e., no sugar
   added) fruit: apricots, peaches, pears, plums, pineapple chunks
1 cup dried Kadota or Elmira figs
1 (14-ounce) package frozen unsweetened blueberries
⅓ cup brandy
2 tablespoons packed brown sugar
1 (14-ounce) package almond macaroon cookies
2 cups canned or frozen black Bing cherries, for garnish

1. Drain all the fruit thoroughly in a colander. Place the drained fruit, figs, and blueberries in a large ovenproof serving dish. Preheat oven to 350°.
2. Heat the brandy and brown sugar together just long enough to dissolve the sugar. Mix this into the fruit.
3. Crush half the macaroon cookies and sprinkle over the top of the fruit.
4. Bake for about 30 minutes, or until the fruit bubbles.
5. Sprinkle the remainder of the crushed macaroons on top of the cooked fruit and garnish with the cherries. Heat until the cherries are defrosted and warm.

*To Serve:* Spoon the hot fruit mixture onto dessert plates and accompany with a scoop of lemon sorbet with a meat meal, or nonfat frozen yogurt with a dairy meal.

NOTE: This may be cooked through step 4 a few days in advance. Cover and store in the refrigerator. Top with the second layer of macaroons and cherries and heat just before serving.

---
PER SERVING
---

| | | | |
|---|---|---|---|
| 2.4 gm total fat | .23 gm saturated fat | 3.8 gm fiber | 241 calories |
| 0 mg cholesterol | 8.5% fat | 12 mg sodium | 22 calories from fat |

# ❦ Lekvar (Plum Butter) ❦

## (PAREVE)

*Yield: 6 to 7 pints (2 tablespoons = 1 serving)*

This preparation is not for the faint-hearted. In fact, it helps if you're a bit of an insomniac. My sisters and I still take turns hosting this craziness each fall. It's worth it, because nothing tastes quite as delicious as homemade lekvar in blintzes, coffee cake, and *delco* (danish).

**10 pounds Italian prune plums**

1. Wash, halve, and pit the plums.
2. Place the plums in a heavy nonaluminum stockpot or Dutch oven. Do not add water. The water that clings to the fruit will be sufficient. Cook, covered, over moderate heat until very tender. Stir from time to time.
3. Transfer to a nonaluminum casserole, if necessary, and cook in a 250° oven overnight. Stir every hour or so to be sure that the mixture does not stick.
4. When adequately cooked, the lekvar will be about the consistency of peanut butter.

*To Store:* Cool, transfer to glass jars or crocks, and refrigerate or freeze (see Note).

NOTE: If you intend to store the lekvar for a long period of time, pour about ¼ inch of melted paraffin over the top of the cooled lekvar and insert a loop of string into the liquefied wax. This seals the jar and facilitates removal of the wax when you are ready to use the lekvar. When cooking with lekvar, taste and adjust flavors with added sugar if necessary. If you have ripe plums with good flavor to begin with, no added sugar should be necessary.

| PER SERVING | | | |
|---|---|---|---|
| .3 gm total fat | .02 gm saturated fat | 4.3 gm fiber | 141 calories |
| 0 mg cholesterol | 1.7% fat | 2 mg sodium | 3 calories from fat |

# 🌿 Rhubarb Sauce 🌿
## (PAREVE)
*Yield: 3 cups (¼ cup = 1 serving)*

Tender young red stalks of rhubarb are generally grown in hothouses and have a sweeter flavor than the large woody field-grown variety. Either way, this sauce is delicious for dipping with cookies.

   4 cups (about 8 stalks) fresh rhubarb, cut into ½-inch pieces
 ¾ cup fresh orange juice
     Grated zest of ½ orange
   2 tablespoons light brown sugar
 12 strawberries, washed, hulled, and sliced (optional)

1. Mix the rhubarb, orange juice and zest, and brown sugar in a large microwave-safe bowl. Cover with plastic wrap.

2. Microwave on High for 2 minutes; stir and microwave an additional 2 minutes or until the rhubarb is soft (see Note). If desired, strawberries may be added at this time and allowed to stand for about 10 minutes in the hot sauce.

3. Stir with a fork (do not purée). Taste and adjust seasonings. Chill.

NOTE: Microwave cooking expert Barbara Kafka suggests using a double thickness of plastic wrap and slitting the wrap with a knife. Stir through the slit in the wrap with a wooden spoon and then patch the plastic wrap with fresh square to make a tight seal.

--- PER SERVING ---

| | | | |
|---|---|---|---|
| .1 gm total fat | .02 gm saturated fat | .3 gm fiber | 21 calories |
| 0 mg cholesterol | 3.6% fat | 2 mg sodium | 1 calorie from fat |

# THE BAKER'S "DEADLY" DOZEN

Hungarian Butter Horns   415

Pogachels or Pogácsa (Hungarian Butter Biscuits)   417

Mama's Danish   418

Hungarian Fluden   422

Never-Fail Pie Crust   423

Mile-High Lemon Meringue Pie   425

My Best Babka   426

Mrs. Katz's Devil's Food Cake (Now My Sister Ruth's)   428

Sea Foam Frosting   429

Lemon Squares   430

Eir Kichlach   431

The Ultimate Cheesecake   432

For more years than I can count, I prepared these rich, delicious morsels with devoted regularity. I always enjoyed not only the preparation but also the loving spirit in which they were baked, eaten, and appreciated.

Now, in all good conscience, I cannot often prepare these classic desserts because of their very high fat and cholesterol content. The recipes that follow are now reserved for *very* special occasions.

## ⸙ Hungarian Butter Horns ⸙
### (DAIRY)
*Yield: 48 (1 pastry = 1 serving)*

I once used butter, eggs, and cream with abandon. This is one pastry that truly melts in your mouth.

    4 **cups unbleached all-purpose flour**
½ **teaspoon kosher salt**
    1 **package active dry yeast**
    3 **sticks (¾ pound) cold unsalted butter or margarine, cut into ½-inch slices**
    1 **cup (8 ounces) sour cream**
    3 **extra-large egg yolks**

*Meringue Filling:*
>     3 extra-large egg whites, at room temperature
>     1 cup minus 2 tablespoons sugar
>     1 cup finely chopped toasted nuts (walnuts, filberts, and/or almonds)
>  1½ teaspoons pure vanilla extract

Confectioners' sugar

1. Sift the flour with the salt into a food processor.
2. Sprinkle the yeast into the flour. Add the butter (make certain that it is firm).
3. Using a pulsing action, process just until the mixture has the texture of coarse cornmeal.
4. Mix the sour cream and egg yolks and add to the flour mixture. Process just until the pastry *begins* to form a ball.
5. Place the dough on a sheet of plastic wrap, shape into a ball, and divide into 6 disk-shaped portions.
6. Wrap them individually in plastic, then place them all in a zip-lock bag; refrigerate at least 3 hours or overnight, or freeze for future use.
7. Make the meringue filling: Beat the egg whites in a bowl (not plastic) until soft peaks form. Add the sugar gradually, about 2 tablespoons at a time, while continuing to beat. Beat until firm peaks form; fold in the nuts and vanilla.
8. Roll the dough, a disk at a time, into circles ⅛ inch thick on a surface that is lightly sprinkled with confectioners' sugar or between 2 sheets of wax paper. Cut each into 8 pie-shaped wedges.
9. Spread each wedge with meringue filling; roll up from a wide end and shape into crescents. Place on an ungreased baking sheet, cover with a kitchen towel, and let stand 30 minutes at room temperature. Meanwhile, preheat the oven to 400°.
10. Bake in the upper third of the oven for about 12 to 14 minutes, or until lightly browned. Remove from the baking sheet with a spatula immediately and cool on a wire rack. (The pastries will stick if allowed to cool on the baking sheet.)

*To Serve:* Arrange the cooled pastries on a cake platter and sprinkle lightly with confectioners' sugar.

*To Freeze:* Place the cooled pastries in a rectangular plastic freezer container with sheets of foil between the layers and on the top of the last layer. They will keep nicely in the freezer for up to 3 months.

---

PER SERVING

| | | | |
|---|---|---|---|
| 8.9 gm total fat | 4.46 gm saturated fat | .6 gm fiber | 139 calories |
| 31 mg cholesterol | 56.7% fat | 44 mg sodium | 80 calories from fat |

---

# ❦ Pogachels or Pogácsa ❦
# (Hungarian Butter Biscuits)
## (DAIRY)
*Yield: 12 to 16 biscuits (1 biscuit = 1 serving)*

On Fridays, when my mother wanted to prepare a quick cookie she baked *pogachels*. Since we all adored these biscuits and there were so many of us to feed, she used to prepare and store mountains of these treats in a huge blue agate pan. They were covered and hidden away for Sabbath consumption. However, my sister Edie and I used to compete to find the new secret hiding place. After all, Mama would never miss a few—or would she?

- 3 cups unbleached all-purpose flour
- ⅓ cup granulated sugar
- ⅓ cup sifted confectioners' sugar
- 1 tablespoon baking powder
- ⅛ teaspoon kosher salt
- 2 sticks (½ pound) cold unsalted butter (half margarine may be used), cut into cubes
- 3 extra-large egg yolks
- 1 cup minus 2 tablespoons sour cream
- 1 extra-large egg white, beaten until foamy
- ½ cup finely chopped walnuts mixed with 3 tablespoons sugar and 1 teaspoon ground cinnamon

1. Place the flour, sugars, baking powder, and salt in a food processor. Blend. Cut the chilled butter into the dry ingredients with a pulsing action until the mixture resembles coarse cornmeal.

2. Stir egg yolks and sour cream together, then add. Blend just to combine. *Do not overmix.*

3. Turn the dough onto a sheet of plastic wrap. Form into a ball, then pat down into a disk, handling as little as possible.

4. Wrap in plastic and chill at least 1 hour, or overnight.

5. When you are ready to begin baking, preheat the oven to 350°.

6. Place the dough on a surface that has been sprinkled with confectioners' sugar. Pat or roll the dough to ¾-inch thickness.

7. Cut out biscuits with a 2-inch round biscuit cutter (a glass or an empty tomato paste can can be used).

8. Using a pastry brush, coat the tops with egg white and dip the biscuits in the sugar-cinnamon-walnut mixture.

9. Place on an ungreased baking sheet and bake in the upper third of the oven for 20 to 25 minutes or until lightly browned. Cool on a rack before eating. (If frozen, reheat at 200° before serving.)

---
PER SERVING
---

| 17.6 gm total fat | 9.28 gm saturated fat | 1 gm fiber | 286 calories |
| 77 mg cholesterol | 54.5% fat | 32 mg sodium | 158 calories from fat |

# ❦ Mama's Danish ❦

## (DAIRY)

*Yield: About 75 miniature Danish (1 piece = 1 serving)*

There is an old joke my husband tells of an elderly, ailing Jewish gentleman whose son tried to console him by asking if there was any special request he had. He weakly replied, "Yes, I would love to taste some of that Danish I smell baking in the house." The son honored his father's request by calling down to Mama, asking if Papa could have a couple of pastries. "Absolutely not," she replied. "We're saving it for the *shiva* [wake]."

This labor-intensive, high-fat, high-cholesterol delicacy is reserved for special, happy occasions, such as weddings and bar mitzvahs.

*Yeast Dough:*
>    1 cup unbleached all-purpose flour
>    1 teaspoon baking powder
>    ½ teaspoon kosher salt
> 1½ tablespoons sugar
>    2 (½ ounce) packages fresh cake yeast or 2 envelopes active dry yeast, softened in ¼ cup warm (115°) water
>    2 extra-large egg yolks, slightly beaten
>    2 tablespoons apricot brandy
>    2 tablespoons sour cream
>    1 teaspoon grated orange zest, optional

1. Measure the flour and baking powder into a heap on a pastry board or in a bowl.

2. Cream the salt, sugar, and yeast together until syrupy.

3. Make a well in the dry ingredients; add the yeast mixture and the yolks and mix lightly with a fork until the yolks are incorporated into the flour.

4. Sprinkle with the brandy and add the sour cream. Mix with a fork.

5. Knead the dough with your fingertips until well blended. If the dough seems too sticky, add a little extra flour. Form into a compact ball.

6. Wrap the dough in plastic and set aside in the refrigerator while preparing the butter dough.

*Butter Dough:*
>    1 cup unbleached all-purpose flour
>    2 sticks (½ pound) firm unsalted butter

1. Measure the flour onto a pastry board.

2. Cut the butter into eight pieces.

3. Knead with the flour until well blended.

4. Form into a smooth, compact disk.

5. Divide the butter dough into thirds. Dust lightly with flour and wrap each third in plastic. Refrigerate at least 30 minutes.

*To Prepare Pastry:*

1. On a lightly floured surface roll the yeast dough into a 10 × 8-inch rectangle about ½ inch thick.

2. Pat one third of the butter dough on a floured surface into a 7-inch square and

place on top of the yeast dough. Roll with a floured rolling pin just to combine the doughs. Fold the dough into thirds crosswise, then in thirds in the other direction. Roll out into one piece about 10 × 8 inches.

3. Now repeat the process with the second piece of butter dough; and then with the third piece of butter dough.

4. Wrap the finished pastry dough in plastic, then foil.

5. Chill at least 3 to 4 hours or overnight.

6. Divide chilled dough into four pieces. Roll out one piece (keeping remaining dough refrigerated) to ⅛-inch thickness on a lightly floured surface. Cut into 3-inch squares. Repeat with remaining dough, one piece at a time.

7. Place a teaspoon of Lekvar (page 411), or one of the suggested fillings, in the center of each square. Lift up two opposite corners and pinch together over the filling. Repeat with the remaining corners.

8. Place on a nonstick baking sheet or in muffin tins lined with paper liners.

9. Preheat oven to 375°. Meanwhile, chill pastries in refrigerator for 20 to 30 minutes.

10. Bake 15 to 20 minutes or until golden brown.

### Nut Filling
    ½ cup chopped salt-free dry-roasted almonds
    ½ cup chopped toasted walnuts
    ¼ cup sugar
    ¼ cup heavy cream

Combine all the ingredients and use as a filling.

### Cheese Filling
    2 tablespoons golden raisins, plumped in hot water and drained
    1 tablespoon Cognac
    8 ounces cream cheese or hoop cheese, at room temperature
    ¼ cup sugar
    1 tablespoon unbleached all-purpose flour
    1 extra-large egg yolk
    1 teaspoon melted butter
    1 tablespoon sour cream
    ½ teaspoon grated lemon zest
    ½ teaspoon pure vanilla extract

1. Mix the raisins and cognac.
2. Cream together the cheese, sugar, and flour.
3. Add the egg yolk, butter, sour cream, lemon zest, and vanilla. Blend well.
4. Add the cognac-soaked raisins.

VARIATIONS:

*Kipfel:* In step 7 of the pastry preparation (page 420), spread each square with 2 teaspoons Nut Filling (page 420). Starting at one corner, roll the square into a cylinder and then bend it into a crescent shape. Place on a nonstick baking sheet and brush with beaten egg white. Proceed as in step 9.

*Miniature Bear Claws or Cockscombs:* In step 6 of pastry preparation (page 420) roll out 1 piece of dough on a granulated sugar and cinnamon mixture to a rectangular shape 3 inches wide. Spread nut filling on half the dough lengthwise. Fold dough over, making it 1½ inches wide. Cut into 2-inch slices, making ¼-inch cuts into unfilled edge of dough. Place each slice on a nonstick or lightly greased baking sheet; curve slightly to spread the slits. Repeat with remaining dough. Proceed as in step 9.

NOTES:

• Do not attempt to make this pastry in hot weather.

• It is important to keep the dough cold.

• Shaped pastries may be frozen for up to 1 week and then baked.

• Cool baked pastries thoroughly before freezing.

• If possible warm before serving.

---

**DANISH WITH LEKVAR PER SERVING**

| | | | |
|---|---|---|---|
| 3.3 gm total fat | 1.63 gm saturated fat | 1.6 gm fiber | 85 calories |
| 13 mg cholesterol | 68% fat | 16 mg sodium | 29 calories from fat |

# ❧ Hungarian Fluden ❧

## (DAIRY)

*Yield: 20 servings (1 bar = 1 serving)*

Of the many pastries my mother expertly prepared, this one may have been my favorite.

     2 sticks (½ pound) unsalted butter, at room temperature
  1¼ cups sugar
     4 extra-large eggs, separated
     1 tablespoon pure vanilla extract
     3 cups unbleached all-purpose flour
     1 teaspoon baking powder
2 to 3 cups raspberry or apricot preserves or Lekvar (page 411)
     1 cup lightly toasted ground walnuts or filberts

1. Preheat the oven to 350°. Lightly butter a 15 × 10-inch jelly roll pan.
2. Cream the butter and 1 cup of the sugar together in a food processor or electric mixer until fluffy.
3. Add the egg yolks and vanilla; beat thoroughly.
4. Sift together the flour and baking powder. Add to the batter and mix well.
5. Spread the dough in the prepared jelly roll pan. Spread the preserves over the dough. (You may use two kinds of preserves by spreading each over half of the dough.) Sprinkle with half the nuts.
6. Beat the egg whites until soft peaks form. Add the remaining ¼ cup of sugar, 1 tablespoon at a time, beating until stiff and shiny. Gently fold in the remaining nuts and spread on top of the preserves, bringing the meringue to the sides of the pan.
7. Bake for about 30 minutes or until the meringue is golden brown.
8. Use a wet knife to loosen the pastry around the sides of the pan. Cool on a rack in the pan.
9. When cool, use a serrated knife to cut into 20 bars or diamond-shaped pieces.

--- PER SERVING ---

| 9.5 gm total fat | 4.28 gm saturated fat | .8 gm fiber | 212 calories |
| 46 mg cholesterol | 39% fat | 11 mg sodium | 85 calories from fat |

# ❦ Never-Fail Pie Crust ❦

(PAREVE, or DAIRY if butter is used)

*Yield: One 10-inch pie shell*

This recipe is for a 10-inch pie shell, although most people have 8- or 9-inch pie pans. My feeling is that for those infrequent occasions I bake a pie, I'll make it big enough for family *and* friends to enjoy. If you happen to have pie dough scraps leftover, sprinkle with sugar, cinnamon, and raisins and make a few *rugelahs*.

Many cooks are intimidated by the preparation of a pie crust or pastry dough. If you keep in mind the following hints, you'll have sure-fire success:

- When measuring flour, scoop it with a spoon into the measuring cup; level it with a knife.

- Don't add too much liquid—just enough to hold together.

- Don't overmix or overhandle.

- Chill at least 30 minutes before rolling.

- Roll out between 2 sheets of wax paper or plastic wrap. Lift off the paper occasionally, reversing the paper to allow the pastry to expand more easily as it is rolled.

1½ cups unbleached all-purpose flour (see Note)
8 tablespoons (½ cup) vegetable shortening (such as Crisco), chilled
2 tablespoons butter or pareve margarine, chilled and cubed
½ teaspoon salt
¼ cup cold orange juice, apple juice, or water
1 teaspoon distilled white vinegar

1. In a food processor using the steel blade, blend the flour, shortening, butter, and salt until the shortening is the size of peas. Or cut the shortening in with a pastry blender or two knives.

2. Pour the orange juice and vinegar over ice cubes. Add the chilled liquid, 1 tablespoon at a time, to the flour and mix until the dough *just starts* to form a ball away from the sides of the container or bowl.

3. Invert the dough onto a sheet of plastic wrap and flatten into an 8-inch circle. Do not touch directly with your hand, because the heat of your hand will cause the pastry to toughen. Place the wrapped dough in an airtight plastic bag.

4. Chill about 35 minutes before using.

5. Roll the dough to a 12- to 14-inch circle about ⅛ inch thick between 2 sheets of wax paper or plastic wrap.

6. Remove the wax paper on one side and carefully place, dough side down, in a 10-inch pan. Remove the top sheet of paper without stretching the pastry.

7. Make a 1-inch border around the pan, trimming off the excess. Turn the edge under, press the edge to seal, and flute (see Note).

8. For a baked pie shell, prick the sides and bottom of the shell all over with a fork. Chill for 30 minutes. Preheat oven to 400°.

9. Place a double sheet of foil on the dough (do not force into the dough), prick the foil, and fill the sheet with uncooked rice or beans or aluminum pie weights. Bake 15 minutes. Reduce oven to 350°.

10. Carefully remove the foil with the weights and return the crust to the 350° oven for 5 to 10 minutes more or until lightly browned. Cool the crust before using.

NOTES: For an even more tender crust, ½ cup of instantized flour, such as Wondra, may be substituted for ½ cup of all-purpose flour.

Press the thumb and index finger of one hand into the crust edge, spacing 1 inch apart. Press the index finger of the opposite hand into the space between the fingers to make an indentation. Work in this way around the perimeter of the pie crust.

VARIATION: For a 10-inch 2-crust pie, double all recipe ingredients except the liquid (start with 6 tablespoons of juice or water, and add as necessary), and proceed as suggested.

--- PER SERVING ---

| 10.6 gm total fat | 2.53 gm saturated fat | .4 gm fiber | 152 calories |
| 0 mg cholesterol | 62.7% fat | 120 mg sodium | 95 calories from fat |

--- ❧ HARRIET'S HINTS ❧ ---

*Lemons release more juice if warmed in the microwave oven for 20 seconds before being squeezed.*

# ❦ Mile-High Lemon Meringue Pie ❦
## (PAREVE)
### Yield: 12 slices (1 slice = 1 serving)

In the bad old days I frequently substituted whipped cream for the meringue topping.

6 **extra-large egg yolks**
　 **Juice (about ½ cup) and zest of 3 lemons**
　 **Few grains of salt**
1 **cup sugar**
1 **tablespoon unsalted butter**

*Meringue Topping:*

6 **extra-large egg whites**
　 **Few grains of salt**
¼ **teaspoon cream of tartar**
8 **tablespoons sugar**

1 **baked 10-inch Never-Fail Pie Crust (page 423)**

1. Mix the egg yolks, lemon juice and zest, and salt together in the top part of a double boiler. Place over hot water and stir in the sugar and butter.

2. Cook over hot water, stirring occasionally, until the custard thickens, about 15 minutes.

3. Remove from the heat and place plastic wrap directly on the surface to keep a skin from forming. Allow to cool.

4. Meanwhile, make the meringue: Beat the egg whites with the salt and cream of tartar until the mixture thickens. Gradually add 8 tablespoons of sugar, 1 tablespoon at a time, while beating. Beat until stiff, shiny peaks are formed.

5. Fold one third of the meringue into the cooled custard, folding in carefully until thoroughly combined. Preheat oven to 425°.

6. Turn the custard filling into the prepared pie shell and cover with the remaining meringue, making sure to seal the edges by spreading the meringue completely to the edge of the pastry. Make decorative swirls in the meringue with the back of a spoon.

7. Bake for 5 minutes or until golden brown. Cool in a draft-free place or the meringue may fall.

VARIATION: Melt 2 ounces of semisweet chocolate with 1 teaspoon of shortening in the microwave oven and spread evenly on the bottom of the baked and cooled pie shell, before adding the lemon mixture.

---

PER SERVING

| 13.2 gm total fat | 3.35 gm saturated fat | .4 gm fiber | 298 calories |
| 109 mg cholesterol | 39.3% fat | 151 mg sodium | 119 calories from fat |

---

## ❦ My Best Babka ❦
### (DAIRY)
*Yield: 20 slices (1 slice = 1 serving)*

You can call it *kuchen, kugelhof, babka,* or coffee cake. I call it delicious.

1½ cups cake flour
1¾ cups unbleached all-purpose flour, or as needed
1¼ cups sugar
  1 teaspoon kosher salt
1½ teaspoons grated orange zest
  8 ounces (2 sticks) chilled unsalted butter or margarine, cut into 16 pieces
  1 package active dry yeast
¼ cup warm water (105° to 115°)
  3 extra-large eggs, separated
½ cup whole milk
  1 teaspoon ground cinnamon
  1 cup ground toasted hazelnuts

**To Make the Dough:**
1. Combine the cake flour, 1½ cups of the all-purpose flour, ¼ cup of the sugar, the salt, and orange zest in a food processor. Using the steel blade, cut in the butter, pulsing until the flour has the texture of coarse cornmeal.

2. Dissolve the yeast in the warm water in the large bowl of an electric mixer and allow to proof until foamy, 5 to 10 minutes.

3. Beat the egg yolks with the milk and add to the proofed yeast mixture.

4. Add the flour-butter mixture to the yeast mixture. Mix thoroughly with the dough hook or with a wooden spoon, cover with a kitchen towel, and let stand about 30 minutes.

5. Add about ¼ to ⅓ cup flour to make a workable dough. Knead the dough, with the dough hook or by hand, about 6 to 7 minutes, or until smooth and elastic.

6. Cover the bowl tightly with plastic wrap and refrigerate 12 hours or overnight.

### To Prepare Babka:

1. Beat the 3 egg whites, gradually adding the remaining 1 cup of sugar; when stiffened, add the cinnamon and nuts.

2. Remove the dough from the refrigerator, knead briefly, and roll out on a lightly floured surface into a 20 × 16-inch rectangle. Spread with the egg white mixture, leaving a 2-inch border.

3. Starting with a long end, roll *tightly* as a jelly roll and place in a 2½-quart (9-inch) kugelhof or tube pan that has been lightly greased with butter. Overlap the ends of the roll. Cover with a towel and let rise in a warm place for 2 to 2½ hours, until doubled in bulk. Preheat oven to 325°.

4. Bake on the middle rack of the oven for 1 hour and 15 minutes, or until golden brown.

5. Let cool in the pan for 10 minutes before turning out on a rack. If you can possibly resist, this can be frozen in plastic, then wrapped in foil for future use. If not, enjoy!

NOTE: If you divide the dough in half, this may also be baked in two greased 9 × 5 × 3-inch loaf pans.

VARIATION: Instead of using beaten egg white mixture, use 8 ounces of sugar-free raspberry or apricot preserves, ⅓ cup of sugar mixed with 1 teaspoon of ground cinnamon, and 1 cup of toasted ground walnuts. Roll and proceed as in step 3.

| PER SERVING | | | |
|---|---|---|---|
| 14 gm total fat | 6.38 gm saturated fat | .6 gm fiber | 252 calories |
| 59 mg cholesterol | 49% fat | 132 mg sodium | 126 calories from fat |

# ❦ Mrs. Katz's Devil's Food Cake ❦ (Now My Sister Ruth's)

## (DAIRY)

*Yield: 20 servings (1 square = 1 serving)*

This recipe originated with Mrs. Annie Katz, a friend of my mother's. She was a neighbor of ours in a small iron and steel town called Rankin, on the banks of the Monongahela River near Pittsburgh, Pennsylvania. This was one of the few batter-based cakes that my mother prepared. No cake was ever frosted at our house; my mother thought that frosting only appeared on store-bought cakes! If you like, however, you may use chocolate frosting or the delicious Sea Foam Frosting on page 429.

    1 cup hydrogenated vegetable shortening, such as Crisco
    3 cups sugar
    2 teaspoons pure vanilla extract
    3 large eggs, slightly beaten with a fork
    4 (1-ounce) squares unsweetened baking chocolate, melted
 3½ cups sifted cake flour
    2 teaspoons baking soda
    2 cups buttermilk
      Confectioners' sugar, for garnish

1. Preheat the oven to 350°. Grease and lightly flour one 13 × 9 × 2-inch pan and one 7-inch loaf pan. Line the bottoms of the pans with wax paper and grease again.

2. Cream the shortening in an electric mixer; add the sugar and vanilla and beat until fluffy.

3. Add the eggs gradually while beating. Add the melted chocolate and blend.

4. Sift the flour with the baking soda.

5. Add the dry ingredients and liquid ingredients alternately to the chocolate mixture, starting and ending with the flour.

6. Pour and scrape the batter into the large pan first, filling it about two-thirds full, and then fill the loaf pan with the remaining batter (about half full).

7. Bake for about 45 minutes, or until the cake starts to pull slightly away from the side of the pan. (The loaf will be done sooner—in about 25 minutes.)

8. Cool on a rack for about 10 minutes, invert, and remove the cakes from the pans and remove the wax paper. When cooled, place on a cake platter or tray and dust lightly with confectioners' sugar or top with Sea Foam Frosting (below).

VARIATION: Use one buttered 9-inch tube pan, and bake about 55 minutes.

---

**PER SERVING**

| | | | |
|---|---|---|---|
| 14.3 gm total fat | 4.72 gm saturated fat | .1 gm fiber | 327 calories |
| 34 mg cholesterol | 38.4% fat | 162 mg sodium | 129 calories from fat |

---

# ❦ Sea Foam Frosting ❦
## (PAREVE)

*Makes enough to frost top, sides, and in between two 9-inch layer cakes*

This is a delicious frosting for a special occasion.

¾ cup packed light brown sugar
¼ cup light corn syrup
2 tablespoons water
⅛ teaspoon kosher salt
¼ teaspoon cream of tartar
2 extra-large egg whites

1. Combine all the ingredients in the top part of a double boiler.
2. Beat with an electric hand mixer over simmering water for 5 to 7 minutes.
3. Remove when the frosting will hold soft peaks.
4. Frost the sides and the top of the cake. If desired, arrange a border of toasted slivered almonds around the sides.

---

**PER SERVING**

| | | | |
|---|---|---|---|
| 0 gm total fat | 0 gm saturated fat | 0 gm fiber | 35 calories |
| 0 mg cholesterol | 0% fat | 30 mg sodium | 0 calories from fat |

# ❦ Lemon Squares ❦
## (DAIRY)
### Yield: 48 squares (1 square = 1 serving)

Lemon is a favorite flavor in our house (second only to chocolate), whether it's pie, cake, or lemon bars. These squares have always been popular for everything from *brith millahs* to bar mitzvahs. They are not only delicious to taste but easy to make, and they freeze beautifully. The bad news is they are high in fat and cholesterol. The good news is that even a small serving is satisfying.

*Cookie Crust:*
   2 cups sifted unbleached all-purpose flour
   ½ cup confectioners' sugar
   7 ounces (2 sticks minus 2 tablespoons) unsalted butter, cut into 14 pieces

*Filling:*
   4 extra-large eggs
   2 cups granulated sugar
   ¼ cup unbleached all-purpose flour
   1 teaspoon baking powder
   ½ cup fresh lemon juice
   1 tablespoon grated lemon zest

   **Confectioners' sugar, for garnish**

1. Make the crust: Place the flour and sugar in the bowl of a blender or food processor. Add the cubed butter and process with a pulsing action until the flour has the consistency of coarse meal. Preheat the oven to 350°.
2. Press into the bottom of a 13 × 9 × 2-inch glass baking dish.
3. Bake for 20 minutes.
4. Make the filling: While the crust is baking, beat the eggs with an electric mixer. Add the sugar and continue beating until light.
5. Add the flour, baking powder, lemon juice and zest and beat until smooth.
6. Spread the filling on the hot crust and return to the oven. Bake for another 20 minutes.
7. Let cool completely before cutting into 1½-inch squares.
8. Dust with confectioners' sugar before serving.

NOTE: I like to bake and serve these in miniature colored-paper baking cups.

---
**PER SERVING**
---

| | | | |
|---|---|---|---|
| 3.8 gm total fat | 2.23 gm saturated fat | .1 gm fiber | 93 calories |
| 27 mg cholesterol | 36.7% fat | 6 mg sodium | 35 calories from fat |

---

 **❦ HARRIET'S HINTS ❦**

*Wash oranges or lemons before using, especially if using the zest. This will remove any residual pesticides that may remain on the rind.*

---

# ❦ Eir Kichlach ❦
## (PAREVE)
### *Yield: 90 to 100 cookies (1 cookie = 1 serving)*

Traditionally served on the Sabbath, these innocent-looking cookies fill baskets in every Jewish bakery and grace tables at every temple kiddush. This recipe came from my mother-in-law, Mollie Roth, whose brown, aged recipe was preserved in plastic by her daughter, Helen Kolatch. It has been kitchen-tested by another daughter, Nanette Nathanson, and flavor-and-texture tested by yet another daughter, Tillie Mostov.

    12 extra-large eggs
     1 teaspoon kosher salt
    ½ cup sugar, plus additional for garnish
   1¼ cups canola oil
     5 cups unbleached all-purpose flour
     2 tablespoons sesame seeds (optional)
    ½ cup fine poppy seeds (optional)

1. Preheat the oven to 325°. Spray one or more baking sheets with vegetable oil cooking spray.

2. Beat the eggs and salt in an electric mixer until lemon-colored and fluffy, about 10 to 15 minutes at medium-high speed.

3. Gradually add the ½ cup sugar and oil, and beat until blended.

4. Beat in the flour (and poppy seeds, if using) gradually; continue beating until very smooth.

5. Drop by teaspoons onto the prepared baking sheets, about 2 inches apart. Cookies will spread and puff.

6. Sprinkle with sugar or with sesame seeds, if desired.

7. Bake for 15 to 20 minutes or until puffed and lightly browned. Cool on a rack.

VARIATION: One-half cup of poppy seeds may be added to the batter with the flour.
This exact recipe may be prepared without the canola oil. This lowers the fat content considerably, although the cookies will still contain some cholesterol and fat from the egg yolks.

---

PER SERVING

| | | | |
|---|---|---|---|
| 4.5 gm total fat | .53 gm saturated fat | .2 gm fiber | 83 calories |
| 35 mg cholesterol | 49.7% fat | 42 mg sodium | 41 calories from fat |

---

# ❦ The Ultimate Cheesecake ❦
## (DAIRY)
### Serves: 20

My friend and former neighbor Ann Nisenson loves to cook and entertain. She does both beautifully. She now lives in Santa Barbara, but has left behind many warm memories that I cherish. This delicious recipe is one of them, although I have to try to forget its enormously high fat content.

    1 (6-ounce) package zwieback or graham crackers, crushed into fine crumbs
    1 cup finely chopped walnuts or pecans
    5 tablespoons butter, melted
    1 cup sugar
    3 (8-ounce) packages cream cheese, at room temperature
    ¼ teaspoon salt
    2 teaspoons pure vanilla extract
    2 teaspoons grated lemon zest
    4 extra-large eggs, separated, at room temperature

**1 cup heavy cream, whipped**
**½ cup sifted unbleached all-purpose flour**

1. Preheat the oven to 325°. Lightly grease the bottom and sides of a 10-inch springform pan.

2. Combine the crumbs, nuts, butter, and 2 tablespoons of the sugar. Mix together with your fingers until blended and spread the crumb mixture on the bottom of the springform pan. Press down firmly.

3. Mix the cream cheese with half the remaining sugar, the salt, vanilla, and lemon zest. Beat in the egg yolks.

4. In a large bowl, beat the egg whites until they hold soft peaks. Add the remaining sugar a tablespoon at a time, beating well after each addition. Continue beating until stiff.

5. Add the whipped cream to the stiffly beaten egg whites. Add the cream cheese mixture. Sprinkle the flour on top of all, and fold all together gently until combined.

6. Pour and scrape into the prepared pan and bake for 1 hour and 15 minutes. Do not open the oven door until 1 hour of baking time has passed. When the top of the cake is light golden brown, turn off the oven heat. Let stand in the oven 3 hours. Do not be concerned if the cake cracks slightly.

7. Cover the cake and chill in the refrigerator before serving. If desired, dust with vanilla sugar (see below) and serve with a fresh raspberry or strawberry sauce (page 408). This cheesecake may be kept frozen for 1 month after baking.

---
PER SERVING
---

| | | | |
|---|---|---|---|
| 24.9 gm total fat | 12.68 gm saturated fat | .5 gm fiber | 336 calories |
| 107 mg cholesterol | 65.7% fat | 207 mg sodium | 224 calories from fat |

---

**❧ HARRIET'S HINTS ❧**

*T*o make vanilla sugar: Bury a split vanilla bean in an airtight container of granulated or confectioners' sugar. Cover tightly. Replace the sugar as it is used. Sprinkle on top of pastries and cakes instead of frosting. (After a week, remove the vanilla bean.)

# Metric Equivalents

Here are some standard measurements that every cook will find useful:

*Measurements by volume*

    1 teaspoon = ⅓ tablespoon = 5 milliliters
    1½ teaspoons = ½ tablespoon
    3 teaspoons = 1 tablespoon = 15 milliliters
    4 tablespoons = ¼ cup = 59 milliliters
    5⅓ tablespoons = ⅓ cup = 79 milliliters
    8 tablespoons = ½ cup = 118.4 milliliters
    16 tablespoons = 1 cup = 236 milliliters
    1 cup = 8 fluid ounces = .237 liters (approx. ¼ liter) = 237 milliliters
    2 cups = 1 pint = .473 liters (approx. ½ liter) = 473 milliliters
    4 cups or 2 pints = 1 quart = .9463 liters (approx. 1 liter) = 946 milliliters
    4 quarts = 1 gallon = 3785 milliliters

*Measurements by weight*

    1 ounce = approx. 28 grams
    3½ ounces = 100 grams
    16 ounces = 1 pound
    1 pound = 454 grams
    2.2 pounds = 1 kilogram

*Temperatures*

    degrees Fahrenheit to degrees Celsius subtract 32, then multiply by .56
    degrees Celsius to degrees Fahrenheit multiply by 1.8, then add 32

# Glossary of Yiddish Terms

**adafina**   Sephardic cholent (a long-simmering stew).

**afikoman**   a Greek word meaning "dessert." A piece of the middle matzo that sits on the Passover seder tray. It is hidden during the service, and the children search for it. When found, the leader of the seder must buy it back by promising a gift. It is the last of the foods eaten at the seder meal.

**bagel** or **begel**   a variety of bread roll, made of yeast dough formed into a small doughnutlike shape, cooked in simmering water, then baked in the oven.

**balabusta**   an efficient housewife or perfect cook.

**b'dikat chametz**   the search through the house for the last remnants of leaven on the night before the first evening of Passover.

**beitza**   roasted hard-cooked egg on the Passover seder plate; symbolizes the offering brought to the temple on festivals.

**bentshen**   the act of blessing or a benediction; specifically, the reciting of grace after a meal or over the Sabbath candles as in "Fentsher licht."

**beryah**   a "jewel" of a homemaker.

**beracha**   a blessing.

**bialy**   a round flat breakfast roll with a center of onion and poppy seeds.

**bisel**   a little.

**blintzes**   very thin pancakes rolled and filled with a variety of fillings, most popularly with cheese.

**borscht**   any of a variety of soups originating in Russia, but popularly a beet soup made with or without meat and served hot or cold. Cabbage or spinach borschts are popular variations of this dish. On Passover it is customary to make a hot meat borscht from soured beet juice (**russel**).

**brit milah**   ceremony of circumcision performed on a male child on the eighth day after birth.

**carnatzlach**   a highly seasoned ground-meat dish of Rumanian origin. The meat is formed into small sausagelike shapes and broiled.

**challah** or **hallah**   braided loaves of egg bread prepared for the Sabbath. Also made in a variety of forms for the various holidays of the year.

**Chanukah** or **Hanukkah**   the Feast of Lights, celebrated for eight days. It commemorates the heroic victory of the Maccabees over the Syrians in the year 165 B.C.E. In the search for oil to rekindle the Eternal Light of the Temple in Jerusalem, a bottle was found with only enough oil to burn for only one day—yet it lasted eight days. Today the eight days are celebrated by lighting eight candles, one the first day, two the second day, etc. A ninth candle, the *shammes,* is used to light the others. Among the traditional foods served are potato latkes. Gifts are given to children.

**cholent**   a Sabbath dish prepared on Friday and cooked overnight in a very slow oven.

**chrain**   ground horseradish.

**chremsel** or **chemslach**   a Passover fritter or pancake.

**dolma**   an combination of meat, rice, vegetables, and spices, popular in Turkey, Syria, and other Near Eastern countries.

**einbrenne**   a roux; a thickening for stews, soups, tzimmes, and other dishes, made by lightly browning flour in melted fat and stirring in some of the liquid from the stew.

**eir kichlach** or **eir kichel**   egg cookies, sometimes made without sweetener and used as a canapé base.

**erev yomtov**   the day or days immediately preceding a holiday.

**esslefel**   tablespoon.

**ey**   egg.

**farfel**   noodle dough chopped into rice-shaped grains.

**ferbrendt**   burned.

**fleischig**   meat or meat derivatives, or dishes made with them.

**forshpeis**   an appetizer.

**galuptze**   Russian term for chopped meat rolled in cabbage leaves; also called prokes, holishkes.

**gebrattens**   roasted meat.

**gefilte** (or **gefüllte**) **fish**   literally, stuffed fish. Some variation of this fish is prepared by Jews in every country of Central and Eastern Europe.

**gehackte**   chopped.

**griebenes** or **grieben**   cracklings which are strained from rendered chicken fat or goose fat.

**gupel**   fork.

**haggadah**   literally, a telling. The narration of the Passover, read at each seder.

**hamantasch(en)**   triangular cakes filled with honey and poppy seed filling, eaten at Purim. The triangular shape of the cakes recalls the triangular hat Haman is supposed to have worn.

**haroset** or **charoses**   a mixture of nuts, apple, and wine served at the Passover seder; it symbolizes the mortar used by the Israelite slaves in the erection of the pyramids of ancient Egypt.

**havdalah**   ceremony marking the end of the Sabbath or of holidays. Prayer recited by the head of the household over a cup of wine, a spice box, and a newly lit special braided candle.

**helzel**   a neck, especially with reference to the neck skin of a chicken, duck, etc., filled with various stuffings.

**karpas**   vegetable such as parsley, radish, celery, or potato on the seder plate; symbolizes spring, the season of hope and growth. It is dipped in salt water before eating.

**kasha**   cooked buckwheat groats.

**kasher**   to soak and salt meats and poultry before cooking, in accordance with the laws of kashruth.

**kashruth**   the Jewish dietary laws.

**khametz**   leavened bread, or any food or utensil regarded as not kosher for Passover.

**kiddush**   the benediction over the wine on the Sabbath and holidays.

**kishke (derma)**   a large beef intestine, stuffed with various savory fillings and roasted. The most common filling is made of flour and fat seasoned with onions, salt, and pepper.

**knaidel** or **knaidlach**   a dumpling.

**knish**   a baked dumpling or patty made of a thinly rolled or stretched dough with fillings of seasoned chopped meat, mashed potatoes, or kasha.

**knubble**   garlic.

**Kol Nidre**   prayer of atonement recited at the beginning of the Yom Kippur eve services.

**kosher**   literally, fit; used to designate foods that have been selected and prepared in accordance with the Jewish dietary laws.

**kosher l'Pesach**   fit for Passover use.

**kreplach**   noodle dough cut into small squares, filled with meat, cheese, or potatoes, and cooked in soups. Kreplach is traditionally eaten on Purim.

**kubik**   cup.

**kuchen**   cake; specifically, a coffee cake.

**kugel** or **kigel**   a pudding, especially one made of potatoes, noodles, rice, or fruit and baked.

**latkes**   pancakes, especially pancakes made of grated raw potato or of matzo meal. Traditionally served at Chanukah.

**l'chayim**   "To life and your good health!"—a toast.

**lefl**   spoon.

**lekach**   honey cake. Traditionally served at Rosh Hoshanah and Yom Kippur.

**linzen**   lentils, or lentil soup.

**lokshen** or **lukshen**   noodles.

**lox**   smoked salmon.

**Magen David**   literally, the shield of David, a six-pointed star that is the national symbol of Israel.

**mandelbrot**   an almond-flavored pastry baked in a long roll, then cut into thin slices which are browned in the oven.

**mashgiakh**   an inspector employed by the community to see that kosher meat markets, etc., conform to the laws of kashruth.

**matzo** or **matzoh**   unleavened bread eaten during Passover. In the Israelites' haste to depart from Egypt, they carried dough with them which was still unleavened. As a yearly reminder of this "bread of affliction," Jews eat only unleavened bread for one week during Passover.

**maven** or **mavin**   a connoisseur, expert, or gourmet.

**mazeltov**   "Good luck!" An expression of congratulation.

**megillah**   a scroll; any of the five books of the Hagiographa, especially the Book of Esther, read at Purim.

**meichel** or **michal**   an especially tasty or savory dish; a special concoction.

**menorah**   the eight-branched candelstick used during Chanukah.

**meshiterein**   "Throw it in."

**messir**   knife.

**milchig**   dairy products, or dishes made with them.

**miltz**   spleen.

**minyan**   the minimum group of ten adults required for the holding of congregational services.

**mitzvah**   a meritorious act.

**mohn**   poppy seeds.

**moror** or **maror**   bitter herbs, usually horseradish, on the Passover seder plate; symbolize the bitter lives endured by the Israelites when enslaved in Egypt.

**nahit**   chick-peas or garbanzo beans.

**nosh**   to nibble or snack.

**orech**   a guest. It is a traditional and prescribed custom to invite at least one orech, especially a traveler or stranger in the city, for the Sabbath and holiday meals.

**oysesn**   to eat out.

**pareve** or **parve**   neither *milchig* nor *fleischig* (neither a dairy nor a meat dish); such as fish, fruit, grains, and vegetables.

**Pesachdig**   for Passover use.

**piroshki** or **pirogen**   baked or fried dumplings made of yeast dough or pastry dough, with various fillings; served with soup, or as canapés.

**rabbi**   literally, my master. An ordained teacher of the Jewish law, authorized to decide questions of law and ritual and to perform marriages, etc., now usually the spiritual head of a congregation.

**raihtuch**   radish.

**reebahzen**   grater.

**russel**   a soured beet juice, used to make Passover borscht.

**schav**   a cold borscht made of sorrel, spinach, etc.

**schmaltz**   rendered chicken fat or goose fat.

**schmooze**   warm and friendly chat or gossip.

**schvester**   sister

**seder**   literally, order or arrangement. The feast commemorating the Exodus of the Jews from Egypt, observed in the home on the eve of the first day (and by Orthodox Jews also the eve of the second day) of Passover.

**Shabbat** or **Shabbos**   the Sabbath, lasting from sundown Friday to sundown Saturday.

**shalachmonos**   the sending of gifts, platters of cakes, and baked goods, exchanged at Purim.

**shalom alcichem**   peace unto you.

**shekhitah**   the method of slaughtering animals or fowl in accordance with the Jewish dietary laws.

**shisl**   bowl.

**shofar**   a ram's horn. In ancient times, the shofar was sounded to herald the arrival of a new month. It is now sounded in the synagogue to announce the New Year at the close of Yom Kippur services.

**shokhet**   an observant Jew trained and authorized to slaughter animals or fowl in accordance with the rituals of shekhitah.

**shomlefl**   slotted spoon to remove foam.

**strudel**   a pastry of stretched or rolled dough, with various fillings.

**sukkah**   a temporary outdoor dwelling in which one eats throughout the holiday of Sukkot.

**synagogue**   the place of assembly used for religious worship by a Jewish community.

**tallit**   prayer shawl.

**Talmud**   the collection of writings constituting the Jewish civil and religious law. It consists of two parts, the *Mishnah* (text) and the *Gemara* (commentary), but the term is sometimes restricted to mean the *Gemara*.

**tam**   taste, especially a savory taste.

**teiglach**   a confection made of pieces of dough cooked in honey.

**teler**   plate.

**tepl**   small pot.

**tish**   table.

**top**   pot.

**t'refah**   not kosher; not in accordance with Jewish dietary laws.

**tsibele** or **zwiebel**   onion.

**tzedaka**   the giving of charity.

**tzimmes**   a sweet dish of fruit and/or vegetables, prepared especially for the Sabbath, Rosh Hashanah, or before the Yom Kippur fast.

**varnishkes**   bowtie–shaped pasta, traditionally served with kasha.

**verenikis**   filled rounds of noodle dough, similar to kreplach.

**yahrzeit**   observance of the anniversary of a death.

**yarmulke**   skullcap worn by the Jews.

**zero'a**   roasted shankbone or neck of fowl on the Passover seder plate; symbolizes the Pascal lamb eaten on Passover by all families in Temple times.

# Bibliography

### Books

*Bowes and Church's Food Values of Portions Commonly Used*, 16th ed. Lippincott, 1994.

*The Holy Scriptures*. The Jewish Publication Society.

Jacobson, Michael, and Marder, Bruce. *What Are We Feeding Our Kids?* Workman, 1994.

Kolatch, Rabbi Alfred J. *The Jewish Book of Why*, vols. I and II. Jonathan David Publishers, 1981.

———. *The Jewish Home Advisor*. Jonathan David Publishers, 1990.

Ornish, Dean, M.D. *Stress, Diet, and Your Heart*. Signet Books, 1984.

Pritikin, Nathan. *The Pritikin Promise: 28 Days to A Longer, Healthier Life*. Simon & Schuster, 1983.

———. *The New Pritikin Program*. Pocket Books, 1991.

### Institutes and Their Publications

Center for Science in the Public Interest, 1501 16th Street, NW, Washington, DC 20036.

    *Eating Smart Fat Guide*

    *Eating Smart Fast Food Guide*

    *Eating Smart Additive Guide*

National Cholesterol Education Program, c/o National Institutes of Health, C-200, Bethesda, MD 20892.

> *So You Have High Blood Cholesterol*
> *Eating to Lower Your Blood Cholesterol*

National Heart, Lung, and Blood Institute, c/o National Institutes of Health, Bethesda, MD 20205.

> *Exercise and Your Heart*, NIH Publication #81-1677

U.S. Department of Agriculture

> *Nutritive Value of Foods*, Home and Garden Bulletin #72, 1992–1993 edition.
> *Making Healthy Food Choices*, 1993 edition.


## Recommended Periodicals and Newsletters

*Environmental Nutrition*, P. O. Box 420451, Palm Coast, FL 32142-0451.

*Harvard Medical School Health Letter*, P. O. Box 10945, Des Moines, IA 50340.

*Johns Hopkins Medical Letter: Health After 50*, P. O. Box 420179, Palm Crest, FL 32142, or call 904-446-4675.

*Mayo Clinic Health Letter*, P. O. Box 53889, Boulder, CO 80322-3889.

*Nutrition Action Newsletter*, c/o Center for Science in the Public Interest, 1501 16th Street, NW, Washington, DC 20036.

*Tufts University Diet and Nutrition Letter*, call 1-800-247-5470.

*University of California/Berkeley Wellness Letter*, P.O. Box 10922, Des Moines, IA 50340.

*University of Texas Lifetime Health Letter*, 7000 Tannen, DCT 12012, Houston, TX 77030.

# Index

Almond(s)
  *in* Apple-Carrot Passover Pudding, Jean
      Berenson's, 81–82
  Apricots and, Syrian Gelatin Mold with, 21–25
  *in* Apricot Squares, 95–96
  *in* Baked Apples Muscatel, 401–402
  *in* Chocolate Trifle, 396
  *in* Dessert Wafers, Harriet Greenwald's, 389–90
  *in* Hungarian Butter Horns, 415–16
  *in* Mandelbrot, My Favorite, 385–86
  *in* Marbled Mandelbrot, 386–87
  *in* Oat Nut Slices with Jam, 383
  *in* Passover Brownies, 90–91
  *in* Passover Chocolate Torte, Almost Dorothy
      Hartstein's, 72–74, 88–90
  *in* Passover Granola, 99
  *in* Pesach Mandelbrot, 92
  *in* Rhubarb Bars, Dorothy Essick's, 392–93
Antipasto
  Herring, 119–20
  Tuna and White Bean, 118
Appetizers
  Artichoke Squares, 124–25
  Baba Ghanouj, 107–108
  Cabbage Strudel, 359
  Chicken Fricassee with Dumplings, Mollie
      Roth's, 120–21
  Chinese Chicken Drumettes, 133–34
  Eggs and Onions, 28–29
  Hummus, 123–24

Kasha Knishes, 352
Kibbe, Renée Holland's, 23–24
Little Meatballs, 128–29
Middle Eastern Chopped Eggplant, 121–22
Mini Knishes, 351–52
Onion
  Cheese Roll, 353
  Leek Strudel, 359
Passover Canapés, 97
Petcha, 127
Potato
  Latkes with Dill Sauce, Quick and Easy,
      125–26
  Onion Strudel, 360
Ricotta
  and Artichoke Flowers, 354
  and Sun-dried Tomato Phyllo Cups, 355–56
Salmon
  Mousse Metz, 286–87
  Smoked, Tartare, 116–17
Spinach
  Cups, 122–23
  Strudel, 358–59
Syrian Meatballs and Cherries, 131–32
Tuna and White Bean Antipasto, 118
Vegetarian Knishes, 132–33
  *see also* Dips; Spreads; Herring
Apple(s)
  *in* Ashkenazi Haroset, Sally's, 70
  Baked, Muscatel, 401–402

Apple(s) (cont.)
    Cabbage Salad, 192–93
    -Carrot Passover Pudding, Jean Berenson's,
        81–82
    in Cranapple Sauce, 53–54
    Date Salad, 182
    in Fruited Sweet Potato Tart, 51–52
    in Fruit Kugel, Helen Kolatch's, 43
    in Herring in Cream, 118–19
    Horseradish, Relish, 73–74
    Kugel, Mama's, 365–66
    in Sephardic Haroset, 70–71
    Slices, Poached, 407
    in Spiced Fruit in Wine, 406–407
    Strudel, No-Fat, Gisele Pollak's, 364–65
Apricot(s)
    and Almonds, Syrian Gelatin Mold with, 24–25
    Chicken, Cyrus Faridi's, 312–13
    dried
        in Fruit Kugel, Helen Kulatch's, 43
        in Stuffed Grape Leaves, 223–24
    Glaze, Stuffed Chicken Breasts with, Nanette
        Nathanson's, 85–86
    in Hot Brandied Fruit, Phyllis's, 410–11
    preserves
        in Apricot Squares, 95–96
        in Hungarian Fluden, 42
        in Mock or Simple Strudel, My Favorite,
            38–39
        in Oat Nut Slices with Jam, 383
        in Special Kugel, Phyllis's, 222–23
    Prune, Filling, 65
        in Spiced Fruit in Wine, 406–407
Artichoke hearts
    in Artichoke Squares, 124–25
    or bottoms, in Chopped Salad, 185–86
    in Herring Antipasto, 119–20
    in Marinated Bean Salad, 183–84
    in Ricotta and Artichoke Flowers, 354
    in Vegetarian Sandwich, 276–77
Arugula, in Red and Green Chopped Salad, 186
Asparagus
    Farfel and, Risotto, 78–79
    Fresh, Soup, Barbara Bernstein's, 151–52
    in Hungarian Vegetable Salad, 193–94
Atlanta Honey Cake, 35–36
Atlanta Pilaf with Pine Nuts, Pinto Beans, and
    Scallions, 224

Baba Ghanouj, 107–108
Babka, My Best, 426–27
Bagels
    Herbed, 375
    Raisin, 375
    Twisted, 375
    Water, Sam Mackler's, 373–75
Baked Apples Muscatel, 401–402
Baked Chicken with Bing Cherries, 306
Baked Fish Hungarian Style, 294
Baked Salmon with Carrot-Zucchini Stuffing,
    288–89
Baking
    low-fat, substituting in, 372–73
    notes on, 372
    powder, substitute for, 373
Bamieh, 261
Banana(s)
    Fillet of Sole with, Annette's, 293–94
    in Fruited Sweet Potato Tart, 51–52
    Pineapple Sherbet, 408–409
    squash. See Squash
    in Strawberry Rhubarb Jumble, 402–403
Barley
    cooking times for, 206
    Lima Bean and, Soup, with Mushrooms,
        Sarah's, 155–56
    and Red Pepper Pilaf, 214–15
    in Vegetarian Stuffed Cabbage, 248–49
Bars
    Cream Cheese Squares, 390–91
    Date
        Dr. Harvey Mendress's Mother's, 65–66
        and Nut, from West Bloomfield, 93
    Lemon Squares, 430–31
    Passover Brownies, 90–91
    Rhubarb, Dorothy Essick's, 392–93
Bean(s)
    black
        cooking times for, 236
        in Marinated Bean Salad, 183–84
        in Vegetarian Chili, 263–64
    Bulgur and, 207–208
    cannellini
        in Lamb Shanks and Beans, 345–46
        in Marinated Bean Salad, 183–84
        in Pasta and Beans, 215–16
        in Sephardic Leeks and Beans, 259–60
        in Tuna and White Bean Antipasto, 118
        in Vegetable and Bean Soup, Connie Reif's,
            166–67
    dried
        cooking times for, 236
        to prepare, 235–36
    garbanzo (chick-peas)
        in Bulgur and Beans, 207–208
        in Chopped Salad, 185–86

cooking times for, 236
*in* Herring Antipasto, 119–20
*in* Hummus, 123–24
*in* Marinated Bean Salad, 183–84
*in* Minestrone, 154–55
*in* Nahit, 274
*in* Syrian Stuffed Eggplant, 324–25
*in* Vegetarian Chili, 263–64
*in* Vegetarian Stew, 258–59
Great Northern
or navy, cooking times for, 236
*in* Sephardic Leeks and Beans, 259–60
*in* Vegetarian Stew, 258–59
green. *See* Green beans
Leeks and, Sephardic, 259–60
lima
and Barley Soup with Mushrooms, Sarah's,
155–56
*in* Cholent, 9–10
cooking times for, 236
for a Crowd, Cousin Pearly's, 268–69
Marinated, Salad, 183–84
Pasta and, 215–16
pinto
cooking times for, 36
Pine Nuts, and Scallions, Atlanta Pilaf with,
224
red kidney
cooking times for, 236
*in* Herring Antipasto, 119–20
*in* Marinated Bean Salad, 183–84
*in* Vegetarian Chili, 263–64
*in* Vegetarian Stew, 258–59
turtle. *See* Beans, black, *above*
Vegetable and, Soup, Connie Reif's, 166–67
white. *See* Beans, cannellini, *above*
*see also* Black-eyed peas
Bear Claws, Miniature, 421
Beef
brisket
cooked, *in* Kreplach, 208–209
Edie Wahl's, 337–38
Mrs. Rubenstein's, 335–36
Roast, with Prunes and Garlic, Marilyn
Lewis's, 58–59
flanken, *in* Lima Beans for a Crowd, Cousin
Pearly's, 268–69
ground
*in* Hungarian Stuffed Cabbage, 321
*in* Kibbe, Renée Holland's, 23–24
*in* Sweet and Sour Stuffed Cabbage,
41–42
steak. *See* Steak

Beet(s)
borscht. *See* Borscht
-Gefilte Fish Mold, 34–35
Horseradish, Homemade, 73–74
*in* Low-Calorie Cabbage Borscht, 172–73
Sweet and Sour, Dorothy Essick's, 266–67
Bell peppers. *See* Peppers
Berries
notes on, 403
as topping, to prepare, 229
*see also* Names of berries
Beta-carotene, sources of, 234
Bialys, 374
Bing cherries. *See* Cherries
Biscuits, Butter, Hungarian, 417–18
Black beans. *See* Beans
Black-eyed peas, cooking times for, 236
Blatlach, Pareve, 102
Blender Beet Borscht, 145
Blintzes
Never-Fail, 101–103
Sandwich, 228–29
Blueberries
dried, *in* Passover Granola, 99
*in* Hot Brandied Fruit, Phyllis's, 410
*in* Lokshen Kugel, Ruth Litt's, 221
*in* Mini Fruit Tarts, 39
Bok choy
for cabbage, *in* Chinese Cabbage with
Mushrooms, 276
*in* Vegetarian Fried Brown Rice, 226–27
Bombay Chicken Breasts, 308–309
Borscht(s)
beet
Blender, 145
Jellied, Salad, 236–37
quick, to make, 159–60
Cabbage
Harriet Friedman's Mother's, 171–72
Low-Calorie, 172–73
Green Bean and Potato, My Mother's, 145–46
Schav, 147–48
Boston lettuce, *in* Hungarian Vegetable Salad,
193–94
Bouillon cubes, sodium-reduced, to make, 259
Bouquet garni, notes on, 138
Braised Lamb Shanks, 344–45
Bran Muffins, Easy, 380–81
Brandy, *in* Hot Brandied Fruit, Phyllis's, 410–11
Bread Stuffing, My Mother's, 304
Bread(s)
Date and Nut, Mother's, 377–78
My Best Babka, 426–27

Bread(s) (*cont.*)
see also Bagels; Challah; Muffins; Rolls
Brisket. *See* Beef; Veal
Broccoli
Kugel, 270–71
in Layered Vegetable Kugel, 52–53
in Mixed Fresh Vegetable Salad, 180–81
Noodle Kugel, 219–20
Broiled Salmon with Mustard Sauce, 285
Broth(s)
to defat, 137
Turkey, 140
Vegetable, 141–42
see also Soups; Stocks
Brown and Wild Rice Pilaf, 206–207
Brownies, Passover, 90–91
Brussels Sprouts, Roast Chicken with, 29–30
Buckwheat groats. *See* Kasha
Bulgur
and Beans, 207–208
cooking times for, 206
Busy Day Chocolate Cake, 395–96
Butter
Biscuits, Hungarian, 417–18
Horns, Hungarian, 415–17
melted, substitutes for, 373
Plum, 411
substitutes for, 372
Buttermilk
in Easy Bran Muffins, 380–81
in Devil's Food Cake, Mrs. Katz's, 428–29
notes on, 392
in Ranch-Style Dressing, 196

Cabbage
Apple, Salad, 192–93
borscht. *See* Borscht
Chinese, with Mushrooms, 276
in Minestrone, 154–55
Mustard, 267–68
and Noodles, 212–13
Onion, Slaw, 108–109
red
Ellen Batzdorf's, 240–41
in Hungarian Caraway Slaw, 191
savoy
in Hungarian Gulyás, 340
in Vegetarian Stuffed Cabbage, 248–49
Strudel, 360
Stuffed
Hungarian, 321–22
Sweet and Sour, 41–42
Vegetarian, 248–49

in Vegetarian Vegetable Soup, 160–61
Cake(s)
Chiffon, Honey, Mollie Roth's, 17–18
Chocolate
Busy Day, 395–96
A Very Good, 391–92
Coffee, Streusel, Edie's, 109–10
Devil's Food, Mrs. Katz's, 428–29
Honey, Atlanta, 35–37
meal. *See* Matzo cake meal
No-Fat Honey Tea Loaf, 379–80
Ultimate Cheesecake, The, 432–33
see also Breads; Kuchen; Tortes
Calf's Foot, Jellied, 97
Cancer, cruciferous vegetables and, 234
Cannellini beans. *See* Beans
Caraway
Seeds, Chicken in Sauerkraut with, 319–20
Slaw, Hungarian, 191
Soup, 164–65
Carbohydrates
complex, notes on, xxii
sources of, 234
Carnatzlach, 327–28
Carp, *in* Jellied Sweet and Sour Fish, 297
Carrot(s)
Apple-, Passover Pudding, Jean Berenson's,
81–82
in Garlic Chicken, Gayle Kohl's, 310–11
in Gingered Cucumbers, 188
in Israeli Vegetable Salad, 184–85
in Layered Vegetable Kugel, 52–53
in Onion Cabbage Slaw, 108–109
in Passover Tzimmes with Mini Matzo Balls,
87–88
and Prune Tzimmes, 272
Ring, 247–48
in Stuffed Zucchini, Nita Williams', 277–78
in Tzimmes, 260
in Vegetarian Chili, 263–64
in Vegetarian Fried Brown Rice, 226–27
in Vegetarian Stew, 258–59
in Vegetarian Stuffed Cabbage, 248–49
in Vegetarian Vegetable Soup, 160–61
Vichyssoise, 148
-Zucchini Stuffing, Baked Salmon with, 288–89
Casserole(s)
Corn and Okra, Creole, 262–63
Spinach Noodle, 213–14
Cauliflower
in Layered Vegetable Kugel, 52–53
in Mixed Fresh Vegetable Salad, 180–81
and Pea Salad, Crunchy, 181

*in* Vegetable and Bean Soup, Connie Reif's, 166–67
Celery
Minced, Parsley and, Salad Vinaigrette, 189–90
Radish, and Cucumber Salad, 187
*in* Vegetarian Chili, 263–64
*in* Vegetarian Vegetable Soup, 160–61
Challah
No-Cholesterol, Mother Mollie's, 5–7
Round, with Raisins, 12–13
Chanukah
menu for, 57
notes on, 56–57
Cheese
Filling, *for* Danish, Mama's, 420–21
Kuchen, 33
Onion, Roll, 353
yogurt. *See* Yogurt cheese
*see also* Names of cheeses
Cheesecake, The Ultimate, 432–33
Cherry(ies)
Bing
Baked Chicken with, 306
*in* Hot Brandied Fruit, Phyllis's, 410
dried
*in* Easy Bran Muffins, 380–81
*in* Hungarian Sour Cherry Muffins, 382
*in* Passover Granola, 99
Meatballs and, Syrian, 131–32
Sour, Hungarian, Muffins, 382
*in* Spiced Fruit in Wine, 406–407
tomatoes. *See* Tomatoes
Chicken
Apricot, Cyrus Faridi's, 312–13
with Bing Cherries, Baked, 306
breasts
Bombay, 308–309
*in* Chicken with Plum Sauce, 313
*in* Garlic Chicken, Gayle Kohl's, 310–11
ground, *in* Falsher Fish, 74–75
Middle Eastern, 313–14
*in* Oven-fried Chicken, 309–10
in Phyllo, 356–57
*in* Shurba, 173–74
Stuffed, with Apricot Glaze, Nanette Nathanson's, 85–87
Ten Easy Pieces of, 311–12
*in* Cholent, 9–10
cooked
*in* Chicken with Potatoes and Red Peppers, 320–21
*in* Chicken Strudel, 350–51
*in* Chopped Salad, 185–86

*in* Hot Cold Noodles, Connie Reif's, 225
*in* Kreplach, 208–209
Drumettes, Chinese, 133–34
Fricassee with Dumplings, Mollie Roth's, 120–21
Garlic, Gayle Kohl's, 310–11
gizzards, *in* Chicken Fricassee with Dumplings, Mollie Roth's, 120–21
Honey Glazed, 315–16
Indoor Barbecued, 317
"Jewish," 307
Lemon, for a Crowd, 314–15
Neck, Stuffed, 305
nutritional notes on, 301–302
Oven-fried, 309–10
Paprikash with Rice, My Favorite, 318–19
with Plum Sauce, 313
with Potatoes and Red Peppers, 320–21
Rizib, 22–23
Roast
with Brussels Sprouts, 29–30
Stuffed, My Mother's, 303–304
in Sauerkraut with Caraway Seeds, 319–20
soup. *See* Soups
Strudel, 350–51
Chick-peas. *See* Beans, garbanzo
Chili, Vegetarian, 263–64
Chilled Tomato Soup, 149–50
Chinese Cabbage with Mushrooms, 276
Chinese Chicken Drumettes, 133–34
Chocolate
cakes. *See* Cakes
*in* Devil's Food Cake, Mrs. Katz's, 428–29
substitutes for, 373
Torte, Passover, Almost Dorothy Hartstein's, 88–90
Trifle, 396
Cholent, 8–10
Cholesterol, notes on, xix
Chopped Salad, 185–86
Red and Green, 186
Chrain, 73–74
Cockscombs, 421
Coffee Cake, Streusel, Edie's, 109–10
Cold Cucumber Soup, 143–44
Compote, Prune-Apricot, 400–401
Concasse, Tomato and Garlic, Fish Fillets with, 292–93
Cookies
Dessert Wafers, Harriet Greenwald's, 389–90
Eir Kichlach, 431–32
Ginger, Spiced, 384
Oat Nut Slices with Jam, 383

Cookies (*cont.*)
    Poppy Seed Crisps, Dorothy Essick's, 388
    Poppy Seed Komitzbrodt, 66–67
    Pogachells or Pogácsa, 417–18
    Russian Raisin Nut Slices, 111
    Spicy Meringues, 91
    *see also* Bars; Mandelbrot
Corn
    *in* Marinated Bean Salad, 183–84
    and Okra Casserole, Creole, 262
    Pudding, 265–66
    Soup, Nanette Nathanson's, 170–71
    *in* Stuffed Peppers, 245–46
    *in* Vegetable and Bean Soup, Connie Reif's,
        166–67
Cornflakes, *in* Oven-fried Chicken, 309–10
Cornish hen(s)
    with Ginger Plum Sauce, 331
    with Sweet and Sour Glaze, 329–30
Cornmeal, Yellow, Mush, 227–28
Cottage cheese (nonfat)
    *in* Blintz Sandwich, 228–29
    *in* Lokshen Kugel, Ruth Litt's, 220–21
    *in* Mini Knishes, 351–52
    *in* Never-Fail Blintzes, 101–103
    *in* Special Kugel, Phyllis's, 222–23
    *in* Spinach Soufflé, Renée Holland's, 103
Court Bouillon, 287
Cracked wheat
    Dip, 20–21
    *see also* Bulgur
Cranapple Sauce, 54–55
Cranberries
    *in* Cranapple Sauce, 53–54
    dried
        *in* Easy Bran Muffins, 380–81
        *in* Passover Granola, 99
    Pear, Strudel, Jackie Keller's, 366–67
Cream, Herring in, 118–19
Cream cheese
    *in* Cheese Filling, *for* Danish, Mama's, 420
    fat-reduced (light)
        *in* Cream Cheese Squares, 390–91
        *in* Reformed Rugelach, 37–39
    nonfat
        *in* Green Pea Dip with Fresh Vegetables,
            130–31
        *in* Never-Fail Blintzes, 101–103
        *in* Orange-flavored Cream Cheese, 378
        *in* Quick and Easy Potato Latkes with Dill
            Sauce, 125–26
    Orange-flavored, 378
    substitutes for, 372

*in* The Ultimate Cheesecake, 432–33
Creamy Tofu Dressing, 198–99
Creole Corn and Okra Casserole, 262
Crepes
    Dessert, 102
    Lemon, 103
    Meat-filled, 102
    Pareve Blatlach, 102
    *see also* Blintzes
Crisp, Italian Plum, 394–95
Croquettes, Salmon, 104–105
Crunchy Cauliflower and Pea Salad, 181
Cucumber(s)
    Gingered, 188
    *in* Hungarian Vegetable Salad, 193–94
    *in* Israeli Vegetable Salad, 184–85
    Marinated, 178
    *in* Middle Eastern Chopped Eggplant, 121–22
    Radish, Celery, and, Salad, 187
    Salad, 179–80
    Soup, Cold, 143–44
Currants
    Lentils and, Rice with, 221
    *in* Stuffed Peppers, 245–46

Danish, Mama's, 418–21
Date(s)
    Apple, Salad, 182
    *in* Baked Apples Muscatel, 401–402
    Bars, Dr. Harvey Mendess's Mother's, 65–66
    to chop, 182
    and Nut
        Bars from West Bloomfield, 93
        Bread, Mother's, 377–78
    Nut Spread, 70–71
    *in* Passover Granola, 99
    *in* Spicy Meringues, 91
    *in* Streusel Coffee Cake, Edie's, 109–10
Day of Atonement. *See* Yom Kippur
Dessert(s)
    Apple Kugel, Mama's, 365–66
    Baked Apples Muscatel, 401–02
    Banana Pineapple Sherbet, 408–409
    Chocolate Trifle, 396
    Crepes, 102
    Fresh Orange Sorbet, 405–406
    Hot Brandied Fruit, Phyllis's, 410
    Italian Plum Crisp, 394–95
    Lemon Crepes, 103
    Mile-High Lemon Meringue Pie, 425
    No-Fat Apple Strudel, Gisele Pollak's, 364–65
    Pear Cranberry Strudel, Jackie Keller's,
        366–67

Poached Apple Slices, 407
Poached Pears with Raspberries, 409
Prune
  -Apricot Compote, 400–401
  Whip, 404
Salad, Fresh Peach, 112
Sliced Oranges in Marmalade, 399–400
Spiced Baked Pears, 404–405
Spiced Fruit in Wine, 406–407
Strawberry Rhubarb Jumble, 402–403
Strudel, Almost Aunt Dora's, 362–63
Wafers, Harriet Greenwald's, 389–90
see also Bars; Cakes; Cookies; Pastries
Devil's Food Cake, Mrs. Katz's, 428–29
Dill
  Pickles, Kosher, Mrs. Rubenstein's, 237–38
  Sauce, Quick and Easy Potato Latkes with,
    125–26
  Tofu, Dip, 46–47
Dip(s)
  Cracked Wheat, 20–21
  Green Pea, with Fresh Vegetables, 130–31
  Tofu Dill, 46–47
Dolmas, 323–24
Dressing(s)
  Asian, Light, Connie Reif's, 201
  Ranch-Style, 196
  Russian, 199
  Tahini, Lemony, 198
  Tofu, Creamy, 198–99
  Tomato, Low-Cal, 197
  Vinaigrette, Light, 200
Dried fruit. See Fruit
Dumplings
  Chicken Fricassee with, Mollie Roth's, 120–21
  Krupen, 244
  Potato, 243–44
  Schliskas from Aunt Ella Markell, 243–44
  see also Knaidlach

Easy Bran Muffins, 380–81
Egg(s)
  Drop Soup, 143
  and egg yolks, substitutes for, 372–73
  notes on, 378
  and Onions, 28–29
Eggplant
  in Baba Ghanouj, 107–108
  Chopped, Middle Eastern, 121–22
  Parmesan, 238–39
  Pasta with, 211
  in Ratatouille, 264–65
  Stuffed, Syrian, 324–25

in Vegetarian Chili, 263–64
in Vegetarian Chopped Liver, 7–8
in Vegetarian Stew, 258–59
"Egg Salad" Spread, 195
Einlauf, 143
Eir Kichlach, 431–32
Elbow macaroni, in Minestrone, 154

Falsher Fish, 74
Farfel
  and Asparagus Risotto, 78–79
  matzo. See Matzo farfel
  Ring, 15–16
  Salad, 190
Farmer cheese, in Never-Fail Blintzes, 101–103
Fat
  calories, notes on, xvii–xviii
  percentage of calorie intake, to calculate,
    xviii–xix
  saturated, notes on, xviii
Fennel
  in Green Pea Dip with Fresh Vegetables,
    130–31
  in Marinated Vegetables, 239–40
  in Red and Green Chopped Salad, 186
Feta cheese, in Chopped Salad, 185–86
Figs
  in Apple-Carrot Passover Pudding, Jean
    Berenson's, 81–82
  in Hot Brandied Fruit, Phyllis's, 410
  in Sephardic Haroset, 70–71
Filling(s)
  for Danish, Mama's, 420–21
  Poppy Seed, 64
  Prune Apricot, 65
  see also Lekvar; Stuffings
Fish
  acceptable as kosher, 283–84
  Baked, Hungarian Style, 294
  to buy, 282
  to cook, 282
  Falsher, 74–75
  fat content of, 284
  Fillets
    in Phyllo, 357
    with Tomato and Garlic Concasse, 292–93
  frozen, notes on, 298
  gefilte. See Gefilte fish
  to grind, 72
  nutritional notes on, 281
  Paprikash, 284–85
  Poached, Horseradish Sauce for, 73
  raw, dangers of, 281

Fish (*cont.*)
  Stock, 142–43
  to store and handle, 282
  Sweet and Sour, Jellied, 297
  *see also* Names of fish
Flounder
  *in* Baked Fish Hungarian Style, 294
  Oven-fried, 291–92
Flour
  as thickener, substitutes for, 373
  white, substitutes for, 373
Fluden, Hungarian, 422
Foods, processed
  kosher, xxv–xxvi
  sodium and, xxi
Fourth of July, menu for, 107
French Onion Soup, 153
Fresh Orange Sorbet, 405–406
Fresh Peach Dessert Salad, 112
Fresh Tomato Sauce, 54
Frosting, Sea Foam, 429
Fruit(s)
  canned
    *in* Hot Brandied Fruit, Phyllis's, 410
    *in* Spiced Fruit in Wine, 406–407
  dried
    to chop, 182
    to plump, 110
    *see also* Names of dried fruits
  Hot Brandied, Phyllis's, 410
  Kugel, Helen Kolatch's, 43
  notes on, 399
  Spiced, in Wine, 406–407
  Tarts, Mini, 39
  *see also* Names of fruits
Fruited Sweet Potato Tart, 51–52

Garbanzo beans. *See* Beans
Garlic
  Chicken, Gayle Kohl's, 310–11
  odor, to remove, 154
  *in* Onion Helper, 254–55
  Onions and, Mashed Potatoes with, 242–43
  to peel, 243
  Prunes and, Roast Brisket with, Marilyn Lewis's, 58–59
  Tomato and, Concasse, Fish Fillets with, 292–93
Gayle Kohl's Garlic Chicken, 310–11
Gefilte Fish
  balls, 72
  Beet-, Mold, 34–35
  from jars, to improve, 35

Loaf, 71–72
Mock, 74–75
Roll, 289–90
Gefilte Helzel, 305
Gehackte Hering, 129–30
Gelatin Mold, Syrian, with Apricots and Almonds, 24–25
Ginger
  Cookies, Spiced, 384
  Plum Sauce, Cornish Hens with, 331
Gingered Cucumbers, 188
Gingersnaps, *in* Cabbage Borscht, Harriet Friedman's Mother's, 171–72
Gizzards. *See* Chicken
Glaze(s)
  Apricot, Stuffed Chicken Breasts with, Nanette Nathanson's, 85–87
  Sweet and Sour, Cornish Hen with, 329–30
Glazed Salmon Fillets, 290–91
Grains, to prepare, 205–206
Green bean(s)
  *in* Hungarian Vegetable Salad, 193–94
  *in* Marinated Bean Salad, 183–84
  and Potato Borscht, My Mother's, 145
  Sweet and Sour, My Mother's, 272–73
  *in* Vegetarian Vegetable Soup, 160–61
Green peas. *See* Peas
Green Sauce, 296
Green Split Pea Soup, 163
Granola, Passover, 99
Grape(s)
  *in* Fruited Sweet Potato Tart, 51–52
  Leaves, stuffed, 323–24
  *in* Spiced Fruit in Wine, 406–407
Gravy(ies)
  Turkey, 49–50
  to use, 307
Gulyás, Hungarian, 340–41

Halibut
  *in* Fish Fillets in Phyllo, 357
  *in* Fish Paprikash, 284–85
Hamantaschen, 63–65
Hamburgers, Broiled, Rumanian, 327–28
Harold's Matzo Brei, 97–98
Haroset
  Ashkenazi, Sally's, 70
  Sephardic, 70–71
Hazelnuts
  *in* My Best Babka, 426–27
  *in* Oat Nut Slices with Jam, 383
  *in* Streusel Coffee Cake, Edie's, 109–10
Herbed Bagels, 375

Herbs, notes on, xxxii–xxxiii
Herring
    Antipasto, 119–20
    Chopped, Mrs. Schneider's, 129–30
    in Cream, 118–19
    nutritional notes on, 130
Homemade Beet Horseradish, 73–74
Hoop cheese, in Never-Fail Blintzes, 101–103
Honey
    Cake, Atlanta, 35–37
    Chiffon Cake, 17–18
    crystallized, to melt, 391
    Glazed Chicken, 315–16
    Tea Loaf, No-Fat, 379–80
Horseradish
    Apple Relish, 73–74
    Beet, Homemade, 73
    Sauce for Poached Fish, 73
Hummus, 123–24
Hungarian Butter Biscuits, 417–18
Hungarian Butter Horns, 415–17
Hungarian Caraway Slaw, 191
Hungarian Fluden, 422
Hungarian Gulyás, 340–41
Hungarian Lecsó, Gisele Pollak's, 269
Hungarian Sauerkraut Soup, 169–70
Hungarian Sour Cherry Muffins, 382
Hungarian Stuffed Cabbage, 321–22
Hungarian Vegetable Salad, 193–94
Hungarian Wilted Lettuce and Tomato Salad,
    191–92

Indoor Barbecued Chicken, 317
Israeli Steak Sandwich, 338–39
Israeli Vegetable Salad, 184–85
Italian plums. See Plums

Jam, Oat Nut Slices with, 383
Jellied Beet Borscht Salad, 236–37
Jellied Calf's Foot, 127
Jellied Sweet and Sour Fish, 297
"Jewish" Chicken, 307
Jicama, in Mixed Fresh Vegetable Salad, 180–81
Jumble, Strawberry Rhubarb, 402–403

Kasha, 217
    cooking times for, 206
    Knishes, 352
    Varnishkes, 218
    in Vegetarian Stuffed Cabbage, 248–49
Kibbe, Renée Holland's, 23–24
Kidney beans. See Beans, red kidney
Kipfel, 421

Kishka, in Cholent, 9–10
Kiwis, in Fresh Peach Dessert Salad, 112
Knaidlach, 76–77
    Potato, 75–76
    see also Dumplings
Knishes
    Kasha, 352
    Mini, 351–52
    Vegetarian, 132–33
Knives, to clean, 134
Kohlrabi, in Vegetarian Vegetable Soup, 160–61
Komitzbrodt, Poppy Seed, 66–67
Kosher
    Dill Pickles, Mrs. Rubenstein's, 237–38
    kitchen, notes on, xxiv
    notes on, xxiii–xxiv
    processed foods, xxv–xxvi
Kraut Pletzlach, 212–13
Kreplach, 208–209
Krupen, 244
Kuchen
    Cheese, 33
    Never-Fail, 30–33
    Today's, 31–33
    Yesterday's, 30–31, 32–33
Kugel(s)
    Apple, Mama's, 365–66
    Broccoli, 270
    Fruit, Helen Kolatch's, 43
    Lokshen, Ruth Litt's, 220–21
    Matzo
        Lillian Tabor's, 82–83
        Marge Taylor's, 80
        Pear Pineapple, 83–84
    Pineapple Upside-Down, No-Cholesterol, 210
    Potato, 256–57
        Individual, 257
    Rice, Sarah's, 218–19
    Special, Phyllis's, 222–23
    Spinach, 16–17
    Vegetable, Layered, 52–53
    see also Puddings

Lamb shanks
    and Beans, 345–46
    Braised, 344–45
Latkes, 59–61
    Potato, Quick and Easy, with Dill Sauce,
        125–26
Layered Vegetable Kugel, 52–53
Lecsó, Hungarian, Gisele Pollak's, 269
Leek(s)
    and Beans, Sephardic, 259–60

Leek(s) (*cont.*)
  Onion Strudel, 259
  *in* Spinach Kugel, 16–17
Lekach, 35–37
  Low-Fat, No-Cholesterol, 17–18
Lekvar, 411
  *in* Danish, Mama's, 420
  *in* Hungarian Fluden, 422
Lemon
  Chicken for a Crowd, 314–15
  Crepes, 103
  Meringue Pie, Mile-High, 425
  notes on, 431
  Squares, 430–31
Lemony Tahini Dressing, 198
Lentil(s)
  cooking times for, 236
  and Currants, Rice with, 221–22
  old, to cook, 222
  to prepare, 235–36
  Soup, Vegetarian, 158–59
  *in* Vegetarian Chopped Liver, 7–8
Lettuce
  Boston, *in* Hungarian Vegetable Salad, 193–94
  *in* Israeli Vegetable Salad, 184–85
  romaine, *in* Chopped Salad, 185–86
  Wilted, and Tomato Salad, 191–92
Light Vinaigrette Dressing, 200
Lima beans. *See* Beans
Little Meatballs, 128–29
Liver, Chopped, Vegetarian, 7–8
Lokshen Kugel, Ruth Litt's, 220–21
Low-Calorie Cabbage Borscht, 172–73
Low-Cal Tomato Dressing, 197
Low-Fat, No-Cholesterol Lekach, 17–18

Macaroons, *in* Hot Brandied Fruit, Phyllis's, 410
Mamaliga, 227–28
Mama's Apple Kugel, 365–66
Mama's Danish, 418–21
Mandelbrot
  Marbled, 386–87
  My Favorite, 385–86
  Pesach, 92
Marbled Mandelbrot, 386–87
Margarine
  melted, substitutes for, 373
  substitutes for, 372
Marinades, notes on, 315
Marinated Bean Salad, 183–84
Marinated Cucumbers, 178
Marinated Vegetables, 239–40
Marvelous Matzo Balls, 76–77

Mashed Potatoes with Onions and Garlic, 242–43
Matzo(s)
  Balls
    Feather-light, Bootsie Segal's, 77–78
    Marvelous, 76–77
    Mini, Passover Tzimmes with, 87–88
    Yellow Split Pea Soup with, 162
  Brei, Harold's, 97–98
  cake meal
    *in* Apricot Squares, 95–96
    *in* Date and Nut Bars from West Bloomfield, 93
    *in* Passover Rolls, Dorothy Essick's, 96–97
    *in* Pesach Mandelbrot, 92
    *in* Vienna Torte, Dorothy Essick's, 94
  farfel
    *in* Broccoli Kugel, 270
    *in* Farfel and Asparagus Risotto, 78–79
    *in* Matzo Kugel, Marge Taylor's, 80
    *in* Matzo Stuffing, 84–85
    *in* Spinach Kugel, 16–17
    *in* Stuffed Chicken Breasts with Apricot Glaze, Nanette Nathanson's, 85–86
  kugels. *See* Kugels
  meal
    *in* Apple-Carrot Pudding, Jean Berenson's, 81–82
    *in* Artichoke Squares, 124–25
    *in* Corn Pudding, 265–66
    *in* Feather-light Matzo Balls, Bootsie Segal's, 77–78
    *in* Gefilte Fish Loaf, 71–72
    *in* Fruit Kugel, Helen Kolatch's, 43
    *in* Layered Vegetable Kugel, 52–53
    *in* Marvelous Matzo Balls, 76–77
    *in* Passover Brownies, 90–91
    *in* Passover Onion Puff, Dorothy Hartstein's, 79–80
    *in* Passover Rolls, Dorothy Essick's, 96–97
    *in* Pesach Mandelbrot, 92
    *in* Potato Knaidlach, 75–76
    *in* Sephardic Haroset, 70–71
    *in* Turkey Meat Loaf, My Family's Favorite, 326–27
    *in* Vegetarian Knishes, 132–33
  *in* Passover Granola, 99
  Stuffing, 84–85
Mayonnaise (nonfat)
  *in* Green Sauce, 296
  *in* Russian Dressing, 199
Measuring, notes on, 372
Meat
  -filled Crepes, 102

Loaf, Turkey, My Family's Favorite, 326–27
safety, notes on, 337
*see also* Names of meats
Meatballs
    and Cherries, Syrian, 131–32
    Crescent-shaped, 23–24
    Little, 128–29
Mechshe, 21–22
Meringue(s)
    Lemon, Pie, Mile-High, 425–26
    Spicy, 91
Middle Eastern Chicken Breasts, 313–14
Middle Eastern Chopped Eggplant, 121–22
Mile-High Lemon Meringue Pie, 425
Milk, whole, substitutes for, 372
Minestrone, 154–55
Miniature Bear Claws, 421
Mini Fruit Tarts, 39
Mini Knishes, 351–52
Mixed Fresh Vegetable Salad, 180–81
Mock Gefilte Fish, 74–75
Mohn, 64–65
Mold(s)
    Beet-Gefilte Fish, 34–35
    Gelatin, Syrian, with Apricots and Almonds,
        24–25
Mousse, Salmon, Metz, 286–87
Mozzarella cheese, *in* Eggplant Parmesan, 238–39
Muffins
    Bran, Easy, 380–81
    Hungarian Sour Cherry, 382
Mullet, ground, *in* Gefilte Fish Loaf, 71–72
Muscatel, Baked Apples, 401–402
Mush, Yellow Cornmeal, 227–28
Mushroom(s)
    *in* Barley and Red Pepper Pilaf, 215–16
    *in* Brown and Wild Rice Pilaf, 206–207
    *in* Chicken Breasts in Phyllo, 356–57
    Chinese Cabbage with, 276
    *in* Farfel Ring, 15–16
    *in* Hungarian Vegetable Salad, 193–94
    *in* Kasha Varnishkes, 217–18
    Lima Beans and Barley Soup with, Sarah's,
        155–56
    *in* Quick Soup, Mollie Roth's, 159–60
    *in* Stuffed Chicken Breasts with Apricot Glaze,
        Nanette Nathanson's, 85–86
    *in* Stuffed Peppers, 245–46
    -Stuffed Tomatoes, 250
    *in* Turkey Meat Loaf, My Family's Favorite,
        326–27
    *in* Vegetarian Chopped Liver, 7–8
    *in* Vegetarian Stuffed Cabbage, 248–49

    *in* Vegetarian Vegetable Soup, 160–61
Mustard
    Cabbage, 267–68
    Sauce, Broiled Salmon with, 285
My Best Babka, 426–27
My Family's Favorite Turkey Meat Loaf, 326–27
My Family's Favorite Veal Roast, 342–43
My Favorite Chicken Paprikash with Rice,
    318–19
My Favorite Mandelbrot, 385–86
My Favorite Mock or Simple Strudel, 38–39
My Mother's Bread Stuffing, 304
My Mother's Chicken Soup, 138–39
My Mother's Green Bean and Potato Borscht,
    145–46
My Mother's Potato Soup, 156–57
My Mother's Roast Stuffed Chicken, 303–304
My Mother's Sweet and Sour Green Beans,
    272–73

Nahit, 274
Neck, Stuffed, 305
Never-Fail Blintzes, 101–103
Never-Fail Kuchen, 30–33
Never-Fail Pie Crust, 423–24
No-Cholesterol Pineapple Upside-Down Kugel,
    210
No-Fat Honey Tea Loaf, 379–80
Noodles (no-yolk)
    *in* Broccoli Kugel, 270
    *in* Cabbage and Noodles, 212–13
    *in* No-Cholesterol Pineapple Upside-Down
        Kugel, 210
    *in* Noodle Broccoli Kugel, 219–20
    *in* Lokshen Kugel, Ruth Litt's, 220–21
    *in* Special Kugel, Phyllis's, 222–23
    *in* Spinach and Noodle Casserole, 213–14
    *in* Spinach Noodle Ring, 214
Nut(s)
    Date
        and, Bars from West Bloomfield, 93
        and, Bread, Mother's, 377–78
        Spread, 70–71
    Filling, *for* Mama's Danish, 420
    Oat, Slices with Jam, 383
    Raisin, Slices, Russian, 111
    substitutes for, 373
    toasted, notes on, 363
    *see also* Names of nuts

Oat(s)
    *in* Date Bars, Dr. Harvey Mendess's Mother's,
        65–66

Oat(s) (*cont.*)
  *in* Easy Bran Muffins, 380–81
  *in* Italian Plum Crisp, 394
  Nut Slices with Jam, 383
  *in* Rhubarb Bars, Dorothy Essick's, 392–93
  *in* Streusel Coffee Cake, Edie's, 109–10
Okra, 261
  Corn and, Casserole, Creole, 262
Olive Oil, Onion-flavored, 255–56
Omelet, Smoked Salmon, 298
Onion(s)
  Baked, Rosy, 253–54
  Cabbage Slaw, 108–109
  Cheese Roll, 353
  to cook, 139
  Eggs and, 28–29
  -flavored Olive Oil, 255–56
  and Garlic, Mashed Potatoes with, 242–43
  Helper, 254–55
  *in* Hungarian Lecsó, Gisele Pollak's, 269
  Leek Strudel, 359
  *in* Marinated Vegetables, 239–40
  odor, to remove, 154
  to peel, 253
  Potato Strudel, 360
  Potted Shoulder Steak with, 339–40
  Puff, Passover, Dorothy Hartstein's, 79–80
  *in* Ratatouille, 264–65
  red, *in* Herring Antipasto, 119–20
  Red Salmon, Tomato, and, Spread, 117
  Soup, French, 153
  *in* Spinach Strudel, 358–59
  *in* Vegetarian Chili, 263–64
  *in* Vegetarian Sandwich, 276–77
Orange(s)
  -flavored Cream Cheese, 378
  Fresh, Sorbet, 405–406
  marmalade, *in* Sliced Oranges in Marmalade, 399–400
  notes on, 431
  Sliced, in Marmalade, 399–400
Orzo, *in* Quick Soup, Mollie Roth's, 159–60
Oven-fried Chicken, 309–10
Oven-fried Flounder, 291

Pancakes
  Potato, Mollie's, 59–61
  *see also* Crepes; Latkes
Pantry supplies, basic, xxviii–xxxii
Pareve Blatlach, 102
Parsley
  *in* Green Sauce, 296
  and Minced Celery Vinaigrette, 189–90

Parsnips
  *in* Chicken Soups, My Mother's, 138–39
  *in* Vegetarian Vegetable Soup, 160–61
Passover
  Apricot Squares, 95
  Basic Matzo Stuffing, 84–85
  Beet Horseradish, Homemade, 73
  Brownies, 90–91
  Canapés, 97
  Chocolate Torte, Almost Dorothy Hartstein's, 88–89
  Date and Nut Bars from West Bloomfield, 93
  Dessert Puffs, 97
  Falsher Fish, 74
  Farfel and Asparagus Risotto, 78–79
  Feather-light Matzo Balls, Bootsie Segal's, 77–78
  Gefilte Fish Loaf, 71
  Granola, 99
  Haroset
    Ashkenazi, Sally's, 70
    Sephardic Date Nut Spread, 70
  Marvelous Matzo Balls, 76–77
  Matzo Brei, Harold's, 97–98
  Matzo Kugel. *See* Kugels
  menu for, 69
  notes on, 68
  Onion Puff, Dorothy Hartstein's, 79–80
  Pesach Mandelbrot, 92
  Potato Knaidlach, 75–76
  Pudding, Apple-Carrot, Jean Berenson's, 81–82
  rolls for. *See* Rolls
  Spicy Meringues, 91
  Stuffed Chicken Breasts with Apricot Glaze, Nanette Nathanson's, 85–86
  Tzimmes with Mini Matzo Balls, 87–88
  Vienna Torte, Dorothy Essick's, 94
Pasta
  and Beans, 215–16
  with Eggplant, 211
  *in* Kasha Varnishkes, 217
  shells, *in* Minestrone, 154–55
  *see also* Names of pastas; Noodles
Pastries
  Apricot Squares, 95–96
  Cockscombs, 421
  Hamantaschen, 63–65
  Hungarian Butter Horns, 415–17
  Hungarian Fluden, 422
  Kipfel, 421
  Mama's Danish, 418–21
  Miniature Bear Claws, 421
  Mini Fruit Tarts, 39

Passover Dessert Puffs, 97
Pear Strudel Squares, 367–68
Reformed Rugelach, 37–39
*see also* Bars; Pastry; Strudels
Pastry
    crust, substitutes for, 373
    *see also* Phyllo; Pie crust
Pea(s)
    black-eyed, cooking times for, 236
    dried, to prepare, 235–36
    green
        *in* Crunchy Cauliflower and Pea Salad, 181
        Dip with Fresh Vegetables, 130–31
        *in* Quick Soup, Mollie Roth's, 159–60
        Soup, 150
        *in* Stuffed Peppers, 245–46
        *in* Two-Pea Salad, 179
        *in* Vegetarian Fried Brown Rice, 226–27
        *in* Vegetarian Vegetable Soup, 160–61
    split
        cooking times for, 236
        Green, Soup, 163
        Yellow, Soup, with Matzo Balls, 162
Peach(es)
    Fresh, Dessert Salad, 112
    *in* Hot Brandied Fruit, Phyllis's, 410–11
    preserves
        *in* Special Kugel, Phyllis's, 222–23
        *in* Strudel, My Favorite, Mock or Simple, 38–39
    *in* Spiced Fruit in Wine, 406–407
Pear(s)
    Cranberry Strudel, Jackie Keller's, 366–67
    *in* Fruited Sweet Potato Tart, 51–52
    *in* Hot Brandied Fruit, Phyllis's, 410
    -Pineapple Matzo Kugel, 83–84
    Poached, with Raspberries, 409
    Spiced Baked, 404–405
    *in* Spiced Fruits in Wine, 406–407
    Strudel Squares, 367–68
Pecans
    *in* Cream Cheese Squares, 390–91
    *in* Passover Chocolate Torte, Almost Dorothy Hartstein's, 88–90
    *in* Passover Granola, 99
    *in* Sephardic Haroset, 70–71
    *in* Strudel, Almost Aunt Dora's, 362–63
    *in* The Ultimate Cheesecake, 432–33
    *in* Vienna Torte, Dorothy Essick's, 94
Pepper(s)
    bell (red and/or green)
        *in* Barley and Red Pepper Pilaf, 214–15
        *in* Chicken with Potatoes and Peppers, 320–21

*in* Chicken in Sauerkraut with Caraway Seeds, 319–20
*in* Fish Paprikash, 284–85
*in* Herring Antipasto, 119–20
*in* Herring in Cream, 118–19
*in* Hungarian Vegetable Salad, 193–94
*in* Israeli Vegetable Salad, 184–85
*in* Lamb Shanks and Beans, 345–46
*in* Marinated Vegetables, 239–40
*in* Middle Eastern Chopped Eggplant, 121–22
*in* Mixed Fresh Vegetable Salad, 180–81
*in* Ratatouille, 264–65
*in* Roasted Peppers, 246–47
*in* Stuffed Peppers, 245–46
*in* Vegetarian Stew, 258–59
    long (frying)
        *in* Hungarian Gulyás, 340–41
        *in* Hungarian Lecsó, Gisele Pollak's, 269–78
Pesach Mandelbrot, 92
Petcha, 127
Phyllo
    Chicken Breasts in, 356–57
    Cups, Ricotta and Sun-dried Tomato, 355–56
    Fish Fillets in, 357
    *in* Mini Knishes, 351–52
    notes on, 349–50
    *in* Onion Cheese Roll, 353
    *in* Ricotta and Artichoke Flowers, 354
    *see also* Strudels
Pickles, Dill, Kosher, Mrs. Rubenstein's, 237–38
Pie
    Crust, Never-Fail, 423–24
    Lemon Meringue, Mile-High, 425
Pike, ground, *in* Gefilte Fish Loaf, 71–72
Pilaf(s)
    Atlanta, with Pine Nuts, Pinto Beans, and Scallions, 224
    Barley and Red Pepper, 214–15
    Brown and Wild Rice, 206
Pineapple
    Banana, Sherbet, 408–409
    *in* Brown and Wild Rice Pilaf, 206
    *in* Fruit Kugel, Helen Kolatch's, 43
    *in* Hot Brandied Fruit, Phyllis's, 410
    *in* Passover Tzimmes with Mini Matzo Balls, 87–88
    Pear-, Matzo Kugel, 83–84
    Upside-Down Kugel, No-Cholesterol, 210
Pine nuts
    Pinto Beans, and Scallions, Atlanta Pilaf with, 224
    *in* Rizib Chicken, 22–23
Pinto beans. *See* Beans

Plum(s)
  Butter, 411
  Damson, preserves, *in* Strudel, Almost Aunt
      Dora's, 362–63
  Ginger, Sauce, Cornish Hens with, 331
  *in* Hot Brandied Fruit, Phyllis's, 410
  Italian
      Crisp, 394
      *in* Lekvar, 411
  Sauce, Chicken with, 313
  *in* Spiced Fruit in Wine, 406–407
Poached Apple Slices, 407
Poached Pears with Raspberries, 409
Poached Salmon, 295–96
Pogachels or Pogácsa, 417–18
Poppy seed(s)
  Crisps, Dorothy Essick's, 388
  *in* Eir Kichlach, 431–32
  Filling, 64–65
  Komitzbrodt, 66–67
Potato(es)
  *in* Carrot Soup, 168
  *in* Cholent, 9–10
  Dumplings, 243–44
  Green Bean and, Borscht, My Mother's, 145–46
  *in* Hungarian Gulyás, 340–41
  Knaidlach, 75–76
  Kugel(s), 256–57
      Individual, 257
  Mashed, with Onions and Garlic, 242–43
  *in* Mini Knishes, 351–52
  Onion Strudel, 360
  Pancakes
      Mollie's, 59–61
      *see also* Latkes
  and Red Peppers, Chicken with, 320–21
  Salad, Syrian-Style, 194
  *in* Savory Veal Brisket, 343–44
  Soup, My Mother's, 156–57
  sweet. *See* Sweet potatoes
Potted Shoulder Steak with Onions, 339–40
Poultry
  to buy, 302
  kosher, sodium and, 302
  nutritional notes on, 301–302
  safety, notes on, 302–303
  *see also* Names of poultry
Prune(s)
  -Apricot
      Compote, 400–401
      Filling, 65
  Carrot and, Tzimmes, 272
  *in* Fruited Sweet Potato Tart, 51–52

and Garlic, Roast Brisket with, Marilyn Lewis's,
    58–59
*in* Passover Tzimmes with Mini Matzo Balls,
    87–88
and Rice Tzimmes, 275
*in* Tzimmes, 260
Whip, 404
Pudding(s)
  Corn, 265–66
  Passover, Apple-Carrot, Jean Berenson's, 81–82
  *see also* Kugels
Purim
  menu for, 63
  notes on, 62

Quick and Easy Potato Latkes with Dill Sauce,
    125–26
Quick Sauce, A, 408
Quick Tomato Soup, 152
Quinoa, cooking times for, 206

Radicchio, *in* Red and Green Chopped Salad, 186
Radish(es)
  Celery, and Cucumber Salad, 187
  *in* Green Pea Dip with Fresh Vegetables,
      130–31
  *in* Israeli Vegetable Salad, 184–85
Raisin(s)
  *in* Apple Kugel, Mama's, 365–66
  Bagels, 375
  *in* Brown and Wild Rice Pilaf, 207
  Cinnamon, Rolls, 375–76
  *in* Dessert Wafers, Harriet Greenwald's, 389–90
  *in* Easy Bran Muffins, 380–81
  golden
  *in* Matzo Kugel, Marge Taylor's, 80
  *in* No-Fat Apple Strudel, Gisele Pollak's,
      364–65
  Nut Slices, Russian, 111
  *in* Pear-Pineapple Matzo Kugel, 83–84
  *in* Reformed Rugelach, 37–39
  *in* Rice Kugel, Sarah's, 218–19
  *in* Rosy Baked Onions, 253–54
  Round Challah with, 12–13
  *in* Streusel Coffee Cake, Edie's, 109–10
  *in* Strudel, Almost Aunt Dora's, 362–63
  *in* Stuffed Peppers, 245–46
  *in* Today's Kuchen, 31–32
  *in* Yesterday's Kuchen, 30–33
Ranch-Style Dressing, 196
Raspberry(ies)
  jam, *in* Vienna Torte, Dorothy Essick's, 94
  *in* Mini Fruit Tarts, 39

Poached Pears with, 409
preserves
    in Chocolate Trifle, 396
    in Hungarian Fluden, 422
    in Oat Nut Slices with Jam, 383
    in A Quick Sauce, 408
Ratatouille, 264–65
Red cabbage. See Cabbage
Red and Green Chopped Salad, 186
Red kidney beans. See Beans
Red Salmon, Tomato, and Onion Spread, 117
Red snapper, in Fish Fillets with Tomato and
        Garlic Concasse, 292–93
Reformed Rugelach, 37–39
Relish, Horseradish Apple, 73–74
Rhubarb
    Bars, Dorothy Essick's, 392–93
    Sauce, 412
Rice
    Arborio, in Vegetable and Bean Soup, Connie
        Reif's, 166–67
    brown
        cooking times for, 206
        Fried, Vegetarian, 226–27
        in Hungarian Stuffed Cabbage. 321–22
        in Stuffed Grape Leaves, 323–24
        in Stuffed Peppers, 245–46
        in Vegetarian Stuffed Cabbage, 248–49
        and Wild, Pilaf, 206–207
    Chicken Paprikash with, My Favorite, 318–19
    converted, cooking times for, 206
    cooking times for, 206
    in Hungarian Stuffed Cabbage, 321–22
    Kugel, Sarah's, 218–19
    with Lentils and Currants, 221–22
    Prune and, Tzimmes, 275
    in Stuffed Grape Leaves, 323–24
    in Sweet and Sour Stuffed Cabbage, 41–42
    Syrian Chicken and, 22–23
    in Syrian Stuffed Eggplant, 324–25
    Tomato, Soup, Sephardic, 173–74
    Turkey, and Vegetable Soup, 157–58
Ricotta cheese (nonfat)
    in Never-Fail Blintzes, 101–103
    in Ricotta
        and Artichoke Flowers, 354
        and Sun-dried Tomato Phyllo Cups, 355–56
    in Spinach
        Cups, 122–23
        Soufflé, Renée Holland's, 103
        Strudel, 358–59
Risotto, Farfel and Asparagus, 78–79
Rizib Chicken, 22–23

Roast Breast of Turkey, 48–49
Roast Chicken with Brussels Sprouts, 29–30
Roasted Chicken Italian Style, 13–14
Roasted Peppers, 246–47
Rolls
    Cinnamon Raisin, 375–77
    Passover, 96–97
    Onion, 97
    Seeded, 97
Romaine lettuce, in Chopped Salad, 185–86
Rosh Hashanah
    menus for, 12, 19
    notes on, 11
Rosy Baked Onions, 253–54
Round Challah with Raisins, 12–13
Rugelach, Reformed, 37–39
Rumanian Broiled Hamburgers, 327–28
Russian Dressing, 199
Russian Raisin Nut Slices, 111

Salad(s)
    Apple
        Cabbage, 192–93
        Date, 182
    Cauliflower and Pea, Crunchy, 181
    Chopped, 185–86
        Red and Green, 186
    Cucumber, 179–80
    Dessert, Fresh Peach, 112
    "Egg," Spread, 195
    Farfel, 190
    Gingered Cucumbers, 188
    Hungarian Caraway Slaw, 191
    Jellied Beet Borscht, 236–37
    Marinated Bean, 183–84
    Marinated Cucumbers, 178
    Parsley and Minced Celery, Vinaigrette, 189–90
    Potato, Syrian-Style, 194
    Radish, Celery, and Cucumber, 187
    Two-Pea, 179
    Vegetable
        Fresh, Mixed, 180–81
        Hungarian, 193–94
        Israeli, 184–85
    Wilted Lettuce and Tomato, Hungarian,
        191–92
    see also Slaws
Salt
    notes on, xx–xxi
    see also Sodium
Salmon
    Baked, with Carrot-Zucchini Stuffing, 288–89
    Broiled, with Mustard Sauce, 285

Salmon (*cont.*)
  Croquettes, 104–105
  Fillets, Glazed, 290–91
  *in* Fish Fillets in Phyllo, 357
  *in* Jellied Sweet and Sour Fish, 297
  Mousse Metz, 286–87
  Poached, 295–96
  Red, Tomato, and Onion Spread, 117
  Smoked
    Omelet, 298
    Tartare, 116
Sandwich(es)
  Blintz, 228–29
  Steak, Israeli, 338–39
  Vegetarian, 276–77
Sauce(s)
  Cranapple, 54–55
  Ginger Plum, Cornish Hens with, 331
  Green, 296
  Horseradish, for Poached Fish, 73
  Mustard, Broiled Salmon with, 285
  Plum, Chicken with, 313
  Rhubarb, 412
  Tomato
    Fresh, 54
    A Little, 251
    A Lot of, 252
Sauerkraut
  Chicken in, with Caraway Seeds, 319–20
  *in* Hungarian Stuffed Cabbage, 321–22
  Soup, Hungarian, 169–70
Savory Veal Brisket, 343–44
Scallions
  *in* Gingered Cucumbers, 188
  *in* Hot Cold Noodles, Connie Reif's, 225–26
  Pine Nuts, Pinto Beans, and, Atlanta Pilaf
    with, 224
  *in* Spinach Strudel, 358–59
Schalet, 365–66
Schav Borscht, 147–48
Schliskas from Aunt Ella Markell, 243–44
Sea bass, *in* Fish Paprikash, 284–85
Sea Foam Frosting, 429
Sephardic Haroset, 70–71
Sephardic Leeks and Beans, 259–60
Sephardic Tomato Rice Soup, 173–74
Shabbat
  Eve, prayers for, 4
  menus for, 3–5
  notes on, 3–4
Shavuot
  menu for, 100
  notes on, 100

Sherbet, Banana Pineapple, 408–409
Shortening, substitutes for, 373
Shurba, 173–74
Slaw(s)
  Caraway, Hungarian, 191
  Onion Cabbage, 108
Sliced Oranges in Marmalade, 399–400
Smoked salmon. *See* Salmon
Snow peas
  *in* Hot Cold Noodles, Connie Reif's, 226
  *in* Two-Pea Salad, 179
  *in* Vegetarian Fried Brown Rice, 226–27
Sodium
  and kosher poultry, 302
  notes on, xx–xxi
  and processed foods, xxi
Sole, Fillet of, with Banana, 293–94
Sorbet, Fresh Orange, 405–406
Sorrel Soup, 147–48
Soufflé, Spinach, Renée Holland's, 103
Soybeans, cooking times for, 236
Soup(s)
  basic rules for, 137–38
  Caraway, 164–65
  Carrot, 168
    Vichyssoise, 148
  Chicken
    in the Microwave, 165–66
    My Mother's, 138–39
  Corn, Nanette Nathanson's, 170–71
  Cucumber, 143–44
  Egg Drop, 143
  Fresh Asparagus, Barbara Bernstein's, 151
  Green Pea, 150
  Green Split Pea, 163
  Lentil, Vegetarian, 158–59
  Lima Bean and Barley, with Mushrooms,
    Sarah's, 155–56
  Minestrone, 154–55
  Onion, French, 153
  Potato, My Mother's, 156–57
  Quick, Mollie Roth's, 159–60
  Sauerkraut, Hungarian, 169–70
  Sorrel, 147–48
  Tomato
    Chilled, 149–50
    Quick, 152
    Rice, Sephardic, 173–74
  Turkey, Rice, and Vegetable, 157–58
  Vegetable
    and Bean, Connie Reif's, 166–67
    Turkey, Rice, and, 157–58
    Vegetarian, 160–61

Yellow Split Pea, with Matzo Balls, 162
  *see also* Borschts; Broths; Stocks
Sour cream
  nonfat
    *in* Herring in Cream, 118–19
    *in* Lokshen Kugel, Ruth Litt's, 220–21
    *in* Special Kugel, Phyllis's, 222–23
    *in* Streusel Coffee Cake, Edie's, 109–10
  substitutes for, 372
Spaghettini, *in* Hot Cold Noodles, Connie Reif's, 225–26
Specha, 324–25
Spiced Baked Pears, 404–405
Spiced Fruit in Wine, 406–407
Spiced Ginger Cookies, 384–85
Spicy Meringues, 71
Spinach
  for beans and potatoes, *in* Green Bean and Potato Borscht, My Mother's, 145–46
  Cups, 122–23
  Kugel, 16–17
  *in* Layered Vegetable Kugel, 52–53
  Noodle
    Casserole, 213–14
    Ring, 214
  for onions and garlic, *in* Mashed Potatoes with Onions and Garlic, 242
  Soufflé, Renée Holland's, 103
  Strudel, 358–59
Split peas. *See* Peas
Spread(s)
  Date Nut, 70–71
  "Egg Salad," 195
  Orange-flavored Cream Cheese, 378
  Red Salmon, Tomato, and Onion, 117
Squash
  Banana, Strudel, 362
  Strudel, 361–62
  yellow (crookneck)
    *in* Marinated Vegetables, 239–40
    *in* Squash Strudel, 361–62
    *in* Vegetarian Stew, 258–59
  *see also* Zucchini
Steak
  Sandwich, Israeli, 338–39
  Shoulder, Potted, with Onions, 339–40
Stew, Vegetarian, 258–59
Stock(s)
  Court Bouillon, 287
  Fish, 142–43
  *see also* Broths; Soups
Strawberry(ies)
  *in* Mini Fruit Tarts, 39

preserves
  *in* Mock or Simple Strudel, My Favorite, 38–39
  *in* Oat Nut Slices with Jam, 383
  *in* A Quick Sauce, 408–409
  *in* Strudel, Almost Aunt Dora's, 362–63
Rhubarb Jumble, 402–403
  *in* Rhubarb Sauce, 412
Strudel(s)
  Almost Aunt Dora's, 362–63
  Apple, No-Fat, Gisele Pollak's, 364–65
  Banana Squash, 362
  Cabbage, 359
  Chicken, 350–51
  leaves
    notes on, 349–50
    *see also* Phyllo
  Mock or Simple, My Favorite, 38–39
  Onion
    Cheese Roll, 353
    Leek, 359
  Pear Cranberry, Jackie Keller's, 366–67
  Potato Onion, 360
  Spinach, 358–59
  Squares, Pear, 367–68
  Squash, 361–62
Stuffed Grape Leaves, 323–24
Stuffed Neck, 305
Stuffed Peppers, 245–46
Stuffing(s)
  Bread, My Mother's, 303–304
  Carrot-Zucchini, Baked Salmon with, 288–89
  to cook, 49
  Matzo, 84–85
  for poultry, to store, 304
Sugar
  notes on, xxi
  substitutes for, 372
  vanilla, to make, 433
Sukkot
  notes on, 40
  menu for, 40
Sun-dried Tomato, Ricotta and, Phyllo Cups, 355–56
Sweet potato(es)
  *in* Middle Eastern Chicken Breasts, 313–14
  *in* Passover Tzimmes with Mini Matzo Balls, 87–88
  Ring, 271–72
  *in* Schliskas from Aunt Ella Markell, 244
  Tart, Fruited, 51–52
  *see also* Yams
Sweet and Sour Stuffed Cabbage, 41–42

Swiss chard, *in* Minestrone, 154–55
Swiss cheese
  low-fat, *in* Vegetarian Sandwich, 276–77
  sodium-reduced, *in* Onion Cheese Roll, 353
Syrian Chicken and Rice, 22–23
Syrian Gelatin Mold with Apricots and Almonds, 24–25
Syrian Meatballs and Cherries, 131–32
Syrian Stuffed Eggplant, 324–25
Syrian-Style Potato Salad, 194

Tahini
  *in* Baba Ghanouj, 107–108
  Dressing, Lemony, 198
  *in* Hummus, 123–24
Tart(s)
  Fruit, Mini, 39
  Sweet Potato, Fruited, 51–52
Tea Loaf, Honey, No-Fat, 379–80
Ten Easy Pieces of Chicken Breast, 311–12
Thanksgiving, menus for, 45–46
Toast points, to prepare, 116
Today's Kuchen, 31–33
Tofu
  *in* Corn Soup, Nanette Nathanson's, 170–71
  Dressing, Creamy, 198–99
  Dill Dip, 46–47
  *in* "Egg Salad" Spread, 195
  to store, 47
Tomato(es)
  *in* Creole Corn and Okra Casserole, 262
  Dressing, Low-Cal, 197
  and Garlic Concasse, Fish Fillet with, 292–93
  *in* Hungarian Gulyás, 340–41
  *in* Hungarian Lecsó, Gisele Pollak's, 269
  *in* Hungarian Stuffed Cabbage, 321–22
  *in* Lamb Shanks and Beans, 345–46
  *in* Middle Eastern Chopped Eggplant, 121–22
  Mushroom-stuffed, 250
  to peel, 253
  *in* Ratatouille, 264–65
  Red Salmon, and Onion Spread, 117
  sauce. *See* Sauces
  soup. *See* Soups
  Sun-dried, Ricotta and, Phyllo Cups, 355–56
  *in* Vegetable and Bean Soup, Connie Reif's, 166–67
  Wilted Lettuce and, Salad, 191–92
Torte(s)
  Chocolate, Passover, Almost Dorothy Hartstein's, 88–90
  Vienna, Dorothy Essick's, 94
Trifle, Chocolate, 396

Tuna and White Bean Antipasto, 118
Turkey
  Breast of, Roast, 48–49
  Broth, 140
  *in* Carnatzlach, 327–28
  cooked
    for chicken, *in* Chicken Strudel, 350–51
    *in* Chopped Salad, 185–86
  Cutlets or Schnitzel, 328–29
  Gravy, 49–50
  ground
    *in* Cabbage Borscht, Harriet Friedman's Mother's, 171–72
    *in* Carnatzlach, 327–28
    *in* Falsher Fish, 74–75
    *in* Hungarian Stuffed Cabbage, 321
    *in* Kibbe, Renée Holland's, 23–24
    *in* Kreplach, 208–209
    *in* Little Meatballs, 128–29
    *in* Mechshe, 21–22
    *in* Stuffed Grape Leaves, 323–24
    *in* Sweet and Sour Stuffed Cabbage, 41–42
    *in* Syrian Meatballs and Cherries, 131–32
    *in* Syrian Stuffed Eggplant, 324–25
  legs, *in* Cholent, 9–10
  Meat Loaf, My Family's Favorite, 326–27
  nutritional notes on, 301–302
  Rice, and Vegetable Soup, 157–58
Turnips
  *in* Vegetarian Stuffed Cabbage, 248–49
  *in* Vegetarian Vegetable Soup, 160–61
Twisted Bagels, 375
Two-Pea Salad, 179
Tzimmes, 260
  Carrot and Prune, 272
  Passover, with Mini Matzo Balls, 87–88
  Prune and Rice, 275

Ultimate Cheesecake, The, 432–33

Vanilla sugar, to make, 433
Veal
  brisket
    *in* Lima Beans for a Crowd, Cousin Pearly's, 268–69
    Savory, 343–44
  ground
    *in* Hungarian Stuffed Cabbage, 322
    *in* Kibbe, Renée Holland's, 23–24
    *in* Little Meatballs, 128–29
    *in* Sweet and Sour Stuffed Cabbage, 41–42
    *in* Syrian Meatballs and Cherries, 131–32
  *in* Hungarian Gulyás, 340–41

Roast, My Family's Favorite, 342–43
V-8 juice (low-sodium)
    *in* Chilled Tomato Soup, 149
    *in* Low-Cal Tomato Dressing, 197
Vegetable(s)
    and Bean Soup, Connie Reif's, 166–67
    Broth, 141–42
    cruciferous, and cancer, 234
    Fresh
        Green Pea Dip with, 130–31
        Mixed, Salad, 180–81
    frozen mixed
        for fiber, 187
        *in* Spinach Noodle Casserole, 213–14
    Kugel, Layered, 52–53
    Marinated, 239–40
    nutritional notes on, 233–34
    Salad(s)
        Hungarian, 193–94
        Israeli, 184–85
    shortening, substitutes for, 372
    soup. *See* Soups
    *see also* Names of vegetables
Vegetarian
    Chili, 263–64
    Chopped Liver, 7–8
    Fried Brown Rice, 226–27
    Knishes, 132–33
    Lentil Soup, 158–59
    Sandwich, 276–77
    Stew, 258–59
    Stuffed Cabbage, 248–49
    Vegetable Soup, 160–61
Very Good Chocolate Cake, A, 391–92
Vichyssoise, Carrot, 148
Vienna Torte, Dorothy Essick's, 94
Vinaigrette
    Dressing, Light, 200
    Parsley and Minced Celery Salad, 189–90
Vitamin(s)
    A, sources of, 234
    C, sources of, 234

Wafers, Dessert, Harriet Greenwald's, 389–90
Walnuts
    *in* Date and Nut Bars from West Bloomfield, 93
    *in* Date and Nut Bread, Mother's, 377–78
    *in* Nut Filling *for* Danish, Mama's, 420
    *in* Oat Nut Slices with Jam, 383
    *in* Passover Brownies, 90–91
    *in* Passover Chocolate Torte, Almost Dorothy Hartstein's, 88–90
    *in* Reformed Rugelach, 37–39
    *in* Russian Raisin Nut Slices, 111
    *in* Streusel Coffee Cake, Edie's, 109–10
    *in* Vegetarian Chopped Liver, 7–8
    *in* Vienna Torte, Dorothy Essick's, 94
Water Bagels, Sam Mackler's, 373–75
Watercress, *in* Green Sauce, 296
Weight, healthy, to maintain, xxii–xxiii
Wheat, Cracked, Dip, 20–21
Wild Rice, Brown and, Pilaf, 206–207
Whitefish
    *in* Fish Fillets with Tomato and Garlic Concasse, 292–93
    ground, *in* Gefilte Fish Loaf, 71–72
White Bean, Tuna and, Antipasto, 118
Wine, Spiced Fruit in, 406–407

Yams
    *in* Tzimmes, 260
    *see also* Sweet Potatoes
Yaprakis de Oja, 323–24
Yebra, 323–24
Yellow Split Pea Soup with Matzo Balls, 162
Yesterday's Kuchen, 30–33
Yogurt
    cheese
        to make, 355
        for ricotta, *in* Ricotta and Artichoke Flowers, 354
    nonfat
        *in* Baked Fish Hungarian Style, 294
        *in* Fish Paprikash, 284–85
        frozen, *in* Chocolate Trifle, 396
        *in* Green Pea Dip with Fresh Vegetables, 130–31
        *in* Green Sauce, 296
        *in* Herring in Cream, 118–19
        *in* Potato Latkes, Quick and Easy, with Dill Sauce, 125–26
        *in* Russian Dressing, 199
        *in* Streusel Coffee Cake, Edie's, 109–10
Yom Kippur
    menus for, 26, 27
    notes on, 26, 27

Zucchini
    Carrot-, Stuffing, Baked Salmon with, 288–89
    *in* Ratatouille, 264–65
    *in* Squash Strudel, 361–62
    Stuffed, 21–22
        Nita Williams', 277–78
Zwieback, *in* The Ultimate Cheesecake, 432–33

• A NOTE ON THE TYPE •

The typeface used in this book is a version of Goudy (Old Style), originally designed by Frederick W. Goudy (1865–1947), perhaps the best known and certainly one of the most prolific of American type designers, who created over a hundred typefaces—the actual number is unknown because a 1939 fire destroyed many of his drawings and "matrices" (molds from which type is cast). Initially a calligrapher, rather than a type cutter or printer, he represented a new breed of designer made possible by late-nineteenth-century technological advance; later on, in order to maintain artistic control, he supervised the production of matrices himself. He was also a tireless promoter of wider awareness of type, with the paradoxical result that the distinctive style of his influential output tends to be associated with his period and, though still a model of taste, can now seem somewhat dated.